The German Stock Corporation Act

SERIES OF LEGISLATION IN TRANSLATION

In the Series of Legislation in Translation, **The German Stock Corporation Act** is the first title, published by Kluwer Law International and C.H. Beck.

SERIES OF
LEGISLATION IN
TRANSLATION 1

The German Stock Corporation Act

Hannes Schneider

and

Martin Heidenhain

C.H. Beck
München

Kluwer Law International
The Hague • London • Boston

Kluwer Law International
P.O. Box 85889
2508 CN The Hague, The Netherlands

Sold and distributed in Austria, Germany and Switzerland by
Verlag C.H. Beck
Postfach 400340
80703 München, Germany

Sold and distributed in the USA and Canada by
Kluwer Law International
675 Massachusetts Avenue
Cambridge, MA 02139, USA

Sold and distributed in all other countries by
Kluwer Law International
P.O. Box 85889
2508 CN The Hague, The Netherlands

Cover design: Peter Gerretzen

Printed on acid-free paper

ISBN 9065447822 (Kluwer)
ISBN 3406379958 (Beck)

Kluwer Law International incorporates the publishing programmes of Graham & Trotman Ltd, Kluwer Law and Taxation Publishers and Martinus Nijhoff Publishers.

Table of Contents

1 Introduction

Introduction

I. General

The German Stock Corporation Act (the 'Act') regulates the stock corporation, or *Aktiengesellschaft* ('AG'), as well as the *Kommanditgesellschaft auf Aktien* ('KGaA'). Both corporate forms are greatly outnumbered by the limited liability company, or *Gesellschaft mit beschränkter Haftung* ('GmbH'), a more flexible form suited for closely held and subsidiary companies and governed by a separate act. At the end of 1994, there were approximately 3000 AGs and some more than 500 000 GmbHs in existence. The AG is the form used mainly by large companies whose shares are publicly held and traded on a stock exchange. The KGaA is a stock corporation in association with one or more personally liable partners who constitute the corporation's board of management. Generally it is subject to the same provisions as the AG. Supplementary and substitute provisions are contained in Book Two of the Act (§§ 278-290). In view of the rarity of the form, the KGaA is not discussed in this Introduction.

While the history of the stock corporation in Germany dates back to the middle of the 18th century, codification of the law of stock corporations began in the mid-19th century. Incorporation without special dispensation from the state became available in 1870. The stock corporation law was taken out of the general commercial code and separately codified in 1937 in a reform that introduced significant changes to the existing law. The current law, which dates from 1965, is based on the 1937 law but also includes many significant changes and refinements. The Act has been amended frequently since its enactment, most significantly perhaps in 1985 when following the EC Accounting Directive the accounting provisions of the Act were largely repealed and consolidated into the Commercial Code and in 1994 where the former Book Four of the Act dealing with mergers and conversions was repealed and consolidated with other acts in the Transformation Act.

This Introduction reviews some of the major features of the AG, including formation, management and shareholders' meetings, capital, affiliated enterprises, accounting, distribution of profits and dissolution. Before turning to these specific areas, however, we briefly discuss some of the basic principles embodied in the Act.

The AG is a legal entity distinct from its shareholders, with the capacity to acquire and hold rights and to undertake and perform obligations. Shareholders are not personally liable to the corporation or its creditors beyond their duty to fulfil obligations undertaken for stock subscriptions. Shareholders have the right to distributions of profits and to vote in the corporation's shareholders' meeting.

The AG's management board *(Vorstand)* has the exclusive responsibility for managing the corporation. In addition, the AG has a supervisory board *(Aufsichtsrat)*, which is elected by the shareholders' meeting *(Hauptversammlung)* and which in turn appoints and supervises the management board. The two entities are entirely distinct and are not permitted to have overlapping members.

Reflecting the Act's pervasive concern for the protection of the AG's creditors, the concept of stated share capital *(Grundkapital)* is extremely important. With a few exceptions discussed below, the share capital of an AG shown in its articles is equivalent to its outstanding capital, and changes in share capital must be effected by amendments to the articles. Shareholders are obligated to pay the consideration for the shares subscribed to upon formation of the corporation or any increase in share capital. Such obligations cannot be released or extended. Contributions in kind are strictly regulated to ensure the integrity of the AG's share capital. Distributions are strictly limited to balance sheet profits, except in the case of a liquidation or permitted decrease in share capital. Disguised repayments of capital – non-arm's length transactions between the AG and its shareholders – are considered illegal. Repurchases of shares are also strictly limited.

Readers should be cautioned that while this translation should be very useful for foreign lawyers and laymen dealing with legal issues concerning German stock corporations, it is no substitute for the advice of competent counsel. Other statutes and regulations as well as the pertinent case law may be relevant to any particular legal problem. Moreover, in the process of translation there is always some inevitable loss in content, since the words used in the original text often have their own special meaning drawn from an entire body of law that has developed over generations and over the course of many different governments and political systems.

II. Formation

The formation of an *Aktiengesellschaft* is governed by Book One, Part Two (§§ 23-53) of the Act. The formation *(Gründung)* is a complicated process that begins with the establishment of the articles of incorporation *(Satzung)* and minutes of formation in notarial form (§ 23) and ultimately concludes with the registration of the AG in the commercial register *(Handelsregister)* maintained by the local court in the place where the AG is domiciled (§§ 36-40). Prior to the completion of registration, the AG does not as such exist and may not issue or transfer shares. Persons acting in the name of the AG prior to registration have personal liability, although with the prior or subsequent consent of creditors the AG may assume such liability and release such persons. The AG may not, however, assume obligations arising under agreements regarding special benefits, formation expenses or contributions in kind and acquisitions of assets unless they are stipulated in the articles (§§ 26-27).

An AG must have one or more founders (§ 2), who may be individuals or companies and need not be German or domiciled in Germany. The existence of corporate founders and authority of their agents must be appropriately established by certified extracts from the commercial register or other official documents. The founders need not personally appear before the notary who establishes the articles but may appear through an attorney-in-fact who is authorized in a notarized power of attorney (§ 23 (1)).

Fairly extensive mandatory provisions must be contained in the articles of incorporation (§ 23 (3)). The corporate name must relate to the purpose of the corporation or be taken over from a business that the corporation has acquired (§ 4), be sufficiently different from all firms registered at the same place and contain the word *Aktiengesellschaft*. The use of foreign terms, coinages and misleading terms is restricted. All filings are forwarded to the local chamber of industry and commerce for review and it is common to obtain informal approval prior to filing.

The corporation's domicile (*Sitz*), which must also be specified in the Articles (§ 23 (3), No. 1) and is the place of filing, must be within Germany and must be a place where the corporation maintains an operation, where its management is situated or where its administration is conducted (§ 5).

The articles must also specify the AG's corporate purpose (§ 23 (3), No. 2). The articles of a corporation engaged in industry or trade must specify the kinds of products and goods to be produced and traded. This statement of corporate purpose limits the management's authority but not its power to act; management may bind the AG outside the scope of the stated purpose but may find itself liable for damages suffered by the corporation from such acts. The articles must also specify the amount of share capital *(Grundkapital)* of the AG (§ 23 (3), No. 3). Share capital and shares of an AG must be denominated in Deutsche Marks (§ 6) and the minimum capital is DM 100,000 (§ 7). Par value may be five Deutsche Mark or any multiple of five Deutsche Mark. Shares are not divisible (§ 8).

In the articles, the par value, classes (if more than one) and number of shares (or of shares in each class of shares) must be stated (§ 23 (3), Nos. 4, 5). Shares may be issued at a premium but not a discount from their par value (§ 9). Different classes may have different rights and preferences (§ 11), such as dividend and liquidation preferences. Preferred stock may be voting or non-voting, but multiple and preferential voting rights are not permitted (§ 12). Shares may be issued in registered or bearer form (§ 10), as specified in the articles, and may be signed by facsimile (§ 13). The transfer of registered shares may be made subject to prior consent by the AG's management board. Such consent may be made dependent on the approval of the supervisory board or the shareholders' meeting (§ 68 (2)).

Finally, the articles must specify the number of members of the management board or the rules for determining such number (§ 23 (3), No. 6), and must specify the journals in which corporate announcements are to be made (§ 23 (4)). Whether or not so specified, all announcements must also be made in the Federal Gazette *(Bundesanzeiger)* (§ 25).

The articles may contain optional provisions, except regarding matters conclusively dealt with by the Act (§ 23 (5)). Optional provisions often deal with the management and supervisory boards, the shareholders' meeting, the fiscal year and the allocation of annual profits.

As mentioned above, agreements regarding special benefits, formation expenses, contributions in kind and acquisitions of assets must be stipulated in the articles in order to be valid. The failure to make such stipulations renders the agreements invalid, and such invalidity cannot be cured after registration. Such provisions may not be amended for five years after registration or deleted for thirty years (§§ 26-27). Services and undertakings to render services, as well as assets whose economic value is not determinable, may not be contributed in kind (§ 27 (2)). If an agreement regarding a contribution in kind is invalid, the shareholder must pay the issue price of the shares subscribed for in cash (§ 27 (3)). If shares are issued in respect of in-kind capital contributions, a formation audit by court appointed auditors to determine the adequacy of the consideration is required (§ 33 (2)), and the court may refuse the registration if the consideration is inadequate (§ 38 (2)).

The founders appoint the first supervisory board and the auditors for the AG's first fiscal year. The provisions of the various codetermination statutes regulating labor representation on the supervisory board do not apply to the first board, but the management board must announce which statutory codetermination provisions in its opinion will govern the composition of the following supervisory board (§ 30). The Act contains special provisions on the composition of the supervisory board to prevent the circumvention of the codetermination rules in the event that the AG acquires all or part of an enterprise (§ 31). The first supervisory board appoints the first management board (§ 30 (4)).

An important element of the formation of an AG is the formation report *(Gründungsbericht)*, which must be prepared by the founders and discuss the transactions leading up to the formation, acquisition of assets and in-kind capital contributions, special advantages or compensations to management or supervisory board members and the earnings' history of acquired enterprises. The report must also address the extent to which members of the supervisory or management board have subscribed for shares on formation or received a promise of any special benefit or compensation (§ 32). The Act further requires that transactions in connection with the formation be audited by both boards. A formation audit by outside auditors appointed by the court after consultation with the chamber of industry and commerce is required not only in connection with in-kind capital contributions and acquisitions of assets as mentioned above but also if any founder is a member of either board or if a member of either board subscribes to shares or has requested a preference or compensation in connection with the formation of the corporation (§ 33). The audit or audits essentially deal with the accuracy of the formation report and the adequacy of the value of assets acquired or contributed in kind (§ 34). The report of the formation auditors is available for public inspection at the court (§ 34 (3)). The court resolves differences of opinion and sets the level of remuneration for the outside auditors (§ 35).

Once all of the foregoing has been accomplished, all in-kind contributions have been made and the amount called on each share to be paid for in cash has been paid in and such contributions, to the extent not utilized for the payment of fees and taxes, are at the free disposal of the management board, the management and supervisory board members are ready to apply to the court for registration in the commercial register (§ 36). At least one quarter of par value must be paid on shares subscribed for cash. The entire premium to be paid, if any, must be made prior to requesting registration (§ 36a). The application must document the foregoing steps, include any required government authorization, and contain proof that capital contributions have been appropriately made (§ 37). The court will review the application and may reject it or require amendments. Incompleteness or inaccuracy of the formation report or audit report or a finding by the formation auditors or the court that the value of assets contributed in kind or acquired is materially less than the par value of shares to be issued or consideration to be paid can result in denial of the application (§ 38). Such decisions are appealable. Upon approval, an entry containing the principal data concerning the corporation – corporate name and domicile, purpose, amount of share capital, date of establishment of the articles, members of the management board and their authority to act – will be made in the commercial register (§ 39), and the corporation commences its legal existence (§ 41 (1)). The registration is announced in the corporation's journals (§ 40), shares may be issued and transferred, and the corporation may assume liability for the acts of persons on its behalf during the course of formation (§ 41). In connection with the formation, all persons taking part – including founders (§ 46), subscribers (§ 46(5)), members of initial boards (§ 48) and formation auditors (§ 49) – may be jointly and severally liable to the corporation for a wide range of possible deficiencies in the formation and initial capitalization of the AG. The Act makes it difficult to waive damage claims against such persons (§ 50) and there is a five year statute of limitations for claims (§ 51).

The section of the Act on formation concludes with two paragraphs dealing with post-formation acquisitions (§§ 52-53). These provisions, which cover agreements entered into within two years of registration for the acquisition of assets for a consideration exceeding one tenth of the AG's capital, are included to deter the circumvention of the stringent rules on asset acquisitions and in-kind contributions during formation and prevent the mistreatment of minority shareholders and deception of creditors. These provisions make the formation and audit report requirements applicable to post-formation acquisitions and require at least a three fourths majority shareholder approval (based on share capital and not on votes cast) (§ 52). Such acquisitions are subject to court review, registration and publication and the liability provisions covering formation apply accordingly, provided that the members of the management and supervisory boards are liable rather than the incorporators (§ 53).

III. Management Board

The sole responsibility for the management of the AG is vested in its management board *(Vorstand)* (§ 76(1)), whose member or members are appointed by the supervisory board *(Aufsichtsrat)* for terms of up to five years (§ 84(1)). Corporations whose share capital exceeds three million Deutsche Mark must have at least two persons on the management board (§ 76 (2)) if the articles do not provide otherwise. Members of the management board must be natural persons who have not been convicted of a bankruptcy crime within the previous five years and have not been barred from practicing a trade or profession or part thereof engaged by the AG (§ 76 (3)). Management board members may not sit on the supervisory board and *vice versa*, except that the supervisory board may temporarily fill vacancies (up to one year) on the management board with its own members, who during their period of service on the management board may not serve on the supervisory board (§ 105). An appointment to the management board may, during the term of the appointment, only be revoked for cause *(aus wichtigem Grund)*, which includes gross violations of duty or inability to manage the corporation or a vote of no confidence by the shareholders' meeting, unless such vote of no confidence was made for manifestly arbitrary reasons (§ 84 (3)). The dismissed appointee may challenge his dismissal in court. The court may fill vacancies in emergencies (§ 85).

Unless otherwise specified in the articles, all members of the management board must act jointly in both managing the corporation and representing the corporation *vis-à-vis* third parties (§ 77 (1)). It is typical for the articles to provide that any two members, or any one member acting together with a so-called 'Prokurist', a registered authorized officer, may represent the corporation (§ 78 (3)). The management board may have internal rules, which may provide for committees and may spell out the transactions requiring management board consent (§ 77 (2)). While no member or group of members may overrule a majority (§ 77 (1)), it is common to give the chairman a 'casting vote' to break ties. The Act contains further provisions governing signatures by members (§ 79), content of business letters (§ 80) and registration of members in the commercial register (§ 81). The Act contains provisions governing how management rights to profit participation may be calculated and management compensation generally (§§ 86-87). Compensation, including benefits and deferred compensation, must bear a reasonable relationship to the duties of the member and condition of the corporation, and may be reduced if payment becomes a hardship for the corporation (§ 87). The Act prohibits members from competing with the corporation in its line of business and from being on the management board or acting as manager or general partner of another commercial enterprise without the consent of the supervisory board (§ 88). The Act also requires supervisory board consent for credit extended to management board members and their families (§ 89).

Except when the corporation is subject to a 'control agreement' or has been 'integrated' with its parent company – cases which will be discussed below –, the management board has the sole duty to manage the corporation (§ 76 (1)) and such duty cannot be delegated, even to the supervisory board (§ 111 (4)). Absent a control agreement or integration, the management board is independent even of any controlling or majority shareholders. If a controlling shareholder induces the AG to enter into a detrimental transaction it must compensate it for resulting disadvantages and is liable to the AG and its shareholders if it fails to do so (§ 311).

The management board also has the duty to report at specified times to the supervisory board on the affairs of the corporation and must give prior notice if possible of transactions that may materially affect the profitability or solvency of the AG (§ 90). The management board has primary responsibility for calling the shareholders' meeting (§ 121). Further, the management board must call a meeting if losses are expected to reduce the corporation's equity to less than half its share capital (§ 92 (1)) and must notify the court within three weeks of any insolvency or overindebtedness applying for the institution of bankruptcy or composition proceedings (§ 92 (2)). Each member of the management board is required to use the care of a 'diligent and conscientious business executive', and members who breach their duty are jointly and severally liable to the corporation for damages and bear the burden of proving compliance with the standard of care (§ 93 (1)-(3)). The liability is not precluded by supervisory board approval of a transaction, though it is precluded if the transaction is based on a lawful resolution of the shareholders' meeting (§ 93 (4)). Stringent rules apply to waiver and limitations of claims, as in the case of liability based on malfeasance during formation (§ 93 (5)). Members of the management board also have a statutory obligation of confidentiality (§ 404). Certain breaches of such obligation, as well as other breaches of statutory provisions governing the duties of the board, are criminal offenses (§§ 399-404).

IV. Supervisory Board

The supervisory board *(Aufsichtsrat)* controls and supervises the management board but may not participate in the corporation's day to day management (§ 111). The members are chosen by the shareholders' meeting and by the employees, if any of the codetermination statutes applies (§ 101 (1)). The size of the supervisory board depends on the articles and the stated share capital if the AG is not subject to one of the codetermination statutes (§ 95). The Act contains detailed provisions for assuring that the composition of the supervisory board is in compliance with applicable codetermination statutes (§§ 96-99).

Codetermination at the supervisory board level is the subject of four acts: The Shop Constitution Act; the Codetermination Act; the Coal and Steel Codetermination Act; and the Supplementary Codetermination Act.

Under the Shop Constitution Act *(Betriebsverfassungsgesetz)*, the supervisory board of any AG must have employee representatives as one third of its members, unless the AG has fewer than 500 employees or was entered into free commercial register prior to 10 August 1994 and was family controlled. Enterprises which are integrated or subject to enterprise agreements are consolidated for purposes of the Act, and corporations which serve political, labour union, religious, charitable, educational, scientific, artistic or similar purposes, including the media, are exempted from the Act. Employees elect their representatives by general, secret, equal and direct balloting. The Codetermination Act *(Mitbestimmungsgesetz)* applies to all corporations with more than 2000 employees and provides for equal numbers of employee and shareholder representatives on the supervisory board. The chairman of the supervisory board, who has a casting or tie-breaking vote, is as a rule a shareholder representative. The employee representatives on the supervisory board must comprise specific numbers of employees of the corporation and of representatives of labour unions. The Coal and Steel Codetermination Acts *(Montanmitbestimmungsgesetz; Mitbestimmungsergänzungsgesetz)* are applicable to corporations whose principal purpose is the production of coal or iron or the preparation of these materials, and are subject to supervision of the mining authorities. The work force must exceed 1000 employees. The supervisory board is composed of an odd number of shareholder and employee representatives, one of whom is elected by a special procedure designed to ensure that he has the confidence of both sides.

Election of shareholder representatives takes place in the shareholders' meeting, and the articles may specify that up to one third of the shareholders' representatives may be designated by shareholders specified in the articles or by shareholders who hold specified registered shares that under the articles may only be transferred with the corporation's consent (§ 101 (2)).

Supervisory board members must be natural persons (§ 100 (1)) and may serve up to approximately five years (§ 102); the articles or resolutions of appointment may provide for a shorter term. A person may not serve if he already serves on the supervisory boards of ten entities required by law to form such a board, is the legal representative of a controlled enterprise of the corporation or is the legal representative of another entity whose supervisory board includes a member of the AG's management board (§ 100(2)). Members may resign or be recalled (§ 103). The court may recall a member for cause upon application of the supervisory board or by a specified minority in the case of a member elected by shareholders (§ 103(3)); the shareholders electing or designating particular members may recall them with or without cause (§ 103 (2)); in the case of members elected by shareholders, the recall is passed by three quarters of the votes cast at a shareholders' meeting (§ 103 (1)). Designated members may also be recalled by a simple majority if they cease to meet the requirements specified in the articles (§ 103 (2)). The codetermination acts govern the recall of members appointed by employees (§ 103 (4)). Detailed provisions cover the appointment of supervisory board members to fill vacancies in the absence of a quorum (§ 104).

Supervisory board members may only act in person or by submitting votes in writing; they may not delegate a deputy to act in their absence (§§ 108(3), 111(5)). Substitute members may, however, be appointed simultaneously with specific members to replace them in the event they prematurely terminate service on the board. Changes in board composition must be published in the corporation's journals and notified to (but not registered in) the commercial register (§ 106).

The supervisory board elects a chairman and one or more deputy chairmen, who can act for the chairman only if he is incapacitated (§ 10 7(1)). The board may formulate internal rules (§ 82 (2)). The board is expected to meet during each calendar quarter and must meet at least once every half-year (§ 110 (3)). Quorum requirements may be specified in the articles if codetermination does not apply. If the articles are silent, a quorum consists of at least half of the full board, but in any event not less than three members (§ 108 (3)). Generally resolutions require a simple majority of the votes cast. While members may vote on their own election as chairman or deputy chairman, they generally do not vote on transactions or litigation in which they are personally interested. The board may form committees but may not delegate to a committee the power to elect the chairman or deputy chairmen, the establishment of the management board's internal rules, the appointment or dismissal of management board members or the calling of a shareholders' meeting (§ 107 (3)).

The supervisory board is responsible for appointing and dismissing members of the management board (§ 84 (1)) and representing the corporation in its dealings with such board (§ 90), including entering into employment agreements with its members (§ 112). The management board reports to the supervisory board, though the latter is independently entitled to inspect the books, records and properties of the corporation (§ 111(2)). The supervisory board must consent to certain business decisions of the management board if required by the articles or the supervisory board's rules. The supervisory board may not, however, encumber the management board's ability to manage the corporation with excessive consent requirements. If the supervisory board withholds consent, the management board may nevertheless act if it can obtain a three quarters majority of votes cast at the shareholders' meeting (§ 111 (4)).

Another principal function of the supervisory board is its participation in the establishment of the annual financial statements *(Jahresabschluß)*, which are discussed in more detail below.

Commonly, the articles or a shareholder resolution will provide for compensation for supervisory board members, typically including meeting fees and a fixed payment or share of profits. The Act regulates compensation of members of the supervisory board in a manner similar to restrictions on compensation of the management board. Provisions in the articles concerning supervisory board compensation may always be amended by simple majority at the shareholders' meeting (§ 113). Loans to board members and their families as well as agreements between the corporation and a member other than as to his board duties generally require board consent (§§ 114, 115).

Generally supervisory board members are subject to the same standard of care and confidentiality requirements as members of the management board (§§116, 399, 400, 404, 405). The Act contains a special provision imposing liability on persons who use undue influence to cause members of the supervisory or management board to act to the corporation's detriment. The member is jointly and severally liable unless he can show he acted with the care of a diligent and prudent manager. Shareholders have a claim for losses they sustain in addition to the loss sustained by virtue of the damage inflicted on the corporation, and creditors may assert the claim if unable to obtain satisfaction from the corporation (§ 117).

V. Shareholders' Meeting

The shareholders act generally through the shareholders' meeting *(Hauptversammlung)*, which management and supervisory board members (§ 118) and external auditors, if any (§ 176 (2)), are expected to attend.

The functions of the shareholders' meeting are basically limited to passing resolutions concerning the corporation's legal and financial structure, electing and recalling members of the supervisory board, appointing auditors and discharging responsibility of or pursuing claims against board members (§ 119). Resolutions concerning the corporations's legal structure requiring shareholder approval include amendments to the articles, consent to 'enterprise agreements', the integration of the corporation into another corporation, mergers, transformation of legal form, transfer of all assets or (according to case law) transfer of major assets of the corporation. In addition to capital increases and decreases, the shareholders' meeting must consent to the allocation of profit (§ 174).

Ordinarily the shareholders' meeting takes place once every year and at that time passes resolutions on the appropriation of distributable profits, the ratification of the acts of the management and supervisory boards and the appointment of auditors. The ordinary meeting must take place within the first eight months of the fiscal year and is called by the management board upon receipt of the supervisory board's report on the annual financial statements (§ 175). One month's notice is required for all meetings (§ 123). The notice consists of the publication of the date, time and place of the meeting, the agenda and the conditions for the participation of shareholders (§ 121). If all shareholders are known to the corporation, meetings may be called by registered mail (§ 121 (4)). If required by the articles, shareholders must notify the corporation of their intention to attend the meeting and holders of bearer shares must deposit their shares with the corporation, a notary or a bank.

Detailed provisions govern the publication of the agenda for the meeting and prohibit resolutions on items for which publication was improper (§ 124). The management board must publish countermotions and nominations that are timely received and not inconsistent with various statutory requirements (§§ 126, 127).

Rather comprehensive rules deal with the keeping of minutes (§ 130) and lists of participants (§ 129).

Shareholders have the right to such information as is necessary to properly evaluate an agenda item. The management board may only refuse information in limited situations, in particular if it would be likely to cause material damage to the corporation. The denial must be explained in writing upon request and recorded in the minutes of the meeting (§ 131) and is subject to judicial review.

While generally the minimum requirement for passage of a resolution is a simple majority of votes cast, a simple majority of capital represented or higher majorities may be required for certain matters by the Act or the articles (§ 133). Amendments to the articles, for example, require a three fourths majority of capital represented, unless otherwise provided, but changes or amendments of the corporate purpose may not be passed with a smaller majority (§ 179). Class voting may be required in certain circumstances, such as the amendment of the relationship of classes to the disadvantage of any class (§ 179 (3)), and may be accomplished by separate vote or at a separate meeting (§ 138). Resolutions and their results must be recorded in notarized form provided the shares of a corporation are not listed and no resolutions requiring a qualified majority are passed (§ 130 (1)). The minutes of the meeting and appendices must be submitted promptly after the conclusion of the meeting to the commercial register (§ 130 (5)).

While multiple voting rights are only permitted in the event the government grants an exception (§ 12 (2)), voting rights may be limited based on maximum par value or a sliding scale (§ 134). Measures reducing or eliminating voting rights for large holdings do not require the consent of affected shareholders but can be adopted like any other amendment to the articles.

Proxy voting is permissible (§ 134), though proxies granted to banking institutions must be revocable and cannot exceed fifteen months (§ 135). Banks and shareholder associations often vote as proxies and may vote customers' shares within their discretion if they do not receive instructions, but they are to be guided in such case by the shareholders' interests (§ 128). It is not the practice for management to solicit proxies. An agreement whereby a shareholder undertakes to vote in accordance with instructions of the corporation or its management or supervisory board or to vote for the respective proposals of the management or supervisory board is null and void (§ 136 (2)).

VI. Minority Rights

Shareholders holding among them a minimum percentage or fixed amount of the shares have certain rights specified in the Act or the articles. The holders of 5 per cent of share capital, or such lower amount as may be specified in the articles, may request the calling of a special shareholders' meeting (§ 122 (1)). Likewise, shareholders holding 5 per cent or 1 million DM of share capital may require the inclusion on the agenda of a particular item (§ 122 (2)). The shareholders may apply to the court for enforcement of their rights should the management board fail to honour such requests (§ 122(3)). A 10 per cent minority has the power to block a corporation waiver or settlement of various claims it may have against members of the management or supervisory boards or others (§§ 50, 53, 93 (4), 116, 117 (4)) or against dominating companies (§§ 309 (3), 310 (4), 317 (4), 318 (4), 323 (1)). A 10 per cent minority that has held its shares for at least three months can also compel the enforcement of claims in connection with the formation of the corporation and claims for abuse of influence (§ 147). A minority holding of 10 per cent or 2 million DM of share capital may in certain contexts petition the court for appointment of a special auditor (§ 142). A minority holding of 5 per cent or 1 million DM may, on the basis of an important reason, petition the court for the replacement of the corporation's liquidators (§ 265 (3)). A minority holding of 10 per cent or 2 million DM can force separate resolutions on some or all members of the board as to their discharge from responsibility (§ 120 (1)). A similar minority may apply on the basis of an important reason to the court for the dismissal of supervisory board members who are delegated by holders of certain shares (§ 103 (3)). Finally, shareholders holding 25 per cent of share capital plus one share ('blocking minority') may block all resolutions of the shareholders' meeting requiring a three fourths majority of capital represented.

VII. Capital

A. General

As apparent from the above discussion of the financial aspects of formation, the Act places great emphasis on the integrity of the stated share capital. The importance of this aspect is apparent in the following discussion of the relationship of the corporation and its shareholders and of increases and decreases in a corporation's capital.

Corporations may not subscribe to their own shares (§ 56 (1)). Subsidiaries and controlled enterprises likewise may not acquire shares of a parent or controlling enterprise (§ 56 (2)). A corporation may not repay contributions or promise to pay interest to shareholders (§ 57). The acquisition of own shares is limited to six situations:

- to avert severe and imminent damage;
- for reoffer to employees;
- to compensate minority shareholders in connection with entering a control agreement or effecting an integration, merger or division;
- acquisitions without consideration or by a bank in execution of a purchase order;
- as successor in interest by operation of law;
- in case of a credit or financial institution for trading purposes (§ 71 (1)).

The first three cases as well as the last one are subject to volume limitations (§ 71 (2)). The corporation has no right in acquired shares (§ 71b) and must sell illegally acquired shares within one year (§ 71c (1)). Further, the corporation must resell shares not later than three years after acquisition if their aggregate par value exceeds ten per cent of share capital (§ 71c (2)). Shares required to be sold but not sold must be redeemed (§ 71c (3)). The corporation may not extend credit for the purchase of its own shares (§ 71a) or accept a pledge of its own shares (§ 71e).

The articles may impose ancillary obligations upon shareholders in addition to the obligation to make contributions to share capital, and may impose penalties for failure to perform such obligations, so long as they require corporation consent for the transfer of shares (§ 55). Such obligations, as well as the imposition of a consent requirement for transfer of shares, require the consent of all shareholders concerned (§ 180). The corporation may compensate shareholders for required ancillary services whether or not a distributable profit is shown in the balance sheet (§ 61). Shareholders must make restitution for improper benefits received, including dividends received by shareholders who knew or should have known they were not entitled to receive them (§ 62). Late subscription payments are subject to interest at 5 per cent; the corporation may claim further damages and the articles may stipulate penalties (§ 63). After the expiration of certain grace periods the corporation may expel a defaulting shareholder (§ 64) and predecessors of expelled shareholders may be held liable for unpaid subscriptions as well (§ 65 (1), (2)). If the corporation cannot obtain satisfaction it must sell the shares, through a broker if the shares are quoted and otherwise by means of a public auction (§ 65 (3)).

B. Capital increases

Since at any time the share capital set forth in the articles generally corresponds to the outstanding capital, increasing the capital of a corporation consists of essentially two steps: a shareholders' resolution amending the articles and subscription for the shares. Both steps must be notified to the commercial register (§§ 184, 188). Typically, a bank or a syndicate of banks will undertake to subscribe to a capital increase prior to the shareholders' resolution and agree to first offer the shares to the shareholders exercising their pre-emptive rights. Unless the articles specify otherwise, the shareholder's resolution requires a majority of three quarters of votes cast. If more than one class exists, class voting is mandatory. If shares are to be issued for more than their par value, the resolution or resolutions must specify the issue price or a minimum issue price (§ 182 (1)-(3)). The share capital shall not be increased if material amounts of capital contributions are outstanding and collectible (§§ 182(4)). In-kind contributions in respect of capital increases are subject to strict requirements, as in the case of in-kind contributions upon formation, including audit requirements (§ 183). Shareholders have pre-emptive rights relating to share and rights offerings and must be given at least two weeks to exercise such rights after publication of the issue price (§ 186 (1)). Pre-emptive rights can be eliminated by a vote of three quarters of the share capital represented at the shareholders' meeting, or such larger majority as may be stated in the articles (§ 186 (3)). The elimination must be justified by the board of management in writing and can be challenged by the shareholders (§ 186 (4)-(5)). The elimination is deemed to be justified if the capital increase provides for contributions in cash, the amount of the capital increase does not exceed an amount equal to 10 per cent of the existing share capital and the issue price is not significantly lower than the quoted price (§ 186 (3)). Convertible and warrant bonds (bonds that provide holders with a conversion right or stock warrant) as well as dividend bonds (bonds in which the rights of holders are related to dividends paid to shareholders) are subject to the same shareholder approval and pre-emption requirements (§ 221). The rules regarding payment on the shares are similar to those applicable to capital subscriptions on formation (§ 188 (2)). The Act provides for detailed rules regarding registration and announcement (§ 188, 190). The capital increase becomes effective upon registration of completion (§ 189), and new shares may not be issued or transferred prior thereto (§ 191).

C. Conditional capital increases

Conditional capital increases are permitted in connection with the issue of convertible bonds or bonds with warrants, profit sharing plans and business combinations (§ 192 (1), (2)). The aggregate par value of the conditional increase is limited to half of the existing share capital (§ 192 (3)), and the increase requires a three fourths majority or higher vote (§ 193). As in the case of noncontingent increases, the Act contains detailed provisions on in-kind contributions, registration, publication and mechanics of exercise (§§ 194-200). In addition, the management board must annually register the extent of new share issuances pursuant to any outstanding contingent capital increase (§ 201).

D. Authorized capital

The shareholders' meeting may also authorize the management board for five years to increase the share capital up to a specified amount not exceeding one half of share capital as of the date of authorization (§ 202). Issuance requires supervisory board consent (§ 202 (3)). Such authorization may include authority to issue warrant or convertible bonds as well as shares (§ 221 (2)). The management board may determine the rights and conditions of issuance of the new shares (§ 204 (1)). Generally analogous provisions apply to issuance of shares pursuant to such authorizations (§§ 203-206).

E. Other capital increases

Finally, retained earnings may be converted to capital (§ 207) and shareholders may be issued new shares in proportion to their holdings (§ 212). While this type of share capital increase is little more than a bookkeeping measure, it does have the effect of increasing the corporation's creditworthiness since the rules on the preservation of share capital are stricter than the rules regarding reserves. Shares created by the increase, which requires shareholder approval, not claimed by the shareholders entitled thereto may be sold on an exchange, if listed, or at public auction (§ 214). Partially paid shares participate in proportion to par value (§ 215). The Act contains provisions assuring fair treatment of shareholders and third parties (§ 216) and holders of convertible and warrant bonds (§ 218).

F. Capital reductions

Capital reductions, which may be effected by reduction of par value or a reverse stock split, are regulated mainly for the protection of creditors. No reduction may result in shares having a par value other than DM 5 or a multiple of DM 5. Reductions must likewise be approved by resolution of three quarters of the stated share capital, with class voting if more than one class exists, and result in an amendment of the articles (§§ 222-224). Creditors with pre-existing claims have the right to demand security within six months after publication of the reduction. Any distribution to shareholders must be delayed until the six months period has expired and demands for security or claims have been satisfied (§ 225).

In a simplified reduction in capital, the corporation's losses may be restructured without distribution of assets to shareholders and without provision of security to creditors. Prior to the decrease, all free reserves must be used to cover losses (§§ 229, 230). Released funds may be transferred to statutory reserves only to the extent the reserves after the transfer do not exceed 10 per cent of the reduced capital (§ 231). After the decrease, distributions are limited to 4 per cent of share capital until the fiscal year that begins at least two years after the decrease unless creditors are secured (§ 233). Decreases may be made retroactively with the establishment of annual financial statements (§ 234), and may be made simultaneously with a retroactive capital increase if all shares have been fully subscribed and one quarter of the par value plus the entire premium has been paid on each share (§ 235). The function of a combined capital reduction and increase is to enable a corporation whose capital has been impaired to raise additional equity capital; an increase without a reduction would have the effect of depriving the new investors a return on their equity until the prior capital had been replenished by earnings.

Redemptions may be made in accordance with similar rules, the difference being that redemption does not affect all shareholders equally. Mandatory redemption is only permitted if prescribed or permitted in the articles or an amendment made effective prior to issuance of the shares to be redeemed (§ 237). While voluntary redemption requires shareholder approval, mandatory redemption is effected by the board of management invoking the appropriate provisions of the articles.

VIII. Affiliated Enterprises

The Act contains detailed provisions defining 'affiliated enterprises' *(verbundene Unternehmen)*. These provisions do not only apply to AGs but also to all other forms of 'enterprises' *(Unternehmen)* independent of their legal form. Affiliated enterprises are defined to be legally separate entities that

(i) are subsidiary and parent companies;
(ii) controlled and controlling companies;
(iii) members of a group *(Konzern)*;
(iv) enterprises with cross-shareholdings; or
(v) parties to so-called 'enterprise agreements' (§ 15).

A 'subsidiary' is a majority controlled enterprise. The Act outlines how the existence of a majority is to be ascertained (§ 16). 'Controlled enterprises' are entities, including subsidiaries, over which a 'controlling enterprise' is able to exert, directly or indirectly, a controlling influence (§ 17). A 'group' is a group of legally separate enterprises under common direction, whether or not there is a controlling and one or more controlled entities. 'Common direction' can be established by a 'control agreement' or 'integration', as well as by shareholdings (§ 18). 'Enterprises with cross-shareholdings' are enterprises that hold over one fourth of each other's shares (§ 19).

Certain reporting requirements apply in respect of interests in an AG in excess of or which fall below 25 per cent or 50 per cent held by any enterprise (§ 20) and of equivalent interests in a domestic corporation or company (AG, KGaA, GmbH) held by an AG (§ 21).

IX. Enterprise Agreements

'Enterprise agreements' *(Unternehmensverträge)* include 'control agreements' *(Beherrschungsverträge)* and 'profit transfer agreements' *(Gewinnabführungsverträge)* (§ 291), as well as 'profit pool agreements', 'agreements to transfer a share of profits' and 'agreements to lease (or surrender) operations' (§ 292). Under a control agreement, an AG submits to the control of another enterprise, usually but not always its majority or sole shareholder. The controlling enterprise is entitled to instruct the board of management of the controlled AG and may even require that it act to the detriment of the corporation (§ 308 (1)). Profit transfer agreements provide for the transfer of the controlled AG's total profit, net of loss carry-forwards and statutory reserves, as well as losses to the controlling enterprise. To protect creditors, the controlling enterprise in the case of a control or profit transfer agreement must compensate the controlled AG for its losses to the extent not compensated by withdrawals from profit reserves transferred during the term of the agreement (§ 302 (1)). In the case of agreements to lease or surrender operations, the controlling enterprise must compensate losses to the extent the agreed consideration is not adequate (§ 302 (2)). Further, upon cancellation or termination of such agreements, creditors generally have a right to security (§ 303). Minority shareholders, if any, must be guaranteed annual dividends based on past performance and future prospects (§ 304) and be given an opportunity to withdraw for reasonable compensation (§ 305). Both the guaranteed dividend and compensation are subject to court examination (§§ 304, 305).

The management board of a corporation entering into an enterprise agreement has te prepare a report on the agreement (§ 293a) which has to be audited (§ 293b-e) and submitted to the shareholders (§§ 293f, g). All enterprise agreements require approval of three fourths of the AG's capital represented at the shareholders' meeting, or such larger majority specified in the articles (§ 293 (1)), and become effective only upon registration in the commercial register (§ 294). A control agreement or profit transfer agreement becomes effective only if the shareholders' meeting of the other entity (if it is an AG or KGaA) consents as well (§ 293 (2)). Such agreements can terminate by expiration of an agreed upon period or by cancellation (which may only be effective as of the end of an accounting period) (§ 296), or can be terminated for cause, which exists in particular if the other party is likely to be unable to perform (§ 297).

Amendments to enterprise agreements require shareholder approval (§ 295 (1)); cancellations (§ 296 (2)), terminations without cause (§ 297 (2)) and amendments (§ 295 (2)) to terms regarding payments to outside shareholders require the consent of such shareholders.

The controlling enterprise and its representatives, including its management and supervisory boards, may be liable for damages to the controlled AG, its outside shareholders and creditors if they cannot prove that a diligent, conscientious manager would have acted the same way (§§ 309, 310). In the absence of a control agreement, the controlling enterprise is not allowed to use its influence to the detriment of the controlled AG without providing compensation (§ 311). Moreover, in the absence of a control agreement, the board of management of a controlled AG is required to render annually a report on relations with affiliated enterprises (§ 312). Such report (so-called 'dependency report', *Abhängigkeitsbericht)* must be audited if the controlled entity's financial statements are audited (§ 313). The report and any audit report must be examined by the supervisory board (§ 314). Special audits may be required in certain instances (§ 315).

X. Integration

The 'integration '*(Eingliederung)* is in effect similar to a merger of a subsidiary into its parent, but the controlled corporation retains its separate legal identity (§ 319). The principal corporation has the right to instruct the board of management of the controlled corporation (§ 323) and becomes jointly and severally liable for the controlled corporation's obligations (§ 322). The establishment of an integration requires at least

95 percent ownership; minority shareholders must withdraw and are entitled to reasonable compensation (§ 320). As in the case of other transactions that may undermine the corporation's capital, there are provisions for protection of creditors (§ 321). Integration ceases, inter alia, if the principal corporation no longer holds all shares of the integrated corporation (§ 327(1)). Joint and several liability continues generally for five years thereafter (§ 327 (4)).

XI. Financial Statements, Appropriation of Profit

The procedural provisions governing the examination and approval of the annual financial statements as well as the appropriation of profit are contained in §§ 170-174. The management board is required to submit the annual financial statements (balance sheet, profit and loss statement – *Jahresabschluß)* and the annual report *(Lagebericht)* together with an auditor's report, if required, to the supervisory board promptly upon completion (§ 170 (1)). At the same time the management board shall submit to the supervisory board a proposal for appropriation of distributable profits (§ 170 (2)). The supervisory board examines the annual financial statements, the annual report, the proposal for distribution of profits as well as the auditor's report and reports on its findings to the shareholders' meeting within one month after receipt of those documents (§ 171). The annual financial statements are to be approved by the supervisory board (§ 172) or, exceptionally, by the shareholders' meeting if the management and supervisory boards resolve that the statements are to be approved by the shareholders' meeting or if the supervisory board has refused to approve such statements (§ 173 (1)). The shareholders' meeting resolves on the appropriation of distributable profits based on the approved financial statements (§ 174 (1)). The resolution shall specify the amounts to be distributed to the shareholders and transferred to the reserves as well as the amounts of profits carried forward (§ 174 (2)).

The substantive provisions governing the appropriation and distribution of annual net profit are contained in §§ 58-60. The articles may provide that when the shareholders' meeting is to approve the annual financial statements, it may transfer up to one half of annual net profits to other profit reserves (§ 58 (1)). If the management and supervisory boards approve the financial statements, they may also transfer up to one half of the annual net profit to other reserves. The articles may authorize transfers in excess of such amount, but transfers on the basis of such authority may not be made if the other profit reserves exceed, or upon such transfers would exceed, one half of the share capital (§ 58 (2)). The shareholders' meeting may transfer additional amounts to profit reserves or carry such amounts forward as profit (§ 58 (3)). In certain circumstances, if authorized under the articles, the management board may make advance payments of distributable profits to shareholders after the close of the fiscal year (§ 59). Shareholders participate in distributions in proportion to the par value of their shares (§ 60 (1)). If contributions have not been made in the same proportion for all shares, shareholders are first to be paid an amount of 4 per cent of the contributions made, provided the profit is sufficient to make such payments. Otherwise payments are to be made at an appropriately lower percentage (§ 60 (2)). Prior to dissolution of the corporation, only distributable profit may be distributed to shareholders (§ 57 (3)).

A holder or holders of a substantial minority of shares may bring an action to set aside the resolution on the allocation and distribution of profits if the distribution, if any, does not exceed 4 per cent of paid in capital and transfers to reserves and carry forwards of profits were not necessary according to reasonable business judgment to secure the viability of the corporation for a period which is foreseeable with respect to economic and financial circumstances (§ 254). The test allows the shareholders' meeting some leeway and a safe harbor, and of course the action may not be an effective deterrent if no qualified minority holder or block exists.

Moreover, the Act contains certain provisions (§§ 150, 152, 158, 160) expanding upon and to some extent superseding the general principles governing the establishment of the annual financial statements and the annual report set forth in Book Three (§§ 238-339) of the Commercial Code *(Handelsgesetzbuch)*. In particular, the Act requires the establishment of a statutory reserve up to an amount equivalent to 10 per cent of the share capital (§ 150).

XII. Dissolution

A corporation may be dissolved for numerous reasons, such as: upon the occurrence of an event or exercise of a right specified in the articles; resolution by three quarters of the share capital represented at the shareholders' meeting; institution of bankruptcy proceedings; a final decision denying the institution of bankruptcy proceedings for lack of assets sufficient to cover the costs of the proceedings, or a finding that the articles are deficient (§ 262). An AG may also be judicially dissolved if it endangers the public welfare as a result of the conduct of its boards or shareholders' meeting and, in the case of board misconduct, fails to procure the dismissal of the offending board members (§ 396). Dissolution means that the corporation ceases regular business and, except in the case of bankruptcy proceedings, which are covered by another statute, turns to liquidation, though it may continue doing business within the scope of liquidation proceedings (§ 264).

Generally, the former members of the management board become the liquidators, though the articles or shareholders' resolution may specify otherwise (§ 265). The liquidators, which in contrast to the management board may include legal entities, must be registered in the commercial register (§ 266) and are supervised by the supervisory board (§ 268). They must notify creditors to submit their claims (§ 267), establish an opening liquidation balance sheet and issue an opening report (§ 270). Distribution of assets occurs only after a period of time set for satisfaction of claims (§§ 185, 271, 272). The conclusion of liquidation is submitted for registration and the corporation is deleted from the commercial register. The corporation's books and records must be deposited at a secure location for ten years and be open for inspection by former shareholders and creditors (§ 273).

Prior to the distribution of assets, a majority of not less than three fourths of capital represented may resolve to continue the corporation (§ 274).

Acknowledgements

We are exceedingly indebted to Richard A. Kahn, Esq. and Matthias Horbach for their assistance.

Hannes Schneider
Martin Heidenhain

2 Stock Corporation Act
Aktiengesetz

Aktiengesetz

Vom 6. September 1965 (BGBl. I 1089), zuletzt geändert durch Gesetz vom 28. Oktober 1994 (BGBl. I 3210)

Inhaltsübersicht

Stock Corporation Act

of September 6, 1965 (Legal Gazette I 1089), as last amended by the Act of 28 October 1994 (Federal Legal Gazette I 3210)

Table of Contents

Erstes Buch. Aktiengesellschaft

Book One. The Stock Corporation

Erster Teil. Allgemeine Vorschriften

§ 1. Wesen der Aktiengesellschaft

(**1**) Die Aktiengesellschaft ist eine Gesellschaft mit eigener Rechtspersönlichkeit. Für die Verbindlichkeiten der Gesellschaft haftet den Gläubigern nur das Gesellschaftsvermögen.

(**2**) Die Aktiengesellschaft hat ein in Aktien zerlegtes Grundkapital.

§ 2. Gründerzahl

An der Feststellung des Gesellschaftsvertrags (der Satzung) müssen sich eine oder mehrere Personen beteiligen, welche die Aktien gegen Einlagen übernehmen.

§ 3. Die Aktiengesellschaft als Handelsgesellschaft

Die Aktiengesellschaft gilt als Handelsgesellschaft, auch wenn der Gegenstand des Unternehmens nicht im Betrieb eines Handelsgewerbes besteht.

Part One. General Provisions

§ 1. Nature of the Stock Corporation

(**1**) The stock corporation is a company which constitutes a separate legal entity. Liability to creditors with respect to obligations of the company shall be limited to the company's assets.

(**2**) The stock corporation shall have a capital divided into shares.

§ 2. Number of Incorporators

One ore more persons who subscribe to shares against contributions shall establish the company's articles of association (the 'articles').

§ 3. The Stock Corporation as a Commercial Enterprise

The stock corporation shall constitute a commercial enterprise[1] even if the corporate purpose does not comprise commercial activity.[2]

1. Commercial enterprises are companies and general and limited partnerships which are subject to the Commercial Code.
2. As defined by § 1 of the Commercial Code.

§ 4. Firma

(1) Die Firma der Aktiengesellschaft ist in der Regel dem Gegenstand des Unternehmens zu entnehmen. Sie muß die Bezeichnung 'Aktiengesellschaft' enthalten.

(2) Führt die Aktiengesellschaft die Firma eines auf sie übergegangenen Handelsgeschäfts fort (§ 22 des Handelsgesetzbuchs), so muß sie die Bezeichnung 'Aktiengesellschaft' in die Firma aufnehmen.

§ 4. Name

(1) The name of the stock corporation shall as a rule be derived from the corporate purpose. The name shall contain the designation 'Aktiengesellschaft'.

(2) If the stock corporation retains the name of a business which it has acquired (§ 22 of the Commercial Code), it shall add to such name the designation 'Aktiengesellschaft.'

§ 5. Sitz

(1) Sitz der Gesellschaft ist der Ort, den die Satzung bestimmt.

(2) Die Satzung hat als Sitz in der Regel den Ort, wo die Gesellschaft einen Betrieb hat, oder den Ort zu bestimmen, wo sich die Geschäftsleitung befindet oder die Verwaltung geführt wird.

§ 5. Domicile

(1) The company's domicile shall be the location designated in the articles.

(2) The articles shall as a rule designate as domicile the location where the company maintains an operation or the location where its management is situated or its administration is conducted.

§ 6. Grundkapital

Das Grundkapital und die Aktien müssen auf einen Nennbetrag in Deutscher Mark lauten.

§ 6. Share Capital

The share capital and the par value of shares shall be denominated in Deutsche Mark.

§ 7. Mindestnennbetrag des Grundkapitals

Der Mindestnennbetrag des Grundkapitals ist einhunderttausend Deutsche Mark.

§ 7. Minimum Par Value of the Share Capital

The minimum par value of the share capital shall be one hundred thousand Deutsche Mark.

§ 8. Mindestnennbetrag der Aktien

(1) Der Mindestnennbetrag der Aktien ist fünf Deutsche Mark. Aktien über einen geringeren Nennbetrag sind nich-

§ 8. Minimum Par Value of Shares

(1) The minimum par value of shares shall be five Deutsche Mark. Shares with a lower par value shall be null and void.

tig. Für den Schaden aus der Ausgabe sind die Ausgeber den Inhabern als Gesamtschuldner verantwortlich.

The issuer of such shares shall be jointly and severally liable to the holders thereof for any damage resulting from the issue.

(2) Höhere Aktiennennbeträge müssen auf volle fünf Deutsche Mark lauten.

(2) Higher share par values shall be stated in multiples of five Deutsche Mark.

(3) Die Aktien sind unteilbar.

(3) Shares shall not be divisible.

(4) Diese Vorschriften gelten auch für Anteilscheine, die den Aktionären vor der Ausgabe der Aktien erteilt werden (Zwischenscheine).

(4) The foregoing provisions shall also apply to certificates ('interim certificates') issued to shareholders prior to the issue of share certificates.

§ 9. Ausgabebetrag der Aktien

§ 9. Issue Price of Shares

(1) Für einen geringeren Betrag als den Nennbetrag dürfen Aktien nicht ausgegeben werden.

(1) Shares may not be issued at a price lower than par value.

(2) Für einen höheren Betrag ist die Ausgabe zulässig.

(2) Shares may be issued at a price higher than par value.

§ 10. Aktien und Zwischenscheine

§ 10. Share Certificates and Interim Certificates

(1) Die Aktien können auf den Inhaber oder auf Namen lauten.

(1) Share certificates may be in bearer or registered form.

(2) Sie müssen auf Namen lauten, wenn sie vor der vollen Leistung des Nennbetrags oder des höheren Ausgabebetrags ausgegeben werden. Der Betrag der Teilleistungen ist in der Aktie anzugeben.

(2) Share certificates shall be in registered form if they are issued prior to full payment of the par value or higher issue price, as the case may be. The amount of partial payments shall be indicated on the share certificates.

(3) Zwischenscheine müssen auf Namen lauten.

(3) Interim certificates shall be in registered form.

(4) Zwischenscheine auf den Inhaber sind nichtig. Für den Schaden aus der Ausgabe sind die Ausgeber den Inhabern als Gesamtschuldner verantwortlich.

(4) Interim certificates in bearer form shall be null and void. The issuers of such certificates shall be jointly and severally liable to the holders thereof for any damage resulting from the issue.

(5) In der Satzung kann der Anspruch auf Einzelverbriefung der Aktien ausgeschlossen oder eingeschränkt werden.

(5) The right to receive individual share certificates may be excluded or restricted in the articles.

§ 11. Aktien besonderer Gattung

§ 11. Classes of Shares

Die Aktien können verschiedene Rechte gewähren, namentlich bei der Verteilung des Gewinns und des Gesellschaftsvermögens. Aktien mit gleichen Rechten bilden eine Gattung.

Shares may confer different rights, in particular with regard of the distribution of profits and assets. Shares conferring identical rights shall constitute one class.

§ 12. Stimmrecht. Keine Mehrstimmrechte

§ 12. No Multiple Voting Rights

(1) Jede Aktie gewährt das Stimmrecht. Vorzugsaktien können nach den Vorschriften dieses Gesetzes als Aktien ohne Stimmrecht ausgegeben werden.

(1) Each share shall confer voting rights. However, preferred shares which confer no voting rights may be issued in accordance with the provisions of this Act.

(2) Mehrstimmrechte sind unzulässig. Die für Wirtschaft zuständige oberste Behörde des Landes, in dem die Gesellschaft ihren Sitz hat, kann Ausnahmen zulassen, soweit es zur Wahrung überwiegender gesamtwirtschaftlicher Belange erforderlich ist.

(2) Multiple voting rights shall be prohibited. The highest authority with responsibility for economic affairs in the federal state in which the company is domiciled may grant exemptions if required in order to safeguard overriding interests of the public welfare.

§ 13. Unterzeichnung der Aktien

§ 13. Signatures on Share Certificates

Zur Unterzeichnung von Aktien und Zwischenscheinen genügt eine vervielfältigte Unterschrift. Die Gültigkeit der Unterzeichnung kann von der Beachtung einer besonderen Form abhängig gemacht werden. Die Formvorschrift muß in der Urkunde enthalten sein.

For share certificates and interim certificates a facsimile signature shall be sufficient. The validity of the signature may be made contingent upon compliance with prescribed form requirements. Any such form requirements shall be set out in the certificate.

§ 14. Zuständigkeit

§ 14. Jurisdiction

Gericht im Sinne dieses Gesetzes ist, wenn nichts anderes bestimmt ist, das Gericht des Sitzes der Gesellschaft.

Unless otherwise specified, 'court' as used in this Act shall mean the court of the company's domicile.

§ 15. Verbundene Unternehmen

Verbundene Unternehmen sind rechtlich selbständige Unternehmen, die im Verhältnis zueinander in Mehrheitsbesitz stehende Unternehmen und mit Mehrheit beteiligte Unternehmen (§ 16), abhängige und herrschende Unternehmen (§ 17), Konzernunternehmen (§ 18), wechselseitig beteiligte Unternehmen (§ 19) oder Vertragsteile eines Unternehmensvertrags (§§ 291, 292) sind.

§ 15. Affiliated Enterprises

Legally separate enterprises which with respect to each other are subsidiary and parent company (§ 16), controlled or controlling enterprises (§ 17), members of a group (§ 18), enterprises with cross-shareholdings (§ 19), or parties to an enterprise agreement (§§ 291, 292) shall constitute affiliated enterprises.

§ 16. In Mehrheitsbesitz stehende Unternehmen und mit Mehrheit beteiligte Unternehmen

(**1**) Gehört die Mehrheit der Anteile eines rechtlich selbständigen Unternehmens einem anderen Unternehmen oder steht einem anderen Unternehmen die Mehrheit der Stimmrechte zu (Mehrheitsbeteiligung), so ist das Unternehmen ein in Mehrheitsbesitz stehendes Unternehmen, das andere Unternehmen ein an ihm mit Mehrheit beteiligtes Unternehmen.

(**2**) Welcher Teil der Anteile einem Unternehmen gehört, bestimmt sich bei Kapitalgesellschaften nach dem Verhältnis des Gesamtnennbetrags der ihm gehörenden Anteile zum Nennkapital, bei bergrechtlichen Gewerkschaften nach der Zahl der Kuxe. Eigene Anteile sind bei Kapitalgesellschaften vom Nennkapital, bei bergrechtlichen Gewerkschaften von der Zahl der Kuxe abzusetzen. Eigenen Anteilen des Unternehmens stehen Anteile gleich, die einem anderen für Rechnung des Unternehmens gehören.

§ 16. Subsidiaries and Parent Companies

(**1**) If the majority of shares in a legally separate enterprise is held by another enterprise or if another enterprise is entitled to the majority of the voting rights ('majority holding'), such enterprise shall constitute a subsidiary and the other enterprise shall constitute its parent company.

(**2**) The portion of shares which is held by an enterprise shall be determined, in the case of corporations, by the ratio of the aggregate par value of shares held to the aggregate par value of the share capital, and, in the case of mining companies, by the number of shares in the mining company. In the case of corporations, company shares held by the corporation shall be deducted from the share capital; in the case of mining companies, company shares held by the mining company shall be deducted from the number of shares in the mining company. Shares held by another person on behalf of the enterprise shall be deemed to be equivalent to company shares held by the enterprise.

(3) Welcher Teil der Stimmrechte einem Unternehmen zusteht, bestimmt sich nach dem Verhältnis der Zahl der Stimmrechte, die es aus den ihm gehörenden Anteilen ausüben kann, zur Gesamtzahl aller Stimmrechte. Von der Gesamtzahl aller Stimmrechte sind die Stimmrechte aus eigenen Anteilen sowie aus Anteilen, die nach Absatz 2 Satz 3 eigenen Anteilen gleichstehen, abzusetzen.

(3) The portion of the voting rights to which an enterprise is entitled shall be determined by the ratio of number of voting rights exercisable in respect of the shares held by such enterprise to the aggregate number of all voting rights. Voting rights arising from company shares held by the enterprise and shares deemed equivalent to such company shares pursuant to subsection (2) sentence 3 shall be deducted from the aggregate number of all voting rights.

(4) Als Anteile, die einem Unternehmen gehören, gelten auch die Anteile, die einem von ihm abhängigen Unternehmen oder einem anderen für Rechnung des Unternehmens oder eines von diesem abhängigen Unternehmens gehören und, wenn der Inhaber des Unternehmens ein Einzelkaufmann ist, auch die Anteile, die sonstiges Vermögen des Inhabers sind.

(4) Shares held by a controlled enterprise or held by another person on behalf of the enterprise or an enterprise controlled by it and, if the owner of the enterprise is a sole proprietor, shares which constitute private property of the owner, shall be deemed to constitute shares held by the enterprise.

§ 17. Abhängige und herrschende Unternehmen

§ 17. Controlled and Controlling Enterprises

(1) Abhängige Unternehmen sind rechtlich selbständige Unternehmen, auf die ein anderes Unternehmen (herrschendes Unternehmen) unmittelbar oder mittelbar einen beherrschenden Einfluß ausüben kann.

(1) Legally separate enterprises over which another enterprise ('controlling enterprise') is able to exert, directly or indirectly, a controlling influence, shall constitute controlled enterprises.

(2) Von einem in Mehrheitsbesitz stehenden Unternehmen wird vermutet, daß es von dem an ihm mit Mehrheit beteiligten Unternehmen abhängig ist.

(2) A subsidiary shall be presumed to be controlled by its parent company.

§ 18. Konzern und Konzernunternehmen

§ 18. Groups and Members of Groups

(1) Sind ein herrschendes und ein oder mehrere abhängige Unternehmen unter der einheitlichen Leitung des herrschenden Unternehmens zusammengefaßt, so bilden sie einen Konzern; die ein-

(1) If a controlling and one or more controlled enterprises are subject to the common direction of the controlling enterprise, such enterprises shall constitute a group and the individual enterprises

zelnen Unternehmen sind Konzernunternehmen. Unternehmen, zwischen denen ein Beherrschungsvertrag (§ 291) besteht oder von denen das eine in das andere eingegliedert ist (§ 319), sind als unter einheitlicher Leitung zusammengefaßt anzusehen. Von einem abhängigen Unternehmen wird vermutet, daß es mit dem herrschenden Unternehmen einen Konzern bildet.

shall constitute members of such group. If enterprises are parties to a control agreement (§ 291) or if one enterprise has been integrated into another (§ 319), such enterprises shall be deemed to be subject to common direction. A controlled enterprise and its controlling enterprise shall be presumed to constitute a group.

(2) Sind rechtlich selbständige Unternehmen, ohne daß das eine Unternehmen von dem anderen abhängig ist, unter einheitlicher Leitung zusammengefaßt, so bilden sie auch einen Konzern; die einzelnen Unternehmen sind Konzernunternehmen.

(2) If legally separate enterprises are subject to common direction, such enterprises shall constitute a group and the individual enterprises shall constitute members of such group even if none of such enterprises controls the other.

§ 19. Wechselseitig beteiligte Unternehmen

§ 19. Enterprises with Cross-Shareholdings

(1) Wechselseitig beteiligte Unternehmen sind Unternehmen mit Sitz im Inland in der Rechtsform einer Kapitalgesellschaft oder bergrechtlichen Gewerkschaft, die dadurch verbunden sind, daß jedem Unternehmen mehr als der vierte Teil der Anteile des anderen Unternehmens gehört. Für die Feststellung, ob einem Unternehmen mehr als der vierte Teil der Anteile des anderen Unternehmens gehört, gilt § 16 Abs. 2 Satz 1, Abs. 4.

(1) Enterprises which have a domestic domicile and are organized as corporations or mining companies and which are affiliated in such manner that each enterprise holds more than one fourth of the shares of the other shall constitute enterprises with cross-shareholdings. § 16 (2) sentence 1 and (4) shall apply in determining whether an enterprise holds more than one fourth of the shares of the other enterprise.

(2) Gehört einem wechselseitig beteiligten Unternehmen an dem anderen Unternehmen eine Mehrheitsbeteiligung oder kann das eine auf das andere Unternehmen unmittelbar oder mittelbar einen beherrschenden Einfluß ausüben, so ist das eine als herrschendes, das andere als abhängiges Unternehmen anzusehen.

(2) If one of the enterprises with cross-shareholdings has a majority holding in the other enterprise or if one of such enterprises is able to exert, directly or indirectly, a controlling influence over the other, such enterprise shall constitute the controlling and the other the controlled enterprise.

(3) Gehört jedem der wechselseitig beteiligten Unternehmen an dem anderen Unternehmen eine Mehrheitsbeteiligung

(3) If each of the enterprises with cross-shareholdings has a majority holding in the other enterprise, or if each is

oder kann jedes auf das andere unmittelbar oder mittelbar einen beherrschenden Einfluß ausüben, so gelten beide Unternehmen als herrschend und als abhängig.

able to exert, directly or indirectly, a controlling influence over the other, each enterprise shall constitute a controlling and a controlled enterprise.

(4) § 328 ist auf Unternehmen, die nach Absatz 2 oder 3 herrschende oder abhängige Unternehmen sind, nicht anzuwenden.

(4) § 328 shall not apply to enterprises which constitute controlling or controlled enterprises pursuant to subsections (2) or (3).

§ 20. Mitteilungspflichten

§ 20. Disclosure Obligations

(1) Sobald einem Unternehmen mehr als der vierte Teil der Aktien einer Aktiengesellschaft mit Sitz im Inland gehört, hat es dies der Gesellschaft unverzüglich schriftlich mitzuteilen. Für die Feststellung, ob dem Unternehmen mehr als der vierte Teil der Aktien gehört, gilt § 16 Abs. 2 Satz 1, Abs. 4.

(1) As soon as an enterprise shall hold more than one fourth of the shares of a stock corporation with domestic domicile, it shall promptly inform such company thereof in writing. § 16 (2) sentence 1 and (4) shall apply in determining whether the enterprise holds more than one fourth of the shares.

(2) Für die Mitteilungspflicht nach Absatz 1 rechnen zu den Aktien, die dem Unternehmen gehören, auch Aktien,

1. deren Übereignung das Unternehmen, ein von ihm abhängiges Unternehmen oder ein anderer für Rechnung des Unternehmens oder eines von diesem abhängigen Unternehmens verlangen kann;
2. zu deren Abnahme das Unternehmen, ein von ihm abhängiges Unternehmen oder ein anderer für Rechnung des Unternehmens oder eines von diesem abhängigen Unternehmens verpflichtet ist.

(2) For purposes of the disclosure requirement pursuant to subsection (1), shares held by an enterprise shall be deemed to include:

1. shares whose transfer may be required by such enterprise, or an enterprise controlled by it, or any other person on behalf of such enterprise or an enterprise controlled by it, and

2. shares which such enterprise, or an enterprise controlled by it, or any other person on behalf of such enterprise or an enterprise controlled by it, is obligated to acquire.

(3) Ist das Unternehmen eine Kapitalgesellschaft oder bergrechtliche Gewerkschaft, so hat es, sobald ihm ohne Hinzurechnung der Aktien nach Absatz 2 mehr als der vierte Teil der Aktien gehört, auch dies der Gesellschaft unverzüglich schriftlich mitzuteilen.

(3) If such enterprise is organized as a corporation or a mining company, it shall, as soon as it shall hold more than one fourth of the shares of a company, not including any shares attributable to it pursuant to subsection (2), promptly inform such company thereof in writing.

(4) Sobald dem Unternehmen eine Mehrheitsbeteiligung (§ 16 Abs. 1) gehört, hat es auch dies der Gesellschaft unverzüglich schriftlich mitzuteilen.

(4) As soon as any enterprise shall acquire a majority holding (§ 16 (1)), it shall promptly inform such company thereof in writing.

(5) Besteht die Beteiligung in der nach Absatz 1, 3 oder 4 mitteilungspflichtigen Höhe nicht mehr, so ist dies der Gesellschaft unverzüglich schriftlich mitzuteilen.

(5) If the holding shall fall below the level requiring disclosure pursuant to subsections (1), (3) or (4), the company shall be promptly informed thereof in writing.

(6) Die Gesellschaft hat das Bestehen einer Beteiligung, die ihr nach Absatz 1 oder 4 mitgeteilt worden ist, unverzüglich in den Gesellschaftsblättern bekanntzumachen; dabei ist das Unternehmen anzugeben, dem die Beteiligung gehört. Wird der Gesellschaft mitgeteilt, daß die Beteiligung in der nach Absatz 1 oder 4 mitteilungspflichtigen Höhe nicht mehr besteht, so ist auch dies unverzüglich in den Gesellschaftsblättern bekanntzumachen.

(6) The company shall promptly announce in the company's designated journals the existence of a shareholding of which it has been informed pursuant to subsection (1) or (4), disclosing the enterprise holding such shares. If the company has been informed that such shareholding has fallen below the level requiring disclosure pursuant to subsections (1) or (4), such fact shall also be announced promptly in the company's designated journals.

(7) Rechte aus Aktien, die einem nach Absatz 1 oder 4 mitteilungspflichtigen Unternehmen gehören, können für die Zeit, für die das Unternehmen die Mitteilung nicht gemacht hat, durch das Unternehmen, ein von ihm abhängiges Unternehmen oder einen anderen für Rechnung des Unternehmens oder eines von diesem abhängigen Unternehmens nicht ausgeübt werden.

(7) Rights arising from shares which are held by an enterprise required to make disclosure pursuant to subsection (1) or (4) may not, for as long as such enterprise has not made such disclosure, be exercised by such enterprise, by an enterprise controlled by it or by any other person on behalf of such enterprise or an enterprise controlled by it.

§ 21. Mitteilungspflichten der Gesellschaft

§ 21. Disclosure Obligations of the Company

(1) Sobald der Gesellschaft mehr als der vierte Teil der Anteile einer anderen Kapitalgesellschaft oder bergrechtlichen Gewerkschaft mit Sitz im Inland gehört, hat sie dies dem Unternehmen, an dem die Beteiligung besteht, unverzüglich schriftlich mitzuteilen. Für die Feststellung, ob der Gesellschaft mehr als der

(1) As soon as the company shall hold more than one fourth of the shares of another corporation or mining company with domestic domicile, it shall promptly inform such enterprise thereof in writing. § 16 (2) sentence 1 and (4) shall apply analogously in determining whether the company holds more than one fourth of the shares.

vierte Teil der Anteile gehört, gilt § 16 Abs. 2 Satz 1, Abs. 4 sinngemäß.

(2) Sobald der Gesellschaft eine Mehrheitsbeteiligung (§ 16 Abs. 1) an einem anderen Unternehmen gehört, hat sie dies dem Unternehmen, an dem die Mehrheitsbeteiligung besteht, unverzüglich schriftlich mitzuteilen.

(2) As soon as the company shall acquire a majority holding (§ 16 (1)) in another enterprise, it shall promptly inform such enterprise thereof in writing.

(3) Besteht die Beteiligung in der nach Absatz 1 oder 2 mitteilungspflichtigen Höhe nicht mehr, hat die Gesellschaft dies dem anderen Unternehmen unverzüglich schriftlich mitzuteilen.

(3) If the holding shall fall below the level requiring disclosure pursuant to subsections (1) or (2), the company shall promptly inform the other enterprise thereof in writing.

(4) Rechte aus Anteilen, die einer nach Absatz 1 oder 2 mitteilungspflichtigen Gesellschaft gehören, können für die Zeit, für die sie die Mitteilung nicht gemacht hat, nicht ausgeübt werden.

(4) Rights arising from shares which are held by a company required to make disclosure pursuant to subsections (1) or (2) may not be exercised for as long as the company has not made such disclosure.

§ 22. Nachweis mitgeteilter Beteiligungen

Ein Unternehmen, dem eine Mitteilung nach § 20 Abs. 1, 3 oder 4, § 21 Abs. 1 oder 2 gemacht worden ist, kann jederzeit verlangen, daß ihm das Bestehen der Beteiligung nachgewiesen wird.

§ 22. Proof of Disclosed Holdings

An enterprise to which disclosure has been made pursuant to § 20 (1), (3) or (4), or § 21 (1) or (2) may at any time require proof of the existence of the shareholding.

Zweiter Teil. Gründung der Gesellschaft

Part Two. Formation of the Company

§ 23. Feststellung der Satzung

(1) Die Satzung muß durch notarielle Beurkundung festgestellt werden. Bevollmächtigte bedürfen einer notariell beglaubigten Vollmacht.

(2) In der Urkunde sind anzugeben
1. die Gründer;
2. der Nennbetrag, der Ausgabebetrag und, wenn mehrere Gattungen bestehen,

§ 23. Establishment of the Articles

(1) The articles shall be established in the form of a notarial deed. Attorneys-in-fact shall require a power of attorney certified by a notary.

(2) The deed shall specify:
1. the incorporators;
2. the par value, the issue price and, if more than one class of shares exists, the

die Gattung der Aktien, die jeder Gründer übernimmt;

3. der eingezahlte Betrag des Grundkapitals.

(3) Die Satzung muß bestimmen

1. die Firma und den Sitz der Gesellschaft;

2. den Gegenstand des Unternehmens; namentlich ist bei Industrie- und Handelsunternehmen die Art der Erzeugnisse und Waren, die hergestellt und gehandelt werden sollen, näher anzugeben;

3. die Höhe des Grundkapitals;

4. die Nennbeträge der Aktien und die Zahl der Aktien jeden Nennbetrags sowie, wenn mehrere Gattungen bestehen, die Gattung der Aktien und die Zahl der Aktien jeder Gattung;

5. ob die Aktien auf den Inhaber oder auf den Namen ausgestellt werden;

6. die Zahl der Mitglieder des Vorstands oder die Regeln, nach denen diese Zahl festgelegt wird.

(4) Die Satzung muß ferner Bestimmungen über die Form der Bekanntmachungen der Gesellschaft enthalten.

(5) Die Satzung kann von den Vorschriften dieses Gesetzes nur abweichen, wenn es ausdrücklich zugelassen ist. Ergänzende Bestimmungen der Satzung sind zulässig, es sei denn, daß dieses Gesetz eine abschließende Regelung enthält.

§ 24. Umwandlung von Aktien

Die Satzung kann bestimmen, daß auf Verlangen eines Aktionärs seine Inhaberaktie in eine Namensaktie oder seine Namensaktie in eine Inhaberaktie umzuwandeln ist.

class of shares subscribed by each incorporator; and

3. the paid-in amount of the share capital.

(3) The articles shall determine:

1. the company's name and domicile;

2. the corporate purpose; in particular in the case of enterprises engaged in industry and trade, the articles shall specify the kind of products and goods to be produced and traded;

3. the amount of the share capital;

4. the par value of the shares and the number of shares of each par value and, if more than one class of shares exists, the classes of shares and the number of shares in each class;

5. whether shares are to be issued in bearer or registered form; and

6. the number of members of the management board or the rules for determining such number.

(4) In addition, the articles shall contain provisions regarding the form of announcements by the company.

(5) The articles may make different provisions from the provisions of this Act only if this Act explicitly so permits. The articles may contain additional provisions, except as to matters that are conclusively dealt with in this Act.

§ 24. Change of Form of Share Certificate

The articles may provide that, upon request of a shareholder, his bearer share shall be exchanged for a registered share or his registered share shall be exchanged for a bearer share.

§ 25. Bekanntmachungen der Gesellschaft

Bestimmt das Gesetz oder die Satzung, daß eine Bekanntmachung der Gesellschaft durch die Gesellschaftsblätter erfolgen soll, so ist sie in den Bundesanzeiger einzurücken. Daneben kann die Satzung andere Blätter als Gesellschaftsblätter bezeichnen.

§ 25. Announcements by the Company

Whenever provisions of law or the articles determine that announcements by the company shall be made in the company's designated journals, such announcements shall be published in the Federal Gazette. In addition, the articles may stipulate other journals as the company's designated journals.

§ 26. Sondervorteile. Gründungsaufwand

(1) Jeder einem einzelnen Aktionär oder einem Dritten eingeräumte besondere Vorteil muß in der Satzung unter Bezeichnung des Berechtigten festgesetzt werden.

(2) Der Gesamtaufwand, der zu Lasten der Gesellschaft an Aktionäre oder an andere Personen als Entschädigung oder als Belohnung für die Gründung oder ihre Vorbereitung gewährt wird, ist in der Satzung gesondert festzusetzen.

(3) Ohne diese Festsetzung sind die Verträge und die Rechtshandlungen zu ihrer Ausführung der Gesellschaft gegenüber unwirksam. Nach der Eintragung der Gesellschaft in das Handelsregister kann die Unwirksamkeit nicht durch Satzungsänderung geheilt werden.

(4) Die Festsetzungen können erst geändert werden, wenn die Gesellschaft fünf Jahre im Handelsregister eingetragen ist.

(5) Die Satzungsbestimmungen über die Festsetzungen können durch Satzungsänderung erst beseitigt werden, wenn die Gesellschaft dreißig Jahre im Handelsregister eingetragen ist und wenn die Rechtsverhältnisse, die den Festset-

§ 26. Special Benefits; Formation Expenses

(1) Any special benefit granted to a particular shareholder or a third person shall be stipulated in the articles and the beneficiary shall be identified.

(2) The aggregate amount of expenditures to be paid at the expense of the company to shareholders or other persons as compensation or remuneration for the formation or preparation thereof shall be separately stipulated in the articles.

(3) Absent such stipulation any relevant agreements and any transaction in execution thereof shall be invalid with respect to the company. Such invalidity cannot be cured by amendment of the articles once the company has been registered in the commercial register.

(4) Such stipulations may only be amended after the company has been registered in the commercial register for five years.

(5) The provisions in the articles regarding such stipulations may only be deleted by means of amendment of the articles after the company has been registered in the commercial register for thirty years and all legal relationships which

zungen zugrunde liegen, seit mindestens fünf Jahren abgewickelt sind.

constituted the basis for such stipulations have been settled for not less than five years.

§ 27. Sacheinlagen. Sachübernahmen

§ 27. Contributions in Kind; Acquisitions of Assets

(1) Sollen Aktionäre Einlagen machen, die nicht durch Einzahlung des Nennbetrags oder des höheren Ausgabebetrags der Aktien zu leisten sind (Sacheinlagen), oder soll die Gesellschaft vorhandene oder herzustellende Anlagen oder andere Vermögensgegenstände übernehmen (Sachübernahmen), so müssen in der Satzung festgesetzt werden der Gegenstand der Sacheinlage oder der Sachübernahme, die Person, von der die Gesellschaft den Gegenstand erwirbt, und der Nennbetrag der bei der Sacheinlage zu gewährenden Aktien oder die bei der Sachübernahme zu gewährende Vergütung. Soll die Gesellschaft einen Vermögensgegenstand übernehmen, für den eine Vergütung gewährt wird, die auf die Einlage eines Aktionärs angerechnet werden soll, so gilt dies als Sacheinlage.

(1) If shareholders shall be required to make contributions other than by cash payments in the amount of the par value or the higher issue price ('contributions in kind'), or if the company shall be required to acquire existing or future facilities or other assets ('acquisitions of assets'), the articles shall stipulate the object of the contribution in kind or acquisition of assets, the person from whom the company is to acquire such object, and the par value of the shares to be issued for the contribution in kind or the consideration to be granted for the acquisition of assets. If the company shall be required to acquire an asset for which a consideration is to be granted which is to be applied towards the contribution payable by a shareholder, such acquisition shall be deemed to be a contribution in kind.

(2) Sacheinlagen oder Sachübernahmen können nur Vermögensgegenstände sein, deren wirtschaftlicher Wert feststellbar ist; Verpflichtungen zu Dienstleistungen können nicht Sacheinlagen oder Sachübernahmen sein.

(2) Contributions in kind or acquisitions of assets may only comprise assets which have an ascertainable economic value; obligations to provide services may not be made the object of contributions in kind or acquisitions of assets.

(3) Ohne eine Festsetzung nach Absatz 1 sind Verträge über Sacheinlagen und Sachübernahmen und die Rechtshandlungen zu ihrer Ausführung der Gesellschaft gegenüber unwirksam. Ist die Gesellschaft eingetragen, so wird die Gültigkeit der Satzung durch diese Unwirksamkeit nicht berührt. Ist die Vereinbarung einer Sacheinlage unwirksam, so ist der Aktionär verpflichtet, den Nennbetrag oder den höheren Ausgabebetrag der Aktie einzuzahlen.

(3) Absent a stipulation pursuant to subsection (1), any agreement regarding contributions in kind or acquisitions of assets and any transaction in execution thereof shall be invalid with respect to the company. The validity of the articles shall not be affected by such invalidity once the company has been registered in the commercial register. If an agreement regarding a contribution in kind is invalid, the shareholder shall be obligated to pay in

the par value or the higher share issue price.

(4) Nach Eintragung der Gesellschaft in das Handelsregister kann die Unwirksamkeit nicht durch Satzungsänderung geheilt werden.

(4) Such invalidity cannot be cured by amendment of the articles once the company has been registered in the commercial register.

(5) Für die Änderung rechtswirksam getroffener Festsetzungen gilt § 26 Abs. 4, für die Beseitigung der Satzungsbestimmungen § 26 Abs. 5.

(5) § 26 (4) shall apply to the amendment of lawfully made stipulations; § 26 (5) shall apply to the deletion of the relevant provisions in the articles.

§ 28. Gründer

Die Aktionäre, die die Satzung festgestellt haben, sind die Gründer der Gesellschaft.

§ 28. Incorporators

The shareholders who have established the articles shall be the incorporators of the company.

§ 29. Errichtung der Gesellschaft

Mit der Übernahme aller Aktien durch die Gründer ist die Gesellschaft errichtet.

§ 29. Establishment of the Company

The company shall be established upon subscription of all shares by the incorporators.

§ 30. Bestellung des Aufsichtsrats, des Vorstands und des Abschlußprüfers

(1) Die Gründer haben den ersten Aufsichtsrat der Gesellschaft und den Abschlußprüfer für das erste Voll- oder Rumpfgeschäftsjahr zu bestellen. Die Bestellung bedarf notarieller Beurkundung.

(2) Auf die Zusammensetzung und die Bestellung des ersten Aufsichtsrats sind die Vorschriften über die Bestellung von Aufsichtsratsmitgliedern der Arbeitnehmer nicht anzuwenden.

(3) Die Mitglieder des ersten Aufsichtsrats können nicht für längere Zeit als bis zur Beendigung der Hauptver-

§ 30. Appointment of the Supervisory Board, the Management Board and the External Auditors

(1) The incorporators shall appoint the first supervisory board of the company and the external auditors for the first full or partial fiscal year. Such appointments shall be made in the form of a notarial deed.

(2) The provisions governing the appointment of employee representatives to the supervisory board shall not apply to the composition and the appointment of the first supervisory board.

(3) The members of the first supervisory board may not be appointed for a period extending beyond the adjourn-

sammlung bestellt werden, die über die Entlastung für das erste Voll- oder Rumpfgeschäftsjahr beschließt. Der Vorstand hat rechtzeitig vor Ablauf der Amtszeit des ersten Aufsichtsrats bekanntzumachen, nach welchen gesetzlichen Vorschriften der nächste Aufsichtsrat nach seiner Ansicht zusammenzusetzen ist; §§ 96 bis 99 sind anzuwenden.

ment of the shareholders' meeting that resolves on ratification of the acts of management in respect of the first full or partial fiscal year. The management board shall, within a reasonable period of time prior to the expiration of the term of office of the first supervisory board, announce which statutory provisions in its opinion govern the composition of the following supervisory board; §§ 96 to 99 shall apply.

(4) Der Aufsichtsrat bestellt den ersten Vorstand.

(4) The supervisory board shall appoint the first management board.

§ 31. Bestellung des Aufsichtsrats bei Sachgründung

§ 31. Appointment of the Supervisory Board in case of Transfer of Existing Enterprises

(1) Ist in der Satzung als Gegenstand einer Sacheinlage oder Sachübernahme die Einbringung oder Übernahme eines Unternehmens oder eines Teils eines Unternehmens festgesetzt worden, so haben die Gründer nur so viele Aufsichtsratsmitglieder zu bestellen, wie nach den gesetzlichen Vorschriften, die nach ihrer Ansicht nach der Einbringung oder Übernahme für die Zusammensetzung des Aufsichtsrats maßgebend sind, von der Hauptversammlung ohne Bindung an Wahlvorschläge zu wählen sind. Sie haben jedoch, wenn dies nur zwei Aufsichtsratsmitglieder sind, drei Aufsichtsratsmitglieder zu bestellen.

(1) If the articles provide for a contribution in kind or an acquisition of assets to be made by contribution or acquisition of an enterprise in whole or in part, the incorporators shall appoint only as many members of the supervisory board as the shareholders' meeting is to elect, without being bound by nominations pursuant to the statutory provisions which in the opinion of the incorporators govern the composition of the supervisory board following such contribution or acquisition. If, however, such procedure would result in only two members of the supervisory board being appointed, the incorporators shall appoint three members to the supervisory board.

(2) Der nach Absatz 1 Satz 1 bestellte Aufsichtsrat ist, soweit die Satzung nichts anderes bestimmt, beschlußfähig, wenn die Hälfte, mindestens jedoch drei seiner Mitglieder an der Beschlußfassung teilnehmen.

(2) A quorum for the supervisory board appointed pursuant to subsection (1) sentence 1 shall exist if one half, but in no event less than three, of its members participate in the passing of resolutions, unless the articles provide otherwise.

(3) Unverzüglich nach der Einbringung oder Übernahme des Unternehmens oder des Unternehmensteils hat der Vor-

(3) The management board shall promptly upon such contribution or acquisition of an enterprise in whole or in

stand bekanntzumachen, nach welchen gesetzlichen Vorschriften nach seiner Ansicht der Aufsichtsrat zusammengesetzt sein muß. §§ 97 bis 99 gelten sinngemäß. Das Amt der bisherigen Aufsichtsratsmitglieder erlischt nur, wenn der Aufsichtsrat nach anderen als den von den Gründern für maßgebend gehaltenen Vorschriften zusammenzusetzen ist oder wenn die Gründer drei Aufsichtsratsmitglieder bestellt haben, der Aufsichtsrat aber auch aus Aufsichtsratsmitgliedern der Arbeitnehmer zu bestehen hat.

(4) Absatz 3 gilt nicht, wenn das Unternehmen oder der Unternehmensteil erst nach der Bekanntmachung des Vorstands nach § 30 Abs. 3 Satz 2 eingebracht oder übernommen wird.

(5) § 30 Abs. 3 Satz 1 gilt nicht für die nach Absatz 3 bestellten Aufsichtsratsmitglieder der Arbeitnehmer.

§ 32. Gründungsbericht

(1) Die Gründer haben einen schriftlichen Bericht über den Hergang der Gründung zu erstatten (Gründungsbericht).

(2) Im Gründungsbericht sind die wesentlichen Umstände darzulegen, von denen die Angemessenheit der Leistungen für Sacheinlagen oder Sachübernahmen abhängt. Dabei sind anzugeben

1. die vorausgegangenen Rechtsgeschäfte, die auf den Erwerb durch die Gesellschaft hingezielt haben;
2. die Anschaffungs- und Herstellungskosten aus den letzten beiden Jahren;
3. beim Übergang eines Unternehmens auf die Gesellschaft die Betriebserträge aus den letzten beiden Geschäftsjahren.

part announce which statutory provisions in its opinion govern the composition of the supervisory board. §§ 97 to 99 shall apply analogously. The term of office of the previous members of the supervisory board shall expire only if the supervisory board is required to be composed in accordance with statutory provisions other than those which the incorporators considered to be governing, or if the incorporators appointed three members of the supervisory board despite the fact that the supervisory board also is to include employee representatives.

(4) Subsection (3) shall not apply if the enterprise or part thereof is contributed or acquired after the announcement by the management board pursuant to § 30 (3) sentence 2.

(5) § 30 (3) sentence 1 shall not apply to employee representatives on the supervisory board appointed pursuant to subsection (3).

§ 32. Formation Report

(1) The incorporators shall render a written report on the transactions in connection with the formation of the company ('formation report').

(2) The formation report shall set forth the material facts relevant to the adequacy of contributions in kind or acquisitions of assets. The report shall specify:

1. any preceding transactions entered into with a view to such contribution or acquisition;
2. the costs of acquisition and production during the preceding two years; and
3. in case of the transfer of an enterprise to the company, the earnings for the last two fiscal years.

(3) Im Gründungsbericht ist ferner anzugeben, ob und in welchem Umfang bei der Gründung für Rechnung eines Mitglieds des Vorstands oder des Aufsichtsrats Aktien übernommen worden sind und ob und in welcher Weise ein Mitglied des Vorstands oder des Aufsichtsrats sich einen besonderen Vorteil oder für die Gründung oder ihre Vorbereitung eine Entschädigung oder Belohnung ausbedungen hat.

(3) In addition, the formation report shall specify whether and to what extent shares have been subscribed at formation on behalf of any member of the management board or the supervisory board and whether and in what manner any member of the management board or the supervisory board has obtained a promise of any special benefit or any compensation or remuneration for the formation or preparation thereof.

§ 33. Gründungsprüfung. Allgemeines

§ 33. Formation Audit; General Provisions

(1) Die Mitglieder des Vorstands und des Aufsichtsrats haben den Hergang der Gründung zu prüfen.

(1) The members of the management board and the supervisory board shall audit the transactions in connection with the formation of the company.

(2) Außerdem hat eine Prüfung durch einen oder mehrere Prüfer (Gründungsprüfer) stattzufinden, wenn

1. ein Mitglied des Vorstands oder des Aufsichtsrats zu den Gründern gehört oder
2. bei der Gründung für Rechnung eines Mitglieds des Vorstands oder des Aufsichtsrats Aktien übernommen worden sind oder
3. ein Mitglied des Vorstands oder des Aufsichtsrats sich einen besonderen Vorteil oder für die Gründung oder ihre Vorbereitung eine Entschädigung oder Belohnung ausbedungen hat oder
4. eine Gründung mit Sacheinlagen oder Sachübernahmen vorliegt.

(2) In addition, an audit by one or more auditors ('formation auditors') shall be made if:

1. a member of the management board or the supervisory board is one of the incorporators; or
2. shares have been subscribed at formation on behalf of a member of the management board or the supervisory board; or
3. a member of the management board or the supervisory board has obtained a promise of any special benefits or compensation or remuneration for the formation or preparation thereof; or
4. the formation involves contributions in kind or acquisitions of assets.

(3) Die Gründungsprüfer bestellt das Gericht nach Anhörung der Industrie- und Handelskammer. Gegen die Entscheidung ist die sofortige Beschwerde zulässig.

(3) The court shall appoint the formation auditors after consulting the Chamber of Industry and Commerce. An immediate appeal may be made against the decision.

(4) Als Gründungsprüfer sollen, wenn die Prüfung keine anderen Kenntnisse fordert, nur bestellt werden

(4) Unless the audit requires additional expertise, formation auditors shall be:

1. Personen, die in der Buchführung ausreichend vorgebildet und erfahren sind;
2. Prüfungsgesellschaften, von deren gesetzlichen Vertretern mindestens einer in der Buchführung ausreichend vorgebildet und erfahren ist.

1. persons who are sufficiently trained and experienced in accounting;

2. auditing firms at least one of whose legal representatives is sufficiently trained and experienced in accounting.

(5) Als Gründungsprüfer darf nicht bestellt werden, wer nach § 143 Abs. 2 nicht Sonderprüfer sein kann. Gleiches gilt für Personen und Prüfungsgesellschaften, auf deren Geschäftsführung die Gründer oder Personen, für deren Rechnung die Gründer Aktien übernommen haben, maßgebenden Einfluß haben.

(5) No formation auditor may be appointed who does not qualify to serve as special auditor pursuant to § 143 (2). The foregoing shall apply with respect to persons and auditing firms over whose management the incorporators, or persons on whose behalf the incorporators have subscribed to shares, exert a substantial influence.

§ 34. Umfang der Gründungsprüfung

(1) Die Prüfung durch die Mitglieder des Vorstands und des Aufsichtsrats sowie die Prüfung durch die Gründungsprüfer haben sich namentlich darauf zu erstrecken,
1. ob die Angaben der Gründer über die Übernahme der Aktien, über die Einlagen auf das Grundkapital und über die Festsetzungen nach §§ 26 und 27 richtig und vollständig sind;
2. ob der Wert der Sacheinlagen oder Sachübernahmen den Nennbetrag der dafür zu gewährenden Aktien oder den Wert der dafür zu gewährenden Leistungen erreicht.

(2) Über jede Prüfung ist unter Darlegung dieser Umstände schriftlich zu berichten. In dem Bericht ist der Gegenstand jeder Sacheinlage oder Sachübernahme zu beschreiben sowie anzugeben, welche Bewertungsmethoden bei der Ermittlung des Wertes angewandt worden sind.

(3) Je ein Stück des Berichts der Gründungsprüfer ist dem Gericht und

§ 34. Scope of the Formation Audit

(1) The audit by the members of the management board and the supervisory board and the audit by the formation auditors shall extend in particular to:

1. whether the statements of the incorporators concerning the subscription of shares, the contributions to the share capital and the stipulations pursuant to §§ 26 and 27 are accurate and complete; and
2. whether the value of the assets contributed or acquired in connection with the formation equals or exceeds the par value of the shares to be issued or the value of the consideration to be given therefor.

(2) A written report concerning such matters shall be rendered in respect of each audit. Such report shall describe each asset which has been contributed or acquired and shall set out the valuation methods applied in ascertaining the value thereof.

(3) One copy each of the report of the formation auditors shall be submitted to

dem Vorstand einzureichen. Jedermann kann den Bericht bei dem Gericht einsehen.

the court and the management board. The report shall be available for public inspection at the court.

§ 35. Meinungsverschiedenheiten zwischen Gründern und Gründungsprüfern. Vergütung und Auslagen der Gründungsprüfer

§ 35. Differences of Opinion between Incorporators and Formation Auditors; Remuneration and Expenses of Formation Auditors

(1) Die Gründungsprüfer können von den Gründern alle Aufklärungen und Nachweise verlangen, die für eine sorgfältige Prüfung notwendig sind.

(1) The formation auditors may require the incorporators to furnish them with all information and documentation necessary for a conscientious audit.

(2) Bei Meinungsverschiedenheiten zwischen den Gründern und den Gründungsprüfern über den Umfang der Aufklärungen und Nachweise, die von den Gründern zu gewähren sind, entscheidet das Gericht. Die Entscheidung ist unanfechtbar. Solange sich die Gründer weigern, der Entscheidung nachzukommen, wird der Prüfungsbericht nicht erstattet.

(2) The court shall resolve any differences of opinion between the incorporators and the formation auditors regarding the scope of information and documentation to be furnished by the incorporators. Such decision may not be appealed. The audit report shall not be rendered for so long as the incorporators refuse to comply with such decision.

(3) Die Gründungsprüfer haben Anspruch auf Ersatz angemessener barer Auslagen und auf Vergütung für ihre Tätigkeit. Die Auslagen und die Vergütung setzt das Gericht fest. Gegen die Entscheidung ist die sofortige Beschwerde zulässig. Die weitere Beschwerde ist ausgeschlossen. Aus der rechtskräftigen Entscheidung findet die Zwangsvollstreckung nach der Zivilprozeßordnung statt.

(3) The formation auditors shall be entitled to reimbursement of reasonable cash expenses and remuneration for their services. The expenses and the remuneration shall be set by the court. An immediate appeal may be made against the decision. Further appeal shall be precluded. A decision which is final and not subject to appeal shall be enforceable in accordance with the provisions of the Code of Civil Procedure.

§ 36. Anmeldung der Gesellschaft

§ 36. Report of the Company for Registration

(1) Die Gesellschaft ist bei dem Gericht von allen Gründern und Mitgliedern des Vorstands und des Aufsichtsrats zur Eintragung in das Handelsregister anzumelden.

(1) All incorporators and all members of the management board and the supervisory board shall report the company to the court for registration in the commercial register.

(2) Die Anmeldung darf erst erfolgen, wenn auf jede Aktie, soweit nicht Sacheinlagen vereinbart sind, der eingeforderte Betrag ordnungsgemäß eingezahlt worden ist (§ 54 Abs. 3) und, soweit er nicht bereits zur Bezahlung der bei der Gründung angefallenen Steuern und Gebühren verwandt wurde, endgültig zur freien Verfügung des Vorstands steht. Wird die Gesellschaft nur durch eine Person errichtet, so hat der Gründer zusätzlich für den Teil der Geldeinlage, der den eingeforderten Betrag übersteigt, eine Sicherung zu bestellen.

(2) Except in the case of contributions in kind, such report may be made only after the amount called on each share has been duly paid in (§ 54 (3)), and, to the extent not already utilized for the payment of taxes and fees arising in connection with the formation, is at the free disposal of the management board. If the company is incorporated by one person only, the incorporator shall in addition provide security for that part of the contribution in cash which exceeds the amount called on the shares.

§ 36a. Leistung der Einlagen

(1) Bei Bareinlagen muß der eingeforderte Betrag (§ 36 Abs. 2) mindestens ein Viertel des Nennbetrags und bei Ausgabe der Aktien für einen höheren als den Nennbetrag auch den Mehrbetrag umfassen.

(2) Sacheinlagen sind vollständig zu leisten. Besteht die Sacheinlage in der Verpflichtung, einen Vermögensgegenstand auf die Gesellschaft zu übertragen, so muß diese Leistung innerhalb von fünf Jahren nach der Eintragung der Gesellschaft in das Handelsregister zu bewirken sein. Der Wert muß dem Nennbetrag und bei Ausgabe der Aktien für einen höheren als den Nennbetrag auch dem Mehrbetrag entsprechen.

§ 36a. Contributions

(1) In the case of contributions in cash, the amount called on each share (§ 36 (2)) shall be not less than one fourth of the par value plus, in the case of a share issue at a price in excess of par value, such excess.

(2) Contributions in kind shall be made in full. If the contribution in kind consists of an obligation to transfer an asset to the company, such obligation must be capable of being fulfilled within five years after registration of the company in the commercial register. The value of such contributions shall equal the par value plus, in the case of a share issue at a price in excess of par value, such excess.

§ 37. Inhalt der Anmeldung

(1) In der Anmeldung ist zu erklären, daß die Voraussetzungen des § 36 Abs. 2 und des § 36a erfüllt sind; dabei sind der Betrag, zu dem die Aktien ausgegeben werden, und der darauf eingezahlte Betrag anzugeben. Es ist nachzuweisen, daß der eingezahlte Betrag endgültig zur freien Verfügung des Vorstands steht. Ist der

§ 37. Contents of the Report

(1) The report shall state that the requirements of § 36 (2) and § 36a have been met and shall specify the price at which shares have been issued and the amount paid in. Proof shall be furnished that the amount paid in is at the free disposal of the management board. If the amount has been paid in by crediting an

Betrag durch Gutschrift auf ein Konto der Gesellschaft oder des Vorstands bei der Deutschen Bundesbank oder einem Kreditinstitut (§ 54 Abs. 3) eingezahlt worden, so ist der Nachweis durch eine schriftliche Bestätigung des Instituts zu führen. Für die Richtigkeit der Bestätigung ist das Institut der Gesellschaft verantwortlich. Sind von dem eingezahlten Betrag Steuern und Gebühren bezahlt worden, so ist dies nach Art und Höhe der Beträge nachzuweisen.

account of the company or the management board maintained with the German Federal Bank or a credit institution (§ 54 (3)), such proof shall consist of a written confirmation issued by such institution. Such institution shall be liable to the company for the accuracy of such confirmation. If taxes and fees have been defrayed from the amount paid in, evidence as to the nature and amount of such payments shall be furnished.

(2) In der Anmeldung haben die Vorstandsmitglieder zu versichern, daß keine Umstände vorliegen, die ihrer Bestellung nach § 76 Abs. 3 Satz 3 und 4 entgegenstehen, und daß sie über ihre unbeschränkte Auskunftspflicht gegenüber dem Gericht belehrt worden sind. Die Belehrung nach § 51 Abs. 2 des Gesetzes über das Zentralregister und das Erziehungsregister in der Fassung der Bekanntmachung vom 22. Juli 1976 (BGBl. I S. 2005)[1] kann auch durch einen Notar vorgenommen werden.

(2) The members of the management board shall certify in the report that no circumstances prevail which preclude their appointment pursuant to § 76 (3) sentence 3 and 4 and that they have been advised of their obligation to make full disclosure to the court. The advice pursuant to § 51 (2) of the Act on the Central Register and the Education Register in the form of the Announcement dated 22 July, 1976 (Legal Gazette I p. 2005)[1] may also be given by a notary.

(3) In der Anmeldung ist ferner anzugeben, welche Vertretungsbefugnis die Vorstandsmitglieder haben.

(3) The report shall further specify the authority of the members of the management board to represent the company.

(4) Der Anmeldung sind beizufügen

1. die Satzung und die Urkunden, in denen die Satzung festgestellt worden ist und die Aktien von den Gründern übernommen worden sind;

2. im Fall der §§ 26 und 27 die Verträge, die den Festsetzungen zugrunde liegen oder zu ihrer Ausführung geschlossen worden sind, und eine Berechnung des der Gesellschaft zur Last fallenden Gründungsaufwands; in der Berechnung

(4) The following shall be appended to the report:

1. the articles and the deeds establishing the articles and concerning the subscription to the shares by the incorporators;

2. in case of §§ 26 and 27, the agreements on which the stipulations are based or which were entered into in execution thereof, and an account of the formation expenses which are to be borne by the company; such account shall list the kind

1. Nunmehr § 53 Abs. 2 des Bundeszentralregistergesetzes in der Fassung der Bekanntmachung vom 21. September 1984 (BGBl. I S. 1229, bereinigt 1985 I S. 195).

1. Now § 53(2) of the Act on the Federal Central Register in the version as published on 21 September 1984 (Legal Gazette I, p. 1229, corrected in Legal Gazette 1985 I, p. 195).

sind die Vergütungen nach Art und Höhe und die Empfänger einzeln anzuführen;

3. die Urkunden über die Bestellung des Vorstands und des Aufsichtsrats;

4. der Gründungsbericht und die Prüfungsberichte der Mitglieder des Vorstands und des Aufsichtsrats sowie der Gründungsprüfer nebst ihren urkundlichen Unterlagen;

5. wenn der Gegenstand des Unternehmens oder eine andere Satzungsbestimmung der staatlichen Genehmigung bedarf, die Genehmigungsurkunde.

(5) Die Vorstandsmitglieder haben ihre Namensunterschrift zur Aufbewahrung beim Gericht zu zeichnen.

(6) Die eingereichten Schriftstücke werden beim Gericht in Urschrift, Ausfertigung oder öffentlich beglaubigter Abschrift aufbewahrt.

§ 38. Prüfung durch das Gericht

(1) Das Gericht hat zu prüfen, ob die Gesellschaft ordnungsgemäß errichtet und angemeldet ist. Ist dies nicht der Fall, so hat es die Eintragung abzulehnen.

(2) Das Gericht kann die Eintragung auch ablehnen, wenn die Gründungsprüfer erklären oder es offensichtlich ist, daß der Gründungsbericht oder der Prüfungsbericht der Mitglieder des Vorstands und des Aufsichtsrats unrichtig oder unvollständig ist oder den gesetzlichen Vorschriften nicht entspricht. Gleiches gilt, wenn die Gründungsprüfer erklären oder das Gericht der Auffassung ist, daß der Wert der Sacheinlagen oder Sachübernahmen nicht unwesentlich hinter dem

and amount of remuneration and the recipients thereof;

3. the documents relating to the appointment of the management board and the supervisory board;

4. the formation report and the audit reports of the members of the management board and the supervisory board and of the formation auditors, together with underlying documentation; and

5. if the corporate purpose of the enterprise or another provision of the articles requires governmental approval, the document containing such approval.

(5) The members of the management board shall file their specimen signatures with the court.

(6) All documents submitted shall be kept by the court in the form of originals, duplicates or officially certified copies.

§ 38. Examination by the Court

(1) The court shall examine whether or not the company has been duly established and properly reported for registration. If the company has not been duly established and properly reported for registration, the court shall deny registration.

(2) The court may also deny registration if the formation auditors state, or if it is manifest, that the formation report or the audit report of the members of the management board and the supervisory board is inaccurate or incomplete or does not comply with statutory provisions. The foregoing shall also apply if the formation auditors state, or if the court is of the opinion, that the value of assets contributed or acquired is materially less than the par value of the shares to be issued or

Nennbetrag der dafür zu gewährenden Aktien oder dem Wert der dafür zu gewährenden Leistungen zurückbleibt.

the value of the consideration to be given therefor.

§ 39. Inhalt der Eintragung

(1) Bei der Eintragung der Gesellschaft sind die Firma und der Sitz der Gesellschaft, der Gegenstand des Unternehmens, die Höhe des Grundkapitals, der Tag der Feststellung der Satzung und die Vorstandsmitglieder anzugeben. Ferner ist einzutragen, welche Vertretungsbefugnis die Vorstandsmitglieder haben.

(2) Enthält die Satzung Bestimmungen über die Dauer der Gesellschaft oder über das genehmigte Kapital, so sind auch diese Bestimmungen einzutragen.

§ 39. Contents of the Registration

(1) The registration entry of the company shall specify the company's name and domicile, the corporate purpose, the amount of the share capital, the date of establishment of the articles and the members of the management board. In addition, the authority of the members of the management board to represent the company shall be registered.

(2) If the articles contain any provisions regarding the duration of the company or in respect of authorized capital, such provisions shall also be registered.

§ 40. Bekanntmachung der Eintragung

(1) In die Bekanntmachung der Eintragung sind außer deren Inhalt aufzunehmen

1. die Festsetzungen nach § 23 Abs. 3 und 4, §§ 24, 25 Satz 2, §§ 26 und 27 sowie Bestimmungen der Satzung über die Zusammensetzung des Vorstands;

2. der Ausgabebetrag der Aktien;

3. Name, Beruf und Wohnort der Gründer;

4. Name, Beruf und Wohnort der Mitglieder des ersten Aufsichtsrats.

(2) Zugleich ist bekanntzumachen, daß die mit der Anmeldung eingereichten Schriftstücke, namentlich die Prüfungsberichte der Mitglieder des Vorstands und des Aufsichtsrats sowie der Gründungsprüfer, bei dem Gericht eingesehen werden können.

§ 40. Announcement of the Registration

(1) The announcement of registration shall include, in addition to the contents of the registration, the following:

1. the stipulations pursuant to § 23 (3) and (4), §§ 24, 25 sentence 2, §§ 26 and 27 and the provisions of the articles regarding the composition of the management board;

2. the issue price of the shares;

3. name, profession and place of residence of the incorporators; and

4. name, profession and place of residence of the members of the first supervisory board.

(2) The announcement shall further state that the documents submitted with the report for registration, in particular the audit reports of the members of the management board and the supervisory board and of the formation auditors, may be inspected at the court.

§ 41. Handeln im Namen der Gesellschaft vor der Eintragung. Verbotene Aktienausgabe

(1) Vor der Eintragung in das Handelsregister besteht die Aktiengesellschaft als solche nicht. Wer vor der Eintragung der Gesellschaft in ihrem Namen handelt, haftet persönlich; handeln mehrere, so haften sie als Gesamtschuldner.

(2) Übernimmt die Gesellschaft eine vor ihrer Eintragung in ihrem Namen eingegangene Verpflichtung durch Vertrag mit dem Schuldner in der Weise, daß sie an die Stelle des bisherigen Schuldners tritt, so bedarf es zur Wirksamkeit der Schuldübernahme der Zustimmung des Gläubigers nicht, wenn die Schuldübernahme binnen drei Monaten nach der Eintragung der Gesellschaft vereinbart und dem Gläubiger von der Gesellschaft oder dem Schuldner mitgeteilt wird.

(3) Verpflichtungen aus nicht in der Satzung festgesetzten Verträgen über Sondervorteile, Gründungsaufwand, Sacheinlagen oder Sachübernahmen kann die Gesellschaft nicht übernehmen.

(4) Vor der Eintragung der Gesellschaft können Anteilsrechte nicht übertragen, Aktien oder Zwischenscheine nicht ausgegeben werden. Die vorher ausgegebenen Aktien oder Zwischenscheine sind nichtig. Für den Schaden aus der Ausgabe sind die Ausgeber den Inhabern als Gesamtschuldner verantwortlich.

§ 41. Acts in the Name of the Company Prior to Registration; Prohibition of Issue of Shares

(1) The stock corporation shall not exist as such prior to its registration in the commerical register. Any person who acts in the name of the company prior to registration shall be personally liable; if more than one person so acts, such persons shall be jointly and severally liable.

(2) If the company shall assume obligations entered into in its name prior to its registration by agreement with the debtor by substituting itself for such debtor, the validity of such assumption of obligations shall not require the consent of the creditor, provided that such assumption has been agreed upon, and communicated to the creditor by the company or the debtor, within three months from the date of registration of the company.

(3) The company may in no event assume obligations arising under agreements regarding special benefits, formation expenses, or contributions in kind and acquisitions of assets which have not been stipulated in the articles.

(4) Shares may not be transferred and share certificates and interim certificates may not be issued prior to registration of the company in the commercial register. Share certificates and interim certificates issued prior to such registration shall be null and void. The issuers of such certificates shall be jointly and severally liable to the holders thereof for any damage resulting from the issue.

§ 42. Einpersonen-Gesellschaft

Gehören alle Aktien allein oder neben der Gesellschaft einem Aktionär, ist dies

§ 42. Single-member Company

If all shares are owned by one shareholder or by one shareholder and the com-

sowie der Name, Vorname, Beruf und Wohnort des alleinigen Aktionärs unverzüglich bei dem Gericht anzumelden.

pany, such fact as well as the surname, forename, profession and domicile of the sole shareholder shall promptly be reported to the court.

§§ 43-44. (aufgehoben)

§§ 43-44. (repealed)

§ 45. Sitzverlegung

(1) Wird der Sitz der Gesellschaft im Inland verlegt, so ist die Verlegung beim Gericht des bisherigen Sitzes anzumelden.

(2) Wird der Sitz aus dem Bezirk des Gerichts des bisherigen Sitzes verlegt, so hat dieses unverzüglich von Amts wegen die Verlegung dem Gericht des neuen Sitzes mitzuteilen. Der Mitteilung sind die Eintragungen für den bisherigen Sitz sowie die bei dem bisher zuständigen Gericht aufbewahrten Urkunden beizufügen. Das Gericht des neuen Sitzes hat zu prüfen, ob die Verlegung ordnungsgemäß beschlossen und § 30 des Handelsgesetzbuchs beachtet ist. Ist dies der Fall, so hat es die Sitzverlegung einzutragen und hierbei die ihm mitgeteilten Eintragungen ohne weitere Nachprüfung in sein Handelsregister zu übernehmen. Mit der Eintragung wird die Sitzverlegung wirksam. Die Eintragung ist dem Gericht des bisherigen Sitzes mitzuteilen. Dieses hat die erforderlichen Löschungen von Amts wegen vorzunehmen.

(3) Wird in den ersten zwei Jahren nach der Eintragung der Gesellschaft in das Handelsregister des ursprünglichen Sitzes eine Sitzverlegung aus dem Bezirk des Gerichts des bisherigen Sitzes eingetragen, so sind in der Bekanntmachung

§ 45. Transfer of Domicile

(1) A transfer of the company's domicile within Germany shall be reported for registration to the court of the previous domicile.

(2) If the company's domicile is transferred from the district of the court of the previous domicile, such court shall without further application promptly communicate such transfer to the court of the new domicile. The registration entries for the previous domicile and the documents kept by the court which previously had jurisdiction shall be appended to such communication. The court of the new domicile shall examine whether the transfer has been duly resolved and whether § 30 of the Commercial Code has been complied with. If such transfer has been duly resolved and § 30 of the Commercial Code has been complied with, the court shall register the transfer of domicile and enter in its commercial register the matters communicated to it without further examination. The transfer of domicile shall become effective upon registration. Such registration shall be communicated to the court of the previous domicile. Such court shall make the necessary cancellations without further application.

(3) If a transfer of domicile from the district of the court of the previous domicile is registered within two years from the date on which the company was registered in the commercial register of the previous domicile, all matters referred to

der Eintragung alle Angaben nach § 40 Abs. 1 zu veröffentlichen.

(**4**) Wird der Sitz an einen anderen Ort innerhalb des Bezirks des Gerichts des bisherigen Sitzes verlegt, so hat das Gericht zu prüfen, ob die Sitzverlegung ordnungsgemäß beschlossen und § 30 des Handelsgesetzbuchs beachtet ist. Ist dies der Fall, so hat es die Sitzverlegung einzutragen. Mit der Eintragung wird die Sitzverlegung wirksam.

in § 40 (1) shall be set out in the announcement of the registration.

(**4**) If the company's domicile is transferred to another location within the district of the court of the previous domicile, the court shall examine whether the transfer of domicile has been duly resolved and whether § 30 of the Commercial Code has been complied with. If such transfer of domicile has been duly resolved and § 30 of the Commercial Code has been complied with, such court shall register the transfer of domicile. The transfer of domicile shall become effective upon registration.

§ 46. Verantwortlichkeit der Gründer

(**1**) Die Gründer sind der Gesellschaft als Gesamtschuldner verantwortlich für die Richtigkeit und Vollständigkeit der Angaben, die zum Zwecke der Gründung der Gesellschaft über Übernahme der Aktien, Einzahlung auf die Aktien, Verwendung eingezahlter Beträge, Sondervorteile, Gründungsaufwand, Sacheinlagen und Sachübernahmen gemacht worden sind. Sie sind ferner dafür verantwortlich, daß eine zur Annahme von Einzahlungen auf das Grundkapital bestimmte Stelle (§ 54 Abs. 3) hierzu geeignet ist und daß die eingezahlten Beträge zur freien Verfügung des Vorstands stehen. Sie haben, unbeschadet der Verpflichtung zum Ersatz des sonst entstehenden Schadens, fehlende Einzahlungen zu leisten und eine Vergütung, die nicht unter den Gründungsaufwand aufgenommen ist, zu ersetzen.

(**2**) Wird die Gesellschaft von Gründern durch Einlagen, Sachübernahmen oder Gründungsaufwand vorsätzlich oder aus grober Fahrlässigkeit geschädigt, so sind ihr alle Gründer als Gesamtschuldner zum Ersatz verpflichtet.

§ 46. Liability of Incorporators

(**1**) The incorporators shall be jointly and severally liable to the company for the accuracy and completeness of the statements made for purposes of formation and relating to subscription to shares, payments on the shares, appropriation of amounts paid in, special benefits, formation expenses, contributions in kind and acquisitions of assets. The incorporators shall further be liable for ascertaining that the agency designated to receive subscription payments on share capital (§ 54 (3)) is qualified and that any amounts paid in are at the free disposal of the management board. Without prejudice to their liability for compensation of other damages, they shall be required to make up any deficiencies in subscription payments and to reimburse any remuneration which was not included in the formation expenses.

(**2**) If the incorporators intentionally or by gross negligence cause damage to the company through contributions, acquisitions of assets or formation expenses, all incorporators shall be jointly and severally liable to the company for damages.

(3) Von diesen Verpflichtungen ist ein Gründer befreit, wenn er die die Ersatzpflicht begründenden Tatsachen weder kannte noch bei Anwendung der Sorgfalt eines ordentlichen Geschäftsmannes kennen mußte.

(3) An incorporator shall be relieved of such liability if the facts giving rise to liability were not known to him and could not have been known to him even if he had employed the diligence of a prudent businessman.

(4) Entsteht der Gesellschaft ein Ausfall, weil ein Aktionär zahlungsunfähig oder unfähig ist, eine Sacheinlage zu leisten, so sind ihr zum Ersatz als Gesamtschuldner die Gründer verpflichtet, welche die Beteiligung des Aktionärs in Kenntnis seiner Zahlungsunfähigkeit oder Leistungsunfähigkeit angenommen haben.

(4) If the company shall suffer a loss as a result of a shareholder being insolvent or unable to make a contribution in kind, the incorporators who accepted the participation of such shareholder with knowledge of his insolvency or inability to make contributions shall be jointly and severally liable to the company for damages.

(5) Neben den Gründern sind in gleicher Weise Personen verantwortlich, für deren Rechnung die Gründer Aktien übernommen haben. Sie können sich auf ihre eigene Unkenntnis nicht wegen solcher Umstände berufen, die ein für ihre Rechnung handelnder Gründer kannte oder kennen mußte.

(5) Persons on whose behalf the incorporators have subscribed to shares shall have the same liability as the incorporators. Such persons shall not be excused for their own lack of knowledge of facts which an incorporator acting on their behalf knew or should have known.

§ 47. Verantwortlichkeit anderer Personen neben den Gründern

§ 47. Liability of Persons Other than the Incorporators

Neben den Gründern und den Personen, für deren Rechnung die Gründer Aktien übernommen haben, ist als Gesamtschuldner der Gesellschaft zum Schadenersatz verpflichtet,

1. wer bei Empfang einer Vergütung, die entgegen den Vorschriften nicht in den Gründungsaufwand aufgenommen ist, wußte oder nach den Umständen annehmen mußte, daß die Verheimlichung beabsichtigt oder erfolgt war, oder wer zur Verheimlichung wissentlich mitgewirkt hat;

In addition to the incorporators and the persons on whose behalf the incorporators have subscribed to shares, the following persons shall be jointly and severally liable to the company for damages:

1. whoever receives remuneration that was not included in the formation expenses despite the fact that such remuneration is required to be so included by the applicable provisions and who knew or in the circumstances should have known that such receipt of remuneration was concealed or intended to be concealed or who knowingly participated in such concealment;

2. wer im Fall einer vorsätzlichen oder grobfahrlässigen Schädigung der Gesellschaft durch Einlagen oder Sachübernahmen an der Schädigung wissentlich mitgewirkt hat;

3. wer vor Eintragung der Gesellschaft in das Handelsregister oder in den ersten zwei Jahren nach der Eintragung die Aktien öffentlich ankündigt, um sie in den Verkehr einzuführen, wenn er die Unrichtigkeit oder Unvollständigkeit der Angaben, die zum Zwecke der Gründung der Gesellschaft gemacht worden sind (§ 46 Abs. 1), oder die Schädigung der Gesellschaft durch Einlagen oder Sachübernahmen kannte oder bei Anwendung der Sorgfalt eines ordentlichen Geschäftsmannes kennen mußte.

2. whoever knowingly participates in causing damage to the company intentionally or by gross negligence by means of contributions or acquisitions of assets; and

3. whoever, prior to registration of the company in the commercial register or within two years from the date of the registration publicly advertises the shares for distribution and knew or, if he had employed the diligence of a prudent businessman, should have known of the inaccuracy or incompleteness of the statements rendered for purposes of formation (§ 46 (1)) or of damage to the company through contributions or acquisitions of assets.

§ 48. Verantwortlichkeit des Vorstands und des Aufsichtsrats

Mitglieder des Vorstands und des Aufsichtsrats, die bei der Gründung ihre Pflichten verletzen, sind der Gesellschaft zum Ersatz des daraus entstehenden Schadens als Gesamtschuldner verpflichtet; sie sind namentlich dafür verantwortlich, daß eine zur Annahme von Einzahlungen auf die Aktien bestimmte Stelle (§ 54 Abs. 3) hierzu geeignet ist, und daß die eingezahlten Beträge zur freien Verfügung des Vorstands stehen. Für die Sorgfaltspflicht und Verantwortlichkeit der Mitglieder des Vorstands und des Aufsichtsrats bei der Gründung gelten im übrigen §§ 93 und 116 mit Ausnahme von § 93 Abs. 4 Satz 3 und 4 und Abs. 6.

§ 48. Liability of the Management Board and the Supervisory Board

Members of the management board and of the supervisory board who violate their obligations in connection with the formation of the company shall be jointly and severally liable to the company for any resulting damage; in particular, they shall be liable for ascertaining that the agency designated to receive payments on the shares (§ 54 (3)) is qualified and that any amounts paid in are at the free disposal of the management board. With respect to the duty of care and the liability of the members of the management board and the supervisory board in connection with the company's formation, §§ 93 and 116 shall also apply, with the exception of § 93 (4) sentences 3 and 4 and (6).

§ 49. Verantwortlichkeit der Gründungsprüfer

§ 323 Abs. 1 bis 4 des Handelsgesetzbuchs über die Verantwortlichkeit des Abschlußprüfers gilt sinngemäß.

§ 49. Liability of Formation Auditors

§ 323 (1) to (4) of the Commercial Code regarding the liability of external auditors shall apply analogously.

§ 50. Verzicht und Vergleich

Die Gesellschaft kann auf Ersatzansprüche gegen die Gründer, die neben diesen haftenden Personen und gegen die Mitglieder des Vorstands und des Aufsichtsrats (§§ 46 bis 48) erst drei Jahre nach der Eintragung der Gesellschaft in das Handelsregister und nur dann verzichten oder sich über sie vergleichen, wenn die Hauptversammlung zustimmt und nicht eine Minderheit, deren Anteile zusammen den zehnten Teil des Grundkapitals erreichen, zur Niederschrift Widerspruch erhebt. Die zeitliche Beschränkung gilt nicht, wenn der Ersatzpflichtige zahlungsunfähig ist und sich zur Abwendung oder Beseitigung des Konkursverfahrens mit seinen Gläubigern vergleicht.[1]

§ 50. Waiver and Compromise

The company may not waive or compromise claims for damages against the incorporators, any other persons who are liable, and against members of the management board and the supervisory board (§§ 46 to 48) prior to the expiration of three years from the date of the registration of the company in the commercial register, and may only waive or compromise such claims if the shareholders' meeting consents thereto and no minority whose aggregate holding equals or exceeds one tenth of the share capital records an objection in the minutes. The foregoing period of time shall not apply if the person liable for damages is insolvent and enters into a composition with his creditors to avoid or terminate bankruptcy proceedings.[1]

§ 51. Verjährung der Ersatzansprüche

Ersatzansprüche der Gesellschaft nach den §§ 46 bis 49 verjähren in fünf Jahren. Die Verjährung beginnt mit der Eintragung der Gesellschaft in das Handelsregister oder, wenn die zum Ersatz verpflichtende Handlung später begangen worden ist, mit der Vornahme der Handlung.

§ 51. Limitation Period for Damage Claims

Damage claims of the company pursuant to §§ 46 to 49 shall be barred after the expiration of a period of five years. Such period shall commence upon the registration of the company in the commercial register or, if the act giving rise to the liability for damages has been committed thereafter, upon commission of such act.

1. Mit Wirkung vom 1. Januar 1999 ist § 50 Satz 2 wie folgt gefaßt:
'Die zeitliche Beschränkung gilt nicht, wenn der Ersatzpflichtige zahlungsunfähig ist und sich zur Abwendung des Insolvenzverfahrens mit seinen Gläubigern vergleicht oder wenn die Ersatzpflicht in einem Insolvenzplan geregelt wird.'

1. Effective as of 1 January 1999 § 50 sentence 2 will read as follows:
'The foregoing period of time shall not apply if the person liable for damages is insolvent and enters into a composition with his creditors to avoid insolvency proceedings or if the liability is subject to an insolvency plan.'

§ 52. Nachgründung

(**1**) Verträge der Gesellschaft, nach denen sie vorhandene oder herzustellende Anlagen oder andere Vermögensgegenstände für eine den zehnten Teil des Grundkapitals übersteigende Vergütung erwerben soll, und die in den ersten zwei Jahren seit der Eintragung der Gesellschaft in das Handelsregister geschlossen werden, werden nur mit Zustimmung der Hauptversammlung und durch Eintragung in das Handelsregister wirksam. Ohne die Zustimmung der Hauptversammlung oder die Eintragung im Handelsregister sind auch die Rechtshandlungen zu ihrer Ausführung unwirksam.

(**2**) Ein Vertrag nach Absatz 1 bedarf der schriftlichen Form, soweit nicht eine andere Form vorgeschrieben ist. Er ist von der Einberufung der Hauptversammlung an, die über die Zustimmung beschließen soll, in dem Geschäftsraum der Gesellschaft zur Einsicht der Aktionäre auszulegen. Auf Verlangen ist jedem Aktionär unverzüglich eine Abschrift zu erteilen. In der Hauptversammlung ist der Vertrag auszulegen. Der Vorstand hat ihn zu Beginn der Verhandlung zu erläutern. Der Niederschrift ist er als Anlage beizufügen.

(**3**) Vor der Beschlußfassung der Hauptversammlung hat der Aufsichtsrat den Vertrag zu prüfen und einen schriftlichen Bericht zu erstatten (Nachgründungsbericht). Für den Nachgründungsbericht gilt sinngemäß § 32 Abs. 2 und 3 über den Gründungsbericht.

(**4**) Außerdem hat vor der Beschlußfassung eine Prüfung durch einen oder mehrere Gründungsprüfer stattzufinden. § 33 Abs. 3 bis 5, §§ 34, 35 über die Gründungsprüfung gelten sinngemäß.

§ 52. Post-formation Acquisition

(**1**) Agreements entered into by the company that require it to acquire existing or future facilities or other assets for a consideration exceeding one tenth of the share capital and that are entered into within two years from the date of registration of the company in the commercial register shall become effective only upon the consent of the shareholders' meeting and registration of such agreements in the commercial register. Absent such consent and registration, any transaction in execution of such agreements shall be invalid.

(**2**) An agreement pursuant to subsection (1) shall be made in writing unless any other form shall be prescribed. Such agreement shall be displayed for inspection by shareholders at the offices of the company as from the date of notice of the shareholders' meeting resolving on such consent. Each shareholder shall upon request promptly be furnished with a copy. The agreement shall be displayed for inspection at the shareholders' meeting. The management board shall comment thereon at the beginning of the deliberations. The agreement shall be appended to the minutes.

(**3**) Prior to the passing of the resolution by the shareholders' meeting, the supervisory board shall examine the agreement and render a written report ('report on post-formation acquisition'). § 32 (2) and (3) regarding the formation report shall apply analogously to the report on post-formation acquisition.

(**4**) In addition, prior to the passing of such resolution, an audit shall be made by one or more formation auditors. § 33 (3) to (5), §§ 34 and 35 regarding the formation audit shall apply analogously.

(5) Der Beschluß der Hauptversammlung bedarf einer Mehrheit, die mindestens drei Viertel des bei der Beschlußfassung vertretenen Grundkapitals umfaßt. Wird der Vertrag im ersten Jahre nach der Eintragung der Gesellschaft in das Handelsregister geschlossen, so müssen außerdem die Anteile der zustimmenden Mehrheit mindestens ein Viertel des gesamten Grundkapitals erreichen. Die Satzung kann an Stelle dieser Mehrheiten größere Kapitalmehrheiten und weitere Erfordernisse bestimmen.

(5) The resolution of the shareholders' meeting shall require a majority of not less than three fourths of the share capital represented at the passing of the resolution. If the agreement has been entered into within one year from the date of registration of the company in the commercial register, the shares of the consenting majority shall amount to not less than one fourth of the total share capital. The articles may provide for larger capital majorities and additional requirements.

(6) Nach Zustimmung der Hauptversammlung hat der Vorstand den Vertrag zur Eintragung in das Handelsregister anzumelden. Der Anmeldung ist der Vertrag in Urschrift, Ausfertigung oder öffentlich beglaubigter Abschrift mit dem Nachgründungsbericht und dem Bericht der Gründungsprüfer mit den urkundlichen Unterlagen beizufügen.

(6) Upon consent of the shareholders' meeting, the management board shall report the agreement for registration in the commercial register. The agreement shall be appended to the report in original, duplicate or officially certified copy, together with the report on post-formation acquisition and the report of the formation auditors and all underlying documentation.

(7) Bestehen gegen die Eintragung Bedenken, weil die Gründungsprüfer erklären oder weil es offensichtlich ist, daß der Nachgründungsbericht unrichtig oder unvollständig ist oder den gesetzlichen Vorschriften nicht entspricht oder daß die für die zu erwerbenden Vermögensgegenstände gewährte Vergütung unangemessen hoch ist, so kann das Gericht die Eintragung ablehnen.

(7) The court may deny registration if registration would be objectionable because the formation auditors state, or it is manifest that, the report on post-formation acquisition is inaccurate or incomplete or does not comply with statutory provisions, or that the consideration given for the assets to be acquired is unreasonably high.

(8) Bei der Eintragung genügt die Bezugnahme auf die eingereichten Urkunden. In die Bekanntmachung der Eintragung sind aufzunehmen der Tag des Vertragsabschlusses und der Zustimmung der Hauptversammlung sowie der zu erwerbende Vermögensgegenstand, die Person, von der die Gesellschaft ihn erwirbt, und die zu gewährende Vergütung.

(8) A reference to the documents submitted shall suffice for the purpose of registration. The announcement of registration shall include the date of execution of the agreement and of the consent of the shareholders' meeting, the asset to be acquired, the person from whom the company is acquiring such asset and the consideration to be given.

(9) Vorstehende Vorschriften gelten nicht, wenn der Erwerb der Vermögensgegenstände den Gegenstand des Unternehmens bildet oder wenn sie in der Zwangsvollstreckung erworben werden.

(9) The foregoing provisions shall not apply if it is the purpose of the enterprise to acquire such assets or if such assets are acquired in the course of judicial execution.

(10) Ein Vertrag nach Absatz 1 ist, gleichviel ob er vor oder nach Ablauf von zwei Jahren seit der Eintragung der Gesellschaft in das Handelsregister geschlossen ist, nicht deshalb unwirksam, weil ein Vertrag der Gründer über denselben Gegenstand nach § 27 Abs. 3 der Gesellschaft gegenüber unwirksam ist.

(10) An agreement pursuant to subsection (1) entered into by the company, irrespective of whether such agreement was entered into before or after the expiration of two years from the date of registration of the company in the commercial register, shall not be invalid because an agreement entered into by the incorporators on the same subject matter would be invalid as against the company.

§ 53. Ersatzansprüche bei der Nachgründung

Für die Nachgründung gelten die §§ 46, 47, 49 bis 51 über die Ersatzansprüche der Gesellschaft sinngemäß. An die Stelle der Gründer treten die Mitglieder des Vorstands und des Aufsichtsrats. Sie haben die Sorgfalt eines ordentlichen und gewissenhaften Geschäftsleiters anzuwenden. Soweit Fristen mit der Eintragung der Gesellschaft in das Handelsregister beginnen, tritt an deren Stelle die Eintragung des Vertrags über die Nachgründung.

§ 53. Damage Claims in Case of Post-formation Acquisition

§§ 46, 47 and 49 to 51 regarding damage claims of the company shall apply analogously to post-formation acquisitions. With respect to such provisions, the members of the management board and the supervisory board shall be substituted for the incorporators. They shall be required to employ the care of a diligent and conscientious manager. Whenever such provisions stipulate that periods shall commence on the date of registration of the company in the commercial register, such periods shall, for purposes of this provision, commence on the date of registration of the agreement regarding the post-formation acquisition.

Dritter Teil. Rechtsverhältnisse der Gesellschaft und der Gesellschafter

Part Three. Legal Relations of the Company and the Shareholders

§ 53a. Gleichbehandlung der Aktionäre

Aktionäre sind unter gleichen Voraussetzungen gleich zu behandeln.

§ 53a. Equal Treatment of Shareholders

Shareholders shall be treated equally under equivalent circumstances.

§ 54. Hauptverpflichtung der Aktionäre

(1) Die Verpflichtung der Aktionäre zur Leistung der Einlagen wird durch den Nennbetrag oder den höheren Ausgabebetrag der Aktien begrenzt.

(2) Soweit nicht in der Satzung Sacheinlagen festgesetzt sind, haben die Aktionäre den Nennbetrag oder den höheren Ausgabebetrag der Aktien einzuzahlen.

(3) Der vor der Anmeldung der Gesellschaft eingeforderte Betrag kann nur in gesetzlichen Zahlungsmitteln, in von der Deutschen Bundesbank bestätigten Schecks, durch Gutschrift auf ein Konto im Inland bei der Deutschen Bundesbank oder einem Kreditinstitut oder auf ein Postscheckkonto der Gesellschaft oder des Vorstands zu seiner freien Verfügung eingezahlt werden. Forderungen des Vorstands aus diesen Einzahlungen gelten als Forderungen der Gesellschaft.

§ 54. Principal Obligation of Shareholders

(1) The obligation of the shareholders to make contributions shall be limited to the par value or the higher issue price of the shares.

(2) Unless the articles provide for contributions in kind, the shareholders shall pay in the par value or the higher issue price of the shares.

(3) Any amount called prior to the company having been reported for registration in the commercial register may be put at the free disposal of the management board only in legal tender, in cheques confirmed by the German Federal Bank, or by credit to an account maintained in Germany with the German Federal Bank or a credit institution or to a post office cheque account of the company or of the management board. Claims of the management board arising from such payments shall be deemed to constitute claims of the company.

§ 55. Nebenverpflichtungen der Aktionäre

(1) Ist die Übertragung der Aktien an die Zustimmung der Gesellschaft gebunden, so kann die Satzung Aktionären die Verpflichtung auferlegen, neben den Einlagen auf das Grundkapital wiederkehrende, nicht in Geld bestehende Leistungen zu erbringen. Dabei hat sie zu bestimmen, ob die Leistungen entgeltlich oder unentgeltlich zu erbringen sind. Die Verpflichtung und der Umfang der Leistungen sind in den Aktien und Zwischenscheinen anzugeben.

(2) Die Satzung kann Vertragsstrafen

§ 55. Ancillary Obligations of Shareholders

(1) If the transfer of shares requires the consent of the company, the articles may impose upon shareholders, in addition to the obligation to make contributions to share capital, recurring obligations other than the payment of money. The articles shall specify whether such obligations are to be performed for consideration or without consideration. The share certificates and interim certificates shall specify the existence and scope of such obligations.

(2) The articles may provide for penalties in the event such obligation has not

für den Fall festsetzen, daß die Verpflichtung nicht oder nicht gehörig erfüllt wird.

been performed or has been improperly performed.

§ 56. Keine Zeichnung eigener Aktien; Aktienübernahme für Rechnung der Gesellschaft oder durch ein abhängiges oder in Mehrheitsbesitz stehendes Unternehmen

§ 56. No Subscription by the Company for Company Shares; Acquisition of Shares on behalf of the Company or through a Controlled Enterprise or Subsidiary

(1) Die Gesellschaft darf keine eigenen Aktien zeichnen.

(1) The company may not subscribe for company shares.

(2) Ein abhängiges Unternehmen darf keine Aktien der herrschenden Gesellschaft, ein in Mehrheitsbesitz stehendes Unternehmen keine Aktien der an ihm mit Mehrheit beteiligten Gesellschaft als Gründer oder Zeichner oder in Ausübung eines bei einer bedingten Kapitalerhöhung eingeräumten Umtausch- oder Bezugsrechts übernehmen. Ein Verstoß gegen diese Vorschrift macht die Übernahme nicht unwirksam.

(2) A controlled enterprise may not acquire shares of the controlling enterprise, and a subsidiary may not acquire shares of its parent company, either as incorporator or subscriber or by exercising a conversion or pre-emptive right granted in connection with a contingent capital increase. A violation of this provision shall not invalidate such acquisition.

(3) Wer als Gründer oder Zeichner oder in Ausübung eines bei einer bedingten Kapitalerhöhung eingeräumten Umtausch- oder Bezugsrechts eine Aktie für Rechnung der Gesellschaft oder eines abhängigen oder in Mehrheitsbesitz stehenden Unternehmens übernommen hat, kann sich nicht darauf berufen, daß er die Aktie nicht für eigene Rechnung übernommen hat. Er haftet ohne Rücksicht auf Vereinbarungen mit der Gesellschaft oder dem abhängigen oder in Mehrheitsbesitz stehenden Unternehmen auf die volle Einlage. Bevor er die Aktie für eigene Rechnung übernommen hat, stehen ihm keine Rechte aus der Aktie zu.

(3) Any person who acquires a share, whether as incorporator or subscriber or by exercising a conversion or pre-emptive right granted in connection with a contingent capital increase, on behalf of the company or a controlled enterprise or subsidiary, shall not be exempt from liability by virtue of the fact that he did not acquire such share on his own behalf. He shall be liable for the full contribution irrespective of any agreement with the company or the controlled enterprise or subsidiary. For as long as he shall not have acquired the share on his own behalf, he shall not be entitled to any rights arising from the share.

(4) Werden bei einer Kapitalerhöhung Aktien unter Verletzung der Absätze 1 oder 2 gezeichnet, so haftet auch jedes Vorstandsmitglied der Gesellschaft auf die volle Einlage. Dies gilt nicht, wenn

(4) If, in the case of a capital increase, shares are subscribed for in violation of subsections (1) or (2), each member of the management board shall be liable to the company for the full contribution. The foregoing shall not apply if a member of

das Vorstandsmitglied beweist, daß es kein Verschulden trifft.

the management board proves that he has not been at fault.

§ 57. Keine Rückgewähr, keine Verzinsung der Einlagen

§ 57. No Repayment of Capital; No Payment of Interest on Contributions

(1) Den Aktionären dürfen die Einlagen nicht zurückgewährt werden. Als Rückgewähr von Einlagen gilt nicht die Zahlung des Erwerbspreises beim zulässigen Erwerb eigener Aktien.

(1) Contributions may not be repaid to shareholders. The payment of the purchase price in case of a permitted acquisition of company shares shall not be deemed to constitute a repayment of contributions.

(2) Den Aktionären dürfen Zinsen weder zugesagt noch ausgezahlt werden.

(2) Interest may be neither promised nor paid to shareholders.

(3) Vor Auflösung der Gesellschaft darf unter die Aktionäre nur der Bilanzgewinn verteilt werden.

(3) Prior to the dissolution of the company only distributable profit may be distributed to shareholders.

§ 58. Verwendung des Jahresüberschusses

§ 58. Appropriation of Annual Net Profit

(1) Die Satzung kann nur für den Fall, daß die Hauptversammlung den Jahresabschluß feststellt, bestimmen, daß Beträge aus dem Jahresüberschuß in andere Gewinnrücklagen einzustellen sind. Auf Grund einer solchen Satzungsbestimmung kann höchstens die Hälfte des Jahresüberschusses in andere Gewinnrücklagen eingestellt werden. Dabei sind Beträge, die in die gesetzliche Rücklage einzustellen sind, und ein Verlustvortrag vorab vom Jahresüberschuß abzuziehen.

(1) The articles may provide, in respect of those cases where the shareholders' meeting is to approve the annual financial statements, that amounts of the annual net profit are to be transferred to other profit reserves. On the basis of such a provision, amounts not exceeding one half of the annual net profit may be transferred to other profit reserves. Amounts to be transferred to the legal reserve and losses carried forward shall first be deducted from the annual net profit.

(2) Stellen Vorstand und Aufsichtsrat den Jahresabschluß fest, so können sie einen Teil des Jahresüberschusses, höchstens jedoch die Hälfte, in andere Gewinnrücklagen einstellen. Die Satzung kann Vorstand und Aufsichtsrat zur Einstellung eines größeren oder kleineren Teils, bei Gesellschaften, deren Aktien zum Handel an einer Börse zugelassen sind, nur eines größeren Teils des Jahres-

(2) If the management board and the supervisory board approve the annual financial statements, they may transfer to other profit reserves a part of the annual net profits, such part however not to exceed one half of the annual net profit. The articles may authorize the management board and the supervisory board to transfer a greater or smaller part, for companies whose shares are listed on a stock

überschusses ermächtigen. Auf Grund einer solchen Satzungsbestimmung dürfen Vorstand und Aufsichtsrat keine Beträge in andere Gewinnrücklagen einstellen, wenn die anderen Gewinnrücklagen die Hälfte des Grundkapitals übersteigen oder soweit sie nach der Einstellung die Hälfte übersteigen würden. Absatz 1 Satz 3 gilt sinngemäß.

exchange however a greater part only. On the basis of such authorization the management board and the supervisory board may not transfer amounts to other profit reserves if the other profit reserves exceed, or upon such transfer would exceed, one half of the share capital. Subsection (1) sentence 3 shall apply analogously.

(2 a) Unbeschadet der Absätze 1 und 2 können Vorstand und Aufsichtsrat den Eigenkapitalanteil von Wertaufholungen bei Vermögensgegenständen des Anlage- und Umlaufvermögens und von bei der steuerrechtlichen Gewinnermittlung gebildeten Passivposten, die nicht im Sonderposten mit Rücklageanteil ausgewiesen werden dürfen, in andere Gewinnrücklagen einstellen. Der Betrag dieser Rücklagen ist entweder in der Bilanz gesondert auszuweisen oder im Anhang anzugeben.

(2a) Subsections (1) and (2) notwithstanding, the management board and the supervisory board may transfer to other profit reserves the capitalized portion of the increase in value of fixed and current assets or liability items created in connection with the allocation of taxable income that may not be shown in the special items with reserve character. The amount of such reserves shall either be shown separately in the balance sheet or stated in the notes to the financial statements.

(3) Die Hauptversammlung kann im Beschluß über die Verwendung des Bilanzgewinns weitere Beträge in Gewinnrücklagen einstellen oder als Gewinn vortragen. Sie kann ferner, wenn die Satzung sie hierzu ermächtigt, auch eine andere Verwendung als nach Satz 1 oder als die Verteilung unter die Aktionäre beschließen.

(3) In its resolution on the appropriation of distributable profit the shareholders' meeting may transfer additional amounts to profit reserves or carry such amounts forward as profit. If the articles contain appropriate authorization, the shareholders' meeting may also resolve on appropriation of distributable profit other than as provided by sentence 1 or other than by distribution to shareholders.

(4) Die Aktionäre haben Anspruch auf den Bilanzgewinn, soweit er nicht nach Gesetz oder Satzung, durch Hauptversammlungsbeschluß nach Absatz 3 oder als zusätzlicher Aufwand auf Grund des Gewinnverwendungsbeschlusses von der Verteilung unter die Aktionäre ausgeschlossen ist.

(4) The shareholders shall be entitled to receive distributable profit to the extent such profit is not excluded from distribution to shareholders by law, the articles or a resolution of the shareholders' meeting pursuant to subsection (3) or because such profit constitutes an additional expense pursuant to the resolution on the appropriation of profits.

(5) (*aufgehoben*)[1]

(5) (*repealed*)[1]

1. Jetzt § 57 Abs. 3.

1. Now § 57 (3).

§ 59. Abschlagszahlung auf den Bilanzgewinn

(1) Die Satzung kann den Vorstand ermächtigen, nach Ablauf des Geschäftsjahrs auf den voraussichtlichen Bilanzgewinn einen Abschlag an die Aktionäre zu zahlen.

(2) Der Vorstand darf einen Abschlag nur zahlen, wenn ein vorläufiger Abschluß für das vergangene Geschäftsjahr einen Jahresüberschuß ergibt. Als Abschlag darf höchstens die Hälfte des Betrags gezahlt werden, der von dem Jahresüberschuß nach Abzug der Beträge verbleibt, die nach Gesetz oder Satzung in Gewinnrücklagen einzustellen sind. Außerdem darf der Abschlag nicht die Hälfte des vorjährigen Bilanzgewinns übersteigen.

(3) Die Zahlung eines Abschlags bedarf der Zustimmung des Aufsichtsrats.

§ 59. Advance Payment of Distributable Profit

(1) The articles may authorize the management board to make an advance payment on account of the estimated distributable profit to shareholders after the close of the fiscal year.

(2) The management board may make such advance payment only if preliminary financial statements for the past fiscal year show an annual net profit. The advance payment may not in any event exceed one half of the annual net profit after deducting therefrom amounts which are to be transferred to profit reserves pursuant to law or the articles. Moreover, the advance payment may not exceed one half of the distributable profit of the preceding year.

(3) Advance payments shall require the consent of the supervisory board.

§ 60. Gewinnverteilung

(1) Die Anteile der Aktionäre am Gewinn bestimmen sich nach dem Verhältnis der Aktiennennbeträge.

(2) Sind die Einlagen auf das Grundkapital nicht auf alle Aktien in demselben Verhältnis geleistet, so erhalten die Aktionäre aus dem verteilbaren Gewinn vorweg einen Betrag von vier vom Hundert der geleisteten Einlagen. Reicht der Gewinn dazu nicht aus, so bestimmt sich der Betrag nach einem entsprechend niedrigeren Satz. Einlagen, die im Laufe des Geschäftsjahrs geleistet wurden, werden nach dem Verhältnis der Zeit berücksichtigt, die seit der Leistung verstrichen ist.

§ 60. Distribution of Profit

(1) The shareholders shall share in the profits of the company in proportion to the par value of their shares.

(2) If contributions to share capital have not been made in the same proportion for all shares, shareholders shall first be paid from the distributable profit an amount of four per cent of the contributions made. If the profit is insufficient to make such payment, the amount to be paid shall be determined on the basis of an appropriately lower percentage. Contributions which have been made during the course of the fiscal year shall be taken into account in proportion to the time which has elapsed since the date of such contributions.

(3) Die Satzung kann eine andere Art der Gewinnverteilung bestimmen.

(3) The articles may provide for another method of distributing profit.

§ 61. Vergütung von Nebenleistungen

§ 61. Compensation of Ancillary Obligations

Für wiederkehrende Leistungen, zu denen Aktionäre nach der Satzung neben den Einlagen auf das Grundkapital verpflichtet sind, darf eine den Wert der Leistungen nicht übersteigende Vergütung ohne Rücksicht darauf gezahlt werden, ob ein Bilanzgewinn ausgewiesen wird.

The company may pay consideration not exceeding the value of services performed for recurring obligations which shareholders are obligated to perform in addition to contributions to share capital, pursuant to the articles, irrespective of whether or not a distributable profit is shown in the balance sheet.

§ 62. Haftung der Aktionäre beim Empfang verbotener Leistungen

§ 62. Liability of Shareholders for Receipt of Prohibited Benefits

(1) Die Aktionäre haben der Gesellschaft Leistungen, die sie entgegen den Vorschriften dieses Gesetzes von ihr empfangen haben, zurückzugewähren. Haben sie Beträge als Gewinnanteile bezogen, so besteht die Verpflichtung nur, wenn sie wußten oder infolge von Fahrlässigkeit nicht wußten, daß sie zum Bezuge nicht berechtigt waren.

(1) Shareholders shall make restitution to the company for benefits received from the company contrary to the provisions of this Act. If they have received such benefits in the form of dividends, the obligation to make restitution shall exist only if they knew, or as a result of negligence did not know, that they were not entitled to such receipt.

(2) Der Anspruch der Gesellschaft kann auch von den Gläubigern der Gesellschaft geltend gemacht werden, soweit sie von dieser keine Befriedigung erlangen können. Ist über das Vermögen der Gesellschaft das Konkursverfahren eröffnet, so übt während dessen Dauer der Konkursverwalter das Recht der Gesellschaftsgläubiger gegen die Aktionäre aus.[1]

(2) The claim of the company may also be asserted by the company's creditors if they are unable to obtain satisfaction from the company. If bankruptcy proceedings have been instituted over the company's assets, the receiver in bankruptcy shall exercise the rights of the company's creditors against the shareholders during the course of the bankruptcy proceedings.[1]

1. Mit Wirkung vom 1. Januar 1999 ist § 62 Abs. 2 Satz 2 wie folgt gefaßt:
'Ist über das Vermögen der Gesellschaft das Insolvenzverfahren eröffnet, so übt während dessen Dauer der Insolvenzverwalter oder der Sachwalter das Recht der Gesellschaftsgläubiger gegen die Aktionäre aus.'

1. Effective as of 1 January 1999 § 62 (2) sentence 2 will read as follows:
'If insolvency proceedings have been instituted over the company's assets, the receiver or the trustee, as the case may be, shall exercise the rights of the company's creditors against the shareholders during the course of the insolvency proceedings.'

(3) Die Ansprüche nach diesen Vorschriften verjähren in fünf Jahren seit dem Empfang der Leistung.

§ 63. Folgen nicht rechtzeitiger Einzahlung

(1) Die Aktionäre haben die Einlagen nach Aufforderung durch den Vorstand einzuzahlen. Die Aufforderung ist, wenn die Satzung nichts anderes bestimmt, in den Gesellschaftsblättern bekanntzumachen.

(2) Aktionäre, die den eingeforderten Betrag nicht rechtzeitig einzahlen, haben ihn vom Eintritt der Fälligkeit an mit fünf vom Hundert für das Jahr zu verzinsen. Die Geltendmachung eines weiteren Schadens ist nicht ausgeschlossen.

(3) Für den Fall nicht rechtzeitiger Einzahlung kann die Satzung Vertragsstrafen festsetzen.

§ 64. Ausschluß säumiger Aktionäre

(1) Aktionären, die den eingeforderten Betrag nicht rechtzeitig einzahlen, kann eine Nachfrist mit der Androhung gesetzt werden, daß sie nach Fristablauf ihrer Aktien und der geleisteten Einzahlungen für verlustig erklärt werden.

(2) Die Nachfrist muß dreimal in den Gesellschaftsblättern bekanntgemacht werden. Die erste Bekanntmachung muß mindestens drei Monate, die letzte mindestens einen Monat vor Fristablauf ergehen. Zwischen den einzelnen Bekanntmachungen muß ein Zeitraum von mindestens drei Wochen liegen. Ist die Über-

(3) Any claim pursuant to the foregoing provisions shall be barred upon the expiration of five years from the date of receipt of the benefit.

§ 63. Consequences of Delayed Subscription Payments

(1) Shareholders shall be required to pay contributions upon call by the management board. Such call shall be announced in the company's designated journals, unless the articles provide otherwise.

(2) Shareholders who fail to make payment of the amount called within the requisite period of time shall be required to pay interest thereon from the due date at the rate of five per cent per annum. The right to claim further damages shall not be precluded.

(3) The articles may stipulate penalties for late payment.

§ 64. Expulsion of Defaulting Shareholders

(1) Shareholders who fail to make payment of amounts called within the requisite period of time may be granted a period of grace with the warning that upon the expiration of such period their shares and subscription payments will be declared forfeited.

(2) Such grace period shall be announced three times in the company's designated journals. The first announcement shall be made no later than three months, the last no later than one month prior to expiration of such period. Not less than three weeks shall elapse between each announcement. If the transfer

tragung der Aktien an die Zustimmung der Gesellschaft gebunden, so genügt an Stelle der öffentlichen Bekanntmachungen die einmalige Einzelaufforderung an die säumigen Aktionäre; dabei muß eine Nachfrist gewährt werden, die mindestens einen Monat seit dem Empfang der Aufforderung beträgt.

of shares requires the consent of the company, it shall suffice if a single notice is made to each defaulting shareholder in lieu of such announcements; provided that in such case a grace period shall be set which is not less than one month from the date of receipt of such notice.

(3) Aktionäre, die den eingeforderten Betrag trotzdem nicht zahlen, werden durch Bekanntmachung in den Gesellschaftsblättern ihrer Aktien und der geleisteten Einzahlungen zugunsten der Gesellschaft für verlustig erklärt. In der Bekanntmachung sind die für verlustig erklärten Aktien mit ihren Unterscheidungsmerkmalen anzugeben.

(3) Shareholders who nevertheless fail to pay amounts called shall be declared to have forfeited their shares and subscription payments in favour of the company by announcement in the company's designated journals. Such announcement shall specify the shares declared to have been forfeited by serial number and any other distinguishing features.

(4) An Stelle der alten Urkunden werden neue ausgegeben; diese haben außer den geleisteten Teilzahlungen den rückständigen Betrag anzugeben. Für den Ausfall der Gesellschaft an diesem Betrag oder an den später eingeforderten Beträgen haftet ihr der ausgeschlossene Aktionär.

(4) New certificates shall be issued in replacement of old certificates; such new certificates shall state the amount in default and all partial payments made. The expelled shareholder shall be liable to the company for any loss arising from such amount in default or amounts called subsequently.

§ 65. Zahlungspflicht der Vormänner

§ 65. Payment Obligation of Preceding Shareholders

(1) Jeder im Aktienbuch verzeichnete Vormann des ausgeschlossenen Aktionärs ist der Gesellschaft zur Zahlung des rückständigen Betrags verpflichtet, soweit dieser von seinen Nachmännern nicht zu erlangen ist. Von der Zahlungsaufforderung an einen früheren Aktionär hat die Gesellschaft seinen unmittelbaren Vormann zu benachrichtigen. Daß die Zahlung nicht zu erlangen ist, wird vermutet, wenn sie nicht innerhalb eines Monats seit der Zahlungsaufforderung und der Benachrichtigung des Vormanns eingegangen ist. Gegen Zahlung des rück-

(1) Each predecessor of the expelled shareholder entered in the share register shall be liable to the company for payment of the amount in default to the extent that such amount cannot be obtained from his successors. The company shall notify the immediate predecessor of any call for payment made to his successor. It shall be presumed that payment cannot be obtained if such payment has not been received within one month from the date of call for payment and notification of the predecessor. A new certificate shall be issued against payment of the amount in default.

ständigen Betrags wird die neue Urkunde ausgehändigt.

(2) Jeder Vormann ist nur zur Zahlung der Beträge verpflichtet, die binnen zwei Jahren eingefordert werden. Die Frist beginnt mit dem Tage, an dem die Übertragung der Aktie zum Aktienbuch der Gesellschaft angemeldet wird.

(2) Each predecessor shall be liable only for payment of amounts called within a period of two years. Such period shall commence on the date on which the transfer of the share has been reported for registration in the company's share register.

(3) Ist die Zahlung des rückständigen Betrags von Vormännern nicht zu erlangen, so hat die Gesellschaft die Aktie unverzüglich zum amtlichen Börsenpreis durch Vermittlung eines Kursmaklers und beim Fehlen eines Börsenpreises durch öffentliche Versteigerung zu verkaufen. Ist von der Versteigerung am Sitz der Gesellschaft kein angemessener Erfolg zu erwarten, so ist die Aktie an einem geeigneten Ort zu verkaufen. Zeit, Ort und Gegenstand der Versteigerung sind öffentlich bekanntzumachen. Der ausgeschlossene Aktionär und seine Vormänner sind besonders zu benachrichtigen; die Benachrichtigung kann unterbleiben, wenn sie untunlich ist. Bekanntmachung und Benachrichtigung müssen mindestens zwei Wochen vor der Versteigerung ergehen.

(3) If payment of the amount in default cannot be obtained from the predecessors, the company shall promptly sell the share at the official stock exchange quotation through a stockbroker and, in the absence of a stock exchange quotation, by means of public auction. If an adequate result may not be expected from an auction at the company's domicile, the share shall be sold at an appropriate location. The time, location and object of the auction shall be announced. The expelled shareholder and his predecessors shall be notified separately; such notification need not be made if impracticable. Such announcement and notification shall be made not less than two weeks prior to the auction.

§ 66. Keine Befreiung der Aktionäre von ihren Leistungspflichten

§ 66. No Release of Shareholders from their Obligations

(1) Die Aktionäre und ihre Vormänner können von ihren Leistungspflichten nach den §§ 54 und 65 nicht befreit werden. Gegen eine Forderung der Gesellschaft nach den §§ 54 und 65 ist die Aufrechnung nicht zulässig.

(1) The shareholders and their predecessors may not be released from their obligations pursuant to §§ 54 and 65. A set-off against a claim of the company pursuant to §§ 54 and 65 shall not be permitted.

(2) Absatz 1 gilt entsprechend für die Verpflichtung zur Rückgewähr von Leistungen, die entgegen den Vorschriften dieses Gesetzes empfangen sind, für die Ausfallhaftung des ausgeschlossenen

(2) Subsection (1) shall apply analogously to the obligation to make restitution for benefits received contrary to the provisions of this Act, the liability of expelled shareholders for losses and the lia-

Aktionärs sowie für die Schadenersatzpflicht des Aktionärs wegen nicht gehöriger Leistung einer Sacheinlage.

bility of shareholders for damages resulting from not properly making a contribution in kind.

(3) Durch eine ordentliche Kapitalherabsetzung oder durch eine Kapitalherabsetzung durch Einziehung von Aktien können die Aktionäre von der Verpflichtung zur Leistung von Einlagen befreit werden, durch eine ordentliche Kapitalherabsetzung jedoch höchstens in Höhe des Betrags, um den das Grundkapital herabgesetzt worden ist.

(3) Shareholders may be released from the obligation to make contributions by an ordinary capital reduction or by a capital reduction through redemption of shares, provided, however, that in the case of an ordinary capital reduction the amount of such release may not exceed the amount by which the share capital is reduced.

§ 67. Eintragung im Aktienbuch

§ 67. Registration in the Share Register

(1) Namensaktien sind unter Bezeichnung des Inhabers nach Namen, Wohnort und Beruf in das Aktienbuch der Gesellschaft einzutragen.

(1) Registered shares shall be entered in the company's share register stating the name, place of residence and profession of the holder.

(2) Im Verhältnis zur Gesellschaft gilt als Aktionär nur, wer als solcher im Aktienbuch eingetragen ist.

(2) In relation to the company, only persons shall be deemed to be shareholders who have been registered as such in the share register.

(3) Ist jemand nach Ansicht der Gesellschaft zu Unrecht als Aktionär in das Aktienbuch eingetragen worden, so kann die Gesellschaft die Eintragung nur löschen, wenn sie vorher die Beteiligten von der beabsichtigten Löschung benachrichtigt und ihnen eine angemessene Frist zur Geltendmachung eines Widerspruchs gesetzt hat. Widerspricht ein Beteiligter innerhalb der Frist, so hat die Löschung zu unterbleiben.

(3) If, in the opinion of the company, a person has been wrongly registered as shareholder in the share register, the company may cancel the registration only if it has previously notified the persons concerned of the intended cancellation and has granted them a reasonable period of time to make an objection. The cancellation may not be made if a person concerned objects thereto within such period.

(4) Diese Vorschriften gelten sinngemäß für Zwischenscheine.

(4) The foregoing provisions shall apply analogously to interim certificates.

(5) Jedem Aktionär ist auf Verlangen Einsicht in das Aktienbuch zu gewähren.

(5) Each shareholder shall be permitted to inspect the share register upon request.

§ 68. Übertragung von Namensaktien. Umschreibung im Aktienbuch

(1) Namensaktien können durch Indossament übertragen werden. Für die Form des Indossaments, den Rechtsausweis des Inhabers und seine Verpflichtung zur Herausgabe gelten sinngemäß Artikel 12, 13 und 16 des Wechselgesetzes.

(2) Die Satzung kann die Übertragung an die Zustimmung der Gesellschaft binden. Die Zustimmung erteilt der Vorstand. Die Satzung kann jedoch bestimmen, daß der Aufsichtsrat oder die Hauptversammlung über die Erteilung der Zustimmung beschließt. Die Satzung kann die Gründe bestimmen, aus denen die Zustimmung verweigert werden darf.

(3) Geht die Namensaktie auf einen anderen über, so ist dies bei der Gesellschaft anzumelden. Die Aktie ist vorzulegen und der Übergang nachzuweisen. Die Gesellschaft vermerkt den Übergang im Aktienbuch.

(4) Die Gesellschaft ist verpflichtet, die Ordnungsmäßigkeit der Reihe der Indossamente und der Abtretungserklärungen, aber nicht die Unterschriften zu prüfen.

(5) Diese Vorschriften gelten sinngemäß für Zwischenscheine.

§ 68. Transfer of Registered Shares; Registration of Transfers in the Share Register

(1) Registered shares shall be transferable by endorsement. §§ 12, 13 and 16 of the Bills of Exchange Act shall apply analogously to the form of the endorsement, legitimation of the holder and his obligation to surrender.

(2) The articles may provide that the transfer of registered shares shall require the consent of the company. Such consent shall be granted by the management board. The articles may, however, provide that the supervisory board or the shareholders' meeting shall resolve on the granting of consent. The articles may specify the reasons for which consent may be refused.

(3) The company shall be notified of any transfer of a registered share to another person. The share certificate shall be presented and evidence of the transfer shall be furnished. The company shall enter the transfer in the share register.

(4) The company shall be obligated to verify the accuracy of the chain of endorsements and the declarations of assignment, but shall not be required to examine the signatures.

(5) The foregoing provisions shall apply analogously to interim certificates.

§ 69. Rechtsgemeinschaft an einer Aktie

(1) Steht eine Aktie mehreren Berechtigten zu, so können sie die Rechte aus der Aktie nur durch einen gemeinschaftlichen Vertreter ausüben.

§ 69. Common Title to a Share

(1) If more than one person is entitled to a share, they may exercise the rights arising from the share only through a common representative.

(2) Für die Leistungen auf die Aktie haften sie als Gesamtschuldner.

(2) Such persons shall be jointly and severally liable for the obligations in respect of the share.

(3) Hat die Gesellschaft eine Willenserklärung dem Aktionär gegenüber abzugeben, so genügt, wenn die Berechtigten der Gesellschaft keinen gemeinschaftlichen Vertreter benannt haben, die Abgabe der Erklärung gegenüber einem Berechtigten. Bei mehreren Erben eines Aktionärs gilt dies nur für Willenserklärungen, die nach Ablauf eines Monats seit dem Anfall der Erbschaft abgegeben werden.

(3) If the company is required to make a statement with legal effect to shareholders and the persons sharing common title have failed to designate a common representative to the company, it shall suffice if such statement is made to any of the persons sharing common title. In the case of more than one heir of a shareholder, the foregoing shall only apply to such statements made after the expiration of one month following the succession to the inheritance.

§ 70. Berechnung der Aktienbesitzzeit

§ 70. Computation of the Period of Shareholding

Ist die Ausübung von Rechten aus der Aktie davon abhängig, daß der Aktionär während eines bestimmten Zeitraums Inhaber der Aktie gewesen ist, so steht dem Eigentum ein Anspruch auf Übereignung gegen ein Kreditinstitut gleich. Die Eigentumszeit eines Rechtsvorgängers wird dem Aktionär zugerechnet, wenn er die Aktie unentgeltlich, von seinem Treuhänder, als Gesamtrechtsnachfolger, bei Auseinandersetzung einer Gemeinschaft oder bei einer Bestandsübertragung nach § 14 des Versicherungsaufsichtsgesetzes oder § 14 des Gesetzes über Bausparkassen erworben hat.

If the exercise of rights arising from a share shall require that the shareholder has been the holder of such share for a certain period of time, the right to demand transfer of title from a credit institution shall be deemed equivalent to ownership. The period during which the share was owned by a predecessor shall be attributed to the shareholder, provided that he has acquired the share without consideration, from his fiduciary, as a successor in legal interest by operation of law, in connection with the liquidation of a community of interest, or as a result of a transfer of assets pursuant to § 14 of the Insurance Supervision Act or § 14 of the Building Loan Associations Act.

§ 71. Erwerb eigener Aktien

§ 71. Acquisition by the Company of Company Shares

(1) Die Gesellschaft darf eigene Aktien nur erwerben,

1. wenn der Erwerb notwendig ist, um einen schweren, unmittelbar bevorste-

(1) A company may only acquire company shares:

1. if the acquisition is necessary to avert severe and imminent damage to the company;

henden Schaden von der Gesellschaft abzuwenden,

2. wenn die Aktien Personen, die im Arbeitsverhältnis zu der Gesellschaft oder einem mit ihr verbundenen Unternehmen stehen oder standen, zum Erwerb angeboten werden sollen,

3. wenn der Erwerb geschieht, um Aktionäre nach § 305 Abs. 2, § 320b oder nach § 29 Abs. 1, § 125 Satz 1 in Verbindung mit § 29 Abs. 1, § 207 Abs. 1 Satz 1 des Umwandlungsgesetzes abzufinden,

4. wenn der Erwerb unentgeltlich geschieht oder ein Kreditinstitut mit dem Erwerb eine Einkaufskommission ausführt,

5. durch Gesamtrechtsnachfolge,

6. auf Grund eines Beschlusses der Hauptversammlung zur Einziehung nach den Vorschriften über die Herabsetzung des Grundkapitals oder

7. wenn sie ein Kredit- oder Finanzinstitut ist, aufgrund eines Beschlusses der Haputversammlung zum Zwecke des Wertpapierhandels. Der Beschluß muß bestimmen, daß der Handelsbestand der zu diesem Zweck zu erwerbenden Aktien fünf vom Hundert des Grundkapitals am Ende jeden Tages nicht übersteigen darf; er muß den niedrigsten und höchsten Gegenwert festlegen. Die Ermächtigung darf Höchstens 18 Monate gelten.

(2) Der Gesamtnennbetrag der zu den Zwecken nach Absatz 1 Nr. 1 bis 3 und 7 erworbenen Aktien darf zusammen mit dem Betrag anderer Aktien der Gesellschaft, welche die Gesellschaft bereits erworben hat und noch besitzt, zehn vom Hundert des Grundkapitals nicht übersteigen. Dieser Erwerb ist ferner nur zulässig, wenn die Gesellschaft die nach § 272 Abs. 4 des Handelsgesetzbuchs vorgeschriebene Rücklage für eigene Aktien bilden kann, ohne das Grundkapital oder eine nach Gesetz oder Satzung zu bildende Rücklage zu mindern, die nicht

2. if the shares are to be offered for purchase to persons who are or were in an employment relationship with the company or an enterprise affiliated with the company;

3. if the acquisition is made to compensate shareholders pursuant to § 305 (2), § 320b or § 29 (1), § 125 sentence 1 in connection with § 29 (1), § 207 (1) sentence 1 of the Act on Transformation;

4. if the acquisition is made without consideration or made by a credit institution in execution of a purchase order;

5. as successor in legal interest by operation of law;

6. on the basis of a resolution of the shareholders' meeting to redeem shares pursuant to the provisions governing a reduction of share capital; or

7. in case the company is a credit or financial institution, for purposes of securities trading on the basis of a resolution of the shareholders' meeting. Such resolution shall provide that the trading portfolio of shares to be acquired for such purpose shall not exceed five percent of the share capital at the end of each day; it shall fix the lowest and the highest counter value. The authorization may not exceed 18 months.

(2) The aggregate par value of shares acquired for the purposes specified in subsection (1), nos. 1 to 3 and 7, and of any other company shares which the company has already acquired and continues to hold, may not exceed ten per cent of the company's share capital. Moreover, such acquisition shall be permitted only if the company is in a position to create the reserve for company shares held by the company prescribed by § 272 (4) of the Commercial Code without reducing either the share capital or any reserve required to be created by law or the articles

zu Zahlungen an die Aktionäre verwandt werden darf. In den Fällen des Absatzes 1 Nr. 1, 2, 4 und 7 ist der Erwerb nur zulässig, wenn auf die Aktien der Nennbetrag oder der höhere Ausgabebetrag voll geleistet ist.

that may not be used for payments to shareholders. In the cases of subsection (1), Nos. 1, 2, 4 and 7, such acquisition may be made only if the par value or the higher share issue price has been paid in full.

(3) Im Falle des Absatzes 1 Nr. 1 hat der Vorstand die nächste Hauptversammlung über die Gründe und den Zweck des Erwerbs, über die Zahl und den Nennbetrag der erworbenen Aktien, über deren Anteil am Grundkapital sowie über den Gegenwert der Aktien zu unterrichten. Im Falle des Absatzes 1 Nr. 2 sind die Aktien innerhalb eines Jahres nach ihrem Erwerb an die Arbeitnehmer auszugeben.

(3) In the case of subsection (1), No. 1, the management board shall inform the next shareholders' meeting as to the reasons for and purpose of the acquisition, the number and par value of the shares acquired, their percentage of the share capital and the purchase price for the shares. In the case of subsection (1) No. 2, the shares shall be issued to employees within one year after they have been acquired.

(4) Ein Verstoß gegen die Absätze 1 oder 2 macht den Erwerb eigener Aktien nicht unwirksam. Ein schuldrechtliches Geschäft über den Erwerb eigener Aktien ist jedoch nichtig, soweit der Erwerb gegen die Absätze 1 oder 2 verstößt.

(4) A violation of subsections (1) or (2) shall not invalidate the acquisition by the company of company shares. However, the contract constituting the basis for such acquisition of shares shall be null and void to the extent that the acquisition is in violation of subsections (1) or (2).

§ 71a. Umgehungsgeschäfte

(1) Ein Rechtsgeschäft, das die Gewährung eines Vorschusses oder eines Darlehens oder die Leistung einer Sicherheit durch die Gesellschaft an einen anderen zum Zweck des Erwerbs von Aktien dieser Gesellschaft zum Gegenstand hat, ist nichtig. Dies gilt nicht für Rechtsgeschäfte im Rahmen der laufenden Geschäfte von Kreditinstituten sowie für die Gewährung eines Vorschusses oder eines Darlehens oder für die Leistung einer Sicherheit zum Zweck des Erwerbs von Aktien durch Arbeitnehmer der Gesellschaft oder eines mit ihr verbundenen Unternehmens; auch in diesen Fällen ist das Rechtsgeschäft jedoch nichtig, wenn bei einem Erwerb der Aktien durch die Gesellschaft diese die nach § 272 Abs. 4 des

§ 71a. Evasive Transactions

(1) Any transaction providing for the extension of an advance or loan or the provisions of security by the company to another person for the purpose of acquiring shares in the company shall be null and void. The foregoing shall not apply to transactions in the ordinary course of business of credit institutions nor to the extension of an advance or loan or the provision of security for the purpose of the purchase of shares by employees of the company or an affiliated enterprise; provided, however, that such transactions shall also be null and void if, had the company acquired the shares, the company would not have been in a position to create the reserve for company shares held by the company prescribed by § 272 (4)

Handelsgesetzbuchs vorgeschriebene Rücklage für eigene Aktien nicht bilden könnte, ohne das Grundkapital oder eine nach Gesetz oder Satzung zu bildende Rücklage zu mindern, die nicht zu Zahlungen an die Aktionäre verwandt werden darf.

of the Commercial Code without reducing either the share capital or any reserve which is required to be created by law or the articles and which may not be used for payments to shareholders.

(2) Nichtig ist ferner ein Rechtsgeschäft zwischen der Gesellschaft und einem anderen, nach dem dieser berechtigt oder verpflichtet sein soll, Aktien der Gesellschaft für Rechnung der Gesellschaft oder eines abhängigen oder eines in ihrem Mehrheitsbesitz stehenden Unternehmens zu erwerben, soweit der Erwerb durch die Gesellschaft gegen § 71 Abs. 1 oder 2 verstoßen würde.

(2) Any transaction between the company and another person which entitles or obligates such other person to acquire shares in the company on behalf of the company or a controlled enterprise or a subsidiary shall be null and void if the acquisition of the shares by the company would violate § 71 (1) or (2).

§ 71b. Rechte aus eigenen Aktien

§ 71b. Rights Arising from Company Shares Held by the Company

Aus eigenen Aktien stehen der Gesellschaft keine Rechte zu.

The company shall have no rights in respect of company shares which it holds.

§ 71c. Veräußerung und Einziehung eigener Aktien

§ 71c. Sale or Redemption of Company Shares Held by the Company

(1) Hat die Gesellschaft eigene Aktien unter Verstoß gegen § 71 Abs. 1 oder 2 erworben, so müssen sie innerhalb eines Jahres nach ihrem Erwerb veräußert werden.

(1) If the company has acquired company shares in violation of § 71 (1) or (2), such shares shall be sold within one year from the date of their acquisition.

(2) Übersteigt der Gesamtnennbetrag der Aktien, welche die Gesellschaft nach § 71 Abs. 1 in zulässiger Weise erworben hat und noch besitzt, zehn vom Hundert des Grundkapitals, so muß der Teil der Aktien, der diesen Satz übersteigt, innerhalb von drei Jahren nach dem Erwerb der Aktien veräußert werden.

(2) If the aggregate par value of the shares which a company has lawfully acquired pursuant to § 71 (1) and continues to hold shall exceed ten per cent of the company's share capital, the shares in excess of such percentage shall be sold not later than three years from the date of their acquisition.

(3) Sind eigene Aktien innerhalb der in den Absätzen 1 und 2 vorgesehenen

(3) If company shares held by the company have not been sold within the

Fristen nicht veräußert worden, so sind sie nach § 237 einzuziehen.

periods provided in subsections (1) and (2), they shall be redeemed in accordance with § 237.

§ 71d. Erwerb eigener Aktien durch Dritte

Ein im eigenen Namen, jedoch für Rechnung der Gesellschaft handelnder Dritter darf Aktien der Gesellschaft nur erwerben oder besitzen, soweit dies der Gesellschaft nach § 71 Abs. 1 Nr. 1 bis 5 und 7 und Abs. 2 gestattet wäre. Gleiches gilt für den Erwerb oder den Besitz von Aktien der Gesellschaft durch ein abhängiges oder ein im Mehrheitsbesitz der Gesellschaft stehendes Unternehmen sowie für den Erwerb oder den Besitz durch einen Dritten, der im eigenen Namen, jedoch für Rechnung eines abhängigen oder eines im Mehrheitsbesitz der Gesellschaft stehenden Unternehmens handelt. Bei der Berechnung des Gesamtnennbetrags nach § 71 Abs. 2 Satz 1 und § 71c Abs. 2 gelten diese Aktien als Aktien der Gesellschaft. Im übrigen gelten § 71 Abs. 3 und 4, §§ 71a bis 71 c sinngemäß. Der Dritte oder das Unternehmen hat der Gesellschaft auf ihr Verlangen das Eigentum an den Aktien zu verschaffen. Die Gesellschaft hat den Gegenwert der Aktien zu erstatten.

§ 71d. Acquisition by Third Parties of Company Shares Held by the Company

A third party acting in its own name but on behalf of the company may acquire or hold shares in the company only if the company would be permitted to make such acquisition pursuant to § 71 (1) Nos. 1 to 5 and 7 and (2). The foregoing shall apply to the acquisition or holding of shares in the company by a controlled enterprise or a subsidiary of the company and to the acquisition or holding by a third party acting in its own name but on behalf of a controlled enterprise or subsidiary of the company. For purposes of computing the aggregate par value pursuant to § 71 (2) sentence 1 and § 71c (2), such shares shall be deemed to be shares of the company. § 71 (3) and (4) and §§ 71a to 71c shall apply analogously. Such third party, controlled enterprise or subsidiary shall upon demand procure that the company receives title to such shares. The company shall reimburse the purchase price of the shares.

§ 71e. Inpfandnahme eigener Aktien

(1) Dem Erwerb eigener Aktien nach § 71 Abs. 1 und 2, § 71d steht es gleich, wenn eigene Aktien als Pfand genommen werden. Jedoch darf ein Kreditinstitut im Rahmen der laufenden Geschäfte eigene Aktien bis zu dem in § 71 Abs. 2 Satz 1 bestimmten Gesamtnennbetrag als Pfand nehmen. § 71a gilt sinngemäß.

§ 71e. Pledge of Company Shares Held by the Company

(1) The pledge of company shares to the company shall be deemed to be equivalent to an acquisition by the company of company shares pursuant to § 71 (1) and (2) and § 71d. A credit institution may, however, in the ordinary course of business take a pledge of company shares in an amount not exceeding the aggregate par value specified in § 71 (2) sentence 1. § 71a shall apply analogously.

(2) Ein Verstoß gegen Absatz 1 macht die Inpfandnahme eigener Aktien unwirksam, wenn auf sie der Nennbetrag oder der höhere Ausgabebetrag noch nicht voll geleistet ist. Ein schuldrechtliches Geschäft über die Inpfandnahme eigener Aktien ist nichtig, soweit der Erwerb gegen Absatz 1 verstößt.

(2) A violation of subsection (1) shall invalidate the pledge of shares in the company, if the par value or the higher issue price of the pledged shares has not been paid in full. A contract providing for the pledge of company shares to the company shall be null and void if the acquisition of such shares would violate subsection (1).

§ 72. Kraftloserklärung von Aktien im Aufgebotsverfahren

(1) Ist eine Aktie oder ein Zwischenschein abhanden gekommen oder vernichtet, so kann die Urkunde im Aufgebotsverfahren nach der Zivilprozeßordnung für kraftlos erklärt werden. § 799 Abs. 2 und § 800 des Bürgerlichen Gesetzbuchs gelten sinngemäß.

(2) Sind Gewinnanteilscheine auf den Inhaber ausgegeben, so erlischt mit der Kraftloserklärung der Aktie oder des Zwischenscheins auch der Anspruch aus den noch nicht fälligen Gewinnanteilscheinen.

(3) Die Kraftloserklärung einer Aktie nach §§ 73 oder 226 steht der Kraftloserklärung der Urkunde nach Absatz 1 nicht entgegen.

§ 72. Cancellation of Share Certificates by Invalidation Proceedings

(1) A share certificate or interim certificate which has been lost, stolen or destroyed may be cancelled by means of invalidation proceedings in accordance with the Code of Civil Procedure. § 799 (2) and § 800 of the Civil Code shall apply analogously.

(2) The rights arising from dividend coupons issued to bearer which are not yet due shall be cancelled on the date of the cancellation of the share certificate or interim certificate.

(3) The cancellation of a share certificate pursuant to §§ 73 or 226 shall not preclude the cancellation of the certificate pursuant to subsection (1).

§ 73. Kraftloserklärung von Aktien durch die Gesellschaft

(1) Ist der Inhalt von Aktienurkunden durch eine Veränderung der rechtlichen Verhältnisse unrichtig geworden, so kann die Gesellschaft die Aktien, die trotz Aufforderung nicht zur Berichtigung oder zum Umtausch bei ihr eingereicht sind, mit Genehmigung des Gerichts für kraftlos erklären. Beruht die Unrichtigkeit auf einer Änderung des Nennbetrags der Aktien, so können sie nur dann für kraftlos erklärt werden, wenn der Nenn-

§ 73. Cancellation of Share Certificates by the Company

(1) If the wording of share certificates has become inaccurate by reason of a change in legal circumstances, the company may, with the permission of the court, cancel the share certificates which have not been surrendered to it for correction or replacement despite request for surrender. If the inaccuracy arises from a change in the par value of the shares, such certificates may be cancelled only if the par value has been reduced to effect a re-

betrag zur Herabsetzung des Grundkapitals herabgesetzt ist. Namensaktien können nicht deshalb für kraftlos erklärt werden, weil die Bezeichnung des Aktionärs unrichtig geworden ist. Gegen die Entscheidung des Gerichts ist die sofortige Beschwerde zulässig; eine Anfechtung der Entscheidung, durch die die Genehmigung erteilt wird, ist ausgeschlossen.

(2) Die Aufforderung, die Aktien einzureichen, hat die Kraftloserklärung anzudrohen und auf die Genehmigung des Gerichts hinzuweisen. Die Kraftloserklärung kann nur erfolgen, wenn die Aufforderung in der in § 64 Abs. 2 für die Nachfrist vorgeschriebenen Weise bekanntgemacht worden ist. Die Kraftloserklärung geschieht durch Bekanntmachung in den Gesellschaftsblättern. In der Bekanntmachung sind die für kraftlos erklärten Aktien so zu bezeichnen, daß sich aus der Bekanntmachung ohne weiteres ergibt, ob eine Aktie für kraftlos erklärt ist.

(3) An Stelle der für kraftlos erklärten Aktien sind neue Aktien auszugeben und dem Berechtigten auszuhändigen oder, wenn ein Recht zur Hinterlegung besteht, zu hinterlegen. Die Aushändigung oder Hinterlegung ist dem Gericht anzuzeigen.

(4) Soweit zur Herabsetzung des Grundkapitals Aktien zusammengelegt werden, gilt § 226.

§ 74. Neue Urkunden an Stelle beschädigter oder verunstalteter Aktien oder Zwischenscheine

Ist eine Aktie oder ein Zwischenschein so beschädigt oder verunstaltet, daß die Urkunde zum Umlauf nicht mehr geeignet ist, so kann der Berechtigte, wenn der wesentliche Inhalt und die Unterschei-

duction of share capital. Registered shares may not be cancelled solely by reason of the fact that the name of the shareholder is no longer correct. An immediate appeal may be made against the decision of the court; an appeal to set aside a decision granting permission shall be precluded.

(2) The request to surrender share certificates shall give warning of cancellation and make reference to the permission of the court. Cancellation may be made only after such request has been announced in the manner prescribed for the period of grace pursuant to § 64 (2). The cancellation shall be effected by announcement in the company's designated journals. Such announcement shall designate the share certificates which have been cancelled in such a manner that it may be ascertained from the announcement itself whether a certain share certificate has been cancelled.

(3) In lieu of the cancelled share certificates new share certificates shall be issued and delivered to the person entitled thereto or deposited with the court if the company is entitled to make such deposit. The court of the company's domicile shall be notified of such delivery or deposit.

(4) § 226 shall apply if shares are consolidated in connection with a reduction of share capital.

§ 74. New Certificates in Lieu of Damaged or Defaced Share Certificates or Interim Certificates

If a share certificate or interim certificate has been damaged or defaced in such a manner that the certificate is no longer fit for circulation, the person entitled thereto may require the company to issue

dungsmerkmale der Urkunde noch sicher zu erkennen sind, von der Gesellschaft die Erteilung einer neuen Urkunde gegen Aushändigung der alten verlangen. Die Kosten hat er zu tragen und vorzuschießen.

a new certificate against surrender of the old certificate, if the material contents and the distinguishing features of the certificate are still clearly recognizable. Such person shall bear and advance the expenses.

§ 75. Neue Gewinnanteilscheine

Neue Gewinnanteilscheine dürfen an den Inhaber des Erneuerungsscheins nicht ausgegeben werden, wenn der Besitzer der Aktie oder des Zwischenscheins der Ausgabe widerspricht; sie sind dem Besitzer der Aktie oder des Zwischenscheins auszuhändigen, wenn er die Haupturkunde vorlegt.

§ 75. New Dividend Coupons

New dividend coupons may not be issued to the holder of the coupon renewal certificate if the holder of the share certificate or of the interim certificate objects to such issue; such new dividend coupons shall be delivered to the holder of the share certificate or the interim certificate if he presents such certificate.

Vierter Teil. Verfassung der Aktiengesellschaft

Erster Abschnitt. Vorstand

§ 76. Leitung der Aktiengesellschaft

(1) Der Vorstand hat unter eigener Verantwortung die Gesellschaft zu leiten.

(2) Der Vorstand kann aus einer oder mehreren Personen bestehen. Bei Gesellschaften mit einem Grundkapital von mehr als drei Millionen Deutsche Mark hat er aus mindestens zwei Personen zu bestehen, es sei denn, die Satzung bestimmt, daß er aus einer Person besteht. Die Vorschriften über die Bestellung eines Arbeitsdirektors bleiben unberührt.

(3) Mitglied des Vorstands kann nur eine natürliche, unbeschränkt geschäftsfähige Person sein. Ein Betreuter, der bei der Besorgung seiner Vermögensangele-

Part Four. Constitution of the Stock Corporation

Division One. Management Board

§ 76. Management of the Stock Corporation

(1) The management board shall have direct responsibility for the management of the company.

(2) The management board may comprise one or more persons. In the case of companies having a share capital of more than three million Deutsche Mark, the management board shall comprise not less than two persons, unless the articles provide that it shall comprise one person. The provisions governing the appointment of a labour director to the management board shall remain unaffected.

(3) Only a natural person with full legal capacity may be a member of the management board. A person under guardianship whose property affairs are

genheiten ganz oder teilweise einem Einwilligungsvorbehalt (§ 1903 des Bürgerlichen Gesetzbuchs) unterliegt, kann nicht Mitglied des Vorstands sein. Wer wegen einer Straftat nach den §§ 283 bis 283d des Strafgesetzbuchs verurteilt worden ist, kann auf die Dauer von fünf Jahren seit der Rechtskraft des Urteils nicht Mitglied des Vorstands sein; in die Frist wird die Zeit nicht eingerechnet, in welcher der Täter auf behördliche Anordnung in einer Anstalt verwahrt worden ist. Wem durch gerichtliches Urteil oder durch vollziehbare Entscheidung einer Verwaltungsbehörde die Ausübung eines Berufs, Berufszweiges, Gewerbes oder Gewerbezweiges untersagt worden ist, kann für die Zeit, für welche das Verbot wirksam ist, bei einer Gesellschaft, deren Unternehmensgegenstand ganz oder teilweise mit dem Gegenstand des Verbots übereinstimmt, nicht Mitglied des Vorstands sein.

subject, in whole or in part, to consent requirements (§ 1903 of the Civil Code) may not be a member of the management board. A person convicted of a criminal offence pursuant to §§ 283 to 283d of the Penal Code may not be a member of the management board for a period of five years from the date on which the jugdment has become final and may not be appealed; such period shall not include any time during which the convicted person has been confined to an institution by order of the authorities. A person who has been prohibited by judical decision or an enforceable administrative order from engaging in any profession or trade, may not, during the period of such prohibition, be a member of the management board of a company whose corporate purpose encompasses in whole or in part such prohibited activity.

§ 77. Geschäftsführung

(1) Besteht der Vorstand aus mehreren Personen, so sind sämtliche Vorstandsmitglieder nur gemeinschaftlich zur Geschäftsführung befugt. Die Satzung oder die Geschäftsordnung des Vorstands kann Abweichendes bestimmen; es kann jedoch nicht bestimmt werden, daß ein oder mehrere Vorstandsmitglieder Meinungsverschiedenheiten im Vorstand gegen die Mehrheit seiner Mitglieder entscheiden.

(2) Der Vorstand kann sich eine Geschäftsordnung geben, wenn nicht die Satzung den Erlaß der Geschäftsordnung dem Aufsichtsrat übertragen hat oder der Aufsichtsrat eine Geschäftsordnung für den Vorstand erläßt. Die Satzung kann Einzelfragen der Geschäftsordnung bindend regeln. Beschlüsse des Vorstands

§ 77. Management

(1) If the management board comprises more than one person, the members of the management board shall manage the company jointly. The articles or the by-laws for the management board may provide otherwise; however, the articles or by-laws may not provide that one or more members of the management board may resolve differences of opinion within the management board against the majority of its members.

(2) The management board may issue by-laws of the management board unless the articles confer the authority to issue such by-laws upon the supervisory board or the supervisory board issues by-laws for the management board. The articles may make binding provisions in respect of specific matters relating to the by-laws. Resolutions of the management

über die Geschäftsordnung müssen einstimmig gefaßt werden.

board regarding the by-laws shall require a unanimous vote.

§ 78. Vertretung

(1) Der Vorstand vertritt die Gesellschaft gerichtlich und außergerichtlich.

(2) Besteht der Vorstand aus mehreren Personen, so sind, wenn die Satzung nichts anderes bestimmt, sämtliche Vorstandsmitglieder nur gemeinschaftlich zur Vertretung der Gesellschaft befugt. Ist eine Willenserklärung gegenüber der Gesellschaft abzugeben, so genügt die Abgabe gegenüber einem Vorstandsmitglied.

(3) Die Satzung kann auch bestimmen, daß einzelne Vorstandsmitglieder allein oder in Gemeinschaft mit einem Prokuristen zur Vertretung der Gesellschaft befugt sind. Dasselbe kann der Aufsichtsrat bestimmen, wenn die Satzung ihn hierzu ermächtigt hat. Absatz 2 Satz 2 gilt in diesen Fällen sinngemäß.

(4) Zur Gesamtvertretung befugte Vorstandsmitglieder können einzelne von ihnen zur Vornahme bestimmter Geschäfte oder bestimmter Arten von Geschäften ermächtigen. Dies gilt sinngemäß, wenn ein einzelnes Vorstandsmitglied in Gemeinschaft mit einem Prokuristen zur Vertretung der Gesellschaft befugt ist.

§ 78. Representation

(1) The management board shall represent the company in and out of court.

(2) If the management board comprises more than one person, the members of the management board shall represent the company jointly, unless the articles provide otherwise. If a statement with legal effect is to be given to the company, it shall suffice if such statement is made to one member of the management board.

(3) The articles may also provide that particular members of the management board may represent the company by acting either solely or jointly with a registered authorized officer.[1] The supervisory board may also so provide if authorized to do so by the articles. Subsection (2) sentence 2 shall apply analogously in such cases.

(4) Members of the management board who are authorized to represent the company by acting jointly may authorize individual members to engage in certain transactions or kinds of transactions. The foregoing shall apply analogously if a member of the management board is authorized to represent the company by acting jointly with a registered authorized officer.

1. Registered authorized officers ('Prokuristen') are officers whose authority to represent the company is prescribed by §§ 49-50 of the Commercial Code and who are registered as such in the appropriate commercial register.

§ 79. Zeichnung durch Vorstandsmitglieder

Vorstandsmitglieder zeichnen für die Gesellschaft, indem sie der Firma der Gesellschaft oder der Benennung des Vorstands ihre Namensunterschrift hinzufügen.

§ 79. Signatures of Members of the Management Board

Members of the management board shall sign on behalf of the company by adding their signature to the company's name or to the designation 'Management Board'.

§ 80. Angaben auf Geschäftsbriefen

(1) Auf allen Geschäftsbriefen, die an einen bestimmten Empfänger gerichtet werden, müssen die Rechtsform und der Sitz der Gesellschaft, das Registergericht des Sitzes der Gesellschaft und die Nummer, unter der die Gesellschaft in das Handelsregister eingetragen ist, sowie alle Vorstandsmitglieder und der Vorsitzende des Aufsichtsrats mit dem Familiennamen und mindestens einem ausgeschriebenen Vornamen angegeben werden. Der Vorsitzende des Vorstands ist als solcher zu bezeichnen. Werden Angaben über das Kapital der Gesellschaft gemacht, so müssen in jedem Falle das Grundkapital sowie, wenn auf die Aktien der Nennbetrag oder der höhere Ausgabebetrag nicht vollständig eingezahlt ist, der Gesamtbetrag der ausstehenden Einlagen angegeben werden.

(2) Der Angaben nach Absatz 1 Satz 1 und 2 bedarf es nicht bei Mitteilungen oder Berichten, die im Rahmen einer bestehenden Geschäftsverbindung ergehen und für die üblicherweise Vordrucke verwendet werden, in denen lediglich die im Einzelfall erforderlichen besonderen Angaben eingefügt zu werden brauchen.

(3) Bestellscheine gelten als Geschäftsbriefe im Sinne des Absatzes 1. Absatz 2 ist auf sie nicht anzuwenden.

§ 80. Business Letters

(1) All business letters which are directed to a specific recipient shall state the company's legal form and domicile, the court of registration of the company's domicile, the number under which the company has been registered in the commercial register, and the surname and not less than one forename in full of each member of the management board and of the chairman of the supervisory board. The chairman of the management board shall be designated as such. If information is provided regarding the company's capital, the amount of the share capital shall in any event be stated and, if the par value or the higher issue price has not been fully paid, the aggregate amount of the contributions outstanding.

(2) The information pursuant to subsection (1) sentences 1 and 2 need not be given in communications or reports which are made in the course of an existing business relationship and for which forms are customarily used in which only the particulars of the specific transaction need be inserted.

(3) Order forms shall be deemed to be business letters within the meaning of subsection (1). Subsection (2) shall not apply to such order forms.

(4) Auf allen Geschäftsbriefen und Bestellscheinen, die von einer Zweigniederlassung einer Aktiengesellschaft mit Sitz im Ausland verwendet werden, müssen das Register, bei dem die Zweigniederlassung geführt wird, und die Nummer des Registereintrags angegeben werden; im übrigen gelten die Vorschriften der Absätze 1 bis 3, soweit nicht das ausländische Recht Abweichungen nötig macht. Befindet sich die ausländische Gesellschaft in Abwicklung, so sind auch diese Tatsache sowie alle Abwickler anzugeben.

(4) All business letters and order forms which are used by a branch of a stock corporation which is domiciled outside Germany shall state the register into which the branch has been entered and the registration number; in all other respects the provisions of subsections (1) to (3) shall apply except to the extent otherwise required by applicable foreign law. If the foreign company is in the state of liquidation this fact and all liquidators shall also be stated.

§ 81. Änderung des Vorstands und der Vertretungsbefugnis seiner Mitglieder

§ 81. Change in the Management Board and in the Authority of its Members to Represent the Company

(1) Jede Änderung des Vorstands oder der Vertretungsbefugnis eines Vorstandsmitglieds hat der Vorstand zur Eintragung in das Handelsregister anzumelden.

(1) The management board shall report for registration in the commercial register any change in the management board or in the authority of a member of the management board to represent the company.

(2) Der Anmeldung sind die Urkunden über die Änderung in Urschrift oder öffentlich beglaubigter Abschrift für das Gericht des Sitzes der Gesellschaft beizufügen.

(2) The documents concerning such change shall be appended to each report in original or officially certified copy for the court of the company's domicile.

(3) Die neuen Vorstandsmitglieder haben in der Anmeldung zu versichern, daß keine Umstände vorliegen, die ihrer Bestellung nach § 76 Abs. 3 Satz 3 und 4 entgegenstehen, und daß sie über ihre unbeschränkte Auskunftspflicht gegenüber dem Gericht belehrt worden sind. § 37 Abs. 2 Satz 2 ist anzuwenden.

(3) New members of the management board shall certify in the report that no circumstances exist which preclude their appointment pursuant to § 76 (3) sentences 3 and 4 and that they have been advised of their obligation to make full disclosure to the court. § 37 (2) sentence 2 shall apply.

(4) Die neuen Vorstandsmitglieder haben ihre Namensunterschrift zur Aufbewahrung beim Gericht zu zeichnen.

(4) New members of the management board shall file their specimen signatures with the court.

§ 82. Beschränkungen der Vertretungs- und Geschäftsführungsbefugnis

(1) Die Vertretungsbefugnis des Vorstands kann nicht beschränkt werden.

(2) Im Verhältnis der Vorstandsmitglieder zur Gesellschaft sind diese verpflichtet, die Beschränkungen einzuhalten, die im Rahmen der Vorschriften über die Aktiengesellschaft die Satzung, der Aufsichtsrat, die Hauptversammlung und die Geschäftsordnungen des Vorstands und des Aufsichtsrats für die Geschäftsführungsbefugnis getroffen haben.

§ 82. Restrictions on the Authority to Represent and Manage

(1) The authority of the management board to represent the company may not be restricted.

(2) The members of the management board shall be obligated as against the company to comply with the restrictions in respect of the authority to manage the company which, in accordance with the provisions governing the stock corporation, are imposed by the articles, the supervisory board, the shareholders' meeting and the by-laws regarding management issued by the management board and the supervisory board.

§ 83. Vorbereitung und Ausführung von Hauptversammlungsbeschlüssen

(1) Der Vorstand ist auf Verlangen der Hauptversammlung verpflichtet, Maßnahmen, die in die Zuständigkeit der Hauptversammlung fallen, vorzubereiten. Das gleiche gilt für die Vorbereitung und den Abschluß von Verträgen, die nur mit Zustimmung der Hauptversammlung wirksam werden. Der Beschluß der Hauptversammlung bedarf der Mehrheiten, die für die Maßnahmen oder für die Zustimmung zu dem Vertrag erforderlich sind.

(2) Der Vorstand ist verpflichtet, die von der Hauptversammlung im Rahmen ihrer Zuständigkeit beschlossenen Maßnahmen auszuführen.

§ 83. Preparation and Execution of Resolutions of Shareholders' Meeting

(1) The management board shall, at the request of the shareholders' meeting, be obligated to prepare any matter which falls within the competence of the shareholders' meeting. The foregoing shall apply to the preparation and execution of agreements which become effective only with the consent of the shareholders' meeting. The resolution of the shareholders' meeting regarding such preparation and execution shall require the same majority as is required for the resolution on the respective matter or, as the case may be, the granting of consent to such agreements.

(2) The management board shall be obligated to execute any resolution adopted by the shareholders' meeting in respect of matters falling within the competence of the shareholders' meeting.

§ 84. Bestellung und Abberufung des Vorstands

(1) Vorstandsmitglieder bestellt der Aufsichtsrat auf höchstens fünf Jahre. Eine wiederholte Bestellung oder Verlängerung der Amtszeit, jeweils für höchstens fünf Jahre, ist zulässig. Sie bedarf eines erneuten Aufsichtsratsbeschlusses, der frühestens ein Jahr vor Ablauf der bisherigen Amtszeit gefaßt werden kann. Nur bei einer Bestellung auf weniger als fünf Jahre kann eine Verlängerung der Amtszeit ohne neuen Aufsichtsratsbeschluß vorgesehen werden, sofern dadurch die gesamte Amtszeit nicht mehr als fünf Jahre beträgt. Dies gilt sinngemäß für den Anstellungsvertrag; er kann jedoch vorsehen, daß er für den Fall einer Verlängerung der Amtszeit bis zu deren Ablauf weitergilt.

(2) Werden mehrere Personen zu Vorstandsmitgliedern bestellt, so kann der Aufsichtsrat ein Mitglied zum Vorsitzenden des Vorstands ernennen.

(3) Der Aufsichtsrat kann die Bestellung zum Vorstandsmitglied und die Ernennung zum Vorsitzenden des Vorstands widerrufen, wenn ein wichtiger Grund vorliegt. Ein solcher Grund ist namentlich grobe Pflichtverletzung, Unfähigkeit zur ordnungsmäßigen Geschäftsführung oder Vertrauensentzug durch die Hauptversammlung, es sei denn, daß das Vertrauen aus offenbar unsachlichen Gründen entzogen worden ist. Dies gilt auch für den vom ersten Aufsichtsrat bestellten Vorstand. Der Widerruf ist wirksam, bis seine Unwirksamkeit rechtskräftig fest-

§ 84. Appointment and Removal of the Management Board

(1) The supervisory board shall appoint the members of the management board for a period not exceeding five years. Such appointment may be renewed or the term of office may be extended, provided that the term of each such renewal or extension shall not exceed five years. Such renewal or extension shall require a new resolution of the supervisory board which may be adopted not earlier than one year prior to the expiration of the current term of office. The term of office may be extended without a new resolution of the supervisory board only in the case of an appointment for less than five years, provided that the aggregate term of office does not, as a result of such extension, exceed five years. The foregoing shall apply analogously to the contract of employment; such contract may, however, provide that in the event of an extension of the term of office, the contract shall continue in effect until the expiry of such term.

(2) If more than one person is appointed as member of the management board, the supervisory board may appoint one member as chairman of the management board.

(3) The supervisory board may revoke the appointment of a member of the management board or the appointment of a member as chairman of the management board for cause. Such cause shall include in particular a gross breach of duties, inability to manage the company properly, or a vote of no-confidence by the shareholders' meeting, unless such vote of no-confidence was made for manifestly arbitrary reasons. The foregoing shall also apply to the management board appointed by the first supervisory board. Such revocation shall be valid until ren-

gestellt ist. Für die Ansprüche aus dem Anstellungsvertrag gelten die allgemeinen Vorschriften.

dered invalid by a judicial decision which has become final and may not be appealed. Rights arising under the contract of employment shall be governed by general provisions of law.

(**4**) Die Vorschriften des Gesetzes über die Mitbestimmung der Arbeitnehmer in den Aufsichtsräten und Vorständen der Unternehmen des Bergbaus und der Eisen und Stahl erzeugenden Industrie vom 21. Mai 1951 (Bundesgesetzbl. I S. 347) – Montan-Mitbestimmungsgesetz – über die besonderen Mehrheitserfordernisse für einen Aufsichtsratsbeschluß über die Bestellung eines Arbeitsdirektors oder den Widerruf seiner Bestellung bleiben unberührt.

(**4**) The provisions of the Act on the Co-determination of Employees in the Supervisory Board and Management Boards in the Mining and Iron and Steel Producing Industries of 21 May 1951 (Legal Gazette I p. 347) – the 'Coal and Steel Co-determination Act' – regarding the special majority requirements for resolutions of the supervisory board on the appointment of a labour director to the management board or the revocation of such appointment shall remain unaffected.

§ 85. Bestellung durch das Gericht

(**1**) Fehlt ein erforderliches Vorstandsmitglied, so hat in dringenden Fällen das Gericht auf Antrag eines Beteiligten das Mitglied zu bestellen. Gegen die Entscheidung ist die sofortige Beschwerde zulässig.

(**2**) Das Amt des gerichtlich bestellten Vorstandsmitglieds erlischt in jedem Fall, sobald der Mangel behoben ist.

(**3**) Das gerichtlich bestellte Vorstandsmitglied hat Anspruch auf Ersatz angemessener barer Auslagen und auf Vergütung für seine Tätigkeit. Einigen sich das gerichtlich bestellte Vorstandsmitglied und die Gesellschaft nicht, so setzt das Gericht die Auslagen und die Vergütung fest. Gegen die Entscheidung ist die sofortige Beschwerde zulässig. Die weitere Beschwerde ist ausgeschlossen. Aus der rechtskräftigen Entscheidung findet die Zwangsvollstreckung nach der Zivilprozeßordnung statt.

§ 85. Appointment by the Court

(**1**) If the management board does not have the required number of members, the court shall, in urgent cases, make the necessary appointments upon motion by a party concerned. An immediate appeal may be made against such decision.

(**2**) The office of a member of the management board appointed by the court shall terminate as soon as the vacancy is filled.

(**3**) The member of the management board appointed by the court shall be entitled to reimbursement of reasonable cash expenses and remuneration for his services. If the member of the management board appointed by the court and the company do not reach agreement, the court shall fix the amount of expenses and remuneration. An immediate appeal may be made against the decision. Further appeal shall be precluded. A decision which is final and which may not be appealed may be enforced in accordance with the

provisions of the Code of Civil Procedure.

§ 86. Gewinnbeteiligung der Vorstandsmitglieder

(1) Den Vorstandsmitgliedern kann für ihre Tätigkeit eine Beteiligung am Gewinn gewährt werden. Sie soll in der Regel in einem Anteil am Jahresgewinn der Gesellschaft bestehen.

(2) Wird den Vorstandsmitgliedern ein Anteil am Jahresgewinn der Gesellschaft gewährt, so berechnet sich der Anteil nach dem Jahresüberschuß, vermindert um einen Verlustvortrag aus dem Vorjahr und um die Beträge, die nach Gesetz oder Satzung aus dem Jahresüberschuß in Gewinnrücklagen einzustellen sind. Entgegenstehende Festsetzungen sind nichtig.

§ 86. Participation in Profits by Members of the Management Board

(1) Members of the management board may be granted for their services a right to participate in profits. As a rule, such participation shall consist of a share in the company's annual profit.

(2) If members of the management board have been granted a share in the company's annual profit, such share shall be computed on the basis of the annual net profit, reduced by any loss carried forward from the previous year and by any amounts which are to be transferred from annual net profit to profit reserves pursuant to law or the articles. Stipulations to the contrary shall be null and void.

§ 87. Grundsätze für die Bezüge der Vorstandsmitglieder

(1) Der Aufsichtsrat hat bei der Festsetzung der Gesamtbezüge des einzelnen Vorstandsmitglieds (Gehalt, Gewinnbeteiligungen, Aufwandsentschädigungen, Versicherungsentgelte, Provisionen und Nebenleistungen jeder Art) dafür zu sorgen, daß die Gesamtbezüge in einem angemessenen Verhältnis zu den Aufgaben des Vorstandsmitglieds und zur Lage der Gesellschaft stehen. Dies gilt sinngemäß für Ruhegehalt, Hinterbliebenenbezüge und Leistungen verwandter Art.

(2) Tritt nach der Festsetzung eine so wesentliche Verschlechterung in den Verhältnissen der Gesellschaft ein, daß die Weitergewährung der in Absatz 1 Satz 1 aufgeführten Bezüge eine schwere Unbil-

§ 87. Principles Governing Remuneration of Members of the Management Board

(1) The supervisory board shall, in determining the aggregate remuneration of any member of the management board (salary, profit participation, reimbursement of expenses, insurance premiums, commissions and additional benefits of any kind), ensure that such aggregate remuneration bears a reasonable relationship to the duties of such member and the condition of the company. The foregoing shall apply analogously to pensions, payments to surviving dependents and similar payments.

(2) If subsequent to such determination of remuneration the condition of the company deteriorates to such extent that continuation of payment of the remuneration referred to in subsection (1) sen-

ligkeit für die Gesellschaft sein würde, so ist der Aufsichtsrat, im Fall des § 85 Abs. 3 das Gericht auf Antrag des Aufsichtsrats, zu einer angemessenen Herabsetzung berechtigt. Durch eine Herabsetzung wird der Anstellungsvertrag im übrigen nicht berührt. Das Vorstandsmitglied kann jedoch seinen Anstellungsvertrag für den Schluß des nächsten Kalendervierteljahrs mit einer Kündigungsfrist von sechs Wochen kündigen.

(3) Wird über das Vermögen der Gesellschaft das Konkursverfahren eröffnet und kündigt der Konkursverwalter den Anstellungsvertrag eines Vorstandsmitglieds, so kann es Ersatz für den Schaden, der ihm durch die Aufhebung des Dienstverhältnisses entsteht, nur für zwei Jahre seit dem Ablauf des Dienstverhältnisses verlangen. Gleiches gilt, wenn über die Gesellschaft das gerichtliche Vergleichsverfahren eröffnet wird und die Gesellschaft den Anstellungsvertrag kündigt.[1]

§ 88. Wettbewerbsverbot

(1) Die Vorstandsmitglieder dürfen ohne Einwilligung des Aufsichtsrats weder ein Handelsgewerbe betreiben noch im Geschäftszweig der Gesellschaft für eigene oder fremde Rechnung Geschäfte machen. Sie dürfen ohne Einwilligung auch nicht Mitglied des Vorstands oder Geschäftsführer oder persönlich haften-

1. Mit Wirkung vom 1. Januar 1999 ist § 87 Abs. 3 wie folgt gefaßt:
'(3) Wird über das Vermögen der Gesellschaft das Insolvenzverfahren eröffnet und kündigt der Insolvenzverwalter den Anstellungsvertrag eines Vorstandsmitglieds, so kann es Ersatz für den Schaden, der ihm durch die Aufhebung des Dienstverhältnisses entsteht, nur für zwei Jahre seit dem Ablauf des Dienstverhältnisses verlangen.'

tence 1 would constitute a grave inequity for the company, the supervisory board, or, in the case of § 85 (3), the court upon motion by the supervisory board, shall be authorized to make a reasonable reduction. Such reduction shall not affect the other terms of the contract of employment. The member of the management board may, however, terminate his contract of employment as of the end of the next calendar quarter upon giving six weeks' notice.

(3) If bankruptcy proceedings have been instituted over the company's assets and the receiver in bankruptcy has given notice of termination of the contract of employment of a member of the management board, such member may claim compensation of damages arising as a result of such termination only for the period of two years following termination of such employment. The foregoing shall also apply if composition proceedings have been instituted against the company and the company has given notice of termination of the contract of employment.[1]

§ 88. Prohibition of Competition

(1) Absent the consent of the supervisory board, members of the management board may neither engage in any trade nor enter into any transaction in the company's line of business on their own behalf or on behalf of others. Absent such consent they may neither be a member of the management board, nor a manager or

1. Effective as of 1 January 1999 § 87 (3) will read as follows:
'(3) If insolvency proceedings have been instituted over the company's assets and the receiver in insolvency has terminated the contract of employment of a member of the management board, such member may claim compensation of damages arising as a result of such termination only for a period of two years following termination of such employment.'

der Gesellschafter einer anderen Handelsgesellschaft sein. Die Einwilligung des Aufsichtsrats kann nur für bestimmte Handelsgewerbe oder Handelsgesellschaften oder für bestimmte Arten von Geschäften erteilt werden.

general partner of another commercial enterprise. The consent of the supervisory board may be granted only for a specific trade or business, a specific commercial enterprise, or for specific kinds of transactions.

(2) Verstößt ein Vorstandsmitglied gegen dieses Verbot, so kann die Gesellschaft Schadenersatz fordern. Sie kann statt dessen von dem Mitglied verlangen, daß es die für eigene Rechnung gemachten Geschäfte als für Rechnung der Gesellschaft eingegangen gelten läßt und die aus Geschäften für fremde Rechnung bezogene Vergütung herausgibt oder seinen Anspruch auf die Vergütung abtritt.

(2) If a member of the management board violates such prohibition, the company may claim damages. In lieu thereof the company may require that such member treat the transaction made on his own behalf as having been made on behalf of the company and remit any remuneration received for transactions made on behalf of another person or assign his rights to such remuneration.

(3) Die Ansprüche der Gesellschaft verjähren in drei Monaten seit dem Zeitpunkt, in dem die übrigen Vorstandsmitglieder und die Aufsichtsratsmitglieder von der zum Schadenersatz verpflichtenden Handlung Kenntnis erlangen. Sie verjähren ohne Rücksicht auf diese Kenntnis in fünf Jahren seit ihrer Entstehung.

(3) The claims of the company shall be barred after the expiration of three months from the date on which the other members of the management board and the supervisory board obtained knowledge of the act giving rise to the claim for damages. Irrespective of such knowledge, such claims shall be barred upon the expiration of five years after they have arisen.

§ 89. Kreditgewährung an Vorstandsmitglieder

§ 89. Extension of Credit to Members of the Management Board

(1) Die Gesellschaft darf ihren Vorstandsmitgliedern Kredit nur auf Grund eines Beschlusses des Aufsichtsrats gewähren. Der Beschluß kann nur für bestimmte Kreditgeschäfte oder Arten von Kreditgeschäften und nicht für länger als drei Monate im voraus gefaßt werden. Er hat die Verzinsung und Rückzahlung des Kredits zu regeln. Der Gewährung eines Kredits steht die Gestattung einer Entnahme gleich, die über die dem Vorstandsmitglied zustehenden Bezüge hinausgeht, namentlich auch die Gestattung der Entnahme von Vorschüssen auf Bezü-

(1) The company may extend credit to members of the management board only pursuant to a resolution of the supervisory board. Such resolution may authorize only the extension of specific credit transactions or kinds of credit transactions, and for not more than three months in advance. Such resolution shall make provision as to the payment of interest on, and repayment of, any loan. Permission to make drawings in excess of the remuneration due to the member of the management board, in particular permission to draw advances of remuneration, shall constitute an extension of

ge. Dies gilt nicht für Kredite, die ein Monatsgehalt nicht übersteigen.

credit. The foregoing shall not apply to credits which do not exceed an amount equal to one month's salary.

(**2**) Die Gesellschaft darf ihren Prokuristen und zum gesamten Geschäftsbetrieb ermächtigten Handlungsbevollmächtigten Kredit nur mit Einwilligung des Aufsichtsrats gewähren. Eine herrschende Gesellschaft darf Kredite an gesetzliche Vertreter, Prokuristen oder zum gesamten Geschäftsbetrieb ermächtigte Handlungsbevollmächtigte eines abhängigen Unternehmens nur mit Einwilligung ihres Aufsichtsrats, eine abhängige Gesellschaft darf Kredite an gesetzliche Vertreter, Prokuristen oder zum gesamten Geschäftsbetrieb ermächtigte Handlungsbevollmächtigte des herrschenden Unternehmens nur mit Einwilligung des Aufsichtsrats des herrschenden Unternehmens gewähren. Absatz 1 Satz 2 bis 5 gilt sinngemäß.

(**2**) The company may extend credit to its registered authorized officers and general managers[1] only with the consent of the supervisory board. A controlling company may extend credit to legal representatives, registered authorized officers or general managers of a controlled enterprise only with the consent of its supervisory board; a controlled company may extend credit to legal representatives, registered authorized officers or general managers of the controlling enterprise only with the consent of the supervisory board of the controlling enterprise. Subsection (1) sentences 2 to 5 shall apply analogously.

(**3**) Absatz 2 gilt auch für Kredite an den Ehegatten oder an ein minderjähriges Kind eines Vorstandsmitglieds, eines anderen gesetzlichen Vertreters, eines Prokuristen oder eines zum gesamten Geschäftsbetrieb ermächtigten Handlungsbevollmächtigten. Er gilt ferner für Kredite an einen Dritten, der für Rechnung dieser Personen oder für Rechnung eines Vorstandsmitglieds, eines anderen gesetzlichen Vertreters, eines Prokuristen oder eines zum gesamten Geschäftsbetrieb ermächtigten Handlungsbevollmächtigten handelt.

(**3**) Subsection (2) shall also apply to credits to the spouse or a minor child of a member of the management board, or other legal representatives, registered authorized officers or general managers. Moreover, such subsection shall apply to credits extended to any third party acting on behalf of any such persons or on behalf of a member of the management board, other legal representative, registered authorized officer or general manager.

(**4**) Ist ein Vorstandsmitglied, ein Prokurist oder ein zum gesamten Geschäftsbetrieb ermächtigter Handlungsbevollmächtigter zugleich gesetzlicher Vertreter oder Mitglied des Aufsichtsrats

(**4**) If a member of the management board, registered authorized officer or general manager is also a legal representative or member of the supervisory board of another legal entity or member

1. General managers are senior officers who are authorized to represent the company in its entire field of business.

einer anderen juristischen Person oder Gesellschafter einer Personenhandelsgesellschaft, so darf die Gesellschaft der juristischen Person oder der Personenhandelsgesellschaft Kredit nur mit Einwilligung des Aufsichtsrats gewähren; Absatz 1 Satz 2 und 3 gilt sinngemäß. Dies gilt nicht, wenn die juristische Person oder die Personenhandelsgesellschaft mit der Gesellschaft verbunden ist oder wenn der Kredit für die Bezahlung von Waren gewährt wird, welche die Gesellschaft der juristischen Person oder der Personenhandelsgesellschaft liefert.

of a commercial partnership, the company may extend credit to such legal entity or commercial partnership only with the consent of the supervisory board; subsection (1) sentences 2 and 3 shall apply analogously. The foregoing shall not apply if such legal entity or commercial partnership is affiliated with the company or if the company or if the credit is extended to finance the payment of goods which the company supplies to such legal entity or commercial partnership.

(5) Wird entgegen den Absätzen 1 bis 4 Kredit gewährt, so ist der Kredit ohne Rücksicht auf entgegenstehende Vereinbarungen sofort zurückzugewähren, wenn nicht der Aufsichtsrat nachträglich zustimmt.

(5) Any credit extended in violation of the provisions of subsections (1) to (4) shall be repaid immediately, irrespective of any agreement to the contrary, unless the supervisory board subsequently consents.

(6) Ist die Gesellschaft ein Kreditinstitut, so gelten an Stelle der Absätze 1 bis 5 die Vorschriften des Gesetzes über das Kreditwesen.

(6) If the company is a credit institution, the provisions of the Banking Act shall apply in lieu of subsections (1) to (5).

§ 90. Berichte an den Aufsichtsrat

(1) Der Vorstand hat dem Aufsichtsrat zu berichten über
1. die beabsichtigte Geschäftspolitik und andere grundsätzliche Fragen der künftigen Geschäftsführung;
2. die Rentabilität der Gesellschaft, insbesondere die Rentabilität des Eigenkapitals;
3. den Gang der Geschäfte, insbesondere den Umsatz, und die Lage der Gesellschaft;
4. Geschäfte, die für die Rentabilität oder Liquidität der Gesellschaft von erheblicher Bedeutung sein können.

Außerdem ist dem Vorsitzenden des Aufsichtsrats aus sonstigen wichtigen Anlässen zu berichten; als wichtiger Anlaß ist auch ein dem Vorstand bekanntge-

§ 90. Reports to the Supervisory Board

(1) The management board shall report to the supervisory board on:
1. intended business policy and other fundamental matters regarding the future conduct of the company's business;
2. the profitability of the company, in particular the return on equity;
3. the state of business, in particular revenues, and the condition of the company;
4. transactions which may have a material impact upon the profitability or liquidity of the company.

In addition, reports to the chairman of the supervisory board shall be made on the occurrence of other significant developments; such significant developments

wordener geschäftlicher Vorgang bei einem verbundenen Unternehmen anzusehen, der auf die Lage der Gesellschaft von erheblichem Einfluß sein kann.

shall also include circumstances concerning the business of an affiliated enterprise which become known to the management board and which may have a material impact upon the condition of the company.

(2) Die Berichte nach Absatz 1 Satz 1 Nr. 1 bis 4 sind wie folgt zu erstatten:

1. die Berichte nach Nummer 1 mindestens einmal jährlich, wenn nicht Änderungen der Lage oder neue Fragen eine unverzügliche Berichterstattung gebieten;
2. die Berichte nach Nummer 2 in der Sitzung des Aufsichtsrats, in der über den Jahresabschluß verhandelt wird;
3. die Berichte nach Nummer 3 regelmäßig, mindestens vierteljährlich;
4. die Berichte nach Nummer 4 möglichst so rechtzeitig, daß der Aufsichtsrat vor Vornahme der Geschäfte Gelegenheit hat, zu ihnen Stellung zu nehmen.

(2) Reports pursuant to subsection (1) sentence 1 Nos. 1 to 4 shall be made as follows:

1. reports pursuant to No. 1 not less than once a year, unless changes in circumstances or new matters necessitate an immediate report;
2. reports pursuant to No. 2 at the meeting of the supervisory board resolving an approval of the annual financial statements;
3. reports pursuant to No. 3 regularly, but not less than quarterly;
4. reports pursuant to No. 4 sufficiently early, if possible, to enable the supervisory board to express its opinion before such transactions are entered into.

(3) Der Aufsichtsrat kann vom Vorstand jederzeit einen Bericht verlangen über Angelegenheiten der Gesellschaft, über ihre rechtlichen und geschäftlichen Beziehungen zu verbundenen Unternehmen sowie über geschäftliche Vorgänge bei diesen Unternehmen, die auf die Lage der Gesellschaft von erheblichem Einfluß sein können. Auch ein einzelnes Mitglied kann einen Bericht, jedoch nur an den Aufsichtsrat, verlangen; lehnt der Vorstand die Berichterstattung ab, so kann der Bericht nur verlangt werden, wenn ein anderes Aufsichtsratsmitglied das Verlangen unterstützt.

(3) The supervisory board may at any time require a report from the management board on the affairs of the company, on the company's legal and business relationships with affiliated enterprises, and on the circumstances concerning the business of such enterprises which may have a material impact upon the condition of the company. Any member may also request such report, which shall be given, however, to the supervisory board as such; if the management board refuses to give such report, the report may be required only if another member of the supervisory board seconds such request.

(4) Die Berichte haben den Grundsätzen einer gewissenhaften und getreuen Rechenschaft zu entsprechen.

(4) The report shall comply with the principles of conscientious and accurate reporting.

(5) Jedes Aufsichtsratsmitglied hat das Recht, von den Berichten Kenntnis zu

(5) Each member of the supervisory board shall have the right to take cogni-

nehmen. Soweit die Berichte schriftlich erstattet worden sind, sind sie auch jedem Aufsichtsratsmitglied auf Verlangen auszuhändigen, soweit der Aufsichtsrat nichts anderes beschlossen hat. Der Vorsitzende des Aufsichtsrats hat die Aufsichtsratsmitglieder über die Berichte nach Absatz 1 Satz 2 spätestens in der nächsten Aufsichtsratssitzung zu unterrichten.

zance of the reports. If the reports have been made in writing they shall be submitted to each member of the supervisory board upon demand, unless the supervisory board has resolved otherwise. The chairman of the supervisory board shall inform the members of the supervisory board of reports made pursuant to subsection (1) sentence 2 no later than at the next following meeting of the supervisory board.

§ 91. Buchführung

Der Vorstand hat dafür zu sorgen, daß die erforderlichen Handelsbücher geführt werden.

§ 91. Accounting

The management board shall ensure that the requisite books of account are maintained.

§ 92. Vorstandspflichten bei Verlust, Überschuldung oder Zahlungsunfähigkeit

(1) Ergibt sich bei Aufstellung der Jahresbilanz oder einer Zwischenbilanz oder ist bei pflichtmäßigem Ermessen anzunehmen, daß ein Verlust in Höhe der Hälfte des Grundkapitals besteht, so hat der Vorstand unverzüglich die Hauptversammlung einzuberufen und ihr dies anzuzeigen.

(2) Wird die Gesellschaft zahlungsunfähig, so hat der Vorstand ohne schuldhaftes Zögern, spätestens aber drei Wochen nach Eintritt der Zahlungsunfähigkeit, die Eröffnung des Konkursverfahrens oder des gerichtlichen Vergleichsverfahrens zu beantragen. Dies gilt sinngemäß, wenn das Vermögen der Gesellschaft nicht mehr die Schulden deckt. Der Antrag ist nicht schuldhaft verzögert, wenn der Vorstand die Eröffnung des gerichtlichen Vergleichsverfahrens mit der

§ 92. Duties of the Management Board in the Event of Losses, Overindebtedness or Insolvency

(1) If upon preparation of the annual balance sheet or an interim balance sheet it becomes apparent, or if in the exercise of proper judgement it must be assumed, that the company has incurred a loss equal to one half of the share capital, the management board shall promptly call a shareholders' meeting and advise the meeting thereof.

(2) If the company shall become unable to make payments when due, the management board shall file petition for the institution of bankruptcy or judicial composition proceedings without undue delay but in no event later than three weeks after the company became unable to make payments when due. The foregoing shall apply analogously if the company's liabilities shall exceed its assets. Such petition shall not be considered to have been unduly delayed if the manage-

Sorgfalt eines ordentlichen und gewissenhaften Geschäftsleiters betreibt.[1]

(3) Nachdem die Zahlungsunfähigkeit der Gesellschaft eingetreten ist oder sich ihre Überschuldung ergeben hat, darf der Vorstand keine Zahlungen leisten. Dies gilt nicht von Zahlungen, die auch nach diesem Zeitpunkt mit der Sorgfalt eines ordentlichen und gewissenhaften Geschäftsleiters vereinbar sind.

ment board attends to the institution of judicial composition proceedings with the care of a diligent and conscientious manager.[1]

(3) If the company shall become insolvent or overindebted, the management board may not make any payments. The foregoing shall not apply to payments which even after the occurrence of insolvency or overindebtedness are consistent with the care of a diligent and conscientious manager.

§ 93. Sorgfaltspflicht und Verantwortlichkeit der Vorstandsmitglieder

(1) Die Vorstandsmitglieder haben bei ihrer Geschäftsführung die Sorgfalt eines ordentlichen und gewissenhaften Geschäftsleiters anzuwenden. Über vertrauliche Angaben und Geheimnisse der Gesellschaft, namentlich Betriebs- oder Geschäftsgeheimnisse, die ihnen durch ihre Tätigkeit im Vorstand bekanntgeworden sind, haben sie Stillschweigen zu bewahren.

(2) Vorstandsmitglieder, die ihre Pflichten verletzen, sind der Gesellschaft zum Ersatz des daraus entstehenden Schadens als Gesamtschuldner verpflichtet. Ist streitig, ob sie die Sorgfalt eines ordentlichen und gewissenhaften Geschäftsleiters angewandt haben, so trifft sie die Beweislast.

§ 93. Duty of Care and Responsibility of Members of the Management Board

(1) In conducting business the members of the management board shall employ the care of a diligent and conscientious manager. They shall not disclose confidential information and secrets of the company, in particular trade and business secrets, which have become known to them as a result of their service on the management board.

(2) Members of the management board who violate their duties shall be jointly and severally liable to the company for any resulting damage. They shall bear the burden of proof in the event of a dispute as to whether or not they have employed the care of a diligent and conscientious manager.

1. Mit Wirkung vom 1. Januar 1999 ist § 92 Abs. 2 wie folgt gefaßt:
'(2) Wird die Gesellschaft zahlungsunfähig, so hat der Vorstand ohne schuldhaftes Zögern, spätestens aber drei Wochen nach Eintritt der Zahlungsunfähigkeit, die Eröffnung des Insolvenzverfahrens zu beantragen. Dies gilt sinngemäß, wenn sich eine Überschuldung der Gesellschaft ergibt.'

1. Effective as of 1 January 1999 § 92 (2) will read as follows:
'(2) If the company shall become unable to make payments when due, the management board shall file petition for the institution of insolvency proceedings without undue delay but in no event later than three weeks after the company became unable to make payments when due. The foregoing shall apply analogously if an overindebtedness of the company arises.'

(3) Die Vorstandsmitglieder sind namentlich zum Ersatz verpflichtet, wenn entgegen diesem Gesetz

1. Einlagen an die Aktionäre zurückgewährt werden,
2. den Aktionären Zinsen oder Gewinnanteile gezahlt werden,
3. eigene Aktien der Gesellschaft oder einer anderen Gesellschaft gezeichnet, erworben, als Pfand genommen oder eingezogen werden,
4. Aktien vor der vollen Leistung des Nennbetrags oder des höheren Ausgabebetrags ausgegeben werden,
5. Gesellschaftsvermögen verteilt wird,
6. Zahlungen geleistet werden, nachdem die Zahlungsunfähigkeit der Gesellschaft eingetreten ist oder sich ihre Überschuldung ergeben hat,
7. Vergütungen an Aufsichtsratsmitglieder gewährt werden,
8. Kredit gewährt wird,
9. bei der bedingten Kapitalerhöhung außerhalb des festgesetzten Zwecks oder vor der vollen Leistung des Gegenwerts Bezugsaktien ausgegeben werden.

(4) Der Gesellschaft gegenüber tritt die Ersatzpflicht nicht ein, wenn die Handlung auf einem gesetzmäßigen Beschluß der Hauptversammlung beruht. Dadurch, daß der Aufsichtsrat die Handlung gebilligt hat, wird die Ersatzpflicht nicht ausgeschlossen. Die Gesellschaft kann erst drei Jahre nach der Entstehung des Anspruchs und nur dann auf Ersatzansprüche verzichten oder sich über sie vergleichen, wenn die Hauptversammlung zustimmt und nicht eine Minderheit, deren Anteile zusammen den zehnten Teil des Grundkapitals erreichen, zur Niederschrift Widerspruch erhebt. Die zeitliche Beschränkung gilt nicht, wenn der Ersatzpflichtige zahlungsunfähig ist und sich zur Abwendung oder Beseitigung

(3) The members of the management board shall in particular be liable for damages if, contrary to this Act:

1. contributions are repaid to shareholders;
2. shareholders are paid interest or dividends;
3. company shares or shares of another company are subscribed, acquired, taken as a pledge or redeemed;
4. share certificates are issued before the par value or the higher issue price has been fully paid;
5. assets of the company are distributed;
6. payments are made after the company has become insolvent or overindebted;
7. remuneration is paid to members of the supervisory board;
8. credit is extended;
9. in connection with a conditional capital increase, new shares are issued other than for the specified purpose or prior to full payment of the consideration.

(4) The member of the management board shall not be liable to the company for damages if they acted pursuant to a lawful resolution of the shareholders' meeting. However, liability for damages shall not be precluded by the fact that the supervisory board has consented to the act. The company may waive or compromise a claim for damages upon the expiry of three years after the claim has arisen, provided that the shareholders' meeting consents thereto and no minority whose aggregate holding equals or exceeds one tenth of the share capital records an objection in the minutes. The foregoing period of time shall not apply if the person liable for damages is insolvent and enters into a composition with

des Konkursverfahrens mit seinen Gläubigern vergleicht.[1]

(5) Der Ersatzanspruch der Gesellschaft kann auch von den Gläubigern der Gesellschaft geltend gemacht werden, soweit sie von dieser keine Befriedigung erlangen können. Dies gilt jedoch in anderen Fällen als denen des Absatzes 3 nur dann, wenn die Vorstandsmitglieder die Sorgfalt eines ordentlichen und gewissenhaften Geschäftsleiters gröblich verletzt haben; Absatz 2 Satz 2 gilt sinngemäß. Den Gläubigern gegenüber wird die Ersatzpflicht weder durch einen Verzicht oder Vergleich der Gesellschaft noch dadurch aufgehoben, daß die Handlung auf einem Beschluß der Hauptversammlung beruht. Ist über das Vermögen der Gesellschaft das Konkursverfahren eröffnet, so übt während dessen Dauer der Konkursverwalter das Recht der Gläubiger gegen die Vorstandsmitglieder aus.[2]

(6) Die Ansprüche aus diesen Vorschriften verjähren in fünf Jahren.

1. Mit Wirkung vom 1. Januar 1999 ist § 93 Abs. 4 Satz 4 wie folgt gefaßt:
'Die zeitliche Beschränkung gilt nicht, wenn der Ersatzpflichtige zahlungsunfähig ist und sich zur Abwendung des Insolvenzverfahrens mit seinen Gläubigern vergleicht oder wenn die Ersatzpflicht in einem Insolvenzplan geregelt wird.'
2. Mit Wirkung vom 1. Januar 1999 ist § 93 Abs. 5 Satz 4 wie folgt gefaßt:
'Ist über das Vermögen der Gesellschaft das Insolvenzverfahren eröffnet, so übt während dessen Dauer der Insolvenzverwalter oder der Sachwalter das Recht der Gläubiger gegen die Vorstandsmitglieder aus.'

his creditors to avoid or terminate bankruptcy proceedings.[1]

(5) The claim of the company for damages may also be asserted by the company's creditors if they are unable to obtain satisfaction from the company. However, in cases other than those set out in subsection (3), the foregoing shall apply only if the members of the management board have grossly violated the duty of care of a diligent and conscientious manager; subsection (2) sentence 2 shall apply analogously. Liability for damages to the creditors shall be extinguished neither by a waiver nor by a compromise of the company nor by the fact that the act which caused the damage was based on a resolution of the shareholders' meeting. If bankruptcy proceedings have been instituted over the company's assets, the receiver in bankruptcy shall exercise the rights of the creditors against the members of the management board during the course of such proceedings.[2]

(6) Claims under the foregoing provisions shall be barred after the expiration of a period of five years.

1. Effective as of 1 January 1999 § 93 (4) sentence 4 will read as follows:
'The foregoing period of time shall not apply if the person liable for damages is insolvent and enters into a composition with his creditors to avoid insolvency proceedings or if the liability for damages is subject to an insolvency plan.'
2. Effective as of 1 January 1999 § 93 (5) sentence 4 will read as follows:
'If insolvency proceedings have been instituted over the company's assets, the receiver or the trustee, as the case may be, shall exercise the rights of the creditors against the members of the management board during the course of such proceedings.'

§ 94. Stellvertreter von Vorstandsmitgliedern

Die Vorschriften für die Vorstandsmitglieder gelten auch für ihre Stellvertreter.

§ 94. Deputies of Members of the Management Board

The provisions relating to members of the management board shall also apply to their deputies.

Zweiter Abschnitt. Aufsichtsrat

Division Two. Supervisory Board

§ 95. Zahl der Aufsichtsratsmitglieder

Der Aufsichtsrat besteht aus drei Mitgliedern. Die Satzung kann eine bestimmte höhere Zahl festsetzen. Die Zahl muß durch drei teilbar sein. Die Höchstzahl der Aufsichtsratsmitglieder beträgt bei Gesellschaften mit einem Grundkapital

bis zu 3 000 000 Deutsche Mark neun,

von mehr als 3 000 000 Deutsche Mark fünfzehn,

von mehr als 20 000 000 Deutsche Mark einundzwanzig.

Durch die vorstehenden Vorschriften werden hiervon abweichende Vorschriften des Gesetzes über die Mitbestimmung der Arbeitnehmer vom 4. Mai 1976 (Bundesgesetzbl. I S. 1153), des Montan-Mitbestimmungsgesetzes und des Gesetzes zur Ergänzung des Gesetzes über die Mitbestimmung der Arbeitnehmer in den Aufsichtsräten und Vorständen der Unternehmen des Bergbaus und der Eisen und Stahl erzeugenden Industrie vom 7. August 1956 (Bundesgesetzbl. I S. 707) – Mitbestimmungsergänzungsgesetz – nicht berührt.

§ 95. Number of Members of the Supervisory Board

The supervisory board shall comprise three members. The articles may provide for a specified higher number. Such number shall be divisible by three. The maximum number of members of the supervisory board for companies with a share capital of:

up to 3,000,000 Deutsche Mark shall be nine,

more than 3,000,000 Deutsche Mark shall be fifteen,

more than 20,000,000 Deutsche Mark shall be twenty-one.

The foregoing provisions shall be without prejudice to any conflicting provisions that may be contained in the Employees Co-determination Act of 4 May 1976 (Legal Gazette I p. 1153), the Coal and Steel Co-determination Act and the Supplemental Act on the Co-determination of Employees in the Supervisory Boards and Management Boards in the Mining and the Iron and Steel Producing Industries of 7 August 1956 (Legal Gazette I p. 707) – ('the Supplemental Co-determination Act').

§ 96. Zusammensetzung des Aufsichtsrats

(1) Der Aufsichtsrat setzt sich zusammen

bei Gesellschaften, für die das Mitbe-

§ 96. Composition of the Supervisory Board

(1) The supervisory board shall:

in the case of companies to which the

stimmungsgesetz gilt, aus Aufsichtsratsmitgliedern der Aktionäre und der Arbeitnehmer,

bei Gesellschaften, für die das Montan-Mitbestimmungsgesetz gilt, aus Aufsichtsratsmitgliedern der Aktionäre und der Arbeitnehmer und aus weiteren Mitgliedern,

bei Gesellschaften, für die die §§ 5 bis 13 des Mitbestimmungsergänzungsgesetzes gelten, aus Aufsichtsratsmitgliedern der Aktionäre und der Arbeitnehmer und aus einem weiteren Mitglied,

bei Gesellschaften, für die § 76 Abs. 1 des Betriebsverfassungsgesetzes 1952 gilt, aus Aufsichtsratsmitgliedern der Aktionäre und der Arbeitnehmer,

bei den übrigen Gesellschaften nur aus Aufsichtsratsmitgliedern der Aktionäre.

(2) Nach anderen als den zuletzt angewandten gesetzlichen Vorschriften kann der Aufsichtsrat nur zusammengesetzt werden, wenn nach § 97 oder nach § 98 die in der Bekanntmachung des Vorstands oder in der gerichtlichen Entscheidung angegebenen gesetzlichen Vorschriften anzuwenden sind.

§ 97. Bekanntmachung über die Zusammensetzung des Aufsichtsrats

(**1**) Ist der Vorstand der Ansicht, daß der Aufsichtsrat nicht nach den für ihn maßgebenden gesetzlichen Vorschriften zusammengesetzt ist, so hat er dies unverzüglich in den Gesellschaftsblättern und gleichzeitig durch Aushang in sämtlichen Betrieben der Gesellschaft und ihrer Konzernunternehmen bekanntzumachen. In

Co-determination Act applies, comprise representatives of the shareholders and the employees;

in the case of companies to which the Coal and Steel Co-determination Act applies, comprise representatives of the shareholders and the employees and additional members;

in the case of companies to which §§ 5 to 13 of the Supplemental Co-determination Act apply, comprise representatives of the shareholders and the employees and one additional member;

in the case of companies to which § 76 (1) of the Labour Council Act 1952[1] applies, comprise representatives of the shareholders and the employees;

in the case of all other companies, comprise representatives of the shareholders only.

(**2**) The supervisory board shall be composed in accordance with the statutory provisions last applied unless, pursuant to § 97 or § 98, other statutory provisions are to be applied that have been specified in an announcement of the management board or in a judicial decision.

§ 97. Announcement Concerning Composition of the Supervisory Board

(**1**) If the management board is of the opinion that the composition of the supervisory board does not comply with applicable statutory provisions, it shall promptly announce such fact in the company's journal and at the same time by notices displayed in all designated offices of the company and the members of its

1. The Labour Council Act 1952 (Betriebsverfassungsgesetz 1952) has been superseded by the Labour Council Act 1972 but for the provisions relating to employee representation in the supervisory boards of companies of a certain size.

der Bekanntmachung sind die nach Ansicht des Vorstands maßgebenden gesetzlichen Vorschriften anzugeben. Es ist darauf hinzuweisen, daß der Aufsichtsrat nach diesen Vorschriften zusammengesetzt wird, wenn nicht Antragsberechtigte nach § 98 Abs. 2 innerhalb eines Monats nach der Bekanntmachung im Bundesanzeiger das nach § 98 Abs. 1 zuständige Gericht anrufen.

(2) Wird das nach § 98 Abs. 1 zuständige Gericht nicht innerhalb eines Monats nach der Bekanntmachung im Bundesanzeiger angerufen, so ist der neue Aufsichtsrat nach den in der Bekanntmachung des Vorstands angegebenen gesetzlichen Vorschriften zusammenzusetzen. Die Bestimmungen der Satzung über die Zusammensetzung des Aufsichtsrats, über die Zahl der Aufsichtsratsmitglieder sowie über die Wahl, Abberufung und Entsendung von Aufsichtsratsmitgliedern treten mit der Beendigung der ersten Hauptversammlung, die nach Ablauf der Anrufungsfrist einberufen wird, spätestens sechs Monate nach Ablauf dieser Frist insoweit außer Kraft, als sie den nunmehr anzuwendenden gesetzlichen Vorschriften widersprechen. Mit demselben Zeitpunkt erlischt das Amt der bisherigen Aufsichtsratsmitglieder. Eine Hauptversammlung, die innerhalb der Frist von sechs Monaten stattfindet, kann an Stelle der außer Kraft tretenden Satzungsbestimmungen mit einfacher Stimmenmehrheit neue Satzungsbestimmungen beschließen.

(3) Solange ein gerichtliches Verfahren nach §§ 98, 99 anhängig ist, kann eine Bekanntmachung über die Zusammensetzung des Aufsichtsrats nicht erfolgen.

group. The statutory provisions which are applicable in the opinion of the management board shall be specified in such announcement. Such announcement shall state that the supervisory board will be composed in accordance with such provisions, unless parties with standing pursuant to § 98 (2) make motion to the court having jurisdiction pursuant to § 98 (1) within one month from the date of the announcement in the Federal Gazette.

(2) If no motion has been made to the court having jurisdiction pursuant to § 98 (1) within one month from the date of the announcement in the Federal Gazette, the new supervisory board shall be composed in accordance with the statutory provisions specified in the announcement of the management board. The provisions of the articles regarding the composition of the supervisory board, the number of members of the supervisory board and the election, removal and appointment of members of the supervisory board shall, in so far as they conflict with the applicable statutory provisions, cease to be effective as at the closure of the first shareholders' meeting called after the expiration of such one month period, but in any event no more than six months after the expiration of such period. As at the same date the term of office of the previous members of the supervisory board shall expire. A shareholders' meeting held within such six month period may, by simple majority, replace those provisions in the articles which cease to be effective by new provisions.

(3) No announcement concerning the composition of the supervisory board may be made while judicial proceedings pursuant to § 98 and § 99 are pending.

§ 98. Gerichtliche Entscheidung über die Zusammensetzung des Aufsichtsrats

(**1**) Ist streitig oder ungewiß, nach welchen gesetzlichen Vorschriften der Aufsichtsrat zusammenzusetzen ist, so entscheidet darüber auf Antrag ausschließlich das Landgericht (Zivilkammer), in dessen Bezirk die Gesellschaft ihren Sitz hat. Die Landesregierung kann die Entscheidung durch Rechtsverordnung für die Bezirke mehrerer Landgerichte einem der Landgerichte übertragen, wenn dies der Sicherung einer einheitlichen Rechtsprechung dient. Die Landesregierung kann die Ermächtigung auf die Landesjustizverwaltung übertragen.

(**2**) Antragsberechtigt sind

1. der Vorstand,
2. jedes Aufsichtsratsmitglied,
3. jeder Aktionär,
4. der Gesamtbetriebsrat der Gesellschaft oder, wenn in der Gesellschaft nur ein Betriebsrat besteht, der Betriebsrat,
5. der Gesamtbetriebsrat eines anderen Unternehmens, dessen Arbeitnehmer nach den gesetzlichen Vorschriften, deren Anwendung streitig oder ungewiß ist, selbst oder durch Delegierte an der Wahl von Aufsichtsratsmitgliedern der Gesellschaft teilnehmen, oder, wenn in dem anderen Unternehmen nur ein Betriebsrat besteht, der Betriebsrat,
6. mindestens ein Zehntel oder einhundert der Arbeitnehmer, die nach den gesetzlichen Vorschriften, deren Anwendung streitig oder ungewiß ist, selbst oder durch Delegierte an der Wahl von Aufsichtsratsmitgliedern der Gesellschaft teilnehmen,
7. Spitzenorganisationen der Gewerkschaften, die nach den gesetzlichen Vorschriften, deren Anwendung streitig oder ungewiß ist, ein Vorschlagsrecht hätten,

§ 98. Judicial Decision Concerning Composition of the Supervisory Board

(**1**) If it is disputed or uncertain which statutory provisions are to be applied to the composition of the supervisory board, the exclusive jurisdiction to decide such issue, upon motion, shall lie with the district court (civil chamber) of the district in which the company is domiciled. The state government may by regulation transfer jurisdiction for several districts to one district court if required to ensure uniformity of decisions. The state government may transfer such authority to the ministry of justice of such state.

(**2**) The following shall have standing to make such motion:

1. the management board;
2. each member of the supervisory board;
3. each shareholder;
4. the central labour council of the company or, if the company has only one labour council, such labour council;
5. the central labour council of another enterprise whose employees participate directly or through delegates in the election of members of the supervisory board of the company pursuant to the statutory provisions whose application is disputed or uncertain, or, if only one labour council exists in such other enterprise, such labour council;
6. not less than one tenth or one hundred of the employees who participate directly or through delegates in the election of members of the supervisory board of the company pursuant to the statutory provisions whose application is disputed or uncertain;
7. the central organisations of the labour unions which would, pursuant to the statutory provisions whose application is

disputed or uncertain, have a right to nominate members;

8. Gewerkschaften, die nach den gesetzlichen Vorschriften, deren Anwendung streitig oder ungewiß ist, ein Vorschlagsrecht hätten.

Ist die Anwendung des Mitbestimmungsgesetzes oder die Anwendung von Vorschriften des Mitbestimmungsgesetzes streitig oder ungewiß, so sind außer den nach Satz 1 Antragsberechtigten auch je ein Zehntel der wahlberechtigten Arbeiter, der wahlberechtigten in § 3 Abs. 3 Nr. 1 des Mitbestimmungsgesetzes bezeichneten Angestellten oder der wahlberechtigten leitenden Angestellten im Sinne des Mitbestimmungsgesetzes antragsberechtigt.

8. labour unions which would, pursuant to the statutory provisions whose application is disputed or uncertain, have a right to nominate members.

If either the application of the Co-determination Act or the application of certain provisions of the Co-determination Act is disputed or uncertain, then in addition to those having standing to make motion pursuant to sentence 1, one tenth of the workers who are entitled to vote, or one enth of the employees designated in § 3 (3) No. 1 of the Co-determination Act who are entitled to vote, or one tenth of the managerial employees within the meaning of the Co-determination Act who are entitled to vote, shall also have standing to make motion hereunder.

(3) Die Absätze 1 und 2 gelten sinngemäß, wenn streitig ist, ob der Abschlußprüfer das nach § 3 oder § 16 des Mitbestimmungsergänzungsgesetzes maßgebliche Umsatzverhältnis richtig ermittelt hat.

(3) Subsections (1) and (2) shall apply analogously in the event of a dispute as to whether the external auditor has correctly determined the relevant revenue ratios pursuant to § 3 or § 16 of the Supplemental Co-determination Act.

(4) Entspricht die Zusammensetzung des Aufsichtsrats nicht der gerichtlichen Entscheidung, so ist der neue Aufsichtsrat nach den in der Entscheidung angegebenen gesetzlichen Vorschriften zusammenzusetzen. § 97 Abs. 2 gilt sinngemäß mit der Maßgabe, daß die Frist von sechs Monaten mit dem Eintritt der Rechtskraft beginnt.

(4) If the composition of the supervisory board does not comply with the judicial decision, the new supervisory board shall be composed in accordance with the statutory provisions specified in such decision. § 97 (2) shall apply analogously, except that the six month period shall commence on the date on which such decision becomes final and may not be appealed.

§ 99. Verfahren

(1) Auf das Verfahren ist das Gesetz über die Angelegenheiten der freiwilligen Gerichtsbarkeit anzuwenden, soweit in den Absätzen 2 bis 5 nichts anderes bestimmt ist.

§ 99. Procedure

(1) The procedure shall be governed by the provisions of the Act on Court Procedure in Non-litigious Matters, unless subsections (2) to (5) provide otherwise.

(**2**) Das Landgericht hat den Antrag in den Gesellschaftsblättern bekanntzumachen. Der Vorstand und jedes Aufsichtsratsmitglied sowie die nach § 98 Abs. 2 antragsberechtigten Betriebsräte, Spitzenorganisationen und Gewerkschaften sind zu hören.

(**2**) The district court shall cause publication of the motion in the company's designated journals. The management board and each member of the supervisory board as well as the labour councils, central organisations and labour unions which have standing to make motion pursuant to § 98 (2) shall be heard.

(**3**) Das Landgericht entscheidet durch einen mit Gründen versehenen Beschluß. Gegen die Entscheidung findet die sofortige Beschwerde statt. Sie kann nur auf eine Verletzung des Gesetzes gestützt werden; die §§ 550, 551, 561, 563 der Zivilprozeßordnung gelten sinngemäß. Die Beschwerde kann nur durch Einreichung einer von einem Rechtsanwalt unterzeichneten Beschwerdeschrift eingelegt werden. Über sie entscheidet das Oberlandesgericht. § 28 Abs. 2 und 3 des Gesetzes über die Angelegenheiten der freiwilligen Gerichtsbarkeit gilt entsprechend. Die weitere Beschwerde ist ausgeschlossen. Die Landesregierung kann durch Rechtsverordnung die Entscheidung über die Beschwerde für die Bezirke mehrerer Oberlandesgerichte einem der Oberlandesgerichte oder dem Obersten Landesgericht übertragen, wenn dies der Sicherung einer einheitlichen Rechtsprechung dient. Die Landesregierung kann die Ermächtigung auf die Landesjustizverwaltung übertragen.

(**3**) The decision of the district court shall be made by decree setting out the grounds on which the decision is based. An immediate appeal may be made against such decision. Such appeal may be based only on a violation of the law; §§ 550, 551, 561 and 563 of the Code of Civil Procedure shall apply analogously. Such appeal may only be made by filing a notice of appeal signed by an attorney at law. The Appellate Court shall have jurisdiction over such appeal. § 28 (2) and (3) of the Act on Court Procedure in Non-litigious Matters shall apply. Further appeal shall be precluded. The state government may by regulation transfer jurisdiction for several districts to one Appellate Court if required to ensure uniformity of decisions. The state government may transfer such authority to the ministry of justice of such state.

(**4**) Das Gericht hat seine Entscheidung dem Antragsteller und der Gesellschaft zuzustellen. Es hat sie ferner ohne Gründe in den Gesellschaftsblättern bekanntzumachen. Die Beschwerde steht jedem nach § 98 Abs. 2 Antragsberechtigten zu. Die Beschwerdefrist beginnt mit der Bekanntmachung der Entscheidung im Bundesanzeiger, für den Antragsteller und die Gesellschaft jedoch nicht vor der Zustellung der Entscheidung.

(**4**) The court shall serve its decision on the party having made motion and on the company. Furthermore, the court shall announce the decision in the company's designated journals without setting out the grounds on which the decision is based. Appeal may be made by each party having standing to make motion pursuant to § 98 (2). The period for filing the notice of appeal shall commence on the date on which the decision was announced in the Federal Gazette, but, in the case of the party having made motion and the company, not prior to service of the decision.

(5) Die Entscheidung wird erst mit der Rechtskraft wirksam. Sie wirkt für und gegen alle. Der Vorstand hat die rechtskräftige Entscheidung unverzüglich zum Handelsregister einzureichen.

(5) The decision shall become binding only when it has become final and may not be appealed. Such decision shall have effect for and against everyone. The management board shall promptly submit the binding decision to the commercial register.

(6) Für die Kosten des Verfahrens gilt die Kostenordnung. Für das Verfahren des ersten Rechtszugs wird das Vierfache der vollen Gebühr erhoben. Für den zweiten Rechtszug wird die gleiche Gebühr erhoben; dies gilt auch dann, wenn die Beschwerde Erfolg hat. Wird der Antrag oder die Beschwerde zurückgenommen, bevor es zu einer Entscheidung kommt, so ermäßigt sich die Gebühr auf die Hälfte. Der Geschäftswert ist von Amts wegen festzusetzen. Er bestimmt sich nach § 30 Abs. 2 der Kostenordnung mit der Maßgabe, daß der Wert regelmäßig auf einhunderttausend Deutsche Mark anzunehmen ist. Schuldner der Kosten ist die Gesellschaft. Die Kosten können jedoch ganz oder zum Teil dem Antragsteller auferlegt werden, wenn dies der Billigkeit entspricht. Kosten der Beteiligten werden nicht erstattet.

(6) The costs of the proceedings shall be determined by the Act on Court Costs. In proceedings before the court of first instance four times the full fee shall be assessed. In proceedings before the court of second instance the same amount shall be assessed; the foregoing shall also apply if the appeal is successful. If the motion or the appeal is withdrawn before a decision is rendered, the fees shall be reduced by one half. The court shall determine the value of the subject matter of the proceedings.[1] Such value shall be determined in accordance with § 30 (2) of the Act on Court Costs, provided that such value shall as a rule be one hundred thousand Deutsche Mark. The company shall be liable for the costs. The party having made motion shall, however, be liable for the costs, in whole or in part, if equity so requires. The parties' own costs shall not be reimbursed.

§ 100. Persönliche Voraussetzungen für Aufsichtsratsmitglieder

§ 100. Personal Qualifications of Members of the Supervisory Board

(1) Mitglied des Aufsichtsrats kann nur eine natürliche, unbeschränkt geschäftsfähige Person sein. Ein Betreuter, der bei der Besorgung seiner Vermögensangelegenheiten ganz oder teilweise einem Einwilligungsvorbehalt (§ 1903 des

(1) Only a natural person with full legal capacity may be a member of the supervisory board. A person under guardianship whose property affairs are subject, in whole or in part, to consent requirements (§ 1903 of the Civil Code)

1. Under the Act on Court Costs the amount of the fees depends on the value of the subject matter of the proceedings as determined by the court.

Bürgerlichen Gesetzbuchs) unterliegt, kann nicht Mitglied des Aufsichtsrats sein.

may not be a member of the supervisory board.

(2) Mitglied des Aufsichtsrats kann nicht sein, wer

1. bereits in zehn Handelsgesellschaften oder bergrechtlichen Gewerkschaften, die gesetzlich einen Aufsichtsrat zu bilden haben, Aufsichtsratsmitglied ist,

2. gesetzlicher Vertreter eines von der Gesellschaft abhängigen Unternehmens ist, oder

3. gesetzlicher Vertreter einer anderen Kapitalgesellschaft oder bergrechtlichen Gewerkschaft ist, deren Aufsichtsrat ein Vorstandsmitglied der Gesellschaft angehört.

Auf die Höchstzahl nach Satz 1 Nr. 1 sind bis zu fünf Aufsichtsratssitze nicht anzurechnen, die ein gesetzlicher Vertreter (beim Einzelkaufmann der Inhaber) des herrschenden Unternehmens eines Konzerns in zum Konzern gehörenden Handelsgesellschaften und bergrechtlichen Gewerkschaften, die gesetzlich einen Aufsichtsrat zu bilden haben, inne hat.

(2) A person may not be a member of the supervisory board who:

1. is already a member of the supervisory board in ten commercial enterprises or mining companies which are required by law to form a supervisory board;

2. is the legal representative of an enterprise controlled by the company; or

3. is the legal representative of another corporation or mining company whose supervisory board includes a member of the management board of the company.

In determining the maximum number for purposes of sentence 1 no. 1 no account shall be taken of up to five seats which a legal representative (or, in the case of a sole proprietorship, the owner) of the controlling enterprise of a group holds in supervisory boards of commercial enterprises and mining companies which are members of such group and which are required by law to form a supervisory board.

(3) Die anderen persönlichen Voraussetzungen der Aufsichtsratsmitglieder der Arbeitnehmer sowie der weiteren Mitglieder bestimmen sich nach dem Mitbestimmungsgesetz, dem Montan-Mitbestimmungsgesetz, dem Mitbestimmungsergänzungsgesetz und dem Betriebsverfassungsgesetz 1952.

(3) The further personal qualifications of the representatives of the employees and the additional members of the supervisory board shall be determined by the Co-determination Act, the Coal and Steel Co-determination Act, the Supplemental Co-determination Act and the Labour Council Act 1952.

(4) Die Satzung kann persönliche Voraussetzungen nur für Aufsichtsratsmitglieder fordern, die von der Hauptversammlung ohne Bindung an Wahlvorschläge gewählt oder auf Grund der Satzung in den Aufsichtsrat entsandt werden.

(4) The articles may stipulate personal qualifications only for those members of the supervisory board who are elected by the shareholders' meeting without being bound by nominations, or who are appointed to the supervisory board pursuant to the articles.

§ 101. Bestellung der Aufsichtsratsmitglieder

(1) Die Mitglieder des Aufsichtsrats werden von der Hauptversammlung gewählt, soweit sie nicht in den Aufsichtsrat zu entsenden oder als Aufsichtsratsmitglieder der Arbeitnehmer nach dem Mitbestimmungsgesetz, dem Mitbestimmungsergänzungsgesetz oder dem Betriebsverfassungsgesetz 1952 zu wählen sind. An Wahlvorschläge ist die Hauptversammlung nur gemäß §§ 6 und 8 des Montan-Mitbestimmungsgesetzes gebunden.

(2) Ein Recht, Mitglieder in den Aufsichtsrat zu entsenden, kann nur durch die Satzung und nur für bestimmte Aktionäre oder für die jeweiligen Inhaber bestimmter Aktien begründet werden. Inhabern bestimmter Aktien kann das Entsendungsrecht nur eingeräumt werden, wenn die Aktien auf Namen lauten und ihre Übertragung an die Zustimmung der Gesellschaft gebunden ist. Die Aktien der Entsendungsberechtigten gelten nicht als eine besondere Gattung. Die Entsendungsrechte können insgesamt höchstens für ein Drittel der sich aus dem Gesetz oder der Satzung ergebenden Zahl der Aufsichtsratsmitglieder der Aktionäre eingeräumt werden. § 4 Abs. 1 des Gesetzes über die Überführung der Anteilsrechte an der Volkswagenwerk Gesellschaft mit beschränkter Haftung in private Hand vom 21. Juli 1960 (Bundesgesetzbl. I S. 585), zuletzt geändert durch das Zweite Gesetz zur Änderung des Gesetzes über die Überführung der Anteilsrechte an der Volkswagenwerk Gesellschaft mit beschränkter Haftung in private Hand vom 31. Juli 1970 (Bundesgesetzbl. I S. 1149), bleibt unberührt.

(3) Stellvertreter von Aufsichtsratsmitgliedern können nicht bestellt werden. Jedoch kann für jedes Aufsichtsratsmit-

§ 101. Election and Appointment of Members of the Supervisory Board

(1) The members of the supervisory board shall be elected by the shareholders' meeting, unless they are to be appointed to the supervisory board or elected as representatives of the employees pursuant to the Co-determination Act, the Supplemental Co-determination Act, or the Labour Council Act 1952. The shareholders' meeting shall be bound by nominations only pursuant to §§ 6 and 8 of the Coal and Steel Co-determination Act.

(2) The right to appoint members to the supervisory board may only be granted by the articles and only to specific shareholders or the holders from time to time of specific shares. The right to appoint may be granted to holders of specific shares only if the shares are in registered form and if their transfer requires the consent of the company. Shares of holders of the right to appoint shall not be deemed to constitute a separate class. Rights to appoint may be granted only with respect to no more than one third in aggregate of the shareholder representatives in the supervisory board as determined by law or the articles. § 4 (1) of the Act Concerning Privatisation of Volkswagen Gesellschaft mit beschränkter Haftung of 21 July 1960 (Legal Gazette I, p. 585), last amended by the Second Act to Amend the Act Concerning Privatisation of Volkswagen Gesellschaft mit beschränkter Haftung of 31 July 1970 (Legal Gazette I, p. 1149) shall not be affected.

(3) It shall not be permitted to appoint deputies of members of the supervisory board. However, for each member of

glied mit Ausnahme des weiteren Mitglieds, das nach dem Montan-Mitbestimmungsgesetz oder dem Mitbestimmungsergänzungsgesetz auf Vorschlag der übrigen Aufsichtsratsmitglieder gewählt wird, ein Ersatzmitglied bestellt werden, das Mitglied des Aufsichtsrats wird, wenn das Aufsichtsratsmitglied vor Ablauf seiner Amtszeit wegfällt. Das Ersatzmitglied kann nur gleichzeitig mit dem Aufsichtsratsmitglied bestellt werden. Auf seine Bestellung sowie die Nichtigkeit und Anfechtung seiner Bestellung sind die für das Aufsichtsratsmitglied geltenden Vorschriften anzuwenden.

the supervisory board a substitute member may be appointed who shall become a member of the supervisory board if the regular member ceases to hold office prior to the expiration of his term of office, except for the additional member to be elected pursuant to the Coal and Steel Co-determination Act or the Supplemental Co-determination Act upon nomination by the other members of the supervisory board. Such substitute member may only be appointed at the same time as the respective regular member of the supervisory board. The provisions governing regular members of the supervisory board shall govern the appointment and the nullity and voidability of the appointment of substitute members.

§ 102. Amtszeit der Aufsichtsratsmitglieder

(1) Aufsichtsratsmitglieder können nicht für längere Zeit als bis zur Beendigung der Hauptversammlung bestellt werden, die über die Entlastung für das vierte Geschäftsjahr nach dem Beginn der Amtszeit beschließt. Das Geschäftsjahr, in dem die Amtszeit beginnt, wird nicht mitgerechnet.

(2) Das Amt des Ersatzmitglieds erlischt spätestens mit Ablauf der Amtszeit des weggefallenen Aufsichtsratsmitglieds.

§ 102. Term of Office of Members of the Supervisory Board

(1) The members of the supervisory board may not be appointed for a period of time extending beyond the closure of the shareholders' meeting resolving on ratification of the acts of management for the fourth fiscal year following the commencement of their respective term of office. The fiscal year in which such term of office commences shall not be taken into account.

(2) The term of office of a substitute member shall expire not later than the expiration of the term of office of the regular member of the supervisory board who has ceased to hold office.

§ 103. Abberufung der Aufsichtsratsmitglieder

(1) Aufsichtsratsmitglieder, die von der Hauptversammlung ohne Bindung an einen Wahlvorschlag gewählt worden sind, können von ihr vor Ablauf der Amts-

§ 103. Removal of Members of the Supervisory Board

(1) Members of the supervisory board who have been elected by the shareholders' meeting without being bound by nominations may be removed pursuant to

zeit abberufen werden. Der Beschluß bedarf einer Mehrheit, die mindestens drei Viertel der abgegebenen Stimmen umfaßt. Die Satzung kann eine andere Mehrheit und weitere Erfordernisse bestimmen.

resolution of the shareholders' meeting prior to the expiration of their term of office. Such resolution shall require a majority of not less than three fourths of the votes cast. The articles may provide for a different majority and for additional requirements.

(2) Ein Aufsichtsratsmitglied, das auf Grund der Satzung in den Aufsichtsrat entsandt ist, kann von dem Entsendungsberechtigten jederzeit abberufen und durch ein anderes ersetzt werden. Sind die in der Satzung bestimmten Voraussetzungen des Entsendungsrechts weggefallen, so kann die Hauptversammlung das entsandte Mitglied mit einfacher Stimmenmehrheit abberufen.

(2) A member of the supervisory board who has been appointed to the supervisory board pursuant to the articles may at any time be removed and replaced by another person by the person who has the right to appoint. If the requirements specified in the articles in respect of the right to appoint are no longer met, the shareholders' meeting may remove the appointed member by a simple majority of votes.

(3) Das Gericht hat auf Antrag des Aufsichtsrats ein Aufsichtsratsmitglied abzuberufen, wenn in dessen Person ein wichtiger Grund vorliegt. Der Aufsichtsrat beschließt über die Antragstellung mit einfacher Mehrheit. Ist das Aufsichtsratsmitglied auf Grund der Satzung in den Aufsichtsrat entsandt worden, so können auch Aktionäre, deren Anteile zusammen den zehnten Teil des Grundkapitals oder den Nennbetrag von zwei Millionen Deutsche Mark erreichen, den Antrag stellen. Gegen die Entscheidung ist die sofortige Beschwerde zulässig.

(3) Upon motion by the supervisory board the court shall remove a member of the supervisory board for cause relating to the person of such member. The supervisory board shall resolve on such motion by simple majority. If such member of the supervisory board has been appointed to the supervisory board pursuant to the articles, shareholders whose aggregate holding amounts to one tenth of the share capital or to a par value of DM 2 million may also make such motion. An immediate appeal may be made against such decision.

(4) Für die Abberufung der Aufsichtsratsmitglieder, die weder von der Hauptversammlung ohne Bindung an einen Wahlvorschlag gewählt worden sind noch auf Grund der Satzung in den Aufsichtsrat entsandt sind, gelten außer Absatz 3 das Mitbestimmungsgesetz, das Montan-Mitbestimmungsgesetz, das Mitbestimmungsergänzungsgesetz und das Betriebsverfassungsgesetz 1952.

(4) The Co-determination Act, the Coal and Steel Co-determination Act, the Supplemental Co-determination Act and the Labour Council Act 1952 shall apply, in addition to subsection (3), to the removal of members of the supervisory board who were neither elected by the shareholders' meeting without being bound by nominations nor appointed to the supervisory board pursuant to the articles.

(5) Für die Abberufung eines Ersatz-

(5) The provisions governing remov-

mitglieds gelten die Vorschriften über die Abberufung des Aufsichtsratsmitglieds, für das es bestellt ist.

§ 104. Bestellung durch das Gericht

(1) Gehört dem Aufsichtsrat die zur Beschlußfähigkeit nötige Zahl von Mitgliedern nicht an, so hat ihn das Gericht auf Antrag des Vorstands, eines Aufsichtsratsmitglieds oder eines Aktionärs auf diese Zahl zu ergänzen. Der Vorstand ist verpflichtet, den Antrag unverzüglich zu stellen, es sei denn, daß die rechtzeitige Ergänzung vor der nächsten Aufsichtsratssitzung zu erwarten ist. Hat der Aufsichtsrat auch aus Aufsichtsratsmitgliedern der Arbeitnehmer zu bestehen, so können auch den Antrag stellen

1. der Gesamtbetriebsrat der Gesellschaft oder, wenn in der Gesellschaft nur ein Betriebsrat besteht, der Betriebsrat, sowie, wenn die Gesellschaft herrschendes Unternehmen eines Konzerns ist, der Konzernbetriebsrat,
2. der Gesamtbetriebsrat eines anderen Unternehmens, dessen Arbeitnehmer selbst oder durch Delegierte an der Wahl teilnehmen, oder, wenn in dem anderen Unternehmen nur ein Betriebsrat besteht, der Betriebsrat,
3. mindestens ein Zehntel oder einhundert der Arbeitnehmer, die selbst oder durch Delegierte an der Wahl teilnehmen,
4. Spitzenorganisationen der Gewerkschaften, die das Recht haben, Aufsichtsratsmitglieder der Arbeitnehmer vorzuschlagen,
5. Gewerkschaften, die das Recht haben, Aufsichtsratsmitglieder der Arbeitnehmer vorzuschlagen.

Hat der Aufsichtsrat nach dem Mitbestimmungsgesetz auch aus Aufsichtsratsmitgliedern der Arbeitnehmer zu bestehen, so sind außer den nach Satz 3 Antragsberechtigten auch je ein Zehntel der

al of a member of the supervisory board shall also apply to the removal of a substitute member.

§ 104. Judicial Appointment

(1) If the supervisory board does not have the requisite number of members to constitute a quorum, the court shall restore it to the requisite number upon motion by the management board, a member of the supervisory board or a shareholder. The management board shall be obligated to make such motion promptly, unless restoration to such number may be expected to occur prior to the next meeting of the supervisory board. If the supervisory board is required to include representatives of the employees, such motion may also be made by:

1. the central labour council of the company or, if the company has only one labour council, such labour council and, if the company is the controlling enterprise of a group, the group labour council;
2. the central labour council of another enterprise whose employees participate directly or through delegates in the election or, if such other enterprises has only one labour council, such labour council;
3. not less than one tenth or one hundred of the employees who participate in the election directly or through delegates;
4. the central organizations of labour unions which have the right to nominate representatives of the employees to the supervisory board;
5. labour unions which have the right to nominate the supervisory board representatives of the employees.

If the supervisory board is required to include representatives of the employees pursuant to the Co-determination Act, then in addition to those parties having standing to make motion pursuant to sen-

wahlberechtigten Arbeiter, der wahlberechtigten in § 3 Abs. 3 Nr. 1 des Mitbestimmungsgesetzes bezeichneten Angestellten oder der wahlberechtigten leitenden Angestellten im Sinne des Mitbestimmungsgesetzes antragsberechtigt. Gegen die Entscheidung ist die sofortige Beschwerde zulässig.

tence 3, one tenth of the workers who are entitled to vote or one tenth of the employees designated in § 3 (3), No. 1 of the Co-determination Act who are entitled to vote or one tenth of the managerial employees within the meaning of the Co-determination Act who are entitled to vote, shall also have standing to make such motion. An immediate appeal may be made against such decision.

(2) Gehören dem Aufsichtsrat länger als drei Monate weniger Mitglieder als die durch Gesetz oder Satzung festgesetzte Zahl an, so hat ihn das Gericht auf Antrag auf diese Zahl zu ergänzen. In dringenden Fällen hat das Gericht auf Antrag den Aufsichtsrat auch vor Ablauf der Frist zu ergänzen. Das Antragsrecht bestimmt sich nach Absatz 1. Gegen die Entscheidung ist die sofortige Beschwerde zulässig.

(2) If for a period of more than three months the number of members of the supervisory board has been less than the number required by law or the articles, the court shall upon motion restore it to the requisite number. In urgent cases the court shall, upon motion, restore the supervisory board to such number even before such period has expired. Standing to make motion shall be governed by subsection (1). An immediate appeal may be made against the decision.

(3) Absatz 2 ist auf einen Aufsichtsrat, in dem die Arbeitnehmer ein Mitbestimmungsrecht nach dem Mitbestimmungsgesetz, dem Montan-Mitbestimmungsgesetz oder dem Mitbestimmungsergänzungsgesetz haben, mit der Maßgabe anzuwenden,

1. daß das Gericht den Aufsichtsrat hinsichtlich des weiteren Mitglieds, das nach dem Montan-Mitbestimmungsgesetz oder dem Mitbestimmungsergänzungsgesetz auf Vorschlag der übrigen Aufsichtsratsmitglieder gewählt wird, nicht ergänzen kann,

2. daß es stets ein dringender Fall ist, wenn dem Aufsichtsrat, abgesehen von dem in Nummer 1 genannten weiteren Mitglied, nicht alle Mitglieder angehören, aus denen er nach Gesetz oder Satzung zu bestehen hat.

(3) Subsection (2) shall apply to a supervisory board in which the employees are entitled to co-determination pursuant to the provision of the Co-determination Act, the Coal and Steel Co-determination Act or the Supplemental Co-determination Act, provided, however, that:

1. the court may not restore the supervisory board to the requisite number by appointing the additional member who is to be elected pursuant to the Coal and Steel Co-determination Act or the Supplemental Co-determination Act upon nomination by the other members of the supervisory board,

2. it shall always constitute on urgent case, if the supervisory board does not have the full number of members which is required to include pursuant to the law or the articles, except for the additional member referred to in No. 1.

(4) Hat der Aufsichtsrat auch aus Aufsichtsratsmitgliedern der Arbeitnehmer zu bestehen, so hat das Gericht ihn so zu ergänzen, daß das für seine Zusammensetzung maßgebende zahlenmäßige Verhältnis hergestellt wird. Wenn der Aufsichtsrat zur Herstellung seiner Beschlußfähigkeit ergänzt wird, gilt dies nur, soweit die zur Beschlußfähigkeit nötige Zahl der Aufsichtsratsmitglieder die Wahrung dieses Verhältnisses möglich macht. Ist ein Aufsichtsratsmitglied zu ersetzen, das nach Gesetz oder Satzung in persönlicher Hinsicht besonderen Voraussetzungen entsprechen muß, so muß auch das vom Gericht bestellte Aufsichtsratsmitglied diesen Voraussetzungen entsprechen. Ist ein Aufsichtsratsmitglied zu ersetzen, bei dessen Wahl eine Spitzenorganisation der Gewerkschaften, eine Gewerkschaft oder die Betriebsräte ein Vorschlagsrecht hätten, so soll das Gericht Vorschläge dieser Stellen berücksichtigen, soweit nicht überwiegende Belange der Gesellschaft oder der Allgemeinheit der Bestellung des Vorgeschlagenen entgegenstehen; das gleiche gilt, wenn das Aufsichtsratsmitglied durch Delegierte zu wählen wäre, für gemeinsame Vorschläge der Betriebsräte der Unternehmen, in denen Delegierte zu wählen sind.

(4) If the supervisory board is required to include also representatives of the employees, the court shall appoint members in such a manner that the numerical ratio required for the composition of the supervisory board is maintained or re-established. If appointments are to be made to the supervisory board to re-establish a quorum, the foregoing shall apply only if the number of members of the supervisory board required for a quorum permits such ratio to prevail. If a member of the supervisory board is to be replaced who must fulfill special personal qualifications pursuant to the law or the articles, the member of the supervisory board appointed by the court shall also fulfill such qualifications. If a member of the supervisory board is to be replaced whom a central organization of labour unions, a labour union or the labour councils would have the right to nominate, the court shall take into account the nominations of such parties, unless appointment of the nominated person would contravene overriding interests of the company or the general public; in case the member of the supervisory board is to be elected by delegates, the foregoing shall apply to joint nominations by the labour councils of the enterprises in which delegates are to be elected.

(5) Das Amt des gerichtlich bestellten Aufsichtsratsmitglieds erlischt in jedem Fall, sobald der Mangel behoben ist.

(5) The term of office of the member of the supervisory board appointed by the court shall expire in any event as soon as the deficiency in the composition of the supervisory board has been cured.

(6) Das gerichtlich bestellte Aufsichtsratsmitglied hat Anspruch auf Ersatz angemessener barer Auslagen und, wenn den Aufsichtsratsmitgliedern der Gesellschaft eine Vergütung gewährt wird, auf Vergütung für seine Tätigkeit. Auf Antrag des Aufsichtsratsmitglieds setzt das Gericht die Auslagen und die Vergütung fest. Gegen die Entscheidung

(6) The member of the supervisory board appointed by the court shall be entitled to reimbursement of reasonable cash expenses and, if remuneration is granted to regular members of the supervisory board of the company, to remuneration for his services. Upon motion by such member of the supervisory board the court shall stipulate the expenses and re-

ist die sofortige Beschwerde zulässig. Die weitere Beschwerde ist ausgeschlossen. Aus der rechtskräftigen Entscheidung findet die Zwangsvollstreckung nach der Zivilprozeßordnung statt.

muneration. An immediate appeal may be made against such decision. Further appeal shall be precluded. A decision which has become final and may not be appealed may be enforced in accordance with the provisions of the Code of Civil Procedure.

§ 105. Unvereinbarkeit der Zugehörigkeit zum Vorstand und zum Aufsichtsrat

(1) Ein Aufsichtsratsmitglied kann nicht zugleich Vorstandsmitglied, dauernd Stellvertreter von Vorstandsmitgliedern, Prokurist oder zum gesamten Geschäftsbetrieb ermächtigter Handlungsbevollmächtigter der Gesellschaft sein.

(2) Nur für einen im voraus begrenzten Zeitraum, höchstens für ein Jahr, kann der Aufsichtsrat einzelne seiner Mitglieder zu Stellvertretern von fehlenden oder behinderten Vorstandsmitgliedern bestellen. Eine wiederholte Bestellung oder Verlängerung der Amtszeit ist zulässig, wenn dadurch die Amtszeit insgesamt ein Jahr nicht übersteigt. Während ihrer Amtszeit als Stellvertreter von Vorstandsmitgliedern können die Aufsichtsratsmitglieder keine Tätigkeit als Aufsichtsratsmitglied ausüben. Das Wettbewerbsverbot des § 88 gilt für sie nicht.

§ 105. Incompatibility of Membership on the Management Board and the Supervisory Board

(1) A member of the supervisory board may not also be a member of the management board, a permanent deputy member of the management board, a registered authorized officer or general manager of the company.

(2) The supervisory board may appoint certain of its members as deputies for absent or incapacitated members of the management board for a predetermined period of time which may not in any event exceed one year. Such appointment may be renewed or the term of office extended, provided, however, that the aggregate term of office may not exceed one year. The members of the supervisory board may not exercise the functions of a member of the supervisory board during their term of office as deputies of members of the management board. The prohibition of competition pursuant to § 88 shall not apply to such deputies.

§ 106. Bekanntmachung der Änderungen im Aufsichtsrat

Der Vorstand hat jeden Wechsel der Aufsichtsratsmitglieder unverzüglich in den Gesellschaftsblättern bekanntzumachen und die Bekanntmachung zum Handelsregister einzureichen.

§ 106. Announcement of Changes in the Supervisory Board

The management board shall promptly announce any change in the membership of the supervisory board in the company's designated journals and submit such announcement to the commercial register.

§ 107. Innere Ordnung des Aufsichtsrats

(1) Der Aufsichtsrat hat nach näherer Bestimmung der Satzung aus seiner Mitte einen Vorsitzenden und mindestens einen Stellvertreter zu wählen. Der Vorstand hat zum Handelsregister anzumelden, wer gewählt ist. Der Stellvertreter hat nur dann die Rechte und Pflichten des Vorsitzenden, wenn dieser behindert ist.

(2) Über die Sitzungen des Aufsichtsrats ist eine Niederschrift anzufertigen, die der Vorsitzende zu unterzeichnen hat. In der Niederschrift sind der Ort und der Tag der Sitzung, die Teilnehmer, die Gegenstände der Tagesordnung, der wesentliche Inhalt der Verhandlungen und die Beschlüsse des Aufsichtsrats anzugeben. Ein Verstoß gegen Satz 1 oder Satz 2 macht einen Beschluß nicht unwirksam. Jedem Mitglied des Aufsichtsrats ist auf Verlangen eine Abschrift der Sitzungsniederschrift auszuhändigen.

(3) Der Aufsichtsrat kann aus seiner Mitte einen oder mehrere Ausschüsse bestellen, namentlich, um seine Verhandlungen und Beschlüsse vorzubereiten oder die Ausführung seiner Beschlüsse zu überwachen. Die Aufgaben nach Absatz 1 Satz 1, § 59 Abs. 3, § 77 Abs. 2 Satz 1, § 84 Abs. 1 Satz 1 und 3, Abs. 2 und Abs. 3 Satz 1, § 111 Abs. 3, §§ 171, 314 Abs. 2 und 3 sowie Beschlüsse, daß bestimmte Arten von Geschäften nur mit Zustimmung des Aufsichtsrats vorgenommen werden dürfen, können einem Ausschuß nicht an Stelle des Aufsichtsrats zur Beschlußfassung überwiesen werden.

§ 107. Organization of the Supervisory Board

(1) The supervisory board shall elect from among its members a chairman and at least one deputy chairman in accordance with the applicable provisions of the articles. The management board shall report the persons elected to the commercial register. The deputy chairman shall have the rights and duties of the chairman only if the latter is incapacitated.

(2) Minutes shall be kept of the meetings of the supervisory board which shall be signed by the chairman. The minutes shall state the place and date of the meeting, the persons attending, the items on the agenda, the essential contents of the proceedings, and the resolutions of the supervisory board. A violation of the provisions of sentences 1 or 2 shall not invalidate a resolution. A copy of the minutes of the meeting shall be provided upon request to each member of the supervisory board.

(3) The supervisory board may appoint from among its members one or more committees, in particular for purposes of preparing its deliberations and resolutions or for supervising the execution of its resolutions. However, neither the duties pursuant to subsection (1) sentence 1, § 59 (3), § 77 (2) sentence 1, § 84 (1) sentence 1 and 3, (2) and (3) sentence 1, § 111 (3), §§ 171 and 314 (2) and (3) nor resolutions providing that specific types of transactions may be entered into only with the consent of the supervisory board, may be referred to a committee for resolution in lieu of the supervisory board.

§ 108. Beschlußfassung des Aufsichtsrats

(1) Der Aufsichtsrat entscheidet durch Beschluß.

(2) Die Beschlußfähigkeit des Aufsichtsrats kann, soweit sie nicht gesetzlich geregelt ist, durch die Satzung bestimmt werden. Ist sie weder gesetzlich noch durch die Satzung geregelt, so ist der Aufsichtsrat nur beschlußfähig, wenn mindestens die Hälfte der Mitglieder, aus denen er nach Gesetz oder Satzung insgesamt zu bestehen hat, an der Beschlußfassung teilnimmt. In jedem Fall müssen mindestens drei Mitglieder an der Beschlußfassung teilnehmen. Der Beschlußfähigkeit steht nicht entgegen, daß dem Aufsichtsrat weniger Mitglieder als die durch Gesetz oder Satzung festgesetzte Zahl angehören, auch wenn das für seine Zusammensetzung maßgebende zahlenmäßige Verhältnis nicht gewahrt ist.

(3) Abwesende Aufsichtsratsmitglieder können dadurch an der Beschlußfassung des Aufsichtsrats und seiner Ausschüsse teilnehmen, daß sie schriftliche Stimmabgaben überreichen lassen. Die schriftlichen Stimmabgaben können durch andere Aufsichtsratsmitglieder überreicht werden. Sie können auch durch Personen, die nicht dem Aufsichtsrat angehören, übergeben werden, wenn diese nach § 109 Abs. 3 zur Teilnahme an der Sitzung berechtigt sind.

(4) Schriftliche, telegrafische oder fernmündliche Beschlußfassungen des Aufsichtsrats oder eines Ausschusses sind nur zulässig, wenn kein Mitglied diesem Verfahren widerspricht.

§ 108. Resolutions of the Supervisory Board

(1) The supervisory board shall decide by resolution.

(2) The quorum required for the supervisory board may, to the extent not determined by law, be set by the articles. If the quorum is set neither by law nor the articles, a quorum of the supervisory board shall only be present if not less than one half of the number of members which it is required to comprise pursuant to law or the articles take part in the passing of the resolution. In any event at least three members shall be required to take part in the passing of a resolution. The presence of a quorum shall not be prejudiced by the fact that the supervisory board shall comprise fewer members than the number required by law or the articles, even if the numerical ratio required for its composition is not maintained.

(3) Members of the supervisory board who are not present may take part in the passing of a resolution of the supervisory board or of any committee thereof by causing votes in writing to be submitted to the meeting. Such votes may be submitted by other members of the supervisory board. They may also be submitted by persons who are not members of the supervisory board, provided that such persons are entitled to attend the meeting pursuant to § 109 (3).

(4) Resolutions of the supervisory board or of any committee thereof may be adopted in writing, by telegraph or telephone if no member objects to such procedure.

§ 109. Teilnahme an Sitzungen des Aufsichtsrats und seiner Ausschüsse

(1) An den Sitzungen des Aufsichtsrats und seiner Ausschüsse sollen Personen, die weder dem Aufsichtsrat noch dem Vorstand angehören, nicht teilnehmen. Sachverständige und Auskunftspersonen können zur Beratung über einzelne Gegenstände zugezogen werden.

(2) Aufsichtsratsmitglieder, die dem Ausschuß nicht angehören, können an den Ausschußsitzungen teilnehmen, wenn der Vorsitzende des Aufsichtsrats nichts anderes bestimmt.

(3) Die Satzung kann zulassen, daß an den Sitzungen des Aufsichtsrats und seiner Ausschüsse Personen, die dem Aufsichtsrat nicht angehören, an Stelle von verhinderten Aufsichtsratsmitgliedern teilnehmen können, wenn diese sie hierzu schriftlich ermächtigt haben.

(4) Abweichende gesetzliche Vorschriften bleiben unberührt.

§ 109. Attendance of Meetings of the Supervisory Board and its Committees

(1) Persons who are not members of the supervisory board or the management board may not attend meetings of the supervisory board and its committees. Experts and persons needed to give information may be invited for consultation on individual matters.

(2) Members of the supervisory board who are not members of a committee may attend meetings of such committee, unless the chairman of the supervisory board determines otherwise.

(3) The articles may permit persons who are not members of the supervisory board to attend meetings of the supervisory board and its committees in lieu of members of the supervisory board who are unable to attend, provided that such members have authorized such persons to attend in writing.

(4) The foregoing shall not affect statutory provisions which provide otherwise.

§ 110. Einberufung des Aufsichtsrats

(1) Jedes Aufsichtsratsmitglied oder der Vorstand kann unter Angabe des Zwecks und der Gründe verlangen, daß der Vorsitzende des Aufsichtsrats unverzüglich den Aufsichtsrat einberuft. Die Sitzung muß binnen zwei Wochen nach der Einberufung stattfinden.

(2) Wird einem Verlangen, das von mindestens zwei Aufsichtsratsmitgliedern oder vom Vorstand geäußert ist, nicht entsprochen, so können die Antrag-

§ 110. Notice of Supervisory Board Meetings

(1) Each member of the supervisory board or the management board may, upon stating the grounds therefor, request that the chairman of the supervisory board promptly call a meeting of the supervisory board. The meeting shall be held within two weeks from the date on which notice thereof has been given.

(2) If any such request made by two or more members of the supervisory board or by the management board should not be complied with, such members may

steller unter Mitteilung des Sachverhalts selbst den Aufsichtsrat einberufen.

themselves call a meeting of the supervisory board upon stating these facts.

(3) Der Aufsichtsrat soll in der Regel einmal im Kalendervierteljahr, er muß einmal im Kalenderhalbjahr einberufen werden.

(3) Meetings of the supervisory board should as a rule be called once in every calendar quarter and shall be called once in every calendar half year.

§ 111. Aufgaben und Rechte des Aufsichtsrats

§ 111. Duties and Rights of the Supervisory Board

(1) Der Aufsichtsrat hat die Geschäftsführung zu überwachen.

(1) The supervisory board shall supervise the management of the company.

(2) Der Aufsichtsrat kann die Bücher und Schriften der Gesellschaft sowie die Vermögensgegenstände, namentlich die Gesellschaftskasse und die Bestände an Wertpapieren und Waren, einsehen und prüfen. Er kann damit auch einzelne Mitglieder oder für bestimmte Aufgaben besondere Sachverständige beauftragen.

(2) The supervisory board may inspect and examine the books and records of the company as well as the assets of the company, in particular cash, securities and merchandise. The supervisory board may also commission individual members or, with respect to specific assignments, special experts, to carry out such inspection and examination.

(3) Der Aufsichtsrat hat eine Hauptversammlung einzuberufen, wenn das Wohl der Gesellschaft es fordert. Für den Beschluß genügt die einfache Mehrheit.

(3) The supervisory board shall call a shareholders' meeting whenever the interests of the company so require. Any resolution to such effect shall require a simple majority.

(4) Maßnahmen der Geschäftsführung können dem Aufsichtsrat nicht übertragen werden. Die Satzung oder der Aufsichtsrat kann jedoch bestimmen, daß bestimmte Arten von Geschäften nur mit seiner Zustimmung vorgenommen werden dürfen. Verweigert der Aufsichtsrat seine Zustimmung, so kann der Vorstand verlangen, daß die Hauptversammlung über die Zustimmung beschließt. Der Beschluß, durch den die Hauptversammlung zustimmt, bedarf einer Mehrheit, die mindestens drei Viertel der abgegebenen Stimmen umfaßt. Die Satzung kann weder eine andere Mehrheit noch weitere Erfordernisse bestimmen.

(4) Management responsibilities may not be conferred on the supervisory board. However, the articles or the supervisory board may determine that specific types of transactions may be entered into only with the consent of the supervisory board. If the supervisory board refuses to grant consent, the management board may request that a shareholders' meeting resolve whether to grant such consent. The resolution of the shareholders' meeting which grants such consent shall require a majority of not less than three fourths of the votes cast. The articles may neither require a different majority nor provide for additional requirements.

(5) Die Aufsichtsratsmitglieder können ihre Aufgaben nicht durch andere wahrnehmen lassen.

(5) Members of the supervisory board may not confer their responsibilities on other persons.

§ 112. Vertretung der Gesellschaft gegenüber Vorstandsmitgliedern

§ 112. Representation of the Company as against Members of the Management Board

Vorstandsmitgliedern gegenüber vertritt der Aufsichtsrat die Gesellschaft gerichtlich und außergerichtlich.

The supervisory board shall represent the company both in and out of court as against the members of the management board.

§ 113. Vergütung der Aufsichtsratsmitglieder

§ 113. Remuneration of Members of the Supervisory Board

(1) Den Aufsichtsratsmitgliedern kann für ihre Tätigkeit eine Vergütung gewährt werden. Sie kann in der Satzung festgesetzt oder von der Hauptversammlung bewilligt werden. Sie soll in einem angemessenen Verhältnis zu den Aufgaben der Aufsichtsratsmitglieder und zur Lage der Gesellschaft stehen. Ist die Vergütung in der Satzung festgesetzt, so kann die Hauptversammlung eine Satzungsänderung, durch welche die Vergütung herabgesetzt wird, mit einfacher Stimmenmehrheit beschließen.

(1) The members of the supervisory board may receive remuneration for their services. Such remuneration may be determined in the articles or set by the shareholders' meeting. Such remuneration shall bear a reasonable relationship to the duties of the members of the supervisory board and to the condition of the company. If the remuneration is determined in the articles, the shareholders' meeting may, by simple majority resolve on an amendment of the articles by which such remuneration is reduced.

(2) Den Mitgliedern des ersten Aufsichtsrats kann nur die Hauptversammlung eine Vergütung für ihre Tätigkeit bewilligen. Der Beschluß kann erst in der Hauptversammlung gefaßt werden, die über die Entlastung der Mitglieder des ersten Aufsichtsrats beschließt.

(2) Remuneration of the members of the first supervisory board for their services may be granted only pursuant to a resolution of the shareholders' meeting. Such resolution may be adopted only in the shareholders' meeting resolving on ratification of the acts of the members of the first supervisory board.

(3) Wird den Aufsichtsratsmitgliedern ein Anteil am Jahresgewinn der Gesellschaft gewährt, so berechnet sich der Anteil nach dem Bilanzgewinn, vermindert um einen Betrag von mindestens vier vom Hundert der auf den Nennbetrag der

(3) If the members of the supervisory board are granted a share of the annual profit of the company, such share shall be computed on the basis of distributable profit, reduced by an amount of not less than four per cent of the contributions made on the par value of the shares. Any

Aktien geleisteten Einlagen. Entgegenstehende Festsetzungen sind nichtig.

provisions to the contrary shall be null and void.

§ 114. Verträge mit Aufsichtsratsmitgliedern

§ 114. Contracts with Members of the Supervisory Board

(1) Verpflichtet sich ein Aufsichtsratsmitglied außerhalb seiner Tätigkeit im Aufsichtsrat durch einen Dienstvertrag, durch den ein Arbeitsverhältnis nicht begründet wird, oder durch einen Werkvertrag gegenüber der Gesellschaft zu einer Tätigkeit höherer Art, so hängt die Wirksamkeit des Vertrags von der Zustimmung des Aufsichtsrats ab.

(1) If a member of the supervisory board in addition to his services as a member of the supervisory board, enters into a contract with the company for provision of professional services which does not establish an employment relationship, or into a contract with the company to undertake a special assignment, any such contract shall require the consent of the supervisory board in order to be valid.

(2) Gewährt die Gesellschaft auf Grund eines solchen Vertrags dem Aufsichtsratsmitglied eine Vergütung, ohne daß der Aufsichtsrat dem Vertrag zugestimmt hat, so hat das Aufsichtsratsmitglied die Vergütung zurückzugewähren, es sei denn, daß der Aufsichtsrat den Vertrag genehmigt. Ein Anspruch des Aufsichtsratsmitglieds gegen die Gesellschaft auf Herausgabe der durch die geleistete Tätigkeit erlangten Bereicherung bleibt unberührt; der Anspruch kann jedoch nicht gegen den Rückgewähranspruch aufgerechnet werden.

(2) If the company pursuant to any such contract grants remuneration to a member of the supervisory board without the supervisory board having consented to such contract, such member of the supervisory board shall repay such remuneration, unless the supervisory board subsequently approves such contract. A claim of the member of the supervisory board against the company for restitution of the enrichment obtained by the services performed shall remain unaffected; such claim may, however, not be set off against the claim of the company for repayment of remuneration.

§ 115. Kreditgewährung an Aufsichtsratsmitglieder

§ 115. Extension of Credit to Members of the Supervisory Board

(1) Die Gesellschaft darf ihren Aufsichtsratsmitgliedern Kredit nur mit Einwilligung des Aufsichtsrats gewähren. Eine herrschende Gesellschaft darf Kredite an Aufsichtsratsmitglieder eines abhängigen Unternehmens nur mit Einwilligung ihres Aufsichtsrats, eine abhängige Gesellschaft darf Kredite an Aufsichtsratsmitglieder des herrschenden

(1) The company may extend credit to members of the supervisory board only with the consent of the supervisory board. A controlling company may extend credit to members of the supervisory board of a controlled enterprise only with the consent of its supervisory board; a controlled company may extend credit to members of the supervisory board of the control-

Unternehmens nur mit Einwilligung des Aufsichtsrats des herrschenden Unternehmens gewähren. Die Einwilligung kann nur für bestimmte Kreditgeschäfte oder Arten von Kreditgeschäften und nicht für länger als drei Monate im voraus erteilt werden. Der Beschluß über die Einwilligung hat die Verzinsung und Rückzahlung des Kredits zu regeln. Betreibt das Aufsichtsratsmitglied ein Handelsgewerbe als Einzelkaufmann, so ist die Einwilligung nicht erforderlich, wenn der Kredit für die Bezahlung von Waren gewährt wird, welche die Gesellschaft seinem Handelsgeschäft liefert.

ling enterprise only with the consent of the supervisory board of the controlling enterprise. Such consent may be granted only for specific credit transactions or kinds of credit transactions, and for not more than three months in advance. The resolution on such consent shall make provision as to the payment of interest on, and repayment of, any loan. If the member of the supervisory board carries on a business as a sole proprietor, such consent shall not be required if the credit is extended to finance the payment of goods which the company supplies to his business.

(**2**) Absatz 1 gilt auch für Kredite an den Ehegatten oder an ein minderjähriges Kind eines Aufsichtsratsmitglieds und für Kredite an einen Dritten, der für Rechnung dieser Personen oder für Rechnung eines Aufsichtsratsmitglieds handelt.

(**2**) Subsection (1) shall also apply to credits to the spouse or a minor child of a member of the supervisory board and to credits to any third person acting on behalf of any such person or on behalf of a member of the supervisory board.

(**3**) Ist ein Aufsichtsratsmitglied zugleich gesetzlicher Vertreter einer anderen juristischen Person oder Gesellschafter einer Personenhandelsgesellschaft, so darf die Gesellschaft der juristischen Person oder der Personenhandelsgesellschaft Kredit nur mit Einwilligung des Aufsichtsrats gewähren; Absatz 1 Satz 3 und 4 gilt sinngemäß. Dies gilt nicht, wenn die juristische Person oder die Personenhandelsgesellschaft mit der Gesellschaft verbunden ist oder wenn der Kredit für die Bezahlung von Waren gewährt wird, welche die Gesellschaft der juristischen Person oder der Personenhandelsgesellschaft liefert.

(**3**) If a member of the supervisory board is also a legal representative of another legal entity or member of a commercial partnership, the company may extend credit to such legal entity or commercial partnership only with the consent of the supervisory board; subsection (1) sentences 3 and 4 shall apply analogously. The foregoing shall not apply if such legal entity or commercial partnership is affiliated with the company or if the credit is extended to finance the payment of goods which the company supplies to such legal entity or commercial partnership.

(**4**) Wird entgegen den Absätzen 1 bis 3 Kredit gewährt, so ist der Kredit ohne Rücksicht auf entgegenstehende Vereinbarungen sofort zurückzugewähren, wenn nicht der Aufsichtsrat nachträglich zustimmt.

(**4**) Any credit extended in violation of the provisions of subsections (1) to (3), shall be repaid immediately, irrespective of any agreement to the contrary, unless the supervisory board subsequently consents.

(5) Ist die Gesellschaft ein Kreditinstitut, so gelten an Stelle der Absätze 1 bis 4 die Vorschriften des Gesetzes über das Kreditwesen.

(5) If the company is a credit institution, the provisions of the Banking Act shall apply in lieu of subsections (1) to (4).

§ 116. Sorgfaltspflicht und Verantwortlichkeit der Aufsichtsratsmitglieder

§ 116. Duty of Care and Responsibility of Members of the Supervisory Board

Für die Sorgfaltspflicht und Verantwortlichkeit der Aufsichtsratsmitglieder gilt § 93 über die Sorgfaltspflicht und Verantwortlichkeit der Vorstandsmitglieder sinngemäß.

§ 93 regarding the duty of care and responsibility of the members of the management board shall apply analogously to the duty of care and responsibility of the members of the supervisory board.

Dritter Abschnitt. Benutzung des Einflusses auf die Gesellschaft

Division Three. Undue Use of Influence on the Company

§ 117. Schadenersatzpflicht

§ 117. Liability for Damages

(1) Wer vorsätzlich unter Benutzung seines Einflusses auf die Gesellschaft ein Mitglied des Vorstands oder des Aufsichtsrats, einen Prokuristen oder einen Handlungsbevollmächtigten dazu bestimmt, zum Schaden der Gesellschaft oder ihrer Aktionäre zu handeln, ist der Gesellschaft zum Ersatz des ihr daraus entstehenden Schadens verpflichtet. Er ist auch den Aktionären zum Ersatz des ihnen daraus entstehenden Schadens verpflichtet, soweit sie, abgesehen von einem Schaden, der ihnen durch Schädigung der Gesellschaft zugefügt worden ist, geschädigt worden sind.

(1) Any person who, by exerting his influence on the company, willfully induces a member of the management board or the supervisory board, a registered authorized officer or an authorized signatory to act to the disadvantage of the company or its shareholders, shall be liable to the company for any resulting damage. Such person shall also be liable to the shareholders for any resulting damage insofar as they have sustained a loss in addition to the loss which they have sustained by virtue of the damage incurred by the company.

(2) Neben ihm haften als Gesamtschuldner die Mitglieder des Vorstands und des Aufsichtsrats, wenn sie unter Verletzung ihrer Pflichten gehandelt haben. Ist streitig, ob sie die Sorgfalt eines ordentlichen und gewissenhaften Geschäftsleiters angewandt haben, so trifft sie die Beweislast. Der Gesellschaft und auch den Aktionären gegenüber tritt die Ersatzpflicht der Mitglieder des Vorstands und des Aufsichtsrats nicht ein,

(2) In addition to such person, the members of the management board and the supervisory board shall be jointly and severally liable if they have acted in violation of their duties. They shall bear the burden of proof in the event of a dispute as to whether or not they have employed the care of a diligent and conscientious manager. The members of the management board and the supervisory board shall not be liable to the company or the

wenn die Handlung auf einem gesetzmäßigen Beschluß der Hauptversammlung beruht. Dadurch, daß der Aufsichtsrat die Handlung gebilligt hat, wird die Ersatzpflicht nicht ausgeschlossen.

shareholders for damage if they acted pursuant to a lawful resolution of the shareholders' meeting. However, liability for damages shall not be precluded by the fact that the supervisory board has consented to the act.

(3) Neben ihm haftet ferner als Gesamtschuldner, wer durch die schädigende Handlung einen Vorteil erlangt hat, sofern er die Beeinflussung vorsätzlich veranlaßt hat.

(3) In addition to such person, any person who has willfully caused undue influence to be exerted and has obtained an advantage from the act which caused the damage shall also be jointly and severally liable.

(4) Für die Aufhebung der Ersatzpflicht gegenüber der Gesellschaft gilt sinngemäß § 93 Abs. 4 Satz 3 und 4.

(4) § 93 (4) sentences 3 and 4 shall apply analogously to the extinguishment of liability for damages to the company.

(5) Der Ersatzanspruch der Gesellschaft kann auch von den Gläubigern der Gesellschaft geltend gemacht werden, soweit sie von dieser keine Befriedigung erlangen können. Den Gläubigern gegenüber wird die Ersatzpflicht weder durch einen Verzicht oder Vergleich der Gesellschaft noch dadurch aufgehoben, daß die Handlung auf einem Beschluß der Hauptversammlung beruht. Ist über das Vermögen der Gesellschaft das Konkursverfahren eröffnet, so übt während dessen Dauer der Konkursverwalter das Recht der Gläubiger aus.[1]

(5) The claim of the company for damages may also be asserted by the company's creditors if they are unable to obtain satisfaction from the company. Liability for damages to the creditors shall be extinguished neither by a waiver nor by a compromise of the company nor by the fact that the act which caused the damage was based on a resolution of the shareholders' meeting. If bankruptcy proceedings have been instituted over the company's assets, the receiver in bankruptcy shall exercise the rights of the creditors during the course of such proceedings.[1]

(6) Die Ansprüche aus diesen Vorschriften verjähren in fünf Jahren.

(6) Claims under the foregoing provisions shall be barred after the expiration of a period of five years.

(7) Diese Vorschriften gelten nicht, wenn das Mitglied des Vorstands oder des Aufsichtsrats, der Prokurist oder der

(7) The foregoing provisions shall not apply if the member of the management board or the supervisory board, the

1. Mit Wirkung vom 1. Januar 1999 § 117 Abs. 5 Satz 3 wie folgt gefaßt:
'Ist über das Vermögen der Gesellschaft das Insolvenzverfahren eröffnet, so übt während dessen Dauer der Insolvenzverwalter oder der Sachwalter das Recht der Gläubiger aus.'

1. Effective as of 1 January 1999 § 117 (5) sentence 3 will read as follows:
'If insolvency proceedings have been instituted over the company's assets, the receiver or the trustee, as the case may be, shall exercise the rights of the creditors during the course of such proceedings.'

Handlungsbevollmächtigte durch Ausübung

1. des Stimmrechts in der Hauptversammlung,
2. der Leitungsmacht auf Grund eines Beherrschungsvertrags oder
3. der Leitungsmacht einer Hauptgesellschaft (§ 319), in die die Gesellschaft eingegliedert ist, zu der schädigenden Handlung bestimmt worden ist.

registered authorized officer or the authorized signatory was induced to engage in the act causing damage by the exercise of:

1. voting rights at the shareholders' meeting;
2. the right to direct under a control agreement; or
3. the right to direct of an acquiring company (§ 319) into which the company has been integrated.

Vierter Abschnitt. Hauptversammlung

Erster Unterabschnitt. Rechte der Hauptversammlung

§ 118. Allgemeines

(1) Die Aktionäre üben ihre Rechte in den Angelegenheiten der Gesellschaft in der Hauptversammlung aus, soweit das Gesetz nichts anderes bestimmt.

(2) Die Mitglieder des Vorstands und des Aufsichtsrats sollen an der Hauptversammlung teilnehmen.

§ 119. Rechte der Hauptversammlung

(1) Die Hauptversammlung beschließt in den im Gesetz und in der Satzung ausdrücklich bestimmten Fällen, namentlich über

1. die Bestellung der Mitglieder des Aufsichtsrats, soweit sie nicht in den Aufsichtsrat zu entsenden oder als Aufsichtsratsmitglieder der Arbeitnehmer nach dem Mitbestimmungsgesetz, dem Mitbestimmungsergänzungsgesetz oder dem Betriebsverfassungsgesetz 1952 zu wählen sind;

Division Four. Shareholders' Meeting

Subdivision One. Rights of the Shareholders' Meeting

§ 118. General Provisions

(1) The shareholders shall exercise their rights with respect to the company at shareholders' meetings unless this Act provides otherwise.

(2) The members of the management board and the supervisory board should attend the shareholders' meeting.

§ 119. Rights of the Shareholders' Meeting

(1) The shareholders' meeting shall resolve on all matters expressly stated in this Act or the articles, in particular with respect to:

1. the election of members of the supervisory board, to the extent they are not to be appointed to the supervisory board or to be elected as representatives of employees pursuant to the Co-determination Act, the Supplemental Co-determination Act or the Labour Council Act 1952;

2. die Verwendung des Bilanzgewinns;

3. die Entlastung der Mitglieder des Vorstands und des Aufsichtsrats;

4. die Bestellung des Abschlußprüfers;

5. Satzungsänderungen;

6. Maßnahmen der Kapitalbeschaffung und der Kapitalherabsetzung;

7. die Bestellung von Prüfern zur Prüfung von Vorgängen bei der Gründung oder der Geschäftsführung;

8. die Auflösung der Gesellschaft.

(2) Über Fragen der Geschäftsführung kann die Hauptversammlung nur entscheiden, wenn der Vorstand es verlangt.

2. the appropriation of distributable profits;

3. the ratification of the acts of the members of the management board and the supervisory board;

4. the appointment of external auditors;

5. amendments of the articles;

6. measures to increase or reduce the share capital;

7. the appointment of auditors for the examination of matters in connection with the formation or the management of the company;

8. the dissolution of the company.

(2) The shareholders' meeting may decide on matters concerning the management of the company only if required by the management board.

§ 120. Entlastung

(1) Die Hauptversammlung beschließt alljährlich in den ersten acht Monaten des Geschäftsjahrs über die Entlastung der Mitglieder des Vorstands und über die Entlastung der Mitglieder des Aufsichtsrats. Über die Entlastung eines einzelnen Mitglieds ist gesondert abzustimmen, wenn die Hauptversammlung es beschließt oder eine Minderheit es verlangt, deren Anteile zusammen den zehnten Teil des Grundkapitals oder den Nennbetrag von zwei Millionen Deutsche Mark erreichen.

(2) Durch die Entlastung billigt die Hauptversammlung die Verwaltung der Gesellschaft durch die Mitglieder des Vorstands und des Aufsichtsrats. Die Entlastung enthält keinen Verzicht auf Ersatzansprüche.

§ 120. Ratification of the Acts of Management

(1) The shareholders' meeting shall annually, during the first eight months of the fiscal year, resolve on ratification of the acts of the members of the management board and the supervisory board. A separate vote shall be taken with regard to the ratification of the acts of an individual member if so resolved by the shareholders' meeting or so requested by a minority, whose aggregate holding equals or exceeds one tenth of the share capital or a par value of DM 2 million.

(2) Such ratification shall constitute approval by the shareholders' meeting of the company's administration by the members of the management board and the supervisory board. Such ratification shall not constitute a waiver of claims for compensation of damage.

(3) Die Verhandlung über die Entlastung soll mit der Verhandlung über die Verwendung des Bilanzgewinns verbunden werden. Der Vorstand hat den Jahresabschluß, den Lagebericht und den Bericht des Aufsichtsrats der Hauptversammlung vorzulegen. Für die Auslegung dieser Vorlagen und für die Erteilung von Abschriften gilt § 175 Abs. 2 sinngemäß.

(3) The deliberations on ratification shall be combined with the deliberations on the appropriation of distributable profits. The management board shall submit to the shareholders' meeting the annual financial statements, the annual report and the report of the supervisory board. § 175 (2) shall apply analogously to the display of such documents for inspection and to the distribution of copies thereof.

ZWEITER UNTERABSCHNITT. EINBERUFUNG DER HAUPTVERSAMMLUNG

SUBDIVISION TWO. CALLING OF SHAREHOLDERS' MEETING

§ 121. Allgemeines

(1) Die Hauptversammlung ist in den durch Gesetz oder Satzung bestimmten Fällen sowie dann einzuberufen, wenn das Wohl der Gesellschaft es fordert.

(2) Die Hauptversammlung wird durch den Vorstand einberufen, der darüber mit einfacher Mehrheit beschließt. Personen, die in das Handelsregister als Vorstand eingetragen sind, gelten als befugt. Das auf Gesetz oder Satzung beruhende Recht anderer Personen, die Hauptversammlung einzuberufen, bleibt unberührt.

(3) Die Einberufung ist in den Gesellschaftsblättern bekanntzumachen. Sie muß die Firma, den Sitz der Gesellschaft, Zeit und Ort der Hauptversammlung und die Bedingungen angeben, von denen die Teilnahme an der Hauptversammlung und die Ausübung des Stimmrechts abhängen.

(4) Sind die Aktionäre der Gesellschaft namentlicht bekannt, so kann die

§ 121. General Provisions

(1) A shareholders' meeting shall be called in all cases provided for in this Act or the articles or whenever required by the interests of the company.

(2) The shareholders' meeting shall be called by the management board which shall resolve thereon by a simple majority of votes. Persons who are registered in the commercial register as members of the management board shall be deemed to have the requisite authority to call such meeting. The right of any other person based on law or the articles to call a shareholders' meeting shall remain unaffected.

(3) Notice of the shareholders' meeting shall be published in the company's designated journals. Such notice shall state the company's name and domicile, the time and place of the shareholders' meeting, and the conditions governing attendance at the shareholders' meeting and the exercise of voting rights.

(4) If the shareholders are known to the company by name, a shareholders'

Hauptversammlung mit eingeschriebenem Brief einberufen werden; der Tag der Absendung gilt als Tag der Bekanntmachung. Die §§ 125 bis 127 gelten sinngemäß.

meeting may be called by registered letter; the day of posting the notice of the meeting shall be deemed to be the day of publication. §§ 125 to 127 shall apply analogously.

(5) Wenn die Satzung nichts anderes bestimmt, soll die Hauptversammlung am Sitz der Gesellschaft stattfinden. Sind die Aktien der Gesellschaft an einer deutschen Börse zum amtlichen Handel zugelassen, so kann, wenn die Satzung nichts anderes bestimmt, die Hauptversammlung auch am Sitz der Börse stattfinden.

(5) Unless the articles provide otherwise, the shareholders' meeting shall be held at the company's domicile. If the company's shares are listed for official quotation on a German stock exchange, the shareholders' meeting may also be held at the domicile of such stock exchange, unless the articles provide otherwise.

(6) Sind alle Aktionäre erschienen oder vertreten, kann die Hauptversammlung Beschlüsse ohne Einhaltung der Bestimmungen dieses Unterabschnitts fassen, soweit kein Aktionär der Beschlußfassung widerspricht.

(6) If all shareholders are present or represented, a shareholders' meeting may adopt resolutions without complying with the provisions of this Subdivision provided that no shareholder objects to the adoption of the relevant resolution.

§ 122. Einberufung auf Verlangen einer Minderheit

§ 122. Calling of a Meeting at the Request of a Minority

(1) Die Hauptversammlung ist einzuberufen, wenn Aktionäre, deren Anteile zusammen den zwanzigsten Teil des Grundkapitals erreichen, die Einberufung schriftlich unter Angabe des Zwecks und der Gründe verlangen; das Verlangen ist an den Vorstand zu richten. Die Satzung kann das Recht, die Einberufung der Hauptversammlung zu verlangen, an den Besitz eines geringeren Anteils am Grundkapital knüpfen.

(1) A shareholders' meeting shall be called if shareholders whose holding in the aggregate equals or exceeds one twentieth of the share capital demand such meeting in writing, stating the purpose and the reasons of such meeting; such demand shall be addressed to the management board. The articles may provide that the right to demand a shareholders' meeting shall require only the holding of a lower proportion of the share capital.

(2) In gleicher Weise können Aktionäre, deren Anteile zusammen den zwanzigsten Teil des Grundkapitals oder den Nennbetrag von einer Million Deutsche Mark erreichen, verlangen, daß Gegenstände zur Beschlußfassung einer Hauptversammlung bekanntgemacht werden.

(2) In the same manner shareholders, whose shares amount in the aggregate to not less than one twentieth of the share capital or the par value of one million Deutsche Mark, may demand that items on the agenda for decision by the shareholders' meeting be published.

(3) Wird dem Verlangen nicht entsprochen, so kann das Gericht die Aktionäre, die das Verlangen gestellt haben, ermächtigen, die Hauptversammlung einzuberufen oder den Gegenstand bekanntzumachen. Zugleich kann das Gericht den Vorsitzenden der Versammlung bestimmen. Auf die Ermächtigung muß bei der Einberufung oder Bekanntmachung hingewiesen werden. Gegen die Entscheidung ist die sofortige Beschwerde zulässig.

(3) If any such demand is not complied with, the court may authorize the shareholders who have made the demand to call a shareholders' meeting or publish such items. At the same time the court may appoint the chairman of the meeting. The notice of the meeting or the publication shall refer to such authorization. An immediate appeal may be made against the decision of the court.

(4) Die Gesellschaft trägt die Kosten der Hauptversammlung und im Fall des Absatzes 3 auch die Gerichtskosten, wenn das Gericht dem Antrag stattgegeben hat.

(4) The company shall bear the costs of the shareholders' meeting and, in the case of subsection (3), also the court costs if the court has granted such motion.

§ 123. Einberufungsfrist

§ 123. Period for Notice of a Meeting

(1) Die Hauptversammlung ist mindestens einen Monat vor dem Tage der Versammlung einzuberufen.

(1) Notice of the shareholders' meeting shall be given no later than one month prior to the date of the meeting.

(2) Die Satzung kann die Teilnahme an der Hauptversammlung oder die Ausübung des Stimmrechts davon abhängig machen, daß die Aktien bis zu einem bestimmten Zeitpunkt vor der Versammlung hinterlegt werden, ferner davon, daß sich die Aktionäre vor der Versammlung anmelden. Sieht die Satzung eine solche Bestimmung vor, so tritt für die Berechnung der Einberufungsfrist an die Stelle des Tages der Versammlung der Tag, bis zu dessen Ablauf die Aktien zu hinterlegen sind oder sich die Aktionäre vor der Versammlung anmelden müssen.

(2) The articles may provide that attendance at the meeting or the exercise of voting rights shall require the deposit of shares by a specified date prior to the meeting, and in addition, the shareholders' giving notice of their intention to attend prior to the meeting. If the articles contain such provision, for purposes of computing the period of notice the day by the end of which the shares are to be deposited or the shareholders are to give prior notice of their intention to attend shall be substituted for the date of the meeting.

(3) Hängt nach der Satzung die Teilnahme an der Hauptversammlung oder die Ausübung des Stimmrechts davon ab, daß die Aktien bis zu einem bestimmten Zeitpunkt vor der Versammlung hinterlegt werden, so genügt es, wenn sie nicht später als am zehnten Tage vor der Ver-

(3) If attendance at the shareholders' meeting or the exercise of voting rights is subject to the deposit of shares by a specified date prior to the meeting, it shall suffice if the shares are deposited not later than the tenth day prior to the date of the meeting. Deposit of the shares with a no-

sammlung hinterlegt werden. Die Hinterlegung bei einem Notar oder bei einer Wertpapiersammelbank ist ausreichend.

tary or a securities clearing bank shall suffice.

(4) Hängt nach der Satzung die Teilnahme an der Hauptversammlung oder die Ausübung des Stimmrechts davon ab, daß sich die Aktionäre vor der Versammlung anmelden, so genügt es, wenn sie sich nicht später als am dritten Tage vor der Versammlung anmelden.

(4) If the articles provide that attendance at the shareholders' meeting or the exercise of voting rights is subject to the shareholders' giving prior notice of their intention to attend, it shall suffice if such notice is given no later than the third day prior to the date of the meeting.

§ 124. Bekanntmachung der Tagesordnung

§ 124. Publication of the Agenda

(1) Die Tagesordnung der Hauptversammlung ist bei der Einberufung in den Gesellschaftsblättern bekanntzumachen. Hat die Minderheit nach der Einberufung der Hauptversammlung die Bekanntmachung von Gegenständen zur Beschlußfassung der Hauptversammlung verlangt, so genügt es, wenn diese Gegenstände binnen zehn Tagen nach der Einberufung der Hauptversammlung bekanntgemacht werden. § 121 Abs. 4 gilt sinngemäß.

(1) The agenda of the shareholders' meeting shall be published in the company's designated journals together with notice of the meeting. If, after the meeting has been called, a minority has requested publication of items on the agenda for decision by the shareholders' meeting, it shall suffice if such items are published within ten days after notice of the shareholders' meeting has been given. § 121 (4) shall apply analogously.

(2) Steht die Wahl von Aufsichtsratsmitgliedern auf der Tagesordnung, so ist in der Bekanntmachung anzugeben, nach welchen gesetzlichen Vorschriften sich der Aufsichtsrat zusammensetzt, und ob die Hauptversammlung an Wahlvorschläge gebunden ist. Soll die Hauptversammlung über eine Satzungsänderung oder über einen Vertrag beschließen, der nur mit Zustimmung der Hauptversammlung wirksam wird, so ist auch der Wortlaut der vorgeschlagenen Satzungsänderung oder der wesentliche Inhalt des Vertrags bekanntzumachen.

(2) If the agenda includes the election of members of the supervisory board, the publication shall designate the statutory provisions governing the composition of the supervisory board and state whether or not the shareholders' meeting is bound by nominations. If the shareholders' meeting is required to resolve on an amendment of the articles or on an agreement which becomes effective only with the consent of the shareholders' meeting, the text of the proposed amendment of the articles or the essential contents of the agreement shall be published.

(3) Zu jedem Gegenstand der Tagesordnung, über den die Hauptversammlung beschließen soll, haben der Vorstand und der Aufsichtsrat, zur Wahl von Aufsichtsratsmitgliedern und Prüfern nur der

(3) With respect to each item on the agenda which is to be decided by the shareholders' meeting, the management board and the supervisory board, but in the case of the election of members of the

Aufsichtsrat, in der Bekanntmachung der Tagesordnung Vorschläge zur Beschlußfassung zu machen. Dies gilt nicht, wenn die Hauptversammlung bei der Wahl von Aufsichtsratsmitgliedern nach § 6 des Montan-Mitbestimmungsgesetzes an Wahlvorschläge gebunden ist, oder wenn der Gegenstand der Beschlußfassung auf Verlangen einer Minderheit auf die Tagesordnung gesetzt worden ist. Der Vorschlag zur Wahl von Aufsichtsratsmitgliedern oder Prüfern hat deren Namen, Beruf und Wohnort anzugeben. Hat der Aufsichtsrat auch aus Aufsichtsratsmitgliedern der Arbeitnehmer zu bestehen, so bedürfen Beschlüsse des Aufsichtsrats über Vorschläge zur Wahl von Aufsichtsratsmitgliedern nur der Mehrheit der Stimmen der Aufsichtsratsmitglieder der Aktionäre; § 8 des Montan-Mitbestimmungsgesetzes bleibt unberührt.

supervisory board and auditors, only the supervisory board shall in the publication of the agenda make a proposal for the respective resolutions. The foregoing shall not apply if the shareholders' meeting is bound by nominations for the election of members of the supervisory board pursuant to § 6 of the Coal and Steel Co-determination Act, or if the subject matter of the resolution has been put on the agenda upon request by a minority. The proposal for the election of members of the supervisory board or auditors shall state their name, profession and place of residence. If the supervisory board is to comprise representatives of employees, any resolution of the supervisory board regarding proposals for the election of members of the supervisory board shall require only the majority of the votes of the representatives of the shareholders in the supervisory board; § 8 of the Coal and Steel Co-determination Act shall remain unaffected.

(4) Über Gegenstände der Tagesordnung, die nicht ordnungsgemäß bekanntgemacht sind, dürfen keine Beschlüsse gefaßt werden. Zur Beschlußfassung über den in der Versammlung gestellten Antrag auf Einberufung einer Hauptversammlung, zu Anträgen, die zu Gegenständen der Tagesordnung gestellt werden, und zu Verhandlungen ohne Beschlußfassung bedarf es keiner Bekanntmachung.

(4) No resolution may be adopted in respect of items on the agenda which have not been properly published. However, no such publication shall be required for the adoption of a resolution on a motion made to call a shareholders' meeting which is made in the meeting, for motions made in respect of items on the agenda, and for deliberations without resolution.

§ 125. Mitteilungen für die Aktionäre und an Aufsichtsratsmitglieder

(1) Der Vorstand hat binnen zwölf Tagen nach der Bekanntmachung der Einberufung der Hauptversammlung im Bundesanzeiger den Kreditinstituten und den Vereinigungen von Aktionären, die in der letzten Hauptversammlung Stimmrechte für Aktionäre ausgeübt oder die die

§ 125. Communications to Shareholders and Members of the Supervisory Board

(1) The management board shall, within twelve days from the date of publication of the notice of a shareholders' meeting in the Federal Gazette, communicate to those credit institutions and shareholders' associations which have exercised voting rights on behalf of

Mitteilung verlangt haben, die Einberufung der Hauptversammlung, die Bekanntmachung der Tagesordnung und etwaige Anträge und Wahlvorschläge von Aktionären einschließlich des Namens des Aktionärs, der Begründung und einer etwaigen Stellungnahme der Verwaltung mitzuteilen.

shareholders in the preceding shareholders' meeting or which have requested such communication, the notice of the meeting, the publication of the agenda and any motions and nominations made by shareholders, including the name of the respective shareholder, the reasons given therefor, and any opinion expressed by the management thereon.

(2) Die gleiche Mitteilung hat der Vorstand den Aktionären zu übersenden, die

1. eine Aktie bei der Gesellschaft hinterlegt haben,
2. es nach der Bekanntmachung der Einberufung der Hauptversammlung im Bundesanzeiger verlangen oder
3. als Aktionär im Aktienbuch der Gesellschaft eingetragen sind und deren Stimmrechte in der letzten Hauptversammlung nicht durch ein Kreditinstitut ausgeübt worden sind.

(2) The management board shall send the same communication to shareholders who:

1. have deposited a share with the company;
2. so request after notice of the shareholders' meeting has been published in the Federal Gazette; or
3. are registered as shareholders in the company's share register and whose voting rights were not exercised by a credit institution at the previous shareholders' meeting.

(3) Jedes Aufsichtsratsmitglied kann verlangen, daß ihm der Vorstand die gleichen Mitteilungen übersendet.

(3) Each member of the supervisory board may request that the management board send the same communication to him.

(4) Jeder Aktionär, der eine Aktie bei der Gesellschaft hinterlegt oder als Aktionär im Aktienbuch der Gesellschaft eingetragen ist, und jedes Aufsichtsratsmitglied kann verlangen, daß der Vorstand ihm die in der Hauptversammlung gefaßten Beschlüsse schriftlich mitteilt.

(4) Each shareholder who has deposited a share with the company or is registered as a shareholder in the company's share register, and each member of the supervisory board may request that the management board advise him in writing of the resolutions adopted at a shareholders' meeting.

§ 126. Anträge von Aktionären

(1) Anträge von Aktionären brauchen nach § 125 nur mitgeteilt zu werden, wenn der Aktionär binnen einer Woche nach der Bekanntmachung der Einberufung der Hauptversammlung im Bundesanzeiger der Gesellschaft einen Gegenantrag mit Begründung übersandt und dabei mitgeteilt hat, er wolle in der Versamm-

§ 126. Motions by Shareholders

(1) Motions by shareholders need only be communicated pursuant to § 125 if, within one week from the date of publication of the notice of the meeting in the Federal Gazette, the shareholder submits to the company a counter-motion stating the grounds for such motion and advising the company that he intends to oppose a

lung einem Vorschlag des Vorstands und des Aufsichtsrats widersprechen und die anderen Aktionäre veranlassen, für seinen Gegenantrag zu stimmen.

proposal of the management board and the supervisory board in the meeting and to induce the other shareholders to vote for his counter-motion.

(2) Ein Gegenantrag und dessen Begründung brauchen nicht mitgeteilt zu werden,

1. soweit sich der Vorstand durch die Mitteilung strafbar machen würde,

2. wenn der Gegenantrag zu einem gesetz- oder satzungswidrigen Beschluß der Hauptversammlung führen würde,

3. wenn die Begründung in wesentlichen Punkten offensichtlich falsche oder irreführende Angaben oder wenn sie Beleidigungen enthält,

4. wenn ein auf denselben Sachverhalt gestützter Gegenantrag des Aktionärs bereits zu einer Hauptversammlung der Gesellschaft nach § 125 mitgeteilt worden ist,

5. wenn derselbe Gegenantrag des Aktionärs mit wesentlich gleicher Begründung in den letzten fünf Jahren bereits zu mindestens zwei Hauptversammlungen der Gesellschaft nach § 125 mitgeteilt worden ist und in der Hauptversammlung weniger als der zwanzigste Teil des vertretenen Grundkapitals für ihn gestimmt hat,

6. wenn der Aktionär zu erkennen gibt, daß er an der Hauptversammlung nicht teilnehmen und sich nicht vertreten lassen wird, oder

7. wenn der Aktionär in den letzten zwei Jahren in zwei Hauptversammlungen einen von ihm mitgeteilten Gegenantrag nicht gestellt hat oder nicht hat stellen lassen.

Die Begründung braucht nicht mitgeteilt zu werden, wenn sie insgesamt mehr als einhundert Worte beträgt.

(2) A counter-motion and the grounds therefor need not be communicated, if:

1. the management board would by reason of such communication become criminally liable;

2. the counter-motion would result in a resolution of the shareholders' meeting which would be illegal or would violate the articles;

3. the grounds contain statements which are manifestly false or misleading in material respects or which are libelous;

4. a counter-motion of such shareholder based on the same facts has already been communicated with respect to a shareholders' meeting of the company pursuant to § 125;

5. the same counter-motion of such shareholder on essentially identical grounds has already been communicated pursuant to § 125 to at least two shareholders' meetings of the company within the past five years and at such shareholders' meetings less than one twentieth of the share capital represented has voted in favor of such counter-motion;

6. the shareholder indicates that he will neither attend nor be represented at the shareholders' meeting; or

7. within the past two years at two shareholders' meetings the shareholder has failed to make or cause to be made on his behalf a counter-motion communicated by him.

The statement of the grounds need not be communicated if it exceeds one hundred words.

(3) Stellen mehrere Aktionäre zu demselben Gegenstand der Beschlußfas-

(3) If several shareholders make counter-motions for resolution in respect

sung Gegenanträge, so kann der Vorstand die Gegenanträge und ihre Begründungen zusammenfassen.

of the same subject matter, the management board may combine such countermotions and the respective statements of the grounds.

§ 127. Wahlvorschläge von Aktionären

Für den Vorschlag eines Aktionärs zur Wahl von Aufsichtsratsmitgliedern oder von Abschlußprüfern gilt § 126 sinngemäß. Der Wahlvorschlag braucht nicht begründet zu werden. Der Vorstand braucht den Wahlvorschlag auch dann nicht mitzuteilen, wenn der Vorschlag nicht die Angaben nach § 124 Abs. 3 Satz 3 enthält.

§ 127. Nominations by Shareholders

§ 126 shall apply analogously to a nomination by a shareholder for the election of a member of the supervisory board or external auditors. Such nomination need not be supported by a statement of the grounds therefor. The management board also need not communicate such nomination if it fails to contain the particulars required by § 124 (3) sentence 3.

§ 128. Weitergabe der Mitteilungen durch Kreditinstitute und Vereinigungen von Aktionären

(1) Verwahrt ein Kreditinstitut für Aktionäre Aktien der Gesellschaft, so hat es die Mitteilungen nach § 125 Abs. 1 unverzüglich an sie weiterzugeben.

(2) Beabsichtigt das Kreditinstitut, in der Hauptversammlung das Stimmrecht für Aktionäre auszuüben oder ausüben zu lassen, so hat es dem Aktionär außerdem eigene Vorschläge für die Ausübung des Stimmrechts zu den einzelnen Gegenständen der Tagesordnung mitzuteilen. Bei den Vorschlägen hat sich das Kreditinstitut vom Interesse des Aktionärs leiten zu lassen. Das Kreditinstitut hat den Aktionär ferner um Erteilung von Weisungen für die Ausübung des Stimmrechts zu bitten und darauf hinzuweisen, daß es, wenn der Aktionär nicht rechtzeitig eine andere Weisung erteilt, das Stimmrecht entsprechend seinen nach Satz 1 mitgeteilten Vorschlägen ausüben werde. Das Kreditinstitut hat der Bitte um Erteilung von Weisungen ein Formblatt

§ 128. Distribution of Communications by Credit Institutions and Shareholders' Associations

(1) A credit institution which on behalf of shareholders holds in custody shares of the company shall promptly forward to such shareholders any communications received pursuant to § 125 (1).

(2) If such credit institution intends to exercise or cause to be exercised voting rights on behalf of a shareholder at a shareholders' meeting, it shall also communicate to such shareholder its proposals in respect of the exercise of voting rights for each item on the agenda. In making such proposals, the credit institution shall be guided by the interests of the shareholder. Moreover the credit institution shall request from the shareholder instructions for the exercise of voting rights and shall advise the shareholder that it will exercise the voting right in accordance with its proposals communicated to the shareholder pursuant to sentence 1, absent instructions to the contrary within the requisite period of time. The credit institution shall append to its request for in-

beizufügen, durch dessen Ausfüllung der Aktionär Weisungen für die Ausübung des Stimmrechts zu den einzelnen Gegenständen der Tagesordnung erteilen kann. Gehört ein Vorstandsmitglied des Kreditinstituts dem Aufsichtsrat der Gesellschaft oder ein Vorstandsmitglied der Gesellschaft dem Aufsichtsrat des Kreditinstituts an, so hat das Kreditinstitut auch dies mitzuteilen.

structions a form to be completed by the shareholder regarding the exercise of the voting right for each item on the agenda. If a member of the credit institution's management board is also a member of the company's supervisory board or if a member of the company's management board is also a member of the credit institution's supervisory board, the credit institution shall also communicate such fact to the shareholder.

(3) Soweit ein Aktionär nach Einberufung der Hauptversammlung dem Kreditinstitut zu den einzelnen Gegenständen der Tagesordnung schriftlich Weisungen für die Ausübung des Stimmrechts erteilt hat, braucht das Kreditinstitut keine eigenen Vorschläge nach Absatz 2 mitzuteilen und den Aktionär nicht um Erteilung von Weisungen zu bitten.

(3) If a shareholder has, after notice of the shareholders' meeting has been given, issued written instructions to the credit institution regarding the exercise of the voting right for items on the agenda, the credit institution shall not be required to communicate to such shareholder its proposals pursuant to subsection (2) or request such shareholder to issue instructions.

(4) Die Verpflichtung des Kreditinstituts zum Ersatz eines aus der Verletzung der Absätze 1 oder 2 entstehenden Schadens kann im voraus weder ausgeschlossen noch beschränkt werden.

(4) The liability of the credit institution for any damages resulting from a violation of subsections (1) or (2) may neither be waived nor limited in advance.

(5) Gehören einer Vereinigung von Aktionären Aktionäre der Gesellschaft als Mitglieder an, so hat die Vereinigung die Mitteilungen nach § 125 Abs. 1 an diese Mitglieder auf deren Verlangen unverzüglich weiterzugeben. Im übrigen gelten die Absätze 2 bis 4 für Vereinigungen von Aktionären entsprechend.

(5) If shareholders of the company are members of a shareholders' association, the shareholders' association shall upon request promptly forward to such members any communications pursuant to § 125 (1). In all other respects subsections (2) to (4) shall apply analogously to shareholders' associations.

(6) Der Bundesminister der Justiz wird ermächtigt, im Einvernehmen mit dem Bundesminister für Wirtschaft und dem Bundesminister der Finanzen durch Rechtsverordnung

1. ein Formblatt für die Erteilung von Weisungen durch den Aktionär vorzuschreiben, das die Kreditinstitute und die Vereinigungen von Aktionären ihrer Bitte

(6) The Federal Minister of Justice shall be authorized in agreement with the Federal Minister of Economics and the Federal Minister of Finance to prescribe by regulation:

1. a form for instructions by shareholders which credit institutions and shareholders' associations shall append to their request for instructions pursuant to subsection (2) sentence 3;

um Weisungen nach Absatz 2 Satz 3 beizufügen haben,

2. vorzuschreiben, daß die Gesellschaft den Kreditinstituten und den Vereinigungen von Aktionären die Aufwendungen für die Vervielfältigung der Mitteilungen und für ihre Übersendung an die Aktionäre oder an ihre Mitglieder zu ersetzen hat. Zur Abgeltung der Aufwendungen kann für jedes Schreiben nach Absatz 1 ein Pauschbetrag festgesetzt werden.

Die Rechtsverordnung bedarf nicht der Zustimmung des Bundesrates.

2. that the company shall reimburse credit institutions and shareholders' associations for the expenses of copying communications and transmitting them to shareholders or to members. A lump-sum amount may be set to cover the expenses for each communication pursuant to subsection (1).

Such regulation shall not require the consent of the Federal Council.

DRITTER UNTERABSCHNITT. VERHANDLUNGSNIEDERSCHRIFT. AUSKUNFTSRECHT

SUBDIVISION THREE. MINUTES OF PROCEEDINGS; RIGHT TO INFORMATION

§ 129. Verzeichnis der Teilnehmer

(1) In der Hauptversammlung ist ein Verzeichnis der erschienenen oder vertretenen Aktionäre und der Vertreter von Aktionären mit Angabe ihres Namens und Wohnorts sowie des Betrags der von jedem vertretenen Aktien unter Angabe ihrer Gattung aufzustellen.

(2) Sind einem Kreditinstitut oder einer in § 135 Abs. 9 bezeichneten Person Vollmachten zur Ausübung des Stimmrechts erteilt worden und übt der Bevollmächtigte das Stimmrecht im Namen dessen, den es angeht, aus, so sind der Betrag und die Gattung der Aktien, für die ihm Vollmachten erteilt worden sind, zur Aufnahme in das Verzeichnis gesondert anzugeben. Die Namen der Aktionäre, welche Vollmachten erteilt haben, brauchen nicht angegeben zu werden.

(3) Wer von einem Aktionär ermächtigt ist, im eigenen Namen das Stimmrecht für Aktien auszuüben, die ihm nicht gehören, hat den Betrag und die Gattung

§ 129. List of Participants

(1) At the shareholders' meeting a list of shareholders present or represented and of the representatives of shareholders shall be prepared stating their name and place of residence and the amount and class of shares represented by each person.

(2) If proxies to exercise voting rights have been granted to a credit institution or a person designated in § 135 (9) and if the holder of the proxy shall exercise voting rights on behalf of an undisclosed principal, the amount and class of the shares for which the proxies were granted shall be specified separately in the list. The names of the shareholders who have granted the proxies need not be mentioned.

(3) A person who has been authorized by a shareholder to exercise voting rights in his own name in respect of shares which are not held by him, shall specify

dieser Aktien zur Aufnahme in das Verzeichnis gesondert anzugeben. Dies gilt auch für Namensaktien, als deren Aktionär der Ermächtigte im Aktienbuch eingetragen ist.

the amount and class of such shares separately for inclusion in the list. The foregoing shall apply also in respect of registered shares for which such authorized person is registered in the share register as shareholder.

(4) Das Verzeichnis ist vor der ersten Abstimmung zur Einsicht für alle Teilnehmer auszulegen. Es ist vom Vorsitzenden zu unterzeichnen.

(4) The list shall be made available for inspection by all participants prior to the first vote. Such list shall be signed by the chairman.

§ 130. Niederschrift

§ 130. Minutes

(1) Jeder Beschluß der Hauptversammlung ist durch eine über die Verhandlung notariell aufgenommene Niederschrift zu beurkunden. Gleiches gilt für jedes Verlangen einer Minderheit nach § 120 Abs. 1 Satz 2, §§ 137 und 147 Abs. 1. Sind die Aktien der Gesellschaft nicht an einer Börse zum Handel zugelassen, reicht eine vom Vorzitzenden des Aufsichtsrats zu unterzeichnende Niederschrift aus, soweit keine Beschlüsse gefaßt werden, für die das Gesetz eine Dreiviertel- oder größere Mehrheit bestimmt.

(1) Each resolution of the shareholders' meeting shall be recorded in minutes of the proceedings which shall be in the form of a notarial deed. The foregoing shall apply to any request made by a minority pursuant to § 120 (1) sentence 2, §§ 137 and 147 (1). If the shares of the company are not admitted for trading on a stock exchange, it shall suffice if the minutes are signed by the chairman of the supervisory board in so far as no resolutions are adopted for which the law requires a three fourth or a larger majority.

(2) In der Niederschrift sind der Ort und der Tag der Verhandlung, der Name des Notars sowie die Art und das Ergebnis der Abstimmung und die Feststellung des Vorsitzenden über die Beschlußfassung anzugeben.

(2) The minutes shall state the place and date of the meeting, the name of the notary, the form and result of the voting and any determinations of the chairman regarding resolutions.

(3) Das Verzeichnis der Teilnehmer an der Versammlung sowie die Belege über die Einberufung sind der Niederschrift als Anlagen beizufügen. Die Belege über die Einberufung brauchen nicht beigefügt zu werden, wenn sie unter Angabe ihres Inhalts in der Niederschrift aufgeführt werden.

(3) The list of participants and the documents regarding notice of the meeting shall be appended to the minutes. The documents regarding notice of the meeting need not be appended if their contents are recorded in the minutes.

(4) Die Niederschrift ist von dem Notar zu unterschreiben. Die Zuziehung von Zeugen ist nicht nötig.

(4) The minutes shall be signed by the notary. The presence of witnesses shall not be required.

(5) Unverzüglich nach der Versammlung hat der Vorstand eine öffentlich beglaubigte, im Falle des Absatzes 1 Satz 3 eine vom Vorsitzenden der Aufsichtsrats unterzeichnete Abschrift der Niederschrift und ihrer Anlagen zum Handelsregister einzureichen.

(5) The management board shall, promptly upon the closure of the meeting, submit an officially certified copy, in case of subsection (1) sentence 3 a copy signed by the chairman of the supervisory board, of the minutes and the appendices to the commercial register.

§ 131. Auskunftsrecht des Aktionärs

§ 131. Right of Shareholders to Information

(1) Jedem Aktionär ist auf Verlangen in der Hauptversammlung vom Vorstand Auskunft über Angelegenheiten der Gesellschaft zu geben, soweit sie zur sachgemäßen Beurteilung des Gegenstands der Tagesordnung erforderlich ist. Die Auskunftspflicht erstreckt sich auch auf die rechtlichen und geschäftlichen Beziehungen der Gesellschaft zu einem verbundenen Unternehmen. Macht eine Gesellschaft von den Erleichterungen nach § 266 Abs. 1 Satz 3, § 276 oder § 288 des Handelsgesetzbuchs Gebrauch, so kann jeder Aktionär verlangen, daß ihm in der Hauptversammlung über den Jahresabschluß der Jahresabschluß in der Form vorgelegt wird, die er ohne Anwendung dieser Vorschriften hätte.

(1) Each shareholder shall upon request be provided with information at the shareholders' meeting by the management board regarding the company's affairs, to the extent that such information is necessary to permit a proper evaluation of the relevant item on the agenda. The duty to provide information shall also extend to the company's legal and business relations with any affiliated enterprise. If a company makes use of the simplified procedure pursuant to § 266 (1) sentence 3, § 276 or § 288 of the Commercial Code, each shareholder may request that the annual financial statements be presented to him at the shareholders' meeting on such annual financial statements in the form that would have been used if such provisions on simplified procedure were not applied.

(2) Die Auskunft hat den Grundsätzen einer gewissenhaften und getreuen Rechenschaft zu entsprechen.

(2) The information provided shall comply with the principles of conscientious and accurate accounting.

(3) Der Vorstand darf die Auskunft verweigern,

1. soweit die Erteilung der Auskunft nach vernünftiger kaufmännischer Beurteilung geeignet ist, der Gesellschaft oder einem verbundenen Unternehmen einen nicht unerheblichen Nachteil zuzufügen;

(3) The management board may refuse to provide information:

1. to the extent that providing such information is, according to sound business judgment, likely to cause material damage to the company or an affiliated enterprise;

2. soweit sie sich auf steuerliche Wertansätze oder die Höhe einzelner Steuern bezieht;

3. über den Unterschied zwischen dem Wert, mit dem Gegenstände in der Jahresbilanz angesetzt worden sind, und einem höheren Wert dieser Gegenstände, es sei denn, daß die Hauptversammlung den Jahresabschluß feststellt;

4. über die Bilanzierungs- und Bewertungsmethoden, soweit die Angabe dieser Methoden im Anhang ausreicht, um ein den tatsächlichen Verhältnissen entsprechendes Bild der Vermögens-, Finanz- und Ertragslage der Gesellschaft im Sinne des § 264 Abs. 2 des Handelsgesetzbuchs zu vermitteln; dies gilt nicht, wenn die Hauptversammlung den Jahresabschluß feststellt;

5. soweit sich der Vorstand durch die Erteilung der Auskunft strafbar machen würde;

6. soweit bei einem Kreditinstitut Angaben über angewandte Bilanzierungs- und Bewertungsmethoden sowie vorgenommene Verrechnungen im Jahresabschluß, Lagebericht, Konzernabschluß oder Konzernlagebericht nicht gemacht zu werden brauchen.

Aus anderen Gründen darf die Auskunft nicht verweigert werden.

(4) Ist einem Aktionär wegen seiner Eigenschaft als Aktionär eine Auskunft außerhalb der Hauptversammlung gegeben worden, so ist sie jedem anderen Aktionär auf dessen Verlangen in der Hauptversammlung zu geben, auch wenn sie zur sachgemäßen Beurteilung des Gegenstands der Tagesordnung nicht erforderlich ist. Der Vorstand darf die Auskunft nicht nach Absatz 3 Satz 1 Nr. 1 bis 4 verweigern. Sätze 1 und 2 gelten nicht, wenn ein Tochterunternehmen (§ 290 Abs. 1, 2 des Handelsgesetzbuchs), ein Gemeinschaftsunternehmen (§ 310 Abs. 1 des Handelsgesetzbuchs) oder ein assoziiertes Unternehmen (§ 311 Abs. 1 des Han-

2. to the extent that such information relates to tax valuations or the amount of certain taxes;

3. with regard to the difference between the value at which items are shown in the annual balance sheet and the higher market value of such items, unless the shareholders' meeting is to approve the annual financial statements;

4. with regard to the methods of classification and valuation, if disclosure of such methods in the notes suffices to provide a clear view of the actual condition of the company's assets, financial position and profitability within the meaning of § 264 (2) of the Commercial Code; the foregoing shall not apply if the shareholders' meeting is to approve the annual financial statements;

5. if provision thereof would render the management board criminally liable.

6. insofar as, in case of credit institutions, information need not be given on methods of classification and valuation applied and set-offs made in the annual financial statements, annual report, group financial statements or group annual report.

The provision of information may not be refused for other reasons.

(4) If information has been provided to a shareholder by reason of his status as a shareholder outside a shareholders' meeting, such information shall upon request be provided to any other shareholder at the shareholders' meeting, even if such information is not necessary to permit a proper evaluation of an item on the agenda. The management board may not refuse to provide such information on the grounds of subsection (3) sentence 1 Nos. 1 to 4. Sentences 1 and 2 shall not apply if a subsidiary (§ 290 (1) and (2) of the Commercial Code) or an associated enterprise (§ 311 (1) of the Commercial Code) provides information to a parent

delsgesetzbuchs) die Auskunft einem Mutterunternehmen (§ 290 Abs. 1, 2 des Handelsgesetzbuchs) zum Zwecke der Einbeziehung der Gesellschaft in den Konzernabschluß des Mutterunternehmens erteilt und die Auskunft für diesen Zweck benötigt wird.

company for purposes of the inclusion of the Company into the group financial statements of the parent company and such information is needed for such purposes.

(5) Wird einem Aktionär eine Auskunft verweigert, so kann er verlangen, daß seine Frage und der Grund, aus dem die Auskunft verweigert worden ist, in die Niederschrift über die Verhandlung aufgenommen werden.

(5) A shareholder who has been denied information may request that his question and the reason for which the information was denied be recorded in the minutes of the meeting.

§ 132. Gerichtliche Entscheidung über das Auskunftsrecht

§ 132. Judicial Decision on the Right to Information

(1) Ob der Vorstand die Auskunft zu geben hat, entscheidet auf Antrag ausschließlich das Landgericht, in dessen Bezirk die Gesellschaft ihren Sitz hat. Ist bei dem Landgericht eine Kammer für Handelssachen gebildet, so entscheidet diese an Stelle der Zivilkammer. Die Landesregierung kann die Entscheidung durch Rechtsverordnung für die Bezirke mehrerer Landgerichte einem der Landgerichte übertragen, wenn dies der Sicherung einer einheitlichen Rechtsprechung dient. Die Landesregierung kann die Ermächtigung auf die Landesjustizverwaltung übertragen.

(1) The district court of the district of the company's domicile shall have exclusive jurisdiction to decide upon motion whether or not the management board is required to provide information. If the district court maintains a chamber for commercial matters, such chamber shall have jurisdiction in lieu of the chamber for civil matters. The state government may by regulation transfer jurisdiction for several district courts to one district court if such transfer is required to ensure uniformity of decisions. The state government may transfer such authority to the ministry of justice of such state.

(2) Antragsberechtigt ist jeder Aktionär, dem die verlangte Auskunft nicht gegeben worden ist, und, wenn über den Gegenstand der Tagesordnung, auf den sich die Auskunft bezog, Beschluß gefaßt worden ist, jeder in der Hauptversammlung erschienene Aktionär, der in der Hauptversammlung Widerspruch zur Niederschrift erklärt hat. Der Antrag ist binnen zwei Wochen nach der Hauptversammlung zu stellen, in der die Auskunft abgelehnt worden ist.

(2) Each shareholder who has been denied information requested and, if a resolution has been adopted on an item on the agenda for which information was requested, each shareholder who was present at the shareholders' meeting and who has recorded his objection in the minutes at the shareholders' meeting, shall have standing to make such motion. Such motion may be made within two weeks from the date of the shareholders' meeting in which the information was refused.

(3) § 99 Abs. 1, Abs. 3 Satz 1, 2, 4 bis 9 und Abs. 5 Satz 1 und 3 gilt sinngemäß. Die sofortige Beschwerde findet nur statt, wenn das Landgericht sie in der Entscheidung für zulässig erklärt. Es soll sie nur zulassen, wenn dadurch die Klärung einer Rechtsfrage von grundsätzlicher Bedeutung zu erwarten ist.

(3) § 99 (1), (3) sentences 1, 2 and 4 to 9 and (5) sentences 1 and 3 shall apply analogously. Immediate appeal may be made against the decision only if the district court has granted leave to appeal in its decision. The court shall grant such leave only if an issue of law of general significance may be expected to be settled on appeal.

(4) Wird dem Antrag stattgegeben, so ist die Auskunft auch außerhalb der Hauptversammlung zu geben. Aus der Entscheidung findet die Zwangsvollstreckung nach den Vorschriften der Zivilprozeßordnung statt.

(4) If the motion is granted, the information shall be provided even outside a shareholders' meeting. The decision may be enforced in accordance with the provisions of the Code of Civil Procedure.

(5) Für die Kosten des Verfahrens gilt die Kostenordnung. Für das Verfahren des ersten Rechtszugs wird das Doppelte der vollen Gebühr erhoben. Für den zweiten Rechtszug wird die gleiche Gebühr erhoben; dies gilt auch dann, wenn die Beschwerde Erfolg hat. Wird der Antrag oder die Beschwerde zurückgenommen, bevor es zu einer Entscheidung oder einer vom Gericht vermittelten Einigung kommt, so ermäßigt sich die Gebühr auf die Hälfte. Der Geschäftswert ist von Amts wegen festzusetzen. Er bestimmt sich nach § 30 Abs. 2 der Kostenordnung mit der Maßgabe, daß der Wert regelmäßig auf zehntausend Deutsche Mark anzunehmen ist. Das mit dem Verfahren befaßte Gericht bestimmt nach billigem Ermessen, welchem Beteiligten die Kosten des Verfahrens aufzuerlegen sind.

(5) The costs of the proceedings shall be determined by the Act on Court Costs. In proceedings before the court of the first instance twice the full fee shall be assessed. In proceedings before the court of the second instance the same amount shall be assessed; the foregoing shall also apply if the appeal is successful. If the motion or the appeal is withdrawn before a decision is rendered or a settlement through the medium of the court has been made, the fees shall be reduced by one half. The court shall determine the value of the subject matter of the proceedings. Such value shall be determined in accordance with § 30 (2) of the Act on Court Costs, provided that such value shall as a rule be ten thousand Deutsche Mark. The court concerned with the proceedings shall determine at its reasonable discretion which party is to bear the costs of proceedings.

VIERTER UNTERABSCHNITT. STIMMRECHT

SUBDIVISION FOUR. VOTING RIGHTS

§ 133. Grundsatz der einfachen Stimmenmehrheit

§ 133. Principle of Simple Majority of Votes

(1) Die Beschlüsse der Hauptversammlung bedürfen der Mehrheit der ab-

(1) Resolutions of the shareholders' meeting shall require a majority of the

gegebenen Stimmen (einfache Stimmenmehrheit), soweit nicht Gesetz oder Satzung eine größere Mehrheit oder weitere Erfordernisse bestimmen.

votes cast ('simple majority') unless the law or the articles provide for a larger majority or additional requirements.

(2) Für Wahlen kann die Satzung andere Bestimmungen treffen.

(2) The articles may provide for different rules in respect of elections.

§ 134. Stimmrecht

(1) Das Stimmrecht wird nach Aktiennennbeträgen ausgeübt. Für den Fall, daß einem Aktionär mehrere Aktien gehören, kann die Satzung das Stimmrecht durch Festsetzung eines Höchstbetrags oder von Abstufungen beschränken. Die Satzung kann außerdem bestimmen, daß zu den Aktien, die dem Aktionär gehören, auch die Aktien rechnen, die einem anderen für seine Rechnung gehören. Für den Fall, daß der Aktionär ein Unternehmen ist, kann sie ferner bestimmen, daß zu den Aktien, die ihm gehören, auch die Aktien rechnen, die einem von ihm abhängigen oder ihn beherrschenden oder einem mit ihm konzernverbundenen Unternehmen oder für Rechnung solcher Unternehmen einem Dritten gehören. Die Beschränkungen können nicht für einzelne Aktionäre angeordnet werden. Bei der Berechnung einer nach Gesetz oder Satzung erforderlichen Kapitalmehrheit bleiben die Beschränkungen außer Betracht.

(2) Das Stimmrecht beginnt mit der vollständigen Leistung der Einlage. Die Satzung kann bestimmen, daß das Stimmrecht beginnt, wenn auf die Aktie die gesetzliche oder höhere satzungsmäßige Mindesteinlage geleistet ist. In diesem Fall gewährt die Leistung der Mindesteinlage eine Stimme; bei höheren Einlagen richtet sich das Stimmenverhältnis nach der Höhe der geleisteten Einlagen. Bestimmt die Satzung nicht, daß das Stimmrecht vor der vollständigen Leistung der Einlage beginnt, und ist noch

§ 134. Voting Rights

(1) Voting rights shall be exercised in proportion to the par value of shares. The articles may limit voting rights with respect to shareholders holding more than one share by setting a maximum par value or a sliding scale. The articles may also provide that shares held by any other person on behalf of a shareholder shall be deemed to be shares held by such shareholder. If a shareholder constitutes a business enterprise, the articles may further provide that those shares which are held by an enterprise which is controlled or controlling or affiliated in a group or which are held by a third party on behalf of any such enterprises, shall also be deemed to be shares of such shareholder. It may not be provided that any such limitation apply to specific shareholders only. Any limitation shall not be taken into account in the computation of a capital majority required by law or the articles.

(2) Voting rights shall arise as from the date on which contributions have been made in full. The articles may provide, however, that voting rights shall arise as from the date on which the minimum contribution provided by law, or a higher minimum contribution provided in the articles, has been paid. If the articles so provide, payment of the minimum contribution shall give rise to one vote, and, if payments exceed the minimum contribution, the voting rights shall be determined in accordance with the amounts of con-

auf keine Aktie die Einlage vollständig geleistet, so richtet sich das Stimmenverhältnis nach der Höhe der geleisteten Einlagen; dabei gewährt die Leistung der Mindesteinlage eine Stimme. Bruchteile von Stimmen werden in diesen Fällen nur berücksichtigt, soweit sie für den stimmberechtigten Aktionär volle Stimmen ergeben. Die Satzung kann Bestimmungen nach diesem Absatz nicht für einzelne Aktionäre oder für einzelne Aktiengattungen treffen.

tributions paid. If the articles do not provide that voting rights arise prior to contributions having been paid in full and if contributions have not been paid in full in respect of any share, the voting rights shall be determined in relation to the amounts paid; in such event payment of the minimum contribution shall give rise to one vote. In such cases fractions of votes shall be taken into account only to the extent they result in full votes for the shareholder entitled to vote. The articles may not make provisions pursuant to this subsection which apply only to specific shareholders or to specific classes of shares.

(3) Das Stimmrecht kann durch einen Bevollmächtigten ausgeübt werden. Für die Vollmacht ist die schriftliche Form erforderlich und genügend. Die Vollmachtsurkunde ist der Gesellschaft vorzulegen und bleibt in ihrer Verwahrung.

(3) Voting rights may be exercised by proxy. The form of the proxy shall be in writing and such writing shall be sufficient. The form of the proxy shall be submitted to the company and remain in its custody.

(4) Die Form der Ausübung des Stimmrechts richtet sich nach der Satzung.

(4) The manner of the exercise of voting rights shall be governed by the articles.

§ 135. Ausübung des Stimmrechts durch Kreditinstitute und geschäftsmäßig Handelnde

§ 135. Exercise of Voting Rights by Credit Institutions and Professional Agents

(1) Ein Kreditinstitut darf das Stimmrecht für Inhaberaktien, die ihm nicht gehören, nur ausüben oder ausüben lassen, wenn es schriftlich bevollmächtigt ist. In der eigenen Hauptversammlung darf das bevollmächtigte Kreditinstitut das Stimmrecht auf Grund der Vollmacht nur ausüben, soweit der Aktionär eine ausdrückliche Weisung zu den einzelnen Gegenständen der Tagesordnung erteilt hat.

(1) A credit institution may only exercise or cause to be exercised, voting rights arising under bearer shares which it does not hold if it has been authorized to exercise such voting rights by proxy. A credit institution may exercise voting rights at its own shareholders' meeting by virtue of such proxy only to the extent that a shareholder has given express instructions in respect of the various items on the agenda.

(2) Die Vollmacht darf nur einem bestimmten Kreditinstitut und nur für läng-

(2) A proxy may only be issued to a specified credit institution and only for a

stens fünfzehn Monate erteilt werden. Sie ist jederzeit widerruflich. Die Vollmachtsurkunde muß bei der Erteilung der Vollmacht vollständig ausgefüllt sein und darf keine anderen Erklärungen enthalten. Sie soll das Datum der Ausstellung enthalten. Die Frist in Satz 1 beginnt spätestens mit dem Tage der Ausstellung.

period of time not exceeding fifteen months. The proxy shall be revocable at any time. The form of proxy shall be completed in full at the time the proxy is issued and may not contain any other statements. Such form of proxy shall indicate the date of signing. The period mentioned in sentence 1 shall commence no later than the date of signing.

(3) Das bevollmächtigte Kreditinstitut darf Personen, die nicht seine Angestellten sind, nur unterbevollmächtigen, wenn die Vollmacht eine Unterbevollmächtigung ausdrücklich gestattet und das bevollmächtigte Kreditinstitut am Ort der Hauptversammlung keine Niederlassung hat. Gleiches gilt für eine Übertragung der Vollmacht durch das bevollmächtigte Kreditinstitut.

(3) The credit institution so authorized may delegate its authority to persons other than its employees only if the proxy expressly permits such delegation of authority and if the credit institution does not maintain an office at the place where the shareholders' meeting is held. The foregoing shall apply to a transfer of a proxy by the authorized credit institution.

(4) Auf Grund der Vollmacht kann das Kreditinstitut das Stimmrecht unter Benennung des Aktionärs in dessen Namen ausüben. Wenn es die Vollmacht bestimmt, kann das Kreditinstitut das Stimmrecht auch im Namen dessen, den es angeht, ausüben. Übt das Kreditinstitut das Stimmrecht unter Benennung des Aktionärs in dessen Namen aus, ist die Vollmachtsurkunde der Gesellschaft vorzulegen und von dieser zu verwahren. Übt es das Stimmrecht im Namen dessen, den es angeht, aus, genügt zum Nachweis seiner Stimmberechtigung gegenüber der Gesellschaft die Erfüllung der in der Satzung für die Ausübung des Stimmrechts vorgesehenen Erfordernisse; enthält die Satzung darüber keine Bestimmungen, genügt die Vorlegung der Aktien oder einer Bescheinigung über die Hinterlegung der Aktien bei einem Notar oder einer Wertpapiersammelbank.

(4) By virtue of the proxy, the credit institution may exercise the voting rights on behalf of a disclosed principal by stating his name. However, if the proxy so provides, the credit institution may exercise the voting rights also on behalf of an undisclosed principal. If the credit institution exercises the voting rights on behalf of a disclosed principal by stating his name, the proxy shall be submitted to, and further held in custody by, the company. If the credit institution exercises the voting rights on behalf of an undisclosed principal, compliance with the provisions of the articles governing the exercise of voting rights shall constitute sufficient evidence with respect to the company of the credit institution's right to vote; if the articles do not contain provisions with respect to such requirements, presentation of the share certificate or a certificate confirming that the shares have been deposited with a notary or a securities clearing bank shall suffice.

(5) Hat der Aktionär dem Kreditinstitut keine Weisung für die Ausübung des

(5) If the shareholder has not given the credit institution instructions on the

Stimmrechts erteilt, so hat das Kreditinstitut das Stimmrecht entsprechend seinen eigenen, den Aktionären nach § 128 Abs. 2 mitgeteilten Vorschlägen auszuüben, es sei denn, daß das Kreditinstitut den Umständen nach annehmen darf, daß der Aktionär bei Kenntnis der Sachlage die abweichende Ausübung des Stimmrechts billigen würde.

exercise of voting rights, the credit institution shall be required to exercise such voting rights in accordance with its own proposals as communicated to the shareholders pursuant to § 128 (2), unless the credit institution may assume in view of the circumstances prevailing, that the shareholder would, if he had knowledge of the facts, approve a different exercise of the voting rights.

(6) Die Wirksamkeit der Stimmabgabe wird durch einen Verstoß gegen Absatz 1 Satz 2, Absätze 2, 3 und 5 nicht beeinträchtigt.

(6) The validity of votes cast shall not be impaired by a violation of subsections (1) sentence 2, subsections (2), (3) and (5).

(7) Ein Kreditinstitut darf das Stimmrecht für Namensaktien, die ihm nicht gehören, als deren Aktionär es aber im Aktienbuch eingetragen ist, nur auf Grund einer schriftlichen Ermächtigung, wenn es nicht als deren Aktionär eingetragen ist, nur unter Benennung des Aktionärs in dessen Namen auf Grund einer schriftlichen Vollmacht ausüben. Auf die Ermächtigung oder Vollmacht sind Absatz 1 Satz 2, Absätze 2, 3 und 5, auf die Vollmacht außerdem Absatz 4 Satz 3 anzuwenden. Im übrigen gilt Absatz 6.

(7) A credit institution may exercise voting rights arising under registered shares which it does not hold, but with respect to which the credit institution is registered in the share register as shareholder, only pursuant to a written authorization and, if the credit institution is not registered as shareholder, only pursuant to a written proxy on behalf of a disclosed principal by stating his name. Subsection (1) sentence 2 and subsections (2), (3) and (5) shall apply to such authorization or proxy; in addition, subsection (4) sentence 3 shall apply to such proxy. Moreover, subsection (6) shall apply.

(8) Ist das Kreditinstitut bei der Ausübung des Stimmrechts von einer Weisung des Aktionärs oder, wenn der Aktionär keine Weisung erteilt hat, von seinem eigenen, dem Aktionär nach § 128 Abs. 2 mitgeteilten Vorschlag abgewichen, so hat es dies dem Aktionär mitzuteilen und die Gründe anzugeben.

(8) If the credit institution in exercising voting rights has not complied with the shareholders' instructions or, in case the shareholder has not given instructions, the credit institution has not complied with its own proposal as communicated to the shareholder pursuant to § 128 (2), the credit institution shall inform the shareholder thereof and state the reasons therefor.

(9) Die Absätze 1 bis 8 gelten sinngemäß für die Ausübung des Stimmrechts durch

1. Vereinigungen von Aktionären,
2. Geschäftsleiter und Angestellte ei-

(9) Subsections (1) to (8) shall apply analogously to the exercise of voting rights by:

1. shareholders' associations;
2. managers and employees of a credit

nes Kreditinstituts, wenn die ihnen nicht gehörenden Aktien dem Kreditinstitut zur Verwahrung anvertraut sind,

3. Personen, die sich geschäftsmäßig gegenüber Aktionären zur Ausübung des Stimmrechts in der Hauptversammlung erbieten.

Dies gilt nicht, wenn derjenige, der das Stimmrecht ausüben will, gesetzlicher Vertreter oder Ehegatte des Aktionärs oder mit ihm bis zum vierten Grade verwandt oder verschwägert ist.

(**10**) Ein Kreditinstitut ist verpflichtet, den Auftrag eines Aktionärs zur Ausübung des Stimmrechts in einer Hauptversammlung anzunehmen, wenn es für den Aktionär Aktien der Gesellschaft verwahrt und sich gegenüber Aktionären der Gesellschaft zur Ausübung des Stimmrechts in derselben Hauptversammlung erboten hat. Die Verpflichtung besteht nicht, wenn das Kreditinstitut am Ort der Hauptversammlung keine Niederlassung hat und der Aktionär die Übertragung der Vollmacht auf oder die Unterbevollmächtigung von Personen, die nicht Angestellte des Kreditinstituts sind, nicht gestattet hat.

(**11**) Die Verpflichtung des Kreditinstituts zum Ersatz eines aus der Verletzung der Absätze 1 bis 3, 5, 7, 8 oder 10 entstehenden Schadens kann im voraus weder ausgeschlossen noch beschränkt werden.

institution if shares not owned by them have been entrusted to the credit institution for custody;

3. persons who professionally offer shareholders their services in exercising voting rights at shareholders' meeting.

The foregoing shall not apply if the person exercising the voting right is the legal representative or spouse of the shareholder or a related by blood or marriage in the fourth degree of kinship.

(**10**) A credit institution shall be obligated to accept an order of a shareholder to exercise voting rights at a shareholders' meeting if it keeps shares of the company in custody for the shareholder and if it has offered to the company's shareholders to exercise voting rights on their behalf at the same shareholders' meeting. Such obligation shall not exist if the credit institution does not maintain an office at the place where the shareholders' meeting is held and the shareholder has not permitted the transfer or delegation of the proxy to persons other than employees of the bank.

(**11**) The liability of a credit institution for damages resulting from a violation of subsections (1) to (3), (5), (7), (8) or (10) may neither be waived nor limited in advance.

§ 136. Ausschluß des Stimmrechts

(**1**) Niemand kann für sich oder für einen anderen das Stimmrecht ausüben, wenn darüber Beschluß gefaßt wird, ob er zu entlasten oder von einer Verbindlichkeit zu befreien ist oder ob die Gesellschaft gegen ihn einen Anspruch geltend machen soll. Für Aktien, aus denen der Aktionär nach Satz 1 das Stimmrecht

§ 136. Exclusion of Voting Rights

(**1**) No person may exercise voting rights on his own behalf or on behalf of any other person in respect of a resolution concerning ratification of his acts, his discharge from a liability, or enforcement by the company of a claim against him. Voting rights arising from shares which may not be exercised by the shareholder him-

nicht ausüben kann, kann das Stimmrecht auch nicht durch einen anderen ausgeübt werden.

self pursuant to sentence 1 may also not be exercised by any other person.

(2) Ein Vertrag, durch den sich ein Aktionär verpflichtet, nach Weisung der Gesellschaft, des Vorstands oder des Aufsichtsrats der Gesellschaft oder nach Weisung eines abhängigen Unternehmens das Stimmrecht auszuüben, ist nichtig. Ebenso ist ein Vertrag nichtig, durch den sich ein Aktionär verpflichtet, für die jeweiligen Vorschläge des Vorstands oder des Aufsichtsrats der Gesellschaft zu stimmen.

(2) An agreement whereby a shareholder undertakes to exercise voting rights in accordance with the instructions of the company, the management board or the supervisory board of the company or a controlled enterprise shall be null and void. An agreement whereby a shareholder undertakes to vote for the respective proposals of the management board or supervisory board of the company shall likewise be null and void.

§ 137. Abstimmung über Wahlvorschläge von Aktionären

§ 137. Voting on Nomination Made by Shareholders

Hat ein Aktionär einen Vorschlag zur Wahl von Aufsichtsratsmitgliedern nach § 127 gemacht und beantragt er in der Hauptversammlung die Wahl des von ihm Vorgeschlagenen, so ist über seinen Antrag vor dem Vorschlag des Aufsichtsrats zu beschließen, wenn es eine Minderheit der Aktionäre verlangt, deren Anteile zusammen den zehnten Teil des vertretenen Grundkapitals erreichen.

If a shareholder has made a nomination for the election of members of the supervisory board pursuant to § 127 and moves at the shareholders' meeting for the election of the person nominated by him, such motion shall be resolved upon prior to acting on the proposal of the supervisory board, provided that a minority of shareholders whose holding in aggregate equals or exceeds one tenth of the share capital represented at the meeting so requests.

Fünfter Unterabschnitt. Sonderbeschluß

Subdivision Five. Separate Resolutions

§ 138. Gesonderte Versammlung. Gesonderte Abstimmung

§ 138. Separate Meeting; Separate Voting

In diesem Gesetz oder in der Satzung vorgeschriebene Sonderbeschlüsse gewisser Aktionäre sind entweder in einer gesonderten Versammlung dieser Aktionäre oder in einer gesonderten Abstimmung zu fassen, soweit das Gesetz nichts anderes bestimmt. Für die Einberufung der gesonderten Versammlung und die

Where this Act or the articles provide for separate resolutions of certain shareholders, such resolutions shall be adopted either at a separate meeting of such shareholders or by a separate vote, unless the law provides otherwise. The provisions governing shareholders' meetings shall apply analogously to the calling of a sep-

Teilnahme an ihr sowie für das Auskunftsrecht gelten die Bestimmungen über die Hauptversammlung, für die Sonderbeschlüsse die Bestimmungen über Hauptversammlungsbeschlüsse sinngemäß. Verlangen Aktionäre, die an der Abstimmung über den Sonderbeschluß teilnehmen können, die Einberufung einer gesonderten Versammlung oder die Bekanntmachung eines Gegenstands zur gesonderten Abstimmung, so genügt es, wenn ihre Anteile, mit denen sie an der Abstimmung über den Sonderbeschluß teilnehmen können, zusammen den zehnten Teil der Anteile erreichen, aus denen bei der Abstimmung über den Sonderbeschluß das Stimmrecht ausgeübt werden kann.

arate meeting, attendance of such meeting, and the right to information; the provisions governing resolutions of shareholders' meetings shall apply analogously to such separate resolutions. If shareholders who are entitled to take part in the voting on a separate resolution request a separate meeting or announcement of a proposal to be voted on separately, it shall suffice if the shares with which they may take part in the voting on the separate resolution in aggregate equal or exceed one tenth of the shares entitled to vote on such separate resolution.

SECHSTER UNTERABSCHNITT. VORZUGSAKTIEN OHNE STIMMRECHT

§ 139. Wesen

(1) Für Aktien, die mit einem nachzuzahlenden Vorzug bei der Verteilung des Gewinns ausgestattet sind, kann das Stimmrecht ausgeschlossen werden (Vorzugsaktien ohne Stimmrecht).

(2) Vorzugsaktien ohne Stimmrecht dürfen nur bis zu einem Gesamtnennbetrag in Höhe des Gesamtnennbetrags der anderen Aktien ausgegeben werden.

§ 140. Rechte der Vorzugsaktionäre

(1) Die Vorzugsaktien ohne Stimmrecht gewähren mit Ausnahme des Stimmrechts die jedem Aktionär aus der Aktie zustehenden Rechte.

(2) Wird der Vorzugsbetrag in einem Jahr nicht oder nicht vollständig gezahlt und der Rückstand im nächsten Jahr nicht n

SUBDIVISION SIX. NON-VOTING PREFERRED SHARES

§ 139. Nature

(1) Shares which carry the benefit of a cumulative preference right with respect to the distribution of profits may be issued without voting rights ('non-voting preferred shares').

(2) Non-voting preferred shares may be issued only up to an aggregate par value equal to the aggregate par value of all other shares.

§ 140. Rights of Preferred Shareholders

(1) Except for the right to vote, non-voting preferred shares shall convey the same rights as those enjoyed by the other shareholders.

(2) If the preferred dividend is not paid or not paid in full in any given year and if the amounts in arrear are not paid

eben dem vollen Vorzug dieses Jahres nachgezahlt, so haben die Vorzugsaktionäre das Stimmrecht, bis die Rückstände nachgezahlt sind. In diesem Fall sind die Vorzugsaktien auch bei der Berechnung einer nach Gesetz oder Satzung erforderlichen Kapitalmehrheit zu berücksichtigen.

(3) Soweit die Satzung nichts anderes bestimmt, entsteht dadurch, daß der Vorzugsbetrag in einem Jahr nicht oder nicht vollständig gezahlt wird, noch kein durch spätere Beschlüsse über die Gewinnverteilung bedingter Anspruch auf den rückständigen Vorzugsbetrag.

in the next following year, together with the full preferred dividend for such year, the holders of preferred shares shall have voting rights until the amounts in arrear have been paid. In such case, the preferred shares shall also be taken into account in computing any capital majority required by law or the articles.

(3) The fact that a preferred dividend is not paid or not paid in full in any given year shall not give rise to a claim for any preferred dividend in arrear which is contingent upon later resolutions on distribution of profits, unless the articles provide otherwise.

§ 141. Aufhebung oder Beschränkung des Vorzugs

(1) Ein Beschluß, durch den der Vorzug aufgehoben oder beschränkt wird, bedarf zu seiner Wirksamkeit der Zustimmung der Vorzugsaktionäre.

(2) Ein Beschluß über die Ausgabe von Vorzugsaktien, die bei der Verteilung des Gewinns oder des Gesellschaftsvermögens den Vorzugsaktien ohne Stimmrecht vorgehen oder gleichstehen, bedarf gleichfalls der Zustimmung der Vorzugsaktionäre. Der Zustimmung bedarf es nicht, wenn die Ausgabe bei Einräumung des Vorzugs oder, falls das Stimmrecht später ausgeschlossen wurde, bei der Ausschließung ausdrücklich vorbehalten worden war und das Bezugsrecht der Vorzugsaktionäre nicht ausgeschlossen wird.

(3) Über die Zustimmung haben die Vorzugsaktionäre in einer gesonderten Versammlung einen Sonderbeschluß zu fassen. Er bedarf einer Mehrheit, die mindestens drei Viertel der abgegebenen Stimmen umfaßt. Die Satzung kann we-

§ 141. Cancellation or Restriction of Preference Rights

(1) Any resolution cancelling or restricting a preference right shall require the consent of the holders of preferred shares in order to be effective.

(2) Any resolution to issue preferred shares which are to enjoy priority over or the same rights as non-voting preferred shares in respect of the distribution of profits or assets, shall also require the consent of the holders of preferred shares. Such consent shall not be required if such issue was expressly reserved when the preference right was granted or, if the voting rights were later excluded, when such exclusion was made, provided, in any such case, that the pre-emptive rights of the holders of preferred shares are not excluded.

(3) The holders of preferred shares shall at a separate meeting resolve on whether or not to grant such consent by separate resolution. Such resolution shall require a majority of not less than three fourths of the votes cast. The articles may

der eine andere Mehrheit noch weitere Erfordernisse bestimmen. Wird in dem Beschluß über die Ausgabe von Vorzugsaktien, die bei der Verteilung des Gewinns oder des Gesellschaftsvermögens den Vorzugsaktien ohne Stimmrecht vorgehen oder gleichstehen, das Bezugsrecht der Vorzugsaktionäre auf den Bezug solcher Aktien ganz oder zum Teil ausgeschlossen, so gilt für den Sonderbeschluß § 186 Abs. 3 bis 5 sinngemäß.

neither provide for any other majority nor prescribe any additional requirements. If the resolution to issue preferred shares which are to enjoy priority over or the same rights as non-voting preferred shares in respect of the distribution of profits or assets excludes the pre-emptive rights of the holders of preferred shares to subscribe to such shares in whole or in part, § 186 (3) to (5) shall apply analogously to such resolution.

(4) Ist der Vorzug aufgehoben, so gewähren die Aktien das Stimmrecht.

(4) The shares shall carry voting rights if the preference is cancelled.

SIEBENTER UNTERABSCHNITT. SONDERPRÜFUNG. GELTENDMACHUNG VON ERSATZANSPRÜCHEN

SUBDIVISION SEVEN. SPECIAL AUDIT; CLAIMS FOR DAMAGES

§ 142. Bestellung der Sonderprüfer

§ 142. Appointment of Special Auditors

(1) Zur Prüfung von Vorgängen bei der Gründung oder der Geschäftsführung, namentlich auch bei Maßnahmen der Kapitalbeschaffung und Kapitalherabsetzung, kann die Hauptversammlung mit einfacher Stimmenmehrheit Prüfer (Sonderprüfer) bestellen. Bei der Beschlußfassung kann ein Mitglied des Vorstands oder des Aufsichtsrats weder für sich noch für einen anderen mitstimmen, wenn die Prüfung sich auf Vorgänge erstrecken soll, die mit der Entlastung eines Mitglieds des Vorstands oder des Aufsichtsrats oder der Einleitung eines Rechtsstreits zwischen der Gesellschaft und einem Mitglied des Vorstands oder des Aufsichtsrats zusammenhängen. Für ein Mitglied des Vorstands oder des Aufsichtsrats, das nach Satz 2 nicht mitstimmen kann, kann das Stimmrecht auch nicht durch einen anderen ausgeübt werden.

(1) The shareholders' meeting may, by simple majority, appoint auditors ('special auditors') for the examination of matters relating to the formation of the company or the management of the company's business, and also, in particular in connection with capital increases or capital reductions. No member of the management board or the supervisory board may vote on any such resolution either on his own behalf or on behalf of another person, if the audit concerns matters related to ratification of the acts of a member of the management board or the supervisory board or to the institution of litigation between the company and a member of the management board or the supervisory board. If a member of the management board or the supervisory board shall not be entitled to vote pursuant to sentence 2, such person's voting rights may not be exercised by another person on his behalf.

(2) Lehnt die Hauptversammlung einen Antrag auf Bestellung von Sonder-

(2) If the shareholders' meeting shall reject a motion to appoint special auditors

prüfern zur Prüfung eines Vorgangs bei der Gründung oder eines nicht über fünf Jahre zurückliegenden Vorgangs bei der Geschäftsführung ab, so hat das Gericht auf Antrag von Aktionären, deren Anteile zusammen den zehnten Teil des Grundkapitals oder den Nennbetrag von zwei Millionen Deutsche Mark erreichen, Sonderprüfer zu bestellen, wenn Tatsachen vorliegen, die den Verdacht rechtfertigen, daß bei dem Vorgang Unredlichkeiten oder grobe Verletzungen des Gesetzes oder der Satzung vorgekommen sind. Die Antragsteller haben die Aktien bis zur Entscheidung über den Antrag zu hinterlegen und glaubhaft zu machen, daß sie seit mindestens drei Monaten vor dem Tage der Hauptversammlung Inhaber der Aktien sind. Zur Glaubhaftmachung genügt eine eidesstattliche Versicherung vor einem Notar.

to audit any matter relating to the formation of the company or the management of the company's business which has occurred within the past five years, the court shall, upon motion by shareholders whose aggregate holdings equal or exceed one tenth of the share capital or the par value of two million Deutsche Mark, appoint special auditors, provided that facts exist which give reason to suspect that improprieties or gross violations of law or the articles have occured in connection with such matter. The parties making motion shall deposit their shares until a decision on the motion has been rendered and furnish evidence that they have been holders of such shares for not less than three months prior to the date of the shareholders' meeting. An affidavit made before a notary shall constitute sufficient evidence.

(3) Die Absätze 1 und 2 gelten nicht für Vorgänge, die Gegenstand einer Sonderprüfung nach § 258 sein können.

(3) Subsections (1) and (2) shall not apply to matters which may be the subject of a special audit pursuant to § 258.

(4) Hat die Hauptversammlung Sonderprüfer bestellt, so hat das Gericht auf Antrag von Aktionären, deren Anteile zusammen den zehnten Teil des Grundkapitals oder den Nennbetrag von zwei Millionen Deutsche Mark erreichen, einen anderen Sonderprüfer zu bestellen, wenn dies aus einem in der Person des bestellten Sonderprüfers liegenden Grund geboten erscheint, insbesondere, wenn der bestellte Sonderprüfer nicht die für den Gegenstand der Sonderprüfung erforderlichen Kenntnisse hat, oder wenn Besorgnis der Befangenheit oder Bedenken gegen seine Zuverlässigkeit bestehen. Der Antrag ist binnen zwei Wochen seit dem Tage der Hauptversammlung zu stellen.

(4) If the shareholders' meeting has appointed special auditors, the court shall, upon motion by shareholders whose aggregate holdings equal or exceed one tenth of the share capital or the par value of two million Deutsche Mark, appoint another special auditor if this appears necessary for reasons relating to the person of the special auditor appointed, in particular if such auditor lacks the expertise required for the subject matter of the special audit or if concern as to his impartiality or doubts as to his reliability exist. Such motion shall be made within a period of two weeks from the date of the shareholders' meeting.

(5) Das Gericht hat außer den Beteiligten auch den Aufsichtsrat und im Fall des Absatzes 4 den von der Hauptversammlung bestellten Sonderprüfer zu hö-

(5) The court shall hear, in addition to the parties concerned, the supervisory board and, in the case of subsection (4), the special auditor appointed by the

ren. Gegen die Entscheidung ist die sofortige Beschwerde zulässig.

(6) Die vom Gericht bestellten Sonderprüfer haben Anspruch auf Ersatz angemessener barer Auslagen und auf Vergütung für ihre Tätigkeit. Die Auslagen und die Vergütung setzt das Gericht fest. Gegen die Entscheidung ist die sofortige Beschwerde zulässig. Die weitere Beschwerde ist ausgeschlossen. Aus der rechtskräftigen Entscheidung findet die Zwangsvollstreckung nach der Zivilprozeßordnung statt.

shareholders' meeting. An immediate appeal may be made against the decision.

(6) Special auditors appointed by the court shall be entitled to reimbursement of reasonable cash expenses and remuneration for their services. The expenses and remuneration shall be set by the court. An immediate appeal may be made against the decision. Further appeal shall be precluded. A decision which is final and may not be appealed may be enforced in accordance with the Code of Civil Procedure.

§ 143. Auswahl der Sonderprüfer

(1) Als Sonderprüfer sollen, wenn der Gegenstand der Sonderprüfung keine anderen Kenntnisse fordert, nur bestellt werden

1. Personen, die in der Buchführung ausreichend vorgebildet und erfahren sind;
2. Prüfungsgesellschaften, von deren gesetzlichen Vertretern mindestens einer in der Buchführung ausreichend vorgebildet und erfahren ist.

(2) Sonderprüfer darf nicht sein, wer nach § 319 Abs. 2 des Handelsgesetzbuchs nicht Abschlußprüfer sein darf oder während der Zeit, in der sich der zu prüfende Vorgang ereignet hat, hätte sein dürfen. Eine Prüfungsgesellschaft darf nicht Sonderprüfer sein, wenn sie nach § 319 Abs. 3 des Handelsgesetzbuchs nicht Abschlußprüfer sein darf oder während der Zeit, in der sich der zu prüfende Vorgang ereignet hat, hätte sein dürfen.

(3) (*aufgehoben*)

§ 143. Selection of Special Auditors

(1) Unless the subject matter of the special audit requires additional expertise, special auditors shall be:

1. persons who are sufficiently trained and experienced in accounting;
2. auditing firms at least one of whose legal representatives is sufficiently trained and experienced in accounting.

(2) No special auditor may be appointed who does not qualify to serve, or would not have qualified to serve at the time when the matter subject to the audit occurred, as external auditor pursuant to § 319 (2) of the Commercial Code. An auditing firm may not serve as special auditor if it does not qualify to serve, or would not have qualified to serve at the time when the matter subject to the audit occurred, as external auditor pursuant to § 319 (3) of the Commercial Code.

(3) (*repealed*)

§ 144. Verantwortlichkeit der Sonderprüfer

§323 des Handelsgesetzbuchs über die Verantwortlichkeit des Abschlußprüfers gilt sinngemäß.

§ 144. Responsibility of Special Auditors

§ 323 of the Commercial Code concerning the responsibility of external auditors shall apply analogously.

§ 145. Rechte der Sonderprüfer. Prüfungsbericht

(1) Der Vorstand hat den Sonderprüfern zu gestatten, die Bücher und Schriften der Gesellschaft sowie die Vermögensgegenstände, namentlich die Gesellschaftskasse und die Bestände an Wertpapieren und Waren, zu prüfen.

(2) Die Sonderprüfer können von den Mitgliedern des Vorstands und des Aufsichtsrats alle Aufklärungen und Nachweise verlangen, welche die sorgfältige Prüfung der Vorgänge notwendig macht.

(3) Die Sonderprüfer haben die Rechte nach Absatz 2 auch gegenüber einem Konzernunternehmen sowie gegenüber einem abhängigen oder herrschenden Unternehmen.

(4) Die Sonderprüfer haben über das Ergebnis der Prüfung schriftlich zu berichten. Auch Tatsachen, deren Bekanntwerden geeignet ist, der Gesellschaft oder einem verbundenen Unternehmen einen nicht unerheblichen Nachteil zuzufügen, müssen in den Prüfungsbericht aufgenommen werden, wenn ihre Kenntnis zur Beurteilung des zu prüfenden Vorgangs durch die Hauptversammlung erforderlich ist. Die Sonderprüfer haben den Bericht zu unterzeichnen und unverzüglich dem Vorstand und zum Handelsregister des Sitzes der Gesellschaft einzureichen. Auf Verlangen hat der Vorstand jedem Aktionär eine Abschrift des Prüfungsberichts zu erteilen. Der Vorstand

§ 145. Rights of Special Auditors; Audit Report

(1) The management board shall permit the special auditors to audit the company's book and records and its assets, in particular cash, securities and merchandise.

(2) The special auditors may require from the members of the management board and the supervisory board all information and evidence required for a diligent audit of the relevant matters.

(3) The special auditors shall have the rights pursuant to subsection (2) also with respect to any member of the group and any controlled or controlling enterprises.

(4) The special auditors shall report in writing on the result of the audit. The audit report shall include facts whose disclosure is apt to cause material damage to the company or an affiliated enterprise, provided that knowledge of such facts is required for the shareholders' meeting in order to form an opinion as to the matter subject to audit. The special auditors shall sign the report and promptly submit such report to the management board and the commercial register of the company's domicile. The management board shall upon request provide a copy of the audit report to each shareholder. The management board shall present the report to the supervisory board and, when the next

hat den Bericht dem Aufsichtsrat vorzulegen und bei der Einberufung der nächsten Hauptversammlung als Gegenstand der Tagesordnung bekanntzumachen.

shareholders' meeting is called, announce that such report will be an item on the agenda.

§ 146. Kosten

Bestellt das Gericht Sonderprüfer, so trägt die Gesellschaft unbeschadet eines ihr nach den Vorschriften des bürgerlichen Rechts zustehenden Ersatzanspruchs die Gerichtskosten und die Kosten der Prüfung.

§ 146. Costs

If the court appoints special auditors, the company shall bear the court costs and the expenses of the audit without prejudice to any claim for reimbursement which the company may have pursuant to the provisions of civil law.

§ 147. Geltendmachung von Ersatzansprüchen

(1) Die Eratzansprüche der Gesellschaft aus der Gründung gegen die nach den §§ 46 bis 48, 53 verpflichteten Personen oder aus der Geschäftsführung gegen die Mitglieder des Vorstands und des Aufsichtsrats oder aus § 117 müssen geltend gemacht werden, wenn es die Hauptversammlung mit einfacher Stimmenmehrheit beschließt oder es eine Minderheit verlangt, deren Anteile zusammen den zehnten Teil des Grundkapitals erreichen. Das Verlangen der Minderheit ist nur zu berücksichtigen, wenn glaubhaft gemacht wird, daß die Aktionäre, die die Minderheit bilden, seit mindestens drei Monaten vor dem Tage der Hauptversammlung Inhaber der Aktien sind. Zur Glaubhaftmachung genügt eine eidesstattliche Versicherung vor einem Notar.

(2) Der Ersatzanspruch soll binnen sechs Monaten seit dem Tage der Hauptversammlung geltend gemacht werden.

(3) Zur Geltendmachung des Ersatzanspruchs kann die Hauptversammlung

§ 147. Damage Claims

(1) Claims of the company for compensation of damages against persons liable pursuant to §§ 46 to 48 and 53 which have arisen in connection with the formation of the company or which have arisen in connection with the management of the company or pursuant to § 117 against members of the management board or the supervisory board, shall be asserted if the shareholders' meeting so resolves by simple majority or if a minority, whose aggregate holdings equal or exceed one tenth of the share capital, so requests. Such request by a minority shall be acted upon only if evidence is furnished that the shareholders who constitute the minority have been holders of the shares for not less than three months prior to the date of the shareholders' meeting. An affidavit made before a notary shall constitute sufficient evidence.

(2) Any claims for compensation of damages shall be brought within six months from the date of the shareholders' meeting.

(3) The shareholders' meeting may appoint special representatives to assert a

besondere Vertreter bestellen. Hat die Hauptversammlung die Geltendmachung des Ersatzanspruchs beschlossen oder eine Minderheit sie verlangt, so hat das Gericht (§ 14) auf Antrag von Aktionären, deren Anteile zusammen den zehnten Teil des Grundkapitals oder den Nennbetrag von zwei Millionen Deutsche Mark erreichen, als Vertreter der Gesellschaft zur Geltendmachung des Ersatzanspruchs andere als die nach §§ 78, 112 oder nach Satz 1 zur Vertretung der Gesellschaft berufenen Personen zu bestellen, wenn ihm dies für eine gehörige Geltendmachung zweckmäßig erscheint. Gibt das Gericht dem Antrag statt, so trägt die Gesellschaft die Gerichtskosten. Gegen die Entscheidung ist die sofortige Beschwerde zulässig. Die gerichtlich bestellten Vertreter können von der Gesellschaft den Ersatz angemessener barer Auslagen und eine Vergütung für ihre Tätigkeit verlangen. Die Auslagen und die Vergütung setzt das Gericht fest. Gegen die Entscheidung ist die sofortige Beschwerde zulässig. Die weitere Beschwerde ist ausgeschlossen. Aus der rechtskräftigen Entscheidung findet die Zwangsvollstreckung nach der Zivilprozeßordnung statt.

(4) Hat eine Minderheit die Geltendmachung des Ersatzanspruchs verlangt und hat die Gesellschaft, weil sie im Rechtsstreit ganz oder teilweise unterlegen ist, Kosten des Rechtsstreits zu tragen, so ist die Minderheit der Gesellschaft zur Erstattung dieser Kosten verpflichtet. Ist die Gesellschaft ganz unterlegen, so ist die Minderheit der Gesellschaft auch zur Erstattung der Gerichtskosten, die der Gesellschaft durch die Bestellung besonderer Vertreter nach Absatz 3 Satz 3 entstanden sind, sowie der baren Auslagen und der Vergütung der besonderen Vertreter verpflichtet.

claim for damages. If the shareholders' meeting has resolved to assert such claim for damages or a minority has so requested, the court (§ 14) shall, upon motion by shareholders whose aggregate holdings equal or exceed one tenth of the share capital or the par value of two million Deutsche Mark, appoint persons other than those authorized to represent the company pursuant to §§ 78 or 112 or sentence 1 as the company's representatives to assert the claim for damages, if in the opinion of the court such appointment is appropriate for the proper assertion of such claim. If the court grants the motion, the company shall bear the court costs. An immediate appeal may be made against the decision. The court-appointed representatives may request from the company reimbursement of reasonable cash expenses and remuneration for their services. The court shall set such expenses and remuneration. An immediate appeal may be made against the decision. Further appeal shall be precluded. A decision which is final and which may not be appealed may be enforced in accordance with the Code of Civil Procedure.

(4) If a minority has requested that a claim for damages be asserted and the company shall be required to bear the costs of the litigation because it has been unsuccessfull in the litigation in whole or in part, the minority shall be obligated to reimburse such costs to the company. If the company has been completely unsuccessful, the minority shall also reimburse to the company the court costs incurred by the company in connection with the appointment of special representatives pursuant to subsection (3) sentence 3 and the cash expenses and remuneration of such special representatives.

Fünfter Teil. Rechnungslegung. Gewinnverwendung

Erster Abschnitt. Jahresabschluß und Lagebericht

§§ 148-149. (aufgehoben)

§ 150. Gesetzliche Rücklage. Kapitalrücklage

(**1**) In der Bilanz des nach den §§ 242, 264 des Handelsgesetzbuchs aufzustellenden Jahresabschlusses ist eine gesetzliche Rücklage zu bilden.

(**2**) In diese ist der zwanzigste Teil des um einen Verlustvortrag aus dem Vorjahr geminderten Jahresüberschusses einzustellen, bis die gesetzliche Rücklage und die Kapitalrücklagen nach § 272 Abs. 2 Nr. 1 bis 3 des Handelsgesetzbuchs zusammen den zehnten oder den in der Satzung bestimmten höheren Teil des Grundkapitals erreichen.

(**3**) Übersteigen die gesetzliche Rücklage und die Kapitalrücklagen nach § 272 Abs. 2 Nr. 1 bis 3 des Handelsgesetzbuchs zusammen nicht den zehnten oder den in der Satzung bestimmten höheren Teil des Grundkapitals, so dürfen sie nur verwandt werden

1. zum Ausgleich eines Jahresfehlbetrags, soweit er nicht durch einen Gewinnvortrag aus dem Vorjahr gedeckt ist und nicht durch Auflösung anderer Gewinnrücklagen ausgeglichen werden kann;
2. zum Ausgleich eines Verlustvortrags aus dem Vorjahr, soweit er nicht durch einen Jahresüberschuß gedeckt ist und nicht durch Auflösung anderer Gewinnrücklagen ausgeglichen werden kann.

(**4**) Übersteigen die gesetzliche Rücklage und die Kapitalrücklagen nach

Part Five. Accounting; Appropriation of Profit

Division One. Annual Financial Statements and Annual Report

§§ 148-149. (repealed)

§ 150. Legal Reserve; Capital Reserve

(**1**) A legal reserve shall be created in the balance sheet of the annual financial statements to be prepared pursuant to §§ 242 and 264 of the Commercial Code.

(**2**) The amount to be transferred to such reserve shall be one twentieth of annual net profit, after deducting any loss carried forward from the previous year, until the legal reserve and the capital reserves pursuant to § 272 (2) Nos. 1 to 3 of the Commercial Code in aggregate amount to one tenth of the share capital or any higher percentage set by the articles.

(**3**) If the legal reserve and the capital reserves pursuant to § 272 (2) Nos. 1 to 3 of the Commercial Code in aggregate do not exceed one tenth or the share capital or any higher percentage set by the articles, such reserves may be used only:

1. to offset an annual net loss to the extent such loss is not covered by profits carried forward from the previous year and cannot be offset by a transfer from other profit reserves;
2. to offset a loss carried forward from the previous year to the extent such loss is not offset by annual net profit and cannot be offset by a transfer from other profit reserves.

(**4**) If the legal reserve and the capital reserves pursuant to § 272 (2) Nos. 1 to 3

§ 272 Abs. 2 Nr. 1 bis 3 des Handelsgesetzbuchs zusammen den zehnten oder den in der Satzung bestimmten höheren Teil des Grundkapitals, so darf der übersteigende Betrag verwandt werden

1. zum Ausgleich eines Jahresfehlbetrags, soweit er nicht durch einen Gewinnvortrag aus dem Vorjahr gedeckt ist;

2. zum Ausgleich eines Verlustvortrags aus dem Vorjahr, soweit er nicht durch einen Jahresüberschuß gedeckt ist;

3. zur Kapitalerhöhung aus Gesellschaftsmitteln nach den §§ 207 bis 220.

Die Verwendung nach den Nummern 1 und 2 ist nicht zulässig, wenn gleichzeitig Gewinnrücklagen zur Gewinnausschüttung aufgelöst werden.

of the Commercial Code in aggregate exceed one tenth of the share capital or any higher percentage set by the articles, such excess may be used:

1. to cover an annual net loss to the extent such loss is not covered by profits carried forward from the previous year;

2. to cover a loss carried forward from the previous year to the extent such loss is not covered by annual net profit;

3. for an increase of the share capital from the corporation's reserves under §§ 207 to 220.

Such excess may not be used pursuant to Nos. 1 and 2 if at the same time transfers are made from profit reserves for the purpose of payment of dividends.

§§ 150a, 151. (aufgehoben)

§§ 150a, 151. (repealed)

§ 152. Vorschriften zur Bilanz

(1) Das Grundkapital ist in der Bilanz als gezeichnetes Kapital auszuweisen. Dabei sind die Gesamtnennbeträge der Aktien jeder Gattung gesondert anzugeben. Bedingtes Kapital ist mit dem Nennbetrag zu vermerken. Bestehen Mehrstimmrechtsaktien, so sind beim gezeichneten Kapital die Gesamtstimmenzahl der Mehrstimmrechtsaktien und die der übrigen Aktien zu vermerken.

(2) Zu dem Posten 'Kapitalrücklage' sind in der Bilanz oder im Anhang gesondert anzugeben

1. der Betrag, der während des Geschäftsjahrs eingestellt wurde;

2. der Betrag, der für das Geschäftsjahr entnommen wird.

(3) Zu den einzelnen Posten der Gewinnrücklagen sind in der Bilanz oder im Anhang jeweils gesondert anzugeben

1. die Beträge, die die Hauptversamm-

§ 152. Provisions regarding the Balance Sheet

(1) The share capital shall be shown in the balance sheet as subscribed capital. The aggregate par value of shares of each class shall be stated separately. Contingent capital shall be indicated at par value. If shares with multiple voting rights exist, the item 'subscribed capital' shall indicate the aggregate number of votes of shares with multiple voting rights and other shares.

(2) The item 'capital reserve' shall specify in the balance sheet or in the notes:

1. the amount which was transferred to such reserve during the fiscal year;

2. the amount which was withdrawn during the fiscal year.

(3) The individual items for profit reserves shall specify in the balance sheet or in the notes:

1. the amounts which the shareholders'

lung aus dem Bilanzgewinn des Vorjahrs eingestellt hat;

2. die Beträge, die aus dem Jahresüberschuß des Geschäftsjahrs eingestellt werden;

3. die Beträge, die für das Geschäftsjahr entnommen werden.

meeting has transferred to such reserves from the distributable profits of the previous year;

2. the amounts which are transferred to such reserves from the annual net profit for the fiscal year;

3. the amounts which were withdrawn for the fiscal year.

§§ 153 – 157. (aufgehoben)

§§ 153 – 157. (repealed)

§ 158. Vorschriften zur Gewinn- und Verlustrechnung

(**1**) Die Gewinn- und Verlustrechnung ist nach dem Posten 'Jahresüberschuß/Jahresfehlbetrag' in Fortführung der Numerierung um die folgenden Posten zu ergänzen:

1. Gewinnvortrag/Verlustvortrag aus dem Vorjahr
2. Entnahmen aus der Kapitalrücklage
3. Entnahmen aus Gewinnrücklagen
(a) aus der gesetzlichen Rücklage
(b) aus der Rücklage für eigene Aktien
(c) aus satzungsmäßigen Rücklagen
(d) aus anderen Gewinnrücklagen
4. Einstellungen in Gewinnrücklagen
(a) in die gesetzliche Rücklage
(b) in die Rücklage für eigene Aktien
(c) in satzungsmäßige Rücklagen
(d) in andere Gewinnrücklagen
5. Bilanzgewinn/Bilanzverlust.

Die Angaben nach Satz 1 können auch im Anhang gemacht werden.

(**2**) Von dem Ertrag aus einem Gewinnabführungs- oder Teilgewinnabführungsvertrag ist ein vertraglich zu leistender Ausgleich für außenstehende Gesellschafter abzusetzen; übersteigt dieser den Ertrag, so ist der übersteigende Betrag unter den Aufwendungen aus Verlustüber-

§ 158. Provisions regarding the Profit and Loss Statement

(**1**) The profit and loss statement shall after the item 'Annual net profit/annual net loss' in consecutive numeration include the following items:

1. profit carried forward/loss carried forward from the previous year
2. withdrawals from the capital reserve
3. withdrawals from profit reserves
(a) from the legal reserve
(b) from the reserve for company shares held by the company
(c) from reserves pursuant to the articles
(d) from other profit reserves
4. transfers to profit reserves
(a) to the legal reserve
(b) to the reserve for company shares held by the company
(c) to reserves pursuant to the articles
(d) to other profit reserves
5. distributable profits/accumulated loss.

The items in sentence 1 may also be stated in the notes.

(**2**) The compensation to be paid under a profit transfer agreement or agreement to transfer a portion of profits to outside shareholders shall be deducted from the income out of such agreement; if such compensation exceeds the income, the amount in excess shall be

nahme auszuweisen. Andere Beträge dürfen nicht abgesetzt werden.

§ 159. (aufgehoben)

§ 160. Vorschriften zum Anhang

(1) In jedem Anhang sind auch Angaben zu machen über

1. den Bestand und den Zugang an Aktien, die ein Aktionär für Rechnung der Gesellschaft oder eines abhängigen oder eines im Mehrheitsbesitz der Gesellschaft stehenden Unternehmens oder ein abhängiges oder im Mehrheitsbesitz der Gesellschaft stehendes Unternehmen als Gründer oder Zeichner oder in Ausübung eines bei einer bedingten Kapitalerhöhung eingeräumten Umtausch- oder Bezugsrechts übernommen hat; sind solche Aktien im Geschäftsjahr verwertet worden, so ist auch über die Verwertung unter Angabe des Erlöses und die Verwendung des Erlöses zu berichten;

2. den Bestand an eigenen Aktien der Gesellschaft, die sie, ein abhängiges oder im Mehrheitsbesitz der Gesellschaft stehendes Unternehmen oder ein anderer für Rechnung der Gesellschaft oder eines abhängigen oder eines im Mehrheitsbesitz der Gesellschaft stehenden Unternehmens erworben oder als Pfand genommen hat; dabei sind die Zahl und der Nennbetrag dieser Aktien sowie deren Anteil am Grundkapital, für erworbene Aktien ferner der Zeitpunkt des Erwerbs und die Gründe für den Erwerb anzugeben. Sind solche Aktien im Geschäftsjahr erworben oder veräußert worden, so ist auch über den Erwerb oder die Veräußerung unter Angabe der Zahl und des Nennbetrags dieser Aktien, des Anteils am Grundkapital und des Erwerbs- oder Veräußerungspreises, sowie über die Verwendung des Erlöses zu berichten;

3. die Zahl und den Nennbetrag der Aktien jeder Gattung, sofern sich diese An-

shown under expenses from losses. Other amounts may not be deducted.

§ 159. (repealed)

§ 160. Provisions regarding the Notes

(1) The notes shall also include:

1. the shares previously held and acquired by a shareholder on behalf of the company or a controlled enterprise or subsidiary, or by a controlled enterprise or subsidiary, as incorporator or subscriber or by exercise of a conversion or pre-emptive right granted in connection with a contingent capital increase; if such shares were sold during the fiscal year, the sale shall also be reported stating the amount of the proceeds and the use thereof;

2. the company shares which the company, or a controlled enterprise or subsidiary or another person on behalf of the company or a controlled enterprise or a subsidiary has acquired or taken as a pledge; the number and par value of such shares and the portion of share capital represented thereby, and in the case of shares acquired the date of acquisition and reasons for the acquisition shall be stated. If such shares were acquired or sold during the fiscal year, such acquisition or sale shall also be reported stating the number and par value of such shares, the proportion of share capital represented thereby, the acquisition or sales price and the use of the proceeds;

3. the number and par value of shares of each class, to the extent such informa-

gaben nicht aus der Bilanz ergeben; davon sind Aktien, die bei einer bedingten Kapitalerhöhung oder einem genehmigten Kapital im Geschäftsjahr gezeichnet wurden, jeweils gesondert anzugeben;

4. das genehmigte Kapital;

5. die Zahl der Wandelschuldverschreibungen und vergleichbaren Wertpapiere unter Angabe der Rechte, die sie verbriefen;

6. Genußrechte, Rechte aus Besserungsscheinen und ähnliche Rechte unter Angabe der Art und Zahl der jeweiligen Rechte sowie der im Geschäftsjahr neu entstandenen Rechte;

7. das Bestehen einer wechselseitigen Beteiligung unter Angabe des Unternehmens;

8. das Bestehen einer Beteiligung an der Gesellschaft, die ihr nach § 20 Abs. 1 oder 4 mitgeteilt worden ist; dabei ist anzugeben, wem die Beteiligung gehört und ob sie den vierten Teil aller Aktien der Gesellschaft übersteigt oder eine Mehrheitsbeteiligung (§ 16 Abs. 1) ist.

(**2**) Die Berichterstattung hat insoweit zu unterbleiben, als es für das Wohl der Bundesrepublik Deutschland oder eines ihrer Länder erforderlich ist.

§ 161. (aufgehoben)

Zweiter Abschnitt. Prüfung des Jahresabschlusses

ERSTER UNTERABSCHNITT. PRÜFUNG DURCH ABSCHLUßPRÜFER

§§ 162 – 169. (aufgehoben)

tion may not be derived from the balance sheet; shares which were subscribed during the fiscal year in connection with a contingent capital increase or an authorized issue of capital, shall be stated separately;

4. the authorized capital;

5. the number of convertible bonds, warrants and comparable securities describing the rights which they represent;

6. participation rights, rights from contingent participation certificates and similar rights describing the nature and number of the respective rights and the rights newly issued during the fiscal year;

7. the existence of a cross-shareholding indicating the enterprise concerned;

8. the existence of a shareholding in the company which has been communicated to it pursuant to § 20 (1) or (4); it shall be stated who holds the shares and whether such holding exceeds one fourth or a majority (§ 16 (1)) of the company's shares.

(**2**) Such information shall be omitted to the extent the public interest of the Federal Republic of Germany or one of the states thereof so requires.

§ 161. (repealed)

Division Two. Examination of Annual Financial Statements

SUBDIVISION ONE. EXAMINATION BY EXTERNAL AUDITORS

§§ 162 – 169. (repealed)

Zweiter Unterabschnitt. Prüfung durch den Aufsichtsrat

Subdivision Two. Examination by the Supervisory Board

§ 170. Vorlage an den Aufsichtsrat

(1) Der Vorstand hat den Jahresabschluß und den Lagebericht unverzüglich nach ihrer Aufstellung dem Aufsichtsrat vorzulegen. Ist der Jahresabschluß durch einen Abschlußprüfer zu prüfen, so sind diese Unterlagen zusammen mit dem Prüfungsbericht des Abschlußprüfers unverzüglich nach dem Eingang des Prüfungsberichts dem Aufsichtsrat vorzulegen.

(2) Zugleich hat der Vorstand dem Aufsichtsrat den Vorschlag vorzulegen, den er der Hauptversammlung für die Verwendung des Bilanzgewinns machen will. Der Vorschlag ist, sofern er keine abweichende Gliederung bedingt, wie folgt zu gliedern:

1. Verteilung an die Aktionäre ....
2. Einstellung in Gewinnrücklagen......
3. Gewinnvortrag...............................
4. Bilanzgewinn..................................

(3) Jedes Aufsichtsratsmitglied hat das Recht, von den Vorlagen Kenntnis zu nehmen. Die Vorlagen sind auch jedem Aufsichtsratsmitglied auf Verlangen auszuhändigen, soweit der Aufsichtsrat nichts anderes beschlossen hat.

§ 170. Submission to the Supervisory Board

(1) The management board shall promptly submit the annual financial statements and the annual report to the supervisory board upon completion. If the annual financial statements are required to be audited by external auditors, the annual financial statements and the annual report shall be submitted to the supervisory board together with the audit report of the external auditor promptly upon receipt of such audit report.

(2) The management board shall at the same time submit to the supervisory board the proposal for appropriation of distributable profits which is intended to be presented to the shareholders' meeting. The proposal shall, unless circumstances require otherwise, be set out as follows:

1. dividends ....
2. transfer to profit reserves ....
3. profit carried forward ....
4. distributable profits ....

(3) Every member of the supervisory board shall be entitled to take cognizance of the documents submitted. Such documents shall also be delivered upon demand to every member of the supervisory board unless the supervisory board has decided otherwise.

§ 171. Prüfung durch den Aufsichtsrat

(1) Der Aufsichtsrat hat den Jahresabschluß, den Lagebericht und den Vorschlag für die Verwendung des Bilanzge-

§ 171. Examination by the Supervisory Board

(1) The supervisory board shall examine the annual financial statements, the annual report and the proposal for ap-

winns zu prüfen. Ist der Jahresabschluß durch einen Abschlußprüfer zu prüfen, so hat der Abschlußprüfer auf Verlangen des Aufsichtsrats an dessen Verhandlungen über diese Vorlagen teilzunehmen.

(2) Der Aufsichtsrat hat über das Ergebnis der Prüfung schriftlich an die Hauptversammlung zu berichten. In dem Bericht hat der Aufsichtsrat auch mitzuteilen, in welcher Art und in welchem Umfang er die Geschäftsführung der Gesellschaft während des Geschäftsjahrs geprüft hat. Ist der Jahresabschluß durch einen Abschlußprüfer zu prüfen, so hat der Aufsichtsrat ferner zu dem Ergebnis der Prüfung des Jahresabschlusses durch den Abschlußprüfer Stellung zu nehmen. Am Schluß des Berichts hat der Aufsichtsrat zu erklären, ob nach dem abschließenden Ergebnis seiner Prüfung Einwendungen zu erheben sind und ob er den vom Vorstand aufgestellten Jahresabschluß billigt.

(3) Der Aufsichtsrat hat seinen Bericht innerhalb eines Monats, nachdem ihm die Vorlagen zugegangen sind, dem Vorstand zuzuleiten. Wird der Bericht dem Vorstand nicht innerhalb der Frist zugeleitet, hat der Vorstand dem Aufsichtsrat unverzüglich eine weitere Frist von nicht mehr als einem Monat zu setzen. Wird der Bericht dem Vorstand nicht vor Ablauf der weiteren Frist zugeleitet, gilt der Jahresabschluß als vom Aufsichtsrat nicht gebilligt.

propriation of distributable profits. If the financial statements are required to be audited by external auditors, the external auditors shall upon demand by the supervisory board be present at its deliberations regarding such statements.

(2) The supervisory board shall report on the results of its examination in writing to the shareholders' meeting. The supervisory board shall in such report state in which manner and to what extent it has examined the management of the company during the fiscal year. If the annual financial statements are required to be audited by an external auditor, the supervisory board shall in addition state its opinion on the result of the audit of the annual financial statements by the external auditor. The supervisory board shall at the end of its report state whether or not objections are to be raised as a result of the definitive findings of its examination and whether it approves the annual financial statements as prepared by the management board.

(3) The supervisory board shall submit its report to the management board within one month after receipt of such statements. If the report has not been submitted to the management board within such period, the management board shall promplty set an additional period not exceeding one month for the supervisory board. If the report has not been submitted to the management board within such further period, the annual financial statements shall be deemed to have not been approved by the supervisory board.

Dritter Abschnitt. Feststellung des Jahresabschlusses. Gewinnverwendung

Division Three. Approval of Annual Financial Statements. Appropriation of Profits

ERSTER UNTERABSCHNITT. FESTSTELLUNG DES JAHRESABSCHLUSSES

SUBDIVISION ONE. APPROVAL OF ANNUAL FINANCIAL STATEMENTS

§ 172. Feststellung durch Vorstand und Aufsichtsrat

Billigt der Aufsichtsrat den Jahresabschluß, so ist dieser festgestellt, sofern nicht Vorstand und Aufsichtsrat beschließen, die Feststellung des Jahresabschlusses der Hauptversammlung zu überlassen. Die Beschlüsse des Vorstands und des Aufsichtsrats sind in den Bericht des Aufsichtsrats an die Hauptversammlung aufzunehmen.

§ 172. Approval by Management Board and Supervisory Board

The annual financial statements shall be deemed to have been approved upon approval thereof by the supervisory board, unless the management board and the supervisory board shall resolve that the annual financial statements are to be approved by the shareholders' meeting. Such resolution by the management board and supervisory board shall be included in the report of the supervisory board to the shareholders' meeting.

§ 173. Feststellung durch die Hauptversammlung

(1) Haben Vorstand und Aufsichtsrat beschlossen, die Feststellung des Jahresabschlusses der Hauptversammlung zu überlassen, oder hat der Aufsichtsrat den Jahresabschluß nicht gebilligt, so stellt die Hauptversammlung den Jahresabschluß fest.

(2) Auf den Jahresabschluß sind bei der Feststellung die für seine Aufstellung geltenden Vorschriften anzuwenden. Die Hauptversammlung darf bei der Feststellung des Jahresabschlusses nur die Beträge in Gewinnrücklagen einstellen, die nach Gesetz oder Satzung einzustellen sind.

§ 173. Approval by the Shareholders' Meeting

(1) The annual financial statements shall be approved by the shareholders' meeting if the management board and the supervisory board shall have resolved that the annual financial statements are to be approved by the shareholders' meeting or if the supervisory board has not approved the annual financial statements.

(2) The provisions governing the preparation of the annual financial statements shall apply to their approval. In connection with the approval of the annual financial statements the shareholders' meeting may transfer to profit reserves only those amounts which are required to be transferred to such reserves pursuant to law or the articles.

(3) Ändert die Hauptversammlung einen von einem Abschlußprüfer auf Grund gesetzlicher Verpflichtung geprüften Jahresabschluß, so werden vor der erneuten Prüfung nach § 316 Abs. 3 des Handelsgesetzbuchs von der Hauptversammlung gefaßte Beschlüsse über die Feststellung des Jahresabschlusses und die Gewinnverwendung erst wirksam, wenn auf Grund der erneuten Prüfung ein hinsichtlich der Änderungen uneingeschränkter Bestätigungsvermerk erteilt worden ist. Sie werden nichtig, wenn nicht binnen zwei Wochen seit der Beschlußfassung ein hinsichtlich der Änderungen uneingeschränkter Bestätigungsvermerk erteilt wird.

(3) If the shareholders' meeting amends annual financial statements which have been audited by an external auditor in accordance with statutory requirements, resolutions on the approval of the annual financial statements and the appropriation of profits which have been adopted by the shareholders' meeting prior to the new audit pursuant to § 316 (3) Commercial Code, shall become effective only if, as a result of such new audit, an unqualified auditors' certificate has been given with respect to such amendments. Such resolutions shall become null and void if an unqualified auditors' certificate has not been provided with respect to such amendments within two weeks after the passing of such resolutions.

Zweiter Unterabschnitt. Gewinnverwendung

Subdivision Two. Appropriation of Profits

§ 174.

(1) Die Hauptversammlung beschließt über die Verwendung des Bilanzgewinns. Sie ist hierbei an den festgestellten Jahresabschluß gebunden.

(2) In dem Beschluß ist die Verwendung des Bilanzgewinns im einzelnen darzulegen, namentlich sind anzugeben

1. der Bilanzgewinn;
2. der an die Aktionäre auszuschüttende Betrag;
3. die in Gewinnrücklagen einzustellenden Beträge;
4. ein Gewinnvortrag;
5. der zusätzliche Aufwand auf Grund des Beschlusses.

§ 174.

(1) The shareholders' meeting shall resolve on the appropriation of distributable profits. In such connection the annual financial statements as approved shall be binding on the shareholders' meeting.

(2) Such resolution shall specify in detail the appropriation of distributable profits, including in particular the following:

1. the amount of distributable profits;
2. the amount to be distributed to shareholders;
3. the amounts to be transferred to profit reserves;
4. any profit carried forward;
5. any additional expense resulting from such resolution.

(3) Der Beschluß führt nicht zu einer Änderung des festgestellten Jahresabschlusses.

(3) Such resolution shall not be deemed to constitute an amendment to the annual financial statements as approved.

DRITTER UNTERABSCHNITT. ORDENTLICHE HAUPTVERSAMMLUNG

SUBDIVISION THREE. ORDINARY SHAREHOLDERS' MEETING

§ 175. Einberufung

§ 175. Notice

(1) Unverzüglich nach Eingang des Berichts des Aufsichtsrats hat der Vorstand die Hauptversammlung zur Entgegennahme des festgestellten Jahresabschlusses und des Lageberichts sowie zur Beschlußfassung über die Verwendung eines Bilanzgewinns einzuberufen. Die Hauptversammlung hat in den ersten acht Monaten des Geschäftsjahrs stattzufinden.

(1) The management board shall, upon receipt of the report of the supervisory board, promptly give notice of a shareholders' meeting to receive the approved annual financial statements and the annual report and to resolve on the appropriation of distributable profits. Such shareholders' meeting shall be held during the first eight months of the fiscal year.

(2) Der Jahresabschluß, der Lagebericht, der Bericht des Aufsichtsrats und der Vorschlag des Vorstands für die Verwendung des Bilanzgewinns sind von der Einberufung an in dem Geschäftsraum der Gesellschaft zur Einsicht der Aktionäre auszulegen. Auf Verlangen ist jedem Aktionär unverzüglich eine Abschrift der Vorlagen zu erteilen.

(2) The annual financial statements, the annual report, the report of the supervisory board and the proposal of the management board regarding the appropriation of distributable profits shall be displayed for inspection by shareholders at the company's offices as from the date of notice of the meeting. Each shareholder shall upon request be provided with a copy of such documents.

(3) Hat die Hauptversammlung den Jahresabschluß festzustellen, so gelten für die Einberufung der Hauptversammlung zur Feststellung des Jahresabschlusses und für die Auslegung der Vorlagen und die Erteilung von Abschriften die Absätze 1 und 2 sinngemäß. Die Verhandlungen über die Feststellung des Jahresabschlusses und über die Verwendung des Bilanzgewinns sollen verbunden werden.

(3) If the shareholders' meeting is to approve the annual financial statements, subsections (1) and (2) shall apply analogously to notice of the shareholders' meeting for the approval of the annual financial statements, the display of the relevant documents and the provision of copies thereof. The deliberations on the approval of the annual financial statements and the appropriation of distributable profits should be combined.

(4) Mit der Einberufung der Hauptversammlung zur Entgegennahme des

(4) The management board and the supervisory board shall be bound by the

festgestellten Jahresabschlusses oder, wenn die Hauptversammlung den Jahresabschluß festzustellen hat, der Hauptversammlung zur Feststellung des Jahresabschlusses sind Vorstand und Aufsichtsrat an die in dem Bericht des Aufsichtsrats enthaltenen Erklärungen über den Jahresabschluß (§§ 172, 173 Abs. 1) gebunden.

statements regarding the annual financial statements contained in the report of the supervisory board (§§ 172, 173 (1)) as from the date of notice of the shareholders' meeting for receipt of the approved annual financial statements or, if the shareholders' meeting is to approve the annual financial statements, as from the date of the shareholders' meeting for approval of the annual financial statements.

§ 176. Vorlagen. Anwesenheit des Abschlußprüfers

(1) Der Vorstand hat der Hauptversammlung die in § 175 Abs. 2 angegebenen Vorlagen vorzulegen. Zu Beginn der Verhandlung soll der Vorstand seine Vorlagen, der Vorsitzende des Aufsichtsrats den Bericht des Aufsichtsrats erläutern. Der Vorstand soll dabei auch zu einem Jahresfehlbetrag oder einem Verlust Stellung nehmen, der das Jahresergebnis wesentlich beeinträchtigt hat. Satz 3 ist auf Kreditinstitute nicht anzuwenden.

(2) Ist der Jahresabschluß von einem Abschlußprüfer zu prüfen, so hat der Abschlußprüfer an den Verhandlungen über die Feststellung des Jahresabschlusses teilzunehmen. Der Abschlußprüfer ist nicht verpflichtet, einem Aktionär Auskunft zu erteilen.

§ 176. Documents to be Presented, Presence of External Auditors

(1) The management board shall present to the shareholders' meeting the documents specified in § 175 (2). At the beginning of the meeting, the management board shall comment on the documents which have been presented by it and the chairman of the supervisory board shall comment on the report of the supervisory board. The management board shall in such connection also comment on any annual net loss or any loss which has materially adversely affected the annual result. Sentence 3 shall not apply to credit institutions.

(2) If the annual financial statements are required to be audited by an external auditor, the external auditor shall be present at the deliberations on the approval of the annual financial statements. The external auditor shall not be obligated to provide information to any shareholder.

Vierter Abschnitt. Bekanntmachung des Jahresabschlusses

§§ 177, 178. (aufgehoben)

Division Four. Publication of Annual Financial Statements

§§ 177, 178. (repealed)

Sechster Teil. Satzungsänderung. Maßnahmen der Kapitalbeschaffung und Kapitalherabsetzung

Erster Abschnitt. Satzungsänderung

§ 179. Beschluß der Hauptversammlung

(1) Jede Satzungsänderung bedarf eines Beschlusses der Hauptversammlung. Die Befugnis zu Änderungen, die nur die Fassung betreffen, kann die Hauptversammlung dem Aufsichtsrat übertragen.

(2) Der Beschluß der Hauptversammlung bedarf einer Mehrheit, die mindestens drei Viertel des bei der Beschlußfassung vertretenen Grundkapitals umfaßt. Die Satzung kann eine andere Kapitalmehrheit, für eine Änderung des Gegenstands des Unternehmens jedoch nur eine größere Kapitalmehrheit bestimmen. Sie kann weitere Erfordernisse aufstellen.

(3) Soll das bisherige Verhältnis mehrerer Gattungen von Aktien zum Nachteil einer Gattung geändert werden, so bedarf der Beschluß der Hauptversammlung zu seiner Wirksamkeit der Zustimmung der benachteiligten Aktionäre. Über die Zustimmung haben die benachteiligten Aktionäre einen Sonderbeschluß zu fassen. Für diesen gilt Absatz 2.

§ 179a. Verpflichtung zur Übertragung des ganzen Gesellschaftsvermögens

(1) Ein Vertrag, durch den sich eine Aktiengesellschaft zur Übertragung des ganzen Gesellschaftsvermögens verpflichtet, ohne daß die Übertragung unter

Part Six. Amendment of the Articles. Capital Increases and Capital Reductions

Division One. Amendment of the Articles

§ 179. Resolution of the Shareholders' Meeting

(1) Any amendment of the articles shall require a resolution of the shareholders' meeting. The shareholders' meeting may confer upon the supervisory board the authority to make amendments which relate solely to the wording of the articles.

(2) The resolution of the shareholders' meeting shall require a majority of not less than three fourths of the share capital represented at the passing of the resolution. The articles may provide for a different capital majority, however, in the case of an amendment of the corporate purpose, only for a larger capital majority. The articles may provide for additional requirements.

(3) If the existing relationship of more than one class of shares is to be amended to the disadvantage of any class, the resolution of the shareholders' meeting shall require the consent of the shareholders adversely affected in order to be effective. The shareholders adversely affected shall decide on such consent by adopting a separate resolution. Subsection (2) shall apply to such resolution.

§ 179a. Obligation to Transfer the Entire Assets

(1) An agreement by which a stock corporation undertakes to transfer its entire assets, and such transfer not being subject to the provisions of the Act on

die Vorschriften des Umwandlungsgesetzes fällt, bedarf auch dann eines Beschlusses der Hauptversammlung nach § 179, wenn damit nicht eine Änderung des Unternehmensgegenstandes verbunden ist. Die Satzung kann nur eine größere Kapitalmehrheit bestimmen.

Transformation, shall require a resolution of the shareholders' meeting pursuant to § 179 even if a change of the corporate purpose should not be connected with such transfer. The articles may provide only for a larger capital majority.

(2) Der Vertrag ist von der Einberufung der Hauptversammlung an, die über die Zustimmung beschließen soll, in dem Geschäftsraum der Gesellschaft zur Einsicht der Aktionäre auszulegen. Auf Verlangen ist jedem Aktionär unverzüglich eine Abschrift zu erteilen. In der Hauptversammlung ist der Vertrag auszulegen. Der Vorstand hat ihn zu Beginn der Verhandlung zu erläutern. Der Niederschrift ist er als Anlage beizufügen.

(2) As from the date of calling that shareholders' meeting which is to resolve on the consent such agreement shall be made available for inspection by the shareholders in the offices of the company. Upon request each shareholder shall promptly be provided with a copy of such agreement. The agreement shall be displayed at the shareholders' meeting. The management board shall comment on the agreement at the commencement of deliberations. The agreement shall be appended to the minutes.

(3) Wird aus Anlaß der Übertragung des Gesellschaftsvermögens die Gesellschaft aufgelöst, so ist der Anmeldung der Auflösung der Vertrag in Ausfertigung oder öffentlich beglaubigter Abschrift beizufügen.

(3) If the company shall be dissolved in consequence of the transfer of its assets an original or an officially certified copy of the agreement shall be appended to the report on the dissolution.

§ 180. Zustimmung der betroffenen Aktionäre

§ 180. Consent of Shareholders Concerned

(1) Ein Beschluß, der Aktionären Nebenverpflichtungen auferlegt, bedarf zu seiner Wirksamkeit der Zustimmung aller betroffenen Aktionäre.

(1) Any resolution imposing ancillary obligations on shareholders shall require the consent of all shareholders concerned in order to be effective.

(2) Gleiches gilt für einen Beschluß, durch den die Übertragung von Namensaktien oder Zwischenscheinen an die Zustimmung der Gesellschaft gebunden wird.

(2) The foregoing shall apply to any resolution which subjects the transfer of registered or interim share certificates to the company's consent.

§ 181. Eintragung der Satzungsänderung

(1) Der Vorstand hat die Satzungsänderung zur Eintragung in das Handelsregister anzumelden. Der Anmeldung ist der vollständige Wortlaut der Satzung beizufügen; er muß mit der Bescheinigung eines Notars versehen sein, daß die geänderten Bestimmungen der Satzung mit dem Beschluß über die Satzungsänderung und die unveränderten Bestimmungen mit dem zuletzt zum Handelsregister eingereichten vollständigen Wortlaut der Satzung übereinstimmen. Bedarf die Satzungsänderung staatlicher Genehmigung, so ist der Anmeldung die Genehmigungsurkunde beizufügen.

(2) Soweit nicht die Änderung Angaben nach § 39 betrifft, genügt bei der Eintragung die Bezugnahme auf die beim Gericht eingereichten Urkunden. Betrifft eine Änderung Bestimmungen, die ihrem Inhalt nach bekanntzumachen sind, so ist auch die Änderung ihrem Inhalt nach bekanntzumachen.

(3) Die Änderung wird erst wirksam, wenn sie in das Handelsregister des Sitzes der Gesellschaft eingetragen worden ist.

§ 181. Registration of Amendments of the Articles

(1) The management board shall report the amendment of the articles for registration in the commercial register. The full text of the articles shall be appended to such report; such text shall be provided with the certificate of a notary that the provisions of the articles which have been amended conform to the resolution to amend the articles and that the provisions which have not been amended conform to the full text of the articles last submitted to the commercial register. If the amendment of the articles requires governmental approval, the document containing such approval shall be appended to the report.

(2) Unless the amendment relates to the matters set out in § 39, a reference to the documents submitted to the court shall suffice for purposes of registration. If an amendment relates to provisions the contents of which are required to be announced, the contents of such amendment shall likewise be announced.

(3) An amendment shall become effective only upon registration thereof in the commercial register of the company's domicile.

Zweiter Abschnitt. Maßnahmen der Kapitalbeschaffung

ERSTER UNTERABSCHNITT. KAPITALERHÖHUNG GEGEN EINLAGEN

§ 182. Voraussetzungen

(1) Eine Erhöhung des Grundkapitals gegen Einlagen kann nur mit einer Mehrheit beschlossen werden, die min-

Division Two. Capital Increases

SUBDIVISION ONE. CAPITAL INCREASE AGAINST CONTRIBUTIONS

§ 182. General Provisions

(1) A resolution to increase the share capital against contributions shall require a majority of not less than three fourths of

destens drei Viertel des bei der Beschlußfassung vertretenen Grundkapitals umfaßt. Die Satzung kann eine andere Kapitalmehrheit, für die Ausgabe von Vorzugsaktien ohne Stimmrecht jedoch nur eine größere Kapitalmehrheit bestimmen. Sie kann weitere Erfordernisse aufstellen. Die Kapitalerhöhung kann nur durch Ausgabe neuer Aktien ausgeführt werden.

the share capital represented at the passing of the resolution. The articles may provide for a different capital majority, however, in the case of the issue of nonvoting preferred shares, only for a larger capital majority. The articles may provide for additional requirements. Any capital increase may only be carried out by issuance of new shares.

(**2**) Sind mehrere Gattungen von stimmberechtigten Aktien vorhanden, so bedarf der Beschluß der Hauptversammlung zu seiner Wirksamkeit der Zustimmung der Aktionäre jeder Gattung. Über die Zustimmung haben die Aktionäre jeder Gattung einen Sonderbeschluß zu fassen. Für diesen gilt Absatz 1.

(**2**) If more than one class of voting shares is outstanding, resolutions of the shareholders' meeting shall require the consent of the shareholders of each class in order to be effective. The shareholders of each class shall decide on such consent by adopting a separate resolution. Subsection (1) shall apply to such resolution.

(**3**) Sollen die neuen Aktien für einen höheren Betrag als den Nennbetrag ausgegeben werden, so ist der Mindestbetrag, unter dem sie nicht ausgegeben werden sollen, im Beschluß über die Erhöhung des Grundkapitals festzusetzen.

(**3**) If the new shares are to be issued for an amount exceeding the par value, the minimum issue price shall be stipulated in the resolution on the share capital increase.

(**4**) Das Grundkapital soll nicht erhöht werden, solange ausstehende Einlagen auf das bisherige Grundkapital noch erlangt werden können. Für Versicherungsgesellschaften kann die Satzung etwas anderes bestimmen. Stehen Einlagen in verhältnismäßig unerheblichem Umfang aus, so hindert dies die Erhöhung des Grundkapitals nicht.

(**4**) The share capital shall not be increased for as long as contributions to share capital are still outstanding and collectible. In the case of insurance companies the articles may provide otherwise. A share capital increase shall not be precluded if immaterial amounts of contributions are outstanding.

§ 183. Kapitalerhöhung mit Sacheinlagen

§ 183. Capital Increase against Contributions in Kind

(**1**) Wird eine Sacheinlage (§ 27 Abs. 1 und 2) gemacht, so müssen ihr Gegenstand, die Person, von der die Gesellschaft den Gegenstand erwirbt, und der Nennbetrag der bei der Sacheinlage zu gewährenden Aktien im Beschluß über die Erhöhung des Grundkapitals festge-

(**1**) In the case of a contribution in kind (§ 27 (1) and (2)), the resolution on the share capital increase shall stipulate the object, the person from whom the company is to acquire such object and the par value of shares to be granted for the contribution in kind. Such resolution may

setzt werden. Der Beschluß darf nur gefaßt werden, wenn die Einbringung von Sacheinlagen und die Festsetzung nach Satz 1 ausdrücklich und ordnungsgemäß (§ 124 Abs. 1) bekanntgemacht worden sind.

only be adopted if the contribution in kind and the stipulations pursuant to sentence 1 have been explicitly and properly announced (§ 124 (1)).

(2) Ohne diese Festsetzung sind Verträge über Sacheinlagen und die Rechtshandlungen zu ihrer Ausführung der Gesellschaft gegenüber unwirksam. Ist die Durchführung der Erhöhung des Grundkapitals eingetragen, so wird die Gültigkeit der Kapitalerhöhung durch diese Unwirksamkeit nicht berührt. Der Aktionär ist verpflichtet, den Nennbetrag oder den höheren Ausgabebetrag der Aktien einzuzahlen. Die Unwirksamkeit kann durch Satzungsänderung nicht geheilt werden, nachdem die Durchführung der Erhöhung des Grundkapitals in das Handelsregister eingetragen worden ist.

(2) Without such stipulations agreements regarding contributions in kind and legal transactions in execution thereof shall be invalid with respect to the company. If the completion of the share capital increase has been registered, the validity of the capital increase shall not be affected by the invalidity of such agreements. The shareholders shall be obligated to pay the par value or, as the case may be, the higher issue price. Such invalidity shall be incapable of being cured by amendment of the articles once the completion of the share capital increase has been registered in the commercial register.

(3) Bei der Kapitalerhöhung mit Sacheinlagen hat eine Prüfung durch einen oder mehrere Prüfer stattzufinden. § 33 Abs. 3 bis 5, § 34 Abs. 2 und 3, § 35 gelten sinngemäß. Das Gericht kann die Eintragung ablehnen, wenn der Wert der Sacheinlage nicht unwesentlich hinter dem Nennbetrag der dafür zu gewährenden Aktien zurückbleibt.

(3) In the case of a capital increase against contributions in kind, an audit shall be made by one or more auditors. § 33 (3) to (5), § 34 (2) and (3) and § 35 shall apply analogously. The court may deny registration if the value of the contributions in kind is materially less than the par value of the shares to be granted therefor.

§ 184. Anmeldung des Beschlusses

(1) Der Vorstand und der Vorsitzende des Aufsichtsrats haben den Beschluß über die Erhöhung des Grundkapitals zur Eintragung in das Handelsregister anzumelden. Der Bericht über die Prüfung von Sacheinlagen (§ 183 Abs. 3) ist der Anmeldung beizufügen.

(2) In der Anmeldung ist anzugeben, welche Einlagen auf das bisherige Grundkapital noch nicht geleistet sind

§ 184. Registration of the Resolution

(1) The management board and the chairman of the supervisory board shall report the resolution on the share capital increase for registration in the commercial register. The audit report on the contributions in kind (§ 183 (3)) shall be appended to such report.

(2) Such report for registration purposes shall state which contributions to

und warum sie nicht erlangt werden können.

existing share capital are still outstanding and why they are not collectible.

(3) (*aufgehoben*)

(3) (*repealed*)

§ 185. Zeichnung der neuen Aktien

§ 185. Subscription to New Shares

(1) Die Zeichnung der neuen Aktien geschieht durch schriftliche Erklärung (Zeichnungsschein), aus der die Beteiligung nach der Zahl, dem Nennbetrag und, wenn mehrere Gattungen ausgegeben werden, der Gattung der Aktien hervorgehen muß. Der Zeichnungsschein soll doppelt ausgestellt werden. Er hat zu enthalten

1. den Tag, an dem die Erhöhung des Grundkapitals beschlossen worden ist;
2. den Ausgabebetrag der Aktien, den Betrag der festgesetzten Einzahlungen sowie den Umfang von Nebenverpflichtungen;
3. die bei einer Kapitalerhöhung mit Sacheinlagen vorgesehenen Festsetzungen und, wenn mehrere Gattungen ausgegeben werden, den Gesamtnennbetrag einer jeden Aktiengattung;
4. den Zeitpunkt, an dem die Zeichnung unverbindlich wird, wenn nicht bis dahin die Durchführung der Erhöhung des Grundkapitals eingetragen ist.

(1) Subscription to new shares shall be effected by means of a certificate in writing ('subscription form') specifying the number, par value and, if more than one class is being issued, class of shares to be subscribed. The subscription certificate shall be executed in duplicate. It shall specify:

1. the date on which the resolution on the share capital increase was adopted;
2. the share issue price, the amount of payments to be made and the scope of any ancillary obligations;
3. the stipulations required in the case of a capital increase against contributions in kind and, if more than one class is being issued, the aggregate par value of each class of shares; and
4. the date on which the subscription shall cease to be effective, if completion of the share capital increase has not been registered prior thereto.

(2) Zeichnungsscheine, die diese Angaben nicht vollständig oder die außer dem Vorbehalt in Absatz 1 Nr. 4 Beschränkungen der Verpflichtung des Zeichners enthalten, sind nichtig.

(2) Any subscription certificate which does not contain all such particulars or which contains limitations in respect of the obligation of the subscriber, other than the limitation pursuant to subsection (1) No. 4, shall be null and void.

(3) Ist die Durchführung der Erhöhung des Grundkapitals eingetragen, so kann sich der Zeichner auf die Nichtigkeit oder Unverbindlichkeit des Zeichnungsscheins nicht berufen, wenn er auf Grund des Zeichnungsscheins als Aktionär Rechte ausgeübt oder Verpflichtungen erfüllt hat.

(3) A subscriber may not assert the nullity or invalidity of the subscription certificate once the completion of the share capital increase has been registered if he has by virtue of the subscription certificate exercised rights or performed obligations as a shareholder.

(4) Jede nicht im Zeichnungsschein enthaltene Beschränkung ist der Gesellschaft gegenüber unwirksam.

(4) Any limitation not contained in the subscription certificate shall be invalid with respect to the company.

§ 186. Bezugsrecht

§ 186. Pre-emptive Rights

(1) Jedem Aktionär muß auf sein Verlangen ein seinem Anteil an dem bisherigen Grundkapital entsprechender Teil der neuen Aktien zugeteilt werden. Für die Ausübung des Bezugsrechts ist eine Frist von mindestens zwei Wochen zu bestimmen.

(1) Each shareholder shall be entitled, upon demand, to subscribe to new shares in proportion to his holdings in the existing share capital. A period of not less than two weeks shall be set for exercising such pre-emptive rights.

(2) Der Vorstand hat den Ausgabebetrag und zugleich eine nach Absatz 1 bestimmte Frist in den Gesellschaftsblättern bekanntzumachen.

(2) The management board shall announce the issue price and the period set in accordance with subsection (1) in the company's designated journals.

(3) Das Bezugsrecht kann ganz oder zum Teil nur im Beschluß über die Erhöhung des Grundkapitals ausgeschlossen werden. In diesem Fall bedarf der Beschluß neben den in Gesetz oder Satzung für die Kapitalerhöhung aufgestellten Erfordernissen einer Mehrheit, die mindestens drei Viertel des bei der Beschlußfassung vertretenen Grundkapitals umfaßt. Die Satzung kann eine größere Kapitalmehrheit und weitere Erfordernisse bestimmen. Ein Ausschluß des Bezugsrechts ist insbesondere dann zulässig, wenn die Kapitalerhöhung gegen Bareinlagen zehn vom Hundert des Grundkapitals nicht übersteigt und der Ausgabebetrag den Börsenpreis nicht wesentlich unterschreitet.

(3) Pre-emptive rights may be excluded in whole or in part only in the resolution on the share capital increase. The relevant resolution shall require, in addition to the requirements provided by law or the articles for such capital increase, a majority of not less than three fourths of the share capital represented at the passing of the resolution. The articles may provide for a larger capital majority and additional requirements. In particular, the exclusion of pre-emptive rights shall be permitted if a capital increase against contributions in cash does not exceed ten percent of the share capital and the issue price is not materially below the stock exchange price.

(4) Ein Beschluß, durch den das Bezugsrecht ganz oder zum Teil ausgeschlossen wird, darf nur gefaßt werden, wenn die Ausschließung ausdrücklich und ordnungsgemäß (§ 124 Abs. 1) bekanntgemacht worden ist. Der Vorstand hat der Hauptversammlung einen schriftlichen Bericht über den Grund für den teilweisen oder vollständigen Ausschluß

(4) A resolution by which pre-emptive rights are excluded in whole or in part may be adopted only if the proposed exclusion has been explicitly and properly (§ 124 (1)) announced. The management board shall present to the shareholders' meeting a written report stating the grounds for the proposed exclusion, in whole or in part, of pre-emptive rights;

des Bezugsrechts vorzulegen; in dem Bericht ist der vorgeschlagene Ausgabebetrag zu begründen.

such report shall provide an explanation of the proposed issue price.

(5) Als Ausschluß des Bezugsrechts ist es nicht anzusehen, wenn nach dem Beschluß die neuen Aktien von einem Kreditinstitut mit der Verpflichtung übernommen werden sollen, sie den Aktionären zum Bezug anzubieten. Der Vorstand hat das Bezugsangebot des Kreditinstituts unter Angabe des für die Aktien zu leistenden Entgelts und einer für die Annahme des Angebots gesetzten Frist in den Gesellschaftsblättern bekanntzumachen; gleiches gilt, wenn die neuen Aktien von einem anderen als einem Kreditinstitut mit der Verpflichtung übernommen werden sollen, sie den Aktionären zum Bezug anzubieten.

(5) A resolution providing that the new shares are to be acquired by a credit institution with the obligation to offer such shares to the shareholders for subscription, shall not be deemed to constitute an exclusion of pre-emptive rights. The management board shall announce in the company's designated journals the subscription offer of the bank stating the consideration to be paid for the shares and the period set for the acceptance of the offer; the foregoing shall apply if the new shares are to be acquired by a person other than a credit institution with the obligation to offer such shares to the shareholders for subscription.

§ 187. Zusicherung von Rechten auf den Bezug neuer Aktien

§ 187. Offer of Rights to subscribe to New Shares

(1) Rechte auf den Bezug neuer Aktien können nur unter Vorbehalt des Bezugsrechts der Aktionäre zugesichert werden.

(1) Any offer of rights to subscribe to new shares may only be made subject to the pre-emptive rights of the shareholders.

(2) Zusicherungen vor dem Beschluß über die Erhöhung des Grundkapitals sind der Gesellschaft gegenüber unwirksam.

(2) Any such offer made prior to the resolution on the share capital increase shall be invalid with respect to the company.

§ 188. Anmeldung und Eintragung der Durchführung

§ 188. Registration

(1) Der Vorstand und der Vorsitzende des Aufsichtsrats haben die Durchführung der Erhöhung des Grundkapitals zur Eintragung in das Handelsregister anzumelden.

(1) The management board and the chairman of the supervisory board shall report the completion of the share capital increase for registration in the commercial register.

(2) Für die Anmeldung gelten sinngemäß § 36 Abs. 2, § 36a und § 37 Abs. 1. Durch Gutschrift auf ein Konto des Vor-

(2) § 36 (2), § 36a and § 37 (1) shall apply analogously to such report. Subscription payments may not be made by

stands kann die Einzahlung nicht geleistet werden.

credit to an account in the name of the management board.

(3) Der Anmeldung sind für das Gericht des Sitzes der Gesellschaft beizufügen

1. die Zweitschriften der Zeichnungsscheine und ein vom Vorstand unterschriebenes Verzeichnis der Zeichner, das die auf jeden entfallenden Aktien und die auf sie geleisteten Einzahlungen angibt;

2 bei einer Kapitalerhöhung mit Sacheinlagen die Verträge, die den Festsetzungen nach § 183 zugrunde liegen oder zu ihrer Ausführung geschlossen worden sind;

3. eine Berechnung der Kosten, die für die Gesellschaft durch die Ausgabe der neuen Aktien entstehen werden;

4. wenn die Erhöhung des Grundkapitals der staatlichen Genehmigung bedarf, die Genehmigungsurkunde.

(3) The following documents shall be appended to the report for the court of the company's domicile:

1. the duplicates of the subscription certificates and a list of the subscribers signed by the management board and stating the shares issued to each subscriber and the payments made in respect thereof;

2. in the case of a capital increase by contributions in kind, the agreements on which the stipulations pursuant to § 183 were based or which have been entered into in execution thereof;

3. a computation of the expenses which the company will incur through the issue of new shares;

4. if the share capital increase requires governmental approval, the documents containing such approval.

(4) Anmeldung und Eintragung der Durchführung der Erhöhung des Grundkapitals können mit Anmeldung und Eintragung des Beschlusses über die Erhöhung verbunden werden.

(4) The report and registration of the completion of the share capital increase may be made together with the report and registration of the resolution on such increase.

(5) Die eingereichten Schriftstücke werden beim Gericht in Urschrift, Ausfertigung oder öffentlich beglaubigter Abschrift aufbewahrt.

(5) The documents submitted shall be filed with the court in original, duplicate or officially certified copy.

§ 189. Wirksamwerden der Kapitalerhöhung

Mit der Eintragung der Durchführung der Erhöhung des Grundkapitals ist das Grundkapital erhöht.

§ 189. Effectiveness of the Capital Increase

The increase of the share capital shall become effective upon registration of the completion of the share capital increase.

§ 190. Bekanntmachung

In die Bekanntmachung der Eintragung (§ 188) sind außer deren Inhalt der

§ 190. Announcement

The announcement of the registration (§ 188) shall include, in addition to the

Ausgabebetrag der Aktien, die bei einer Kapitalerhöhung mit Sacheinlagen vorgesehenen Festsetzungen und ein Hinweis auf den Bericht über die Prüfung von Sacheinlagen (§ 183 Abs. 3) aufzunehmen. Bei der Bekanntmachung dieser Festsetzungen genügt die Bezugnahme auf die beim Gericht eingereichten Urkunden.

registration entries, the share issue price, the stipulations required in respect of a capital increase against contributions in kind and a reference to the report on the audit of contributions in kind (§ 183 (3)). A reference to the documents submitted to the court shall suffice for purpose of announcement of such stipulations.

§ 191. Verbotene Ausgabe von Aktien und Zwischenscheinen

Vor der Eintragung der Durchführung der Erhöhung des Grundkapitals können die neuen Anteilsrechte nicht übertragen, neue Aktien und Zwischenscheine nicht ausgegeben werden. Die vorher ausgegebenen neuen Aktien und Zwischenscheine sind nichtig. Für den Schaden aus der Ausgabe sind die Ausgeber den Inhabern als Gesamtschuldner verantwortlich.

§ 191. Prohibited Issue of Share Certificates and Interim Certificates

The new shares may not be transferred and new share certificates and interim certificates may not be issued prior to registration of the completion of the share capital increase. New share certificates and interim certificates issued prior to such registration shall be null and void. The issuers shall be jointly and severally liable to the shareholders for any damage resulting from such issue.

ZWEITER UNTERABSCHNITT. BEDINGTE KAPITALERHÖHUNG

§ 192. Voraussetzungen

(1) Die Hauptversammlung kann eine Erhöhung des Grundkapitals beschließen, die nur so weit durchgeführt werden soll, wie von einem Umtausch- oder Bezugsrecht Gebrauch gemacht wird, das die Gesellschaft auf die neuen Aktien (Bezugsaktien) einräumt (bedingte Kapitalerhöhung).

(2) Die bedingte Kapitalerhöhung soll nur zu folgenden Zwecken beschlossen werden:

1. zur Gewährung von Umtausch- oder Bezugsrechten an Gläubiger von Wandelschuldverschreibungen;

2. zur Vorbereitung des Zusammenschlusses mehrerer Unternehmen;

SUBDIVISION TWO. CONTINGENT CAPITAL INCREASE

§ 192. General Provisions

(1) The shareholders' meeting may resolve upon an increase of share capital which shall be carried out only to the extent that conversion rights or stock warrants which obligate the company to issue new shares ('new shares') are exercised ('contingent capital increase').

(2) A resolution on a contingent capital increase may be adopted only for any of the following purposes:

1. to grant conversion rights or stock warrants to holders of convertible bonds or with warrant bonds;

2. to prepare a merger of enterprises;

3. zur Gewährung von Bezugsrechten an Arbeitnehmer der Gesellschaft zum Bezug neuer Aktien gegen Einlage von Geldforderungen, die den Arbeitnehmern aus einer ihnen von der Gesellschaft eingeräumten Gewinnbeteiligung zustehen.

3. to grant rights to employees of the company to subscribe to new shares against the contribution of amounts due to such employees under a profit-sharing plan established by the company.

(3) Der Nennbetrag des bedingten Kapitals darf die Hälfte des Grundkapitals, das zur Zeit der Beschlußfassung über die bedingte Kapitalerhöhung vorhanden ist, nicht übersteigen.

(3) The par value of contingent capital may not exceed one half of the share capital as at the date of the adoption of the resolution on the contingent capital increase.

(4) Ein Beschluß der Hauptversammlung, der dem Beschluß über die bedingte Kapitalerhöhung entgegensteht, ist nichtig.

(4) A resolution of the shareholders' meeting which contravenes the resolution on the contingent capital increase shall be null and void.

(5) Die folgenden Vorschriften über das Bezugsrecht gelten sinngemäß für das Umtauschrecht.

(5) The following provisions regarding stock warrants shall apply analogously to conversion rights.

§ 193. Erfordernisse des Beschlusses

§ 193. Resolution

(1) Der Beschluß über die bedingte Kapitalerhöhung bedarf einer Mehrheit, die mindestens drei Viertel des bei der Beschlußfassung vertretenen Grundkapitals umfaßt. Die Satzung kann eine größere Kapitalmehrheit und weitere Erfordernisse bestimmen. § 182 Abs. 2 und § 187 Abs. 2 gelten.

(1) The resolution on the contingent capital increase shall require a majority of not less than three fourths of the share capital represented at the passing of the resolution. The articles may provide for a larger capital majority and additional requirements. § 182 (2) and § 187 (2) shall apply.

(2) Im Beschluß müssen auch festgestellt werden
1. der Zweck der bedingten Kapitalerhöhung;
2. der Kreis der Bezugsberechtigten;
3. der Ausgabebetrag oder die Grundlagen, nach denen dieser Betrag errechnet wird.

(2) The resolution shall also stipulate:
1. the purpose of the contingent capital increase;
2. the persons entitled to subscribe;
3. the issue price or the basis on which such price is to be computed.

§ 194. Bedingte Kapitalerhöhung mit Sacheinlagen

(1) Wird eine Sacheinlage gemacht, so müssen ihr Gegenstand, die Person, von der die Gesellschaft den Gegenstand erwirbt, und der Nennbetrag der bei der Sacheinlage zu gewährenden Aktien im Beschluß über die bedingte Kapitalerhöhung festgesetzt werden. Als Sacheinlage gilt nicht die Hingabe von Schuldverschreibungen im Umtausch gegen Bezugsaktien. Der Beschluß darf nur gefaßt werden, wenn die Einbringung von Sacheinlagen ausdrücklich und ordnungsgemäß (§ 124 Abs. 1) bekanntgemacht worden ist.

(2) Ohne diese Festsetzung sind Verträge über Sacheinlagen und die Rechtshandlungen zu ihrer Ausführung der Gesellschaft gegenüber unwirksam. Sind die Bezugsaktien ausgegeben, so wird die Gültigkeit der bedingten Kapitalerhöhung durch diese Unwirksamkeit nicht berührt. Der Aktionär ist verpflichtet, den Nennbetrag oder den höheren Ausgabebetrag der Bezugsaktien einzuzahlen. Die Unwirksamkeit kann durch Satzungsänderung nicht geheilt werden, nachdem die Bezugsaktien ausgegeben worden sind.

(3) Die Absätze 1 und 2 gelten nicht für die Einlage von Geldforderungen, die Arbeitnehmern der Gesellschaft aus einer ihnen von der Gesellschaft eingeräumten Gewinnbeteiligung zustehen.

(4) Bei der Kapitalerhöhung mit Sacheinlagen hat eine Prüfung durch einen oder mehrere Prüfer stattzufinden. § 33 Abs. 3 bis 5, § 34 Abs. 2 und 3, § 35 gelten sinngemäß. Das Gericht kann die Eintragung ablehnen, wenn der Wert der Sacheinlage nicht unwesentlich hinter dem Nennbetrag der dafür zu gewährenden Aktien zurückbleibt.

§ 194. Contingent Capital Increase against Contributions in Kind

(1) In the case of a contribution in kind, the resolution on the contingent capital increase shall stipulate the object, the person from whom the company shall acquire the object and the par value of the shares to be granted for the contribution in kind. The delivery of bonds for conversion into new shares shall not be deemed to constitute a contribution in kind. The resolution may only be adopted if the proposed contributions in kind have been explicitly and properly (§ 124 (1)) announced.

(2) Without such stipulations, agreements regarding contributions in kind and legal transactions in execution thereof shall be invalid with respect to the company. If the new shares have been issued, the validity of the contingent capital increase shall not be affected by the invalidity of such agreements. The respective shareholders shall be obligated to pay the par value or the higher issue price of the new shares. Such invalidity shall be incapable of being cured by amendment of the articles once the new shares have been issued.

(3) Subsections (1) and (2) shall not apply to the contribution of amounts due to employees of the company pursuant to a profit-sharing plan established by the company.

(4) In the case of a capital increase against contributions in kind, an audit shall be made by one or more auditors. § 33 (3) to (5), § 34 (2) and (3) and § 35 shall apply analogously. The court may deny registration if the value of contributions in kind is materially less than the par value of the shares to be granted therefor.

§ 195. Anmeldung des Beschlusses

(1) Der Vorstand und der Vorsitzende des Aufsichtsrats haben den Beschluß über die bedingte Kapitalerhöhung zur Eintragung in das Handelsregister anzumelden.

(2) Der Anmeldung sind für das Gericht des Sitzes der Gesellschaft beizufügen

1. bei einer bedingten Kapitalerhöhung mit Sacheinlagen die Verträge, die den Festsetzungen nach § 194 zugrunde liegen oder zu ihrer Ausführung geschlossen worden sind, und der Bericht über die Prüfung von Sacheinlagen (§ 194 Abs. 4);
2. eine Berechnung der Kosten, die für die Gesellschaft durch die Ausgabe der Bezugsaktien entstehen werden;
3. wenn die Kapitalerhöhung der staatlichen Genehmigung bedarf, die Genehmigungsurkunde.

(3) Die eingereichten Schriftstücke werden beim Gericht in Urschrift, Ausfertigung oder öffentlich beglaubigter Abschrift aufbewahrt.

§ 195. Registration of the Resolution

(1) The management board and the chairman of the supervisory board shall report the resolution on the contingent capital increase for registration in the commercial register.

(2) The following documents shall be appended to the report for filing with the court of the company's domicile:

1. in the case of a contingent capital increase against contributions in kind, the articles on which the stipulations pursuant to § 194 were based or which have been entered into in execution thereof and the report on the audit of contributions in kind (§ 194 (4));
2. a computation of the expenses which the company will incur through the issue of new shares;
3. if the capital increase requires governmental approval, the document containing such approval.

(3) The documents submitted shall be filed with the court in original, duplicate or officially certified copy.

§ 196. Bekanntmachung der Eintragung

In die Bekanntmachung der Eintragung des Beschlusses über die bedingte Kapitalerhöhung sind außer deren Inhalt die Feststellungen nach § 193 Abs. 2, die nach § 194 bei der Einbringung von Sacheinlagen vorgesehenen Festsetzungen und ein Hinweis auf den Bericht über die Prüfung von Sacheinlagen (§ 194 Abs. 4) aufzunehmen. Für die Festsetzungen nach § 194 genügt die Bezugnahme auf die beim Gericht eingereichten Urkunden.

§ 196. Announcement of the Registration

The announcement of the registration of the resolution on the contingent capital increase shall include, in addition to the registration entries, the stipulations pursuant to § 193 (2), the stipulations required by § 194 in respect of contributions in kind, and a reference to the report on the audit of contributions in kind (§ 194 (4)). A reference to the documents submitted to the court shall suffice for purposes of announcement of the stipulations required by § 194.

§ 197. Verbotene Aktienausgabe

Vor der Eintragung des Beschlusses über die bedingte Kapitalerhöhung können die Bezugsaktien nicht ausgegeben werden. Ein Anspruch des Bezugsberechtigten entsteht vor diesem Zeitpunkt nicht. Die vorher ausgegebenen Bezugsaktien sind nichtig. Für den Schaden aus der Ausgabe sind die Ausgeber den Inhabern als Gesamtschuldner verantwortlich.

§ 197. Prohibited Issue of Shares

The new shares may not be issued prior to registration of the resolution on the contingent capital increase. A right to subscribe shall not arise prior to such date. New shares issued prior to such registration shall be null and void. The issuers shall be jointly and severally liable to the holders for any damage resulting from such issue.

§ 198. Bezugserklärung

(1) Das Bezugsrecht wird durch schriftliche Erklärung ausgeübt. Die Erklärung (Bezugserklärung) soll doppelt ausgestellt werden. Sie hat die Beteiligung nach der Zahl, dem Nennbetrag und, wenn mehrere Gattungen ausgegeben werden, der Gattung der Aktien, die Feststellungen nach § 193 Abs. 2, die nach § 194 bei der Einbringung von Sacheinlagen vorgesehenen Festsetzungen sowie den Tag anzugeben, an dem der Beschluß über die bedingte Kapitalerhöhung gefaßt worden ist.

(2) Die Bezugserklärung hat die gleiche Wirkung wie eine Zeichnungserklärung. Bezugserklärungen, deren Inhalt nicht dem Absatz 1 entspricht oder die Beschränkungen der Verpflichtung des Erklärenden enthalten, sind nichtig.

(3) Werden Bezugsaktien ungeachtet der Nichtigkeit einer Bezugserklärung ausgegeben, so kann sich der Erklärende auf die Nichtigkeit nicht berufen, wenn er auf Grund der Bezugserklärung als Aktionär Rechte ausgeübt oder Verpflichtungen erfüllt hat.

§ 198. Exercise Notice

(1) Rights to subscribe shall be exercised by means of a written notice. Such notice (‘exercise notice’) shall be executed in duplicate. The exercise notice shall state the number, par value and, if more than one class is being issued, the class of shares, the stipulations required pursuant to § 193 (2), the stipulations required pursuant to § 194 in respect of contributions in kind, and the date on which the resolution on the contingent capital increase was adopted.

(2) The exercise notice shall have the same effect as a subscription certificate. Any exercise notice whose contents do not comply with subsection (1) or which contain limitations in respect of the obligation of the person giving such notice shall be null and void.

(3) If new shares are issued despite the exercise notice being null and void, the person who has given such notice may not assert the nullity of the exercise notice if he has by virtue of such notice exercised rights or performed obligations as a shareholder.

(4) Jede nicht in der Bezugserklärung enthaltene Beschränkung ist der Gesellschaft gegenüber unwirksam.

(4) Any limitation not contained in the exercise notice shall be invalid with respect to the company.

§ 199. Ausgabe der Bezugsaktien

§ 199. Issue of New Shares

(1) Der Vorstand darf die Bezugsaktien nur in Erfüllung des im Beschluß über die bedingte Kapitalerhöhung festgesetzten Zwecks und nicht vor der vollen Leistung des Gegenwerts ausgeben, der sich aus dem Beschluß ergibt.

(1) The management board may issue new shares only in fulfilment of the purpose stipulated in the resolution on the contingent capital increase and in no event prior to full performance of the consideration resulting from such resolution.

(2) Der Vorstand darf Bezugsaktien gegen Wandelschuldverschreibungen nur ausgeben, wenn der Unterschied zwischen dem Ausgabebetrag der zum Umtausch eingereichten Schuldverschreibungen und dem höheren Nennbetrag der für sie zu gewährenden Bezugsaktien aus einer anderen Gewinnrücklage, soweit sie zu diesem Zweck verwandt werden kann, oder durch Zuzahlung des Umtauschberechtigten gedeckt ist. Dies gilt nicht, wenn der Gesamtbetrag, zu dem die Schuldverschreibungen ausgegeben sind, den Gesamtnennbetrag der Bezugsaktien erreicht oder übersteigt.

(2) The management board may issue new shares in exchange for convertible bonds or bonds with warrants only if the difference between the issue price of the bonds surrendered for conversion and the higher par value of the new shares is offset by profit reserves which may be used for such purpose or by an additional payment from the person entitled to conversion. The foregoing shall not apply if the aggregate amount for which the bonds were issued equals or exceeds the aggregate par value of the new shares.

§ 200. Wirksamwerden der bedingten Kapitalerhöhung

§ 200. Effectiveness of the Contingent Capital Increase

Mit der Ausgabe der Bezugsaktien ist das Grundkapital erhöht.

The increase of the share capital shall become effective upon issue of the new shares.

§ 201. Anmeldung der Ausgabe von Bezugsaktien

§ 201. Registration of the Issue of New Shares

(1) Der Vorstand hat innerhalb eines Monats nach Ablauf des Geschäftsjahrs zur Eintragung in das Handelsregister anzumelden, in welchem Umfang im abgelaufenen Geschäftsjahr Bezugsaktien ausgegeben worden sind.

(1) The management board shall, within one month after the expiration of each fiscal year, report as to what extent new shares have been issued in the preceding fiscal year for registration in the commercial register.

(2) Der Anmeldung sind für das Gericht des Sitzes der Gesellschaft die Zweitschriften der Bezugserklärungen und ein vom Vorstand unterschriebenes Verzeichnis der Personen, die das Bezugsrecht ausgeübt haben, beizufügen. Das Verzeichnis hat die auf jeden Aktionär entfallenden Aktien und die auf sie gemachten Einlagen anzugeben.

(2) Duplicates of the exercise notice and a list, signed by the management board, of the persons who have exercised the subscription rights, shall be appended to the report for filing with the court of the company's domicile. Such list shall state the shares attributable to each shareholder and the contribution made in respect thereof.

(3) In der Anmeldung hat der Vorstand zu erklären, daß die Bezugsaktien nur in Erfüllung des im Beschluß über die bedingte Kapitalerhöhung festgesetzten Zwecks und nicht vor der vollen Leistung des Gegenwerts ausgegeben worden sind, der sich aus dem Beschluß ergibt.

(3) The management board shall certify in a report that the new shares were issued solely in fulfilment of the purpose stipulated in the resolution on the contingent capital increase and in no event prior to full performance of the price resulting from such resolution.

(4) Die eingereichten Schriftstücke werden beim Gericht in Urschrift, Ausfertigung oder öffentlich beglaubigter Abschrift aufbewahrt.

(4) The documents submitted shall be filed with the court in original, duplicate or officially certified copy.

DRITTER UNTERABSCHNITT. GENEHMIGTES KAPITAL

SUBDIVISION THREE. AUTHORIZED CAPITAL

§ 202. Voraussetzungen

§ 202. General Provisions

(1) Die Satzung kann den Vorstand für höchstens fünf Jahre nach Eintragung der Gesellschaft ermächtigen, das Grundkapital bis zu einem bestimmten Nennbetrag (genehmigtes Kapital) durch Ausgabe neuer Aktien gegen Einlagen zu erhöhen.

(1) The articles may authorize the management board, for a period not exceeding five years after registration of the company, to increase the share capital up to a specified par value ('authorized capital') by issuing new shares against contributions.

(2) Die Ermächtigung kann auch durch Satzungsänderung für höchstens fünf Jahre nach Eintragung der Satzungsänderung erteilt werden. Der Beschluß der Hauptversammlung bedarf einer Mehrheit, die mindestens drei Viertel des bei der Beschlußfassung vertretenen Grundkapitals umfaßt. Die Satzung kann eine größere Kapitalmehrheit und weitere Erfordernisse bestimmen. § 182 Abs. 2 gilt.

(2) Such authorization may also be granted by amendment of the articles for a period not exceeding five years from the date or registration of such amendment of the articles. The respective resolution of the shareholders' meeting shall require a majority of not less than three fourths of the share capital represented at the passing of the resolution. The articles may provide for a larger capital majority and

additional requirements. § 182 (2) shall apply.

(3) Der Nennbetrag des genehmigten Kapitals darf die Hälfte des Grundkapitals, das zur Zeit der Ermächtigung vorhanden ist, nicht übersteigen. Die neuen Aktien sollen nur mit Zustimmung des Aufsichtsrats ausgegeben werden.

(3) The par value of the authorized capital may not exceed one half of the share capital as of the date of such authorization. The new shares may be issued only with the consent of the supervisory board.

(4) Die Satzung kann auch vorsehen, daß die neuen Aktien an Arbeitnehmer der Gesellschaft ausgegeben werden.

(4) The articles may also provide that the new shares are to be issued to employees of the company.

§ 203. Ausgabe der neuen Aktien

§ 203. Issue of New Shares

(1) Für die Ausgabe der neuen Aktien gelten sinngemäß, soweit sich aus den folgenden Vorschriften nichts anderes ergibt, §§ 185 bis 191 über die Kapitalerhöhung gegen Einlagen. An die Stelle des Beschlusses über die Erhöhung des Grundkapitals tritt die Ermächtigung der Satzung zur Ausgabe neuer Aktien.

(1) §§ 185 to 191 relating to a capital increase against contributions shall apply analogously to the issue of new shares, unless the following provisions provide otherwise. In respect of §§ 185 to 191 the authorization in the articles to issue new shares shall be substituted for the resolution on the share capital increase.

(2) Die Ermächtigung kann vorsehen, daß der Vorstand über den Ausschluß des Bezugsrechts entscheidet. Wird eine Ermächtigung, die dies vorsieht, durch Satzungsänderung erteilt, so gilt § 186 Abs. 4 sinngemäß.

(2) The authorization may provide that the management board shall have the authority to exclude subscription rights. § 186 (4) shall apply analogously if such authorization is contained in an amendment of the articles.

(3) Die neuen Aktien sollen nicht ausgegeben werden, solange ausstehende Einlagen auf das bisherige Grundkapital noch erlangt werden können. Für Versicherungsgesellschaften kann die Satzung etwas anderes bestimmen. Stehen Einlagen in verhältnismäßig unerheblichem Umfang aus, so hindert dies die Ausgabe der neuen Aktien nicht. In der ersten Anmeldung der Durchführung der Erhöhung des Grundkapitals ist anzugeben, welche Einlagen auf das bisherige Grundkapital noch nicht geleistet sind und warum sie nicht erlangt werden können.

(3) The new shares shall not be issued as long as contributions to the previously existing share capital are still outstanding and collectible. In the case of insurance companies, the articles may provide otherwise. The issue of new shares shall not be precluded if immaterial amounts of contributions are outstanding. The first report for registration of the completion of the share capital increase shall state which contributions to the previously existing share capital are still outstanding and why they are not collectible.

(4) Absatz 3 Satz 1 und 4 gilt nicht, wenn die Aktien an Arbeitnehmer der Gesellschaft ausgegeben werden.

(4) Subsection (3) sentences 1 and 4 shall not apply if the shares are issued to employees of the company.

§ 204. Bedingungen der Aktienausgabe

(1) Über den Inhalt der Aktienrechte und die Bedingungen der Aktienausgabe entscheidet der Vorstand, soweit die Ermächtigung keine Bestimmungen enthält. Die Entscheidung des Vorstands bedarf der Zustimmung des Aufsichtsrats; gleiches gilt für die Entscheidung des Vorstands nach § 203 Abs. 2 über den Ausschluß des Bezugsrechts.

(2) Sind Vorzugsaktien ohne Stimmrecht vorhanden, so können Vorzugsaktien, die bei der Verteilung des Gewinns oder des Gesellschaftsvermögens ihnen vorgehen oder gleichstehen, nur ausgegeben werden, wenn die Ermächtigung es vorsieht.

(3) Weist ein Jahresabschluß, der mit einem uneingeschränkten Bestätigungsvermerk versehen ist, einen Jahresüberschuß aus, so können Aktien an Arbeitnehmer der Gesellschaft auch in der Weise ausgegeben werden, daß die auf sie zu leistende Einlage aus dem Teil des Jahresüberschusses gedeckt wird, den nach § 58 Abs. 2 Vorstand und Aufsichtsrat in andere Gewinnrücklagen einstellen können. Für die Ausgabe der neuen Aktien gelten die Vorschriften über eine Kapitalerhöhung gegen Bareinlagen, ausgenommen § 188 Abs. 2. Der Anmeldung der Durchführung der Erhöhung des Grundkapitals ist außerdem der festgestellte Jahresabschluß mit Bestätigungsvermerk beizufügen. Die Anmeldenden haben ferner die Erklärung nach § 210 Abs. 1 Satz 2 abzugeben.

§ 204. Conditions of Share Issues

(1) The management board shall, to the extent that the authorization does not contain provisions thereon, decide as to the rights arising under shares and the conditions of the share issue. The decision of the management board shall require the consent of the supervisory board; the foregoing shall apply to the decision of the management board pursuant to § 203 (2) regarding the exclusion of the subscription rights.

(2) If non-voting preferred shares are outstanding, preferred shares which have priority to or equal standing with respect to the distribution of profits or assets may be issued only if the authorization so provides.

(3) If the annual financial statements, which are provided with an unqualified auditors' certificate, show an annual net profit, shares may also be issued to employees of the company in such manner that the contribution to be made thereupon is covered by that portion of the annual net profit which the management board and the supervisory board may transfer to other profit reserves pursuant to § 58 (2). The provisions regarding a capital increase against contributions in cash shall, with the exception of § 188 (2), apply to the issue of new shares. The approved annual financial statements which are provided with an auditors' certificate shall be appended to the report for registration of the completion of the share capital increase. The persons making such report shall further certify as provided by § 210 (1) sentence 2.

§ 205. Ausgabe gegen Sacheinlagen

(1) Gegen Sacheinlagen dürfen Aktien nur ausgegeben werden, wenn die Ermächtigung es vorsieht.

(2) Der Gegenstand der Sacheinlage, die Person, von der die Gesellschaft den Gegenstand erwirbt, und der Nennbetrag der bei der Sacheinlage zu gewährenden Aktien sind, wenn sie nicht in der Ermächtigung festgesetzt sind, vom Vorstand festzusetzen und in den Zeichnungsschein aufzunehmen. Der Vorstand soll die Entscheidung nur mit Zustimmung des Aufsichtsrats treffen.

(3) Bei Ausgabe der Aktien gegen Sacheinlagen hat eine Prüfung durch einen oder mehrere Prüfer stattzufinden. § 33 Abs. 3 bis 5, § 34 Abs. 2 und 3, § 35 gelten sinngemäß. Das Gericht kann die Eintragung ablehnen, wenn der Wert der Sacheinlage nicht unwesentlich hinter dem Nennbetrag der dafür zu gewährenden Aktien zurückbleibt.

(4) Ohne die vorgeschriebene Festsetzung sind Verträge über Sacheinlagen und die Rechtshandlungen zu ihrer Ausführung der Gesellschaft gegenüber unwirksam. Gleiches gilt, wenn die Festsetzung des Vorstands nicht in den Zeichnungsschein aufgenommen ist. Ist die Durchführung der Erhöhung des Grundkapitals eingetragen, so wird die Gültigkeit der Kapitalerhöhung durch diese Unwirksamkeit nicht berührt. Der Aktionär ist verpflichtet, den Nennbetrag oder den höheren Ausgabebetrag der Aktien einzuzahlen. Die Unwirksamkeit kann durch Satzungsänderung nicht geheilt werden, nachdem die Durchführung der Erhöhung des Grundkapitals in das Handelsregister eingetragen worden ist.

§ 205. Issue against Contributions in Kind

(1) Shares may be issued against contributions in kind only if the authorization so provides.

(2) Unless stipulated in the authorization, the object of the contribution in kind, the person from whom the company is to acquire such object and the par value of the shares to be granted for contribution in kind shall be stipulated by the management board and stated in the subscription notice. The management board shall make such stipulations only with the consent of the supervisory board.

(3) In the case of an issue of shares against contributions in kind an audit shall be made by one or more auditors. § 33 (3) to (5), § 34 (2) and (3) and § 35 apply analogously. The court may deny registration if the value of the contribution in kind is materially less than the par value of the shares to be granted therefor.

(4) Without the required stipulations, agreements regarding contributions in kind and legal transactions in execution thereof shall be invalid with respect to the company. The foregoing shall apply if the stipulations of the management board are not stated in the subscriptions notice. If the completion of the share capital increase has been registered, the validity of the capital increase shall not be affected by the invalidity of such agreements. The respective shareholder shall be obligated to pay the par value or the higher share issue price. Such invalidity shall be incapable of being cured by amendment of the articles once the completion of the share capital increase has been registered in the commercial register.

(5) Die Absätze 2 und 3 gelten nicht für die Einlage von Geldforderungen, die Arbeitnehmern der Gesellschaft aus einer ihnen von der Gesellschaft eingeräumten Gewinnbeteiligung zustehen.

(5) Subsections (2) and (3) shall not apply to the contribution of amounts due to employees of the company under a profit-sharing plan established by the company.

§ 206. Verträge über Sacheinlagen vor Eintragung der Gesellschaft

§ 206. Agreements regarding Contributions in Kind prior to Registration of the Company

Sind vor Eintragung der Gesellschaft Verträge geschlossen worden, nach denen auf das genehmigte Kapital eine Sacheinlage zu leisten ist, so muß die Satzung die Festsetzungen enthalten, die für eine Ausgabe gegen Sacheinlagen vorgeschrieben sind. Dabei gelten sinngemäß § 27 Abs. 3, 5, §§ 32 bis 35, 37 Abs. 4 Nr. 2, 4 und 5, § 38 Abs. 2, § 49 über die Gründung der Gesellschaft. An die Stelle der Gründer tritt der Vorstand und an die Stelle der Anmeldung und Eintragung der Gesellschaft die Anmeldung und Eintragung der Durchführung der Erhöhung des Grundkapitals.

If prior to registration of the company, agreements have been entered into which provide for a contribution in kind to be made on the authorized capital, the articles must contain the stipulations which are required for an issue against contributions in kind. § 27 (3), §§ 32 to 35, § 37 (4) sentences 2, 4 and 5, § 38 (2) and § 49 regarding formation of the company shall apply analogously. In respect of such provisions the management board shall be substituted for the incorporators and the registration of the completion of the share capital increase shall be substituted for the registration of the company.

VIERTER UNTERABSCHNITT. KAPITALERHÖHUNG AUS GESELLSCHAFTSMITTELN

SUBDIVISION FOUR. CAPITAL INCREASE FROM THE COMPANY'S RESERVES

§ 207. Voraussetzungen

§ 207. General Provisions

(1) Die Hauptversammlung kann eine Erhöhung des Grundkapitals durch Umwandlung der Kapitalrücklage und von Gewinnrücklagen in Grundkapital beschließen.

(1) The shareholders' meeting may resolve on an increase of the share capital by means of conversion of the capital reserve or profit reserves into share capital.

(2) Für den Beschluß und für die Anmeldung des Beschlusses gelten § 182 Abs. 1 Satz 1, 2 und 4, § 184 Abs. 1 sinngemäß.

(2) § 182 (1) sentences 1, 2 and 4, and § 184 (1) shall apply analogously to the respective resolution and the registration of such resolution.

(3) Die Erhöhung kann erst beschlossen werden, nachdem der Jahresabschluß für das letzte vor der Beschlußfassung über die Kapitalerhöhung abgelaufene

(3) A resolution on such increase may only be adopted after the annual financial statements for the last fiscal year ended before the adoption of such reso-

Geschäftsjahr (letzter Jahresabschluß) festgestellt ist.

lution on the capital increase ('latest annual financial statements') have been approved.

(4) Dem Beschluß ist eine Bilanz zugrunde zu legen.

(4) The resolution shall be based on a balance sheet.

§ 208. Umwandlungsfähigkeit von Kapital- und Gewinnrücklagen

§ 208. Capital and Profit Reserves Qualifying for Conversion

(1) Die Kapitalrücklage und die Gewinnrücklagen, die in Grundkapital umgewandelt werden sollen, müssen in der letzten Jahresbilanz und, wenn dem Beschluß eine andere Bilanz zugrunde gelegt wird, auch in dieser Bilanz unter 'Kapitalrücklage' oder 'Gewinnrücklagen' oder im letzten Beschluß über die Verwendung des Jahresüberschusses oder des Bilanzgewinns als Zuführung zu diesen Rücklagen ausgewiesen sein. Vorbehaltlich des Absatzes 2 können andere Gewinnrücklagen und deren Zuführungen in voller Höhe, die Kapitalrücklage und die gesetzliche Rücklage sowie deren Zuführungen nur, soweit sie zusammen den zehnten oder den in der Satzung bestimmten höheren Teil des bisherigen Grundkapitals übersteigen, in Grundkapital umgewandelt werden.

(1) The capital reserve and the profit reserves which are to be converted into share capital must have been shown in the latest annual balance sheet and, if the resolution is based on a balance sheet other than the latest balance sheet, also in such balance sheet as 'capital reserve' or 'profit reserves' or, in the last resolution on the appropriation of the annual net profit or distributable profits, as transfer to such reserves. Subject to subsection (2) other profit reserves and transfers thereto may be converted in full into share capital, however, the capital reserve and the legal reserve including transfers thereto only to the extent that in aggregate such items exceed one tenth or a higher proportion of the previously existing share capital which has been determined by the articles.

(2) Die Kapitalrücklage und die Gewinnrücklagen sowie deren Zuführungen können nicht umgewandelt werden, soweit in der zugrunde gelegten Bilanz ein Verlust einschließlich eines Verlustvortrags ausgewiesen ist. Gewinnrücklagen und deren Zuführungen, die für einen bestimmten Zweck bestimmt sind, dürfen nur umgewandelt werden, soweit dies mit ihrer Zweckbestimmung vereinbar ist.

(2) The capital reserve and the profit reserves as well as transfers thereto may not be converted to the extent that the relevant balance sheet shows a loss, including a loss carried forward. Profit reserves and transfers thereto which are designated for a specific purpose may only be converted to the extent that such conversion is compatible with such designated purpose.

§ 209. Zugrunde gelegte Bilanz

(1) Dem Beschluß kann die letzte Jahresbilanz zugrunde gelegt werden, wenn die Jahresbilanz geprüft und die festgestellte Jahresbilanz mit dem uneingeschränkten Bestätigungsvermerk des Abschlußprüfers versehen ist und wenn ihr Stichtag höchstens acht Monate vor der Anmeldung des Beschlusses zur Eintragung in das Handelsregister liegt.

(2) Wird dem Beschluß nicht die letzte Jahresbilanz zugrunde gelegt, so muß die Bilanz §§ 150, 152 dieses Gesetzes, §§ 242 bis 256, 264 bis 274, 279 bis 283 des Handelsgesetzbuchs entsprechen. Der Stichtag der Bilanz darf höchstens acht Monate vor der Anmeldung des Beschlusses zur Eintragung in das Handelsregister liegen.

(3) Die Bilanz muß durch einen Abschlußprüfer darauf geprüft werden, ob sie §§ 150, 152 dieses Gesetzes, §§ 242 bis 256, 264 bis 274, 279 bis 283 des Handelsgesetzbuchs entspricht. Sie muß mit einem uneingeschränkten Bestätigungsvermerk versehen sein.

(4) Wenn die Hauptversammlung keinen anderen Prüfer wählt, gilt der Prüfer als gewählt, der für die Prüfung des letzten Jahresabschlusses von der Hauptversammlung gewählt oder vom Gericht bestellt worden ist. Soweit sich aus der Besonderheit des Prüfungsauftrags nichts anderes ergibt, sind auf die Prüfung § 318 Abs. 1 Satz 3, § 319 Abs. 1 bis 3, § 320 Abs. 1, 2, §§ 321, 322 Abs. 4 und § 323 des Handelsgesetzbuchs entsprechend anzuwenden.

(5) Bei Versicherungsgesellschaften wird der Prüfer vom Aufsichtsrat bestimmt; Absatz 4 Satz 1 gilt sinngemäß. Soweit sich aus der Besonderheit des Prüfungsauftrags nichts anderes ergibt, ist

§ 209. Relevant Balance Sheet

(1) The resolution concerning conversion may be based on the latest balance sheet if such annual balance sheet has been audited and the approved annual balance sheet is provided with an unqualified auditors' certificate and if the balance sheet closing date is not more than eight months prior to the registrations of the resolution in the commercial register.

(2) If the resolution is not based on the latest annual balance sheet, the balance sheet shall comply with §§ 150 and 152 of this Act and §§ 242 to 256, 264 to 274 and 279 to 283 of the Commercial Code. The balance sheet closing date may be not more than eight months prior to the registration of the resolution in the commercial register.

(3) The balance sheet must be audited by an external auditor as to whether it complies with §§ 150 and 152 of this Act and §§ 242 to 256, 264 to 274, 279 to 283 of the Commercial Code. Such balance sheet must be provided with an unqualified auditors' certificate.

(4) Unless the shareholders' meeting elects another auditor, the auditor who was elected by the shareholders' meeting to audit the latest annual financial statements or who was appointed by the court for such purpose shall be deemed to have been elected. Unless the special nature of the audit requires otherwise, § 308 (1) sentence 3, § 319 (1) to (3), § 320 (1), (2), §§ 321, 322 (4) and § 323 of the Commercial Code shall apply analogously to the audit.

(5) In the case of insurance companies the auditor shall be appointed by the supervisory board; subsection (4) sentence 1 shall apply analogously. Unless the special nature of the audit requires

auf die Prüfung § 341k des Handelsgesetzbuchs anzuwenden.

(6) Im Fall der Absätze 2 bis 5 gilt für die Auslegung der Bilanz und für die Erteilung von Abschriften § 175 Abs. 2 sinngemäß.

§ 210. Anmeldung und Eintragung des Beschlusses

(1) Der Anmeldung des Beschlusses zur Eintragung in das Handelsregister ist für das Gericht des Sitzes der Gesellschaft die der Kapitalerhöhung zugrunde gelegte Bilanz mit Bestätigungsvermerk, im Fall des § 209 Abs. 2 bis 6 außerdem die letzte Jahresbilanz, sofern sie noch nicht eingereicht ist, beizufügen. Die Anmeldenden haben dem Gericht gegenüber zu erklären, daß nach ihrer Kenntnis seit dem Stichtag der zugrunde gelegten Bilanz bis zum Tag der Anmeldung keine Vermögensminderung eingetreten ist, die der Kapitalerhöhung entgegenstünde, wenn sie am Tag der Anmeldung beschlossen worden wäre.

(2) Das Gericht darf den Beschluß nur eintragen, wenn die der Kapitalerhöhung zugrunde gelegte Bilanz auf einen höchstens acht Monate vor der Anmeldung liegenden Stichtag aufgestellt und eine Erklärung nach Absatz 1 Satz 2 abgegeben worden ist.

(3) Das Gericht braucht nicht zu prüfen, ob die Bilanzen den gesetzlichen Vorschriften entsprechen.

(4) Bei der Eintragung des Beschlusses ist anzugeben, daß es sich um eine Kapitalerhöhung aus Gesellschaftsmitteln handelt.

otherwise, § 341k of the Commercial Code shall apply to the audit.

(6) In the case of subsections (2) to (5), § 175 (2) shall apply analogously to the display of the balance sheet for inspection and the distribution of copies.

§ 210. Report and Registration of the Resolution

(1) The report of the resolution for registration in the commercial register shall include for the court of the company's domicile the relevant balance sheet for the capital increase together with the auditors' certificate and, in the case of § 209 (2) to (6), in addition the latest annual balance sheet, if not already submitted. The persons reporting shall declare to the court that, to their knowledge, no reduction in value of assets has occurred between the closing date of the relevant balance sheet and the date of the report which would preclude a capital increase if such resolution were to be adopted on the date of the report.

(2) The court may register the resolution only if the record date of the balance sheet on which the capital increase was based was no later than eight months prior to the report and a declaration in accordance with subsection (1) sentence 2 has been given.

(3) The court need not examine whether the balance sheets comply with statutory provisions.

(4) The registration entry of the resolution shall state that the capital increase was made from the company's reserves.

(**5**) Die eingereichten Schriftstücke werden beim Gericht in Urschrift, Ausfertigung oder öffentlich beglaubigter Abschrift aufbewahrt.

(**5**) The documents submitted shall be filed with the court in original, duplicate, or officially certified copy.

§ 211. Wirksamwerden der Kapitalerhöhung

§ 211. Effectiveness of the Capital Increase

(**1**) Mit der Eintragung des Beschlusses über die Erhöhung des Grundkapitals ist das Grundkapital erhöht.

(**1**) The increase of share capital shall become effective upon registration of the resolution on the share capital increase.

(**2**) (*aufgehoben*)

(**2**) (*repealed*)

§ 212. Aus der Kapitalerhöhung Berechtigte

§ 212. Persons Entitled to New Shares

Die neuen Aktien stehen den Aktionären im Verhältnis ihrer Anteile am bisherigen Grundkapital zu. Ein entgegenstehender Beschluß der Hauptversammlung ist nichtig.

The new shares shall be allocated to the shareholders in proportion to their holdings of the previously existing share capital. Any resolution of the shareholders' meeting to the contrary shall be null and void.

§ 213. Teilrechte

§ 213. Fractional Shares

(**1**) Führt die Kapitalerhöhung dazu, daß auf einen Anteil am bisherigen Grundkapital nur ein Teil einer neuen Aktie entfällt, so ist dieses Teilrecht selbständig veräußerlich und vererblich.

(**1**) If the capital increase shall result in only a fraction of a new share being allocated to a holding of the previously existing share capital, such fractional share may be separately disposed of or inherited.

(**2**) Die Rechte aus einer neuen Aktie einschließlich des Anspruchs auf Ausstellung einer Aktienurkunde können nur ausgeübt werden, wenn Teilrechte, die zusammen eine volle Aktie ergeben, in einer Hand vereinigt sind oder wenn sich mehrere Berechtigte, deren Teilrechte zusammen eine volle Aktie ergeben, zur Ausübung der Rechte zusammenschließen.

(**2**) The rights arising under a new share, including the right to receive a share certificate, may be exercised only if fractional shares which in aggregate comprise a full share are held by one person or if several persons, whose fractional shares comprise a full share, exercise such rights jointly.

§ 214. Aufforderung an die Aktionäre

(1) Nach der Eintragung des Beschlusses über die Erhöhung des Grundkapitals hat der Vorstand unverzüglich die Aktionäre aufzufordern, die neuen Aktien abzuholen. Die Aufforderung ist in den Gesellschaftsblättern bekanntzumachen. In der Bekanntmachung ist anzugeben,

1. um welchen Betrag das Grundkapital erhöht worden ist,
2. in welchem Verhältnis auf die alten Aktien neue Aktien entfallen.

In der Bekanntmachung ist ferner darauf hinzuweisen, daß die Gesellschaft berechtigt ist, Aktien, die nicht innerhalb eines Jahres seit der Bekanntmachung der Aufforderung abgeholt werden, nach dreimaliger Androhung für Rechnung der Beteiligten zu verkaufen.

(2) Nach Ablauf eines Jahres seit der Bekanntmachung der Aufforderung hat die Gesellschaft den Verkauf der nicht abgeholten Aktien anzudrohen. Die Androhung ist dreimal in Abständen von mindestens einem Monat in den Gesellschaftsblättern bekanntzumachen. Die letzte Bekanntmachung muß vor dem Ablauf von achtzehn Monaten seit der Bekanntmachung der Aufforderung ergehen.

(3) Nach Ablauf eines Jahres seit der letzten Bekanntmachung der Androhung hat die Gesellschaft die nicht abgeholten Aktien für Rechnung der Beteiligten zum amtlichen Börsenpreis durch Vermittlung eines Kursmaklers und beim Fehlen eines Börsenpreises durch öffentliche Versteigerung zu verkaufen. § 226 Abs. 3 Satz 2 bis 6 gilt sinngemäß.

§ 214. Notice to Shareholders

(1) After registration of the resolution on the share capital increase the management board shall promptly request the shareholders to take delivery of the new share certificates. Such notice shall be published in the company's designated journals. Such publication shall state:

1. the amount by which the share capital has been increased,
2. the proportion in which new shares have been allocated for previously existing shares.

Such announcement shall further state that the company may, after three warnings, sell any shares on behalf of the persons entitled thereto which have not been collected within one year after publication of the notice.

(2) Upon expiration of one year from the date of the notice the company shall warn that any shares not collected may be sold. Such warning shall be published three times in intervals of not less than one month in the company's journals. The last publication must be made prior to the expiration of eighteen months from the date of publication of the notice.

(3) Upon expiration of one year from the date of the last publication of the warning, the company shall sell on behalf of the persons entitled thereto any shares not collected at the official stock exchange quotation through the intermediation of a stock broker and in the absence of a stock exchange quotation by public auction. § 226 (3) sentences 2 to 6 shall apply analogously.

(4) Die Absätze 1 bis 3 gelten sinngemäß für Gesellschaften, die keine Aktienurkunden ausgegeben haben. Die Gesellschaften haben die Aktionäre aufzufordern, sich die neuen Aktien zuteilen zu lassen.

(4) Subsections (1) to (3) shall apply analogously to companies which have not issued share certificates. Such companies shall request the shareholders to accept the allocation of new shares.

§ 215. Eigene Aktien. Teileingezahlte Aktien

§ 215. Company Shares held by the Company; Partially Paid Shares

(1) Eigene Aktien nehmen an der Erhöhung des Grundkapitals teil.

(1) Company shares held by the company shall participate in any increase of share capital.

(2) Teileingezahlte Aktien nehmen entsprechend ihrem Nennbetrag an der Erhöhung des Grundkapitals teil. Bei ihnen kann die Kapitalerhöhung nur durch Erhöhung des Nennbetrags der Aktien ausgeführt werden. Sind neben teileingezahlten Aktien volleingezahlte Aktien vorhanden, so kann bei diesen die Kapitalerhöhung durch Erhöhung des Nennbetrags der Aktien und durch Ausgabe neuer Aktien ausgeführt werden; der Beschluß über die Erhöhung des Grundkapitals muß die Art der Erhöhung angeben. Soweit die Kapitalerhöhung durch Erhöhung des Nennbetrags der Aktien ausgeführt wird, ist sie so zu bemessen, daß durch sie auf keine Aktie Beträge entfallen, die durch eine Erhöhung des Nennbetrags der Aktien nicht gedeckt werden können.

(2) Partially paid shares shall participate in any increase of share capital in proportion to their par value. In such cases the capital increase may be carried out only by increasing the par value of the shares. If fully paid shares exist in addition to partially paid shares, the capital increase in respect of such fully paid shares may be carried out by increasing the par value of the shares and issuing new shares; the resolution on the share capital increase shall specify the manner of the increase. If the capital increase is carried out by increasing the par value of the shares, the amount of such capital increase shall be so computed that the amount allocated to each share is fully covered by the increase in the par value.

§ 216. Wahrung der Rechte der Aktionäre und Dritter

§ 216. Preservation of the Rights of Shareholders and Third Persons

(1) Das Verhältnis der mit den Aktien verbundenen Rechte zueinander wird durch die Kapitalerhöhung nicht berührt. Die Ausgabe neuer Mehrstimmrechtsaktien und die Erhöhung des Stimmrechts von Mehrstimmrechtsaktien auf Grund des Satzes 1 bedürfen keiner Zulassung nach § 12 Abs. 2 Satz 2.

(1) The proportion of rights arising from shares shall not be affected by the capital increase. The issue of new shares with multiple voting rights and the increase of the voting rights of shares with multiple voting rights pursuant to sentence 1 shall not require permission pursuant to § 12 (2) sentence 2.

(2) Soweit sich einzelne Rechte teileingezahlter Aktien, insbesondere die Beteiligung am Gewinn oder das Stimmrecht, nach der auf die Aktie geleisteten Einlage bestimmen, stehen diese Rechte den Aktionären bis zur Leistung der noch ausstehenden Einlagen nur nach der Höhe der geleisteten Einlage, erhöht um den auf den Nennbetrag des Grundkapitals berechneten Hundertsatz der Erhöhung des Grundkapitals zu. Werden weitere Einzahlungen geleistet, so erweitern sich diese Rechte entsprechend. Im Fall des § 271 Abs. 3 gelten die Erhöhungsbeträge als voll eingezahlt.

(2) To the extent that specific rights arising from partially paid shares, in particular the right to participate in the distributions of profit or the right to vote, are determined by the contribution made in respect of each share, the shareholders shall have such rights, until performance of the contributions still outstanding, only in proportion to the amount of the respective contributions made increased by the percentage increase in the share capital which was computed for the par value of the share capital. If further contributions are made, such rights shall increase proportionately. In the case of § 271 (3) the amounts of the increase shall be deemed to be paid in full.

(3) Der wirtschaftliche Inhalt vertraglicher Beziehungen der Gesellschaft zu Dritten, die von der Gewinnausschüttung der Gesellschaft, dem Nennbetrag oder Wert ihrer Aktien oder ihres Grundkapitals oder sonst von den bisherigen Kapital- oder Gewinnverhältnissen abhängen, wird durch die Kapitalerhöhung nicht berührt. Gleiches gilt für Nebenverpflichtungen der Aktionäre.

(3) The financial terms of agreements between the company and third persons which are related to the distribution of the company's profits or the par value or market value of its share capital or the previously existing capital or profitability, shall not be affected by the capital increase. The foregoing shall apply to the ancillary obligations of the shareholders.

§ 217. Beginn der Gewinnbeteiligung

§ 217. Commencement of Participation in Profits

(1) Die neuen Aktien nehmen, wenn nichts anderes bestimmt ist, am Gewinn des ganzen Geschäftsjahrs teil, in dem die Erhöhung des Grundkapitals beschlossen worden ist.

(1) Unless otherwise provided, the new shares shall participate in profits of the entire fiscal year in which the resolution on the share capital increase was adopted.

(2) Im Beschluß über die Erhöhung des Grundkapitals kann bestimmt werden, daß die neuen Aktien bereits am Gewinn des letzten vor der Beschlußfassung über die Kapitalerhöhung abgelaufenen Geschäftsjahrs teilnehmen. In diesem Fall ist die Erhöhung des Grundkapitals zu beschließen, bevor über die Verwendung des Bilanzgewinns des letzten vor

(2) The resolution on the share capital increase may provide that the new shares also participate in the profits of the latest fiscal year ended prior to adoption of the resolution on the capital increase. In such case the resolution on the share capital increase shall be adopted prior to adoption of the resolution on the appropriation of distributable profits of the la-

der Beschlußfassung abgelaufenen Geschäftsjahrs Beschluß gefaßt ist. Der Beschluß über die Verwendung des Bilanzgewinns des letzten vor der Beschlußfassung über die Kapitalerhöhung abgelaufenen Geschäftsjahrs wird erst wirksam, wenn das Grundkapital erhöht ist. Der Beschluß über die Erhöhung des Grundkapitals und der Beschluß über die Verwendung des Bilanzgewinns des letzten vor der Beschlußfassung über die Kapitalerhöhung abgelaufenen Geschäftsjahrs sind nichtig, wenn der Beschluß über die Kapitalerhöhung nicht binnen drei Monaten nach der Beschlußfassung in das Handelsregister eingetragen worden ist. Der Lauf der Frist ist gehemmt, solange eine Anfechtungs- oder Nichtigkeitsklage rechtshängig ist oder eine zur Kapitalerhöhung beantragte staatliche Genehmigung noch nicht erteilt ist.

test fiscal year ended prior to adoption of such resolution on the capital increase. The resolution on the appropriation of the distributable profits of the latest fiscal year ended prior to adoption of the resolution on the capital increase shall become effective only after the share capital has been increased. The resolution on the share capital increase and the resolution on the appropriation of the distributable profits of the last fiscal year ended prior to adoption of the resolution on the capital increase shall be null and void if the resolution on the capital increase has not been registered in the commercial register within three months after adoption of the resolution. The running of such period shall be tolled for as long as an action to set aside or annul the resolution shall be pending or any governmental approval which has been applied for in connection with the capital increase has not yet been granted.

§ 218. Bedingtes Kapital

Bedingtes Kapital erhöht sich im gleichen Verhältnis wie das Grundkapital. Ist das bedingte Kapital zur Gewährung von Umtauschrechten an Gläubiger von Wandelschuldverschreibungen beschlossen worden, so ist zur Deckung des Unterschieds zwischen dem Ausgabebetrag der Schuldverschreibungen und dem höheren Gesamtnennbetrag der für sie zu gewährenden Bezugsaktien eine Sonderrücklage zu bilden, soweit nicht Zuzahlungen der Umtauschberechtigten vereinbart sind.

§ 218. Contingent Capital

Contingent capital shall increase in the same proportion as share capital. If the purpose of the contingent capital is to grant conversion rights to holders of convertible or warrant bonds, a special reserve shall be created in an amount equal to the difference between the issue price of bonds of the higher aggregate par value of the new shares to be issued therefor to the extent that additional payments by the persons entitled to conversion have not been agreed upon.

§ 219. Verbotene Ausgabe von Aktien und Zwischenscheinen

Vor der Eintragung des Beschlusses über die Erhöhung des Grundkapitals in das Handelsregister dürfen neue Aktien

§ 219. Prohibited Issue of Share Certificates and Interim Certificates

New share certificates and interim certificates may not be issued prior to regis-

und Zwischenscheine nicht ausgegeben werden.

tration of the resolution on the share capital increase in the commercial register.

§ 220. Wertansätze

Als Anschaffungskosten der vor der Erhöhung des Grundkapitals erworbenen Aktien und der auf sie entfallenen neuen Aktien gelten die Beträge, die sich für die einzelnen Aktien ergeben, wenn die Anschaffungskosten der vor der Erhöhung des Grundkapitals erworbenen Aktien auf diese und auf die auf sie entfallenen neuen Aktien nach dem Verhältnis der Nennbeträge verteilt werden. Der Zuwachs an Aktien ist nicht als Zugang auszuweisen.

§ 220. Valuation

The costs of acquisition of the shares acquired prior to the share capital increase and the new shares issued therefor shall be deemed to be the amounts attributable to the individual shares after allocation of the costs of acquisition of the shares acquired to the share capital increase between such shares and the new shares issued therefor in proportion to the respective par values. The additional shares may not be shown as newly required shares.

FÜNFTER UNTERABSCHNITT. WANDELSCHULDVERSCHREIBUNGEN. GEWINNSCHULDVERSCHREIBUNGEN

SUBDIVISION FIVE. CONVERTIBLE OR WARRANT BONDS; DIVIDEND BONDS

§ 221.

(1) Schuldverschreibungen, bei denen den Gläubigern ein Umtausch- oder Bezugsrecht auf Aktien eingeräumt wird (Wandelschuldverschreibungen), und Schuldverschreibungen, bei denen die Rechte der Gläubiger mit Gewinnanteilen von Aktionären in Verbindung gebracht werden (Gewinnschuldverschreibungen), dürfen nur auf Grund eines Beschlusses der Hauptversammlung ausgegeben werden. Der Beschluß bedarf einer Mehrheit, die mindestens drei Viertel des bei der Beschlußfassung vertretenen Grundkapitals umfaßt. Die Satzung kann eine andere Kapitalmehrheit und weitere Erfordernisse bestimmen. § 182 Abs. 2 gilt.

(2) Eine Ermächtigung des Vorstandes zur Ausgabe von Wandelschuldverschreibungen kann höchstens für fünf Jahre erteilt werden. Der Vorstand und

§ 221.

(1) Bonds which provide holders with a conversion right or stock warrant ('convertible or warrant bonds') and bonds in which the rights of the holders are related to dividends paid to shareholders ('dividend bonds') may only be issued on the basis of a resolution of the shareholders' meeting. Such resolution shall require a majority of not less than three fourths of the share capital represented at the passing of the resolution. The articles may provide for a different capital majority and additional requirements. § 182 (2) shall apply.

(2) The management board may be authorized for a period of not more than five years to issue convertible or warrant bonds. The management board and the

der Vorsitzende des Aufsichtsrats haben den Beschluß über die Ausgabe der Wandelschuldverschreibungen sowie eine Erklärung über deren Ausgabe beim Handelsregister zu hinterlegen. Ein Hinweis auf den Beschluß und die Erklärung ist in den Gesellschaftsblättern bekanntzumachen.

chairman of the supervisory board shall submit to the commercial register the resolution on the issue of convertible or warrant bonds and a confirmation of their issue. An announcement as to the resolution and the confirmation of issue shall be published in the company's journals.

(3) Absatz 1 gilt sinngemäß für die Gewährung von Genußrechten.

(3) Subsection (1) shall apply analogously to the issue of participation rights.

(4) Auf Wandelschuldverschreibungen, Gewinnschuldverschreibungen und Genußrechte haben die Aktionäre ein Bezugsrecht. § 186 gilt sinngemäß.

(4) Shareholders shall have pre-emptive rights with respect to convertible or warrant bonds, dividend bonds and participation rights. § 186 shall apply analogously.

Dritter Abschnitt. Maßnahmen der Kapitalherabsetzung

Division Three. Capital Reductions

ERSTER UNTERABSCHNITT. ORDENTLICHE KAPITALHERABSETZUNG

SUBDIVISION ONE. ORDINARY CAPITAL REDUCTION

§ 222. Voraussetzungen

§ 222. General Provisions

(1) Eine Herabsetzung des Grundkapitals kann nur mit einer Mehrheit beschlossen werden, die mindestens drei Viertel des bei der Beschlußfassung vertretenen Grundkapitals umfaßt. Die Satzung kann eine größere Kapitalmehrheit und weitere Erfordernisse bestimmen.

(1) A reduction of the share capital shall require a resolution which has been adopted by a majority of not less than three fourths of the share capital represented at the passing of the resolution. The articles may provide for a larger capital majority and additional requirements.

(2) Sind mehrere Gattungen von stimmberechtigten Aktien vorhanden, so bedarf der Beschluß der Hauptversammlung zu seiner Wirksamkeit der Zustimmung der Aktionäre jeder Gattung. Über die Zustimmung haben die Aktionäre jeder Gattung einen Sonderbeschluß zu fassen. Für diesen gilt Absatz 1.

(2) If more than one class of voting shares is outstanding the resolution of the shareholders' meeting shall require the consent of the shareholders of each class in order to be effective. Such consent shall require a separate resolution by the shareholders of each class. Subsection (1) shall apply to such separate resolution.

(3) In dem Beschluß ist festzusetzen, zu welchem Zweck die Herabsetzung stattfindet, namentlich ob Teile des

(3) The resolution shall stipulate the purpose of the capital reduction, in par-

Grundkapitals zurückgezahlt werden sollen.

(4) Das Grundkapital kann herabgesetzt werden
1. durch Herabsetzung des Nennbetrags der Aktien;
2. durch Zusammenlegung der Aktien; diese ist nur zulässig, soweit der Mindestnennbetrag für Aktien nicht innegehalten werden kann.

Der Beschluß muß die Art der Herabsetzung angeben.

ticular whether part of the share capital is to be repaid.

(4) The share capital may be reduced by means of:
1. a reduction of the par value of the shares;
2. a consolidation of shares; such consolidation may only be made if the minimum par value of shares can not be maintained.

The resolution must stipulate in which manner the capital reduction is to be made.

§ 223. Anmeldung des Beschlusses

Der Vorstand und der Vorsitzende des Aufsichtsrats haben den Beschluß über die Herabsetzung des Grundkapitals zur Eintragung in das Handelsregister anzumelden.

§ 223. Registration of the Resolution

The management board and the chairman of the supervisory board shall report the resolution on the reduction of the share capital for registration in the commercial register.

§ 224. Wirksamwerden der Kapitalherabsetzung

Mit der Eintragung des Beschlusses über die Herabsetzung des Grundkapitals ist das Grundkapital herabgesetzt.

§ 224. Effectiveness of the Capital Reduction

The reduction of the share capital shall become effective upon registration of the resolution on the share capital reduction.

§ 225. Gläubigerschutz

(1) Den Gläubigern, deren Forderungen begründet worden sind, bevor die Eintragung des Beschlusses bekanntgemacht worden ist, ist, wenn sie sich binnen sechs Monaten nach der Bekanntmachung zu diesem Zweck melden, Sicherheit zu leisten, soweit sie nicht Befriedigung verlangen können. Die Gläubiger sind in der Bekanntmachung der Eintra-

§ 225. Protection of Creditors

(1) Creditors whose claims arose prior to the date of the announcement of the registration of the resolution shall, upon request within six months of the date of such announcement, be granted security to the extent that they may not demand satisfaction. In the announcement of registration the creditors shall be advised of such right. Creditors

gung auf dieses Recht hinzuweisen. Das Recht, Sicherheitsleistung zu verlangen, steht Gläubigern nicht zu, die im Fall des Konkurses[1] ein Recht auf vorzugsweise Befriedigung aus einer Deckungsmasse haben, die nach gesetzlicher Vorschrift zu ihrem Schutz errichtet und staatlich überwacht ist.

who in the case of bankruptcy[1] have a right to preferential satisfaction from a fund which has been established on the basis of statutory provisions for their protection and which is subject to governmental supervision shall not have the right to demand security.

(2) Zahlungen an die Aktionäre dürfen auf Grund der Herabsetzung des Grundkapitals erst geleistet werden, nachdem seit der Bekanntmachung der Eintragung sechs Monate verstrichen sind und nachdem den Gläubigern, die sich rechtzeitig gemeldet haben, Befriedigung oder Sicherheit gewährt worden ist. Auch eine Befreiung der Aktionäre von der Verpflichtung zur Leistung von Einlagen wird nicht vor dem bezeichneten Zeitpunkt und nicht vor Befriedigung oder Sicherstellung der Gläubiger wirksam, die sich rechtzeitig gemeldet haben.

(2) Payments to shareholders in connection with the reduction of share capital may only be made upon the expiration of six months from the date of the announcement of registration and after those creditors who have made a timely request have been satisfied or granted security. A release of shareholders from the obligation to make contributions shall not be effective prior to the aforementioned date and before the creditors who have made a timely request have been satisfied or granted security.

(3) Das Recht der Gläubiger, Sicherheitsleistung zu verlangen, ist unabhängig davon, ob Zahlungen an die Aktionäre auf Grund der Herabsetzung des Grundkapitals geleistet werden.

(3) The right of creditors to demand security shall not be conditional on payments having been made to shareholders in connection with the reduction of share capital.

§ 226. Kraftloserklärung von Aktien

§ 226. Cancellation of Share Certificates

(1) Sollen zur Durchführung der Herabsetzung des Grundkapitals Aktien durch Umtausch, Abstempelung oder durch ein ähnliches Verfahren zusammengelegt werden, so kann die Gesellschaft die Aktien für kraftlos erklären, die trotz Aufforderung nicht bei ihr eingereicht worden sind. Gleiches gilt für eingereichte Aktien, welche die zum Ersatz durch neue Aktien nötige Zahl nicht erreichen und der Gesellschaft nicht zur Ver-

(1) If share certificates are to be consolidated in connection with the reduction of share capital by exchanging or stamping share certificates or a similar procedure, the company may declare the share certificates which despite notice have been surrendered to have been cancelled. The foregoing shall apply to share certificates surrendered which are insufficient in number for replacement by new share certificates and which have not

1. Mit Wirkung vom 1. Januar 1999 sind die Worte 'des Konkurses' durch die Worte 'des Insolvenzverfahrens' ersetzt.

1. Effective as of 1 January 1999 the word 'bankruptcy' will be substituted by the words 'insolvency proceedings'.

wertung für Rechnung der Beteiligten zur Verfügung gestellt sind.

(2) Die Aufforderung, die Aktien einzureichen, hat die Kraftloserklärung anzudrohen. Die Kraftloserklärung kann nur erfolgen, wenn die Aufforderung in der in § 64 Abs. 2 für die Nachfrist vorgeschriebenen Weise bekanntgemacht worden ist. Die Kraftloserklärung geschieht durch Bekanntmachung in den Gesellschaftsblättern. In der Bekanntmachung sind die für kraftlos erklärten Aktien so zu bezeichnen, daß sich aus der Bekanntmachung ohne weiteres ergibt, ob eine Aktie für kraftlos erklärt ist.

(3) Die neuen Aktien, die an Stelle der für kraftlos erklärten Aktien auszugeben sind, hat die Gesellschaft unverzüglich für Rechnung der Beteiligten zum amtlichen Börsenpreis durch Vermittlung eines Kursmaklers und beim Fehlen eines Börsenpreises durch öffentliche Versteigerung zu verkaufen. Ist von der Versteigerung am Sitz der Gesellschaft kein angemessener Erfolg zu erwarten, so sind die Aktien an einem geeigneten Ort zu verkaufen. Zeit, Ort und Gegenstand der Versteigerung sind öffentlich bekanntzumachen. Die Beteiligten sind besonders zu benachrichtigen; die Benachrichtigung kann unterbleiben, wenn sie untunlich ist. Bekanntmachung und Benachrichtigung müssen mindestens zwei Wochen vor der Versteigerung ergehen. Der Erlös ist den Beteiligten auszuzahlen oder, wenn ein Recht zur Hinterlegung besteht, zu hinterlegen.

§ 227. Anmeldung der Durchführung

(1) Der Vorstand hat die Durchführung der Herabsetzung des Grundkapitals zur Eintragung in das Handelsregister anzumelden.

been submitted to the company for sale on behalf of the persons concerned.

(2) The notice to surrender share certificates shall give warning of cancellation. Cancellation may only be made if the notice has been published in the manner prescribed by § 64 (2) for the additional period. Cancellation shall become effective upon publication in the company's designated journals. In such publication the cancelled shares shall be identified in such manner that the publication alone shall suffice to ascertain whether a share certificate has been cancelled.

(3) The new share certificates which are to be issued in place of the cancelled share certificates shall be promptly sold by the company on behalf of the persons concerned at the official stock exchange quotation through the intermediation of a stock broker and in the absence of a stock exchange quotation by public auction. If adequate results can not be expected from an auction at the company's domicile the shares shall be sold at an appropriate location. The time, place and object of the auction shall be announced. The persons concerned shall be notified separately; such notification may be omitted if not feasible. The announcement and notification must be made not less than two weeks prior to the auction. The proceeds shall be paid to the persons concerned or, if a right to deposit exists, be deposited.

§ 227. Registration

(1) The management board shall report the completion of the share capital reduction for registration in the commercial register.

(2) Anmeldung und Eintragung der Durchführung der Herabsetzung des Grundkapitals können mit Anmeldung und Eintragung des Beschlusses über die Herabsetzung verbunden werden.

(2) The report and registration of the completion of the share capital reduction may be made together with the report and registration of the resolution on the reduction.

§ 228. Herabsetzung unter den Mindestnennbetrag

§ 228. Reduction to Less than the Minimum Par Value

(1) Das Grundkapital kann unter den in § 7 bestimmten Mindestnennbetrag herabgesetzt werden, wenn dieser durch eine Kapitalerhöhung wieder erreicht wird, die zugleich mit der Kapitalherabsetzung beschlossen ist und bei der Sacheinlagen nicht festgesetzt sind.

(1) The share capital may be reduced to less than the minimum par value prescribed in § 7 if the minimum par value is restored by means of a capital increase which has been resolved upon at the same time as the capital reduction and for which contributions in kind have not been stipulated.

(2) Die Beschlüsse sind nichtig, wenn sie und die Durchführung der Erhöhung nicht binnen sechs Monaten nach der Beschlußfassung in das Handelsregister eingetragen worden sind. Der Lauf der Frist ist gehemmt, solange eine Anfechtungs- oder Nichtigkeitsklage rechtshängig ist oder eine zur Kapitalherabsetzung oder Kapitalerhöhung beantragte staatliche Genehmigung noch nicht erteilt ist. Die Beschlüsse und die Durchführung der Erhöhung des Grundkapitals sollen nur zusammen in das Handelsregister eingetragen werden.

(2) Such resolutions shall be null and void if the resolutions and the completion of the increase have not been registered in the commercial register within six months after the date of adoption of the resolutions. The running of such period shall be tolled for as long as an action to set aside or annul the resolution shall be pending or a governmental approval which has been applied for in connection with the capital reduction or capital increase has not yet been granted. The resolutions and the completion of the share capital increase may only be registered at the same time in the commercial register.

ZWEITER UNTERABSCHNITT. VEREINFACHTE KAPITALHERABSETZUNG

SUBDIVISION TWO. SIMPLIFIED PROCEDURE FOR CAPITAL REDUCTION

§ 229. Voraussetzungen

§ 229. General Provisions

(1) Eine Herabsetzung des Grundkapitals, die dazu dienen soll, Wertminderungen auszugleichen, sonstige Verluste zu decken oder Beträge in die Kapitalrücklage einzustellen, kann in vereinfachter Form vorgenommen werden. Im

(1) A simplified procedure may be employed for a share capital reduction for the purpose of compensation for a decline in the value of assets, offsetting other losses or transferring amounts to the capital reserve. The resolution shall stipulate

Beschluß ist festzusetzen, daß die Herabsetzung zu diesen Zwecken stattfindet.

that the reduction is made for such purposes.

(2) Die vereinfachte Kapitalherabsetzung ist nur zulässig, nachdem der Teil der gesetzlichen Rücklage und der Kapitalrücklage, um den diese zusammen über zehn vom Hundert des nach der Herabsetzung verbleibenden Grundkapitals hinausgehen, sowie die Gewinnrücklagen vorweg aufgelöst sind. Sie ist nicht zulässig, solange ein Gewinnvortrag vorhanden ist.

(2) The simplified procedure for capital reduction may only be employed after any amount by which the sum of the legal reserve and the capital reserve exceeds ten per cent of the share capital remaining after such reduction and any amounts in the profit reserves have been released. Such simplified procedure may not be employed for as long as profit carried forward is shown.

(3) § 222 Abs. 1, 2 und 4, §§ 223, 224, 226 bis 228 über die ordentliche Kapitalherabsetzung gelten sinngemäß.

(3) § 222 (1), (2) and (4), §§ 223, 224 and 226 to 228 regarding the ordinary capital reduction shall apply analogously.

§ 230. Verbot von Zahlungen an die Aktionäre

§ 230. Prohibition of Payments to Shareholders

Die Beträge, die aus der Auflösung der Kapital- oder Gewinnrücklagen und aus der Kapitalherabsetzung gewonnen werden, dürfen nicht zu Zahlungen an die Aktionäre und nicht dazu verwandt werden, die Aktionäre von der Verpflichtung zur Leistung von Einlagen zu befreien. Sie dürfen nur verwandt werden, um Wertminderungen auszugleichen, sonstige Verluste zu decken und Beträge in die Kapitalrücklage oder in die gesetzliche Rücklage einzustellen. Auch eine Verwendung zu einem dieser Zwecke ist nur zulässig, soweit sie im Beschluß als Zweck der Herabsetzung angegeben ist.

The amounts which are obtained from the release of the capital and profit reserves and the capital reduction may not be utilized for payments to shareholders or to exempt shareholders from their obligation to make contributions. Such amount may be utilized only to compensate for declines in the value of assets, to offset other losses and to transfer amounts to the capital reserve or the legal reserve. Such amounts may be utilized for such purpose only to the extent that the resolution states that such utilization is the purpose of the reduction.

§ 231. Beschränkte Einstellung in die Kapitalrücklage und in die gesetzliche Rücklage

§ 231. Limited Transfer to the Capital Reserve and the Legal Reserve

Die Einstellung der Beträge, die aus der Auflösung von anderen Gewinnrücklagen gewonnen werden, in die gesetzliche Rücklage und der Beträge, die aus der Kapitalherabsetzung gewonnen werden,

The transfer to the legal reserve of amounts obtained from the release of other profit reserves and to the capital reserve of amounts obtained from the capital reduction may be made only to the

in die Kapitalrücklage ist nur zulässig, soweit die Kapitalrücklage und die gesetzliche Rücklage zusammen zehn vom Hundert des Grundkapitals nicht übersteigen. Als Grundkapital gilt dabei der Nennbetrag, der sich durch die Herabsetzung ergibt, mindestens aber der in § 7 bestimmte Mindestnennbetrag. Bei der Bemessung der zulässigen Höhe bleiben Beträge, die in der Zeit nach der Beschlußfassung über die Kapitalherabsetzung in die Kapitalrücklage einzustellen sind, auch dann außer Betracht, wenn ihre Zahlung auf einem Beschluß beruht, der zugleich mit dem Beschluß über die Kapitalherabsetzung gefaßt wird.

extent that the sum of the capital reserve and the legal reserve does not exceed ten per cent of the share capital. In such case the share capital shall be deemed to be the par value which results from the reduction but not less than the minimum par value prescribed in § 7. In comparing the amounts which may be transferred, amounts which are to be transferred to the capital reserve after the adoption of the resolution on the capital reduction shall not be taken into account even if such transfer is based on a resolution which is adopted at the same time as the resolution on the capital reduction.

§ 232. Einstellung von Beträgen in die Kapitalrücklage bei zu hoch angenommenen Verlusten

Ergibt sich bei Aufstellung der Jahresbilanz für das Geschäftsjahr, in dem der Beschluß über die Kapitalherabsetzung gefaßt wurde, oder für eines der beiden folgenden Geschäftsjahre, daß Wertminderungen und sonstige Verluste in der bei der Beschlußfassung angenommenen Höhe tatsächlich nicht eingetreten oder ausgeglichen waren, so ist der Unterschiedsbetrag in die Kapitalrücklage einzustellen.

§ 232. Transfer of Amounts to the Capital Reserve in the Case of Overestimated Losses

If it becomes apparent in connection with the preparation of the annual balance sheet for the fiscal year in which the resolution on the capital reduction was adopted or for one of the two following fiscal years that declines in the value of assets or other losses have not in fact occurred in the amount estimated when the resolution was adopted or have been offset, the amount of the differences shall be transferred to the capital reserve.

§ 233. Gewinnausschüttung. Gläubigerschutz

(1) Gewinn darf nicht ausgeschüttet werden, bevor die gesetzliche Rücklage und die Kapitalrücklage zusammen zehn vom Hundert des Grundkapitals erreicht haben. Als Grundkapital gilt dabei der Nennbetrag, der sich durch die Herabsetzung ergibt, mindestens aber der in § 7 bestimmte Mindestnennbetrag.

§ 233. Payments of Dividends; Protection of Creditors

(1) Dividends may not be paid for as long as the legal reserve and the capital reserve in aggregate do not amount to ten per cent of the share capital. For such purpose the share capital shall be deemed to be the par value which results from the reduction, but not less than the minimum par value prescribed in § 7.

(2) Die Zahlung eines Gewinnanteils von mehr als vier vom Hundert ist erst für ein Geschäftsjahr zulässig, das später als zwei Jahre nach der Beschlußfassung über die Kapitalherabsetzung beginnt. Dies gilt nicht, wenn die Gläubiger, deren Forderungen vor der Bekanntmachung der Eintragung des Beschlusses begründet worden waren, befriedigt oder sichergestellt sind, soweit sie sich binnen sechs Monaten nach der Bekanntmachung des Jahresabschlusses, auf Grund dessen die Gewinnverteilung beschlossen ist, zu diesem Zweck gemeldet haben. Einer Sicherstellung der Gläubiger bedarf es nicht, die im Fall des Konkurses[1] ein Recht auf vorzugsweise Befriedigung aus einer Deckungsmasse haben, die nach gesetzlicher Vorschrift zu ihrem Schutz errichtet und staatlich überwacht ist. Die Gläubiger sind in der Bekanntmachung nach § 325 Abs. 1 Satz 2 oder Abs. 2 Satz 1 des Handelsgesetzbuchs auf die Befriedigung oder Sicherstellung hinzuweisen.

(2) A dividend exceeding four per cent may not be paid for a fiscal year beginning earlier than two years after the resolution on the capital reduction has been adopted. The foregoing shall not apply if creditors whose claims arose prior to announcement of the registration of such resolution have been satisfied or provided with security, if they have applied for this purpose within six months after publication of the annual financial statements which formed the basis for the resolution on the dividend. It is not necessary to secure creditors who in the case of bankruptcy[1] have a right to preferential satisfaction from a fund which has been established pursuant to statutory provisions for their protection and is subject to governmental supervision. In the announcement pursuant to § 325 (1) sentence 2 or (2) sentence 1 of the Commercial Code the creditors shall be advised of such satisfaction or provision of security.

(3) Die Beträge, die aus der Auflösung von Kapital- und Gewinnrücklagen und aus der Kapitalherabsetzung gewonnen sind, dürfen auch nach diesen Vorschriften nicht als Gewinn ausgeschüttet werden.

(3) The foregoing provisions do not permit the payment of dividends from amounts released from the capital and legal reserves or obtained in connection with the capital reduction.

§ 234. Rückwirkung der Kapitalherabsetzung

(1) Im Jahresabschluß für das letzte vor der Beschlußfassung über die Kapitalherabsetzung abgelaufene Geschäftsjahr können das gezeichnete Kapital sowie die Kapital- und Gewinnrücklagen in der Höhe ausgewiesen werden, in der sie nach der Kapitalherabsetzung bestehen sollen.

§ 234. Retroactive Effect of the Capital Reduction

(1) In the annual financial statements for the latest fiscal year ended prior to adoption of the resolution on the capital reduction the subscribed capital and the capital and legal reserves may be shown in the respective amounts which will prevail upon completion of the capital reduction.

1. Mit Wirkung vom 1. Januar 1999 sind die Worte 'des Konkurses' durch die Worte 'des Insolvenzverfahrens' ersetzt.

1. Effective as of 1 January 1999 the word 'bankruptcy' will be substituted by the words 'insolvency proceedings'.

(2) In diesem Fall beschließt die Hauptversammlung über die Feststellung des Jahresabschlusses. Der Beschluß soll zugleich mit dem Beschluß über die Kapitalherabsetzung gefaßt werden.

(2) In such case the shareholders' meeting shall resolve on approval of the annual financial statements. Such resolution should be adopted together with the resolution on the capital reduction.

(3) Die Beschlüsse sind nichtig, wenn der Beschluß über die Kapitalherabsetzung nicht binnen drei Monaten nach der Beschlußfassung in das Handelsregister eingetragen worden ist. Der Lauf der Frist ist gehemmt, solange eine Anfechtungs- oder Nichtigkeitsklage rechtshängig ist oder eine zur Kapitalherabsetzung beantragte staatliche Genehmigung noch nicht erteilt ist.

(3) The resolution shall be null and void if the resolution on the capital reduction has not been registered in the commercial register within three months of adoption of the resolution. The running of such period shall be tolled for as long as an action to set aside or annul the resolution shall be pending or a governmental approval which has been applied for in connection with the capital reduction has not yet been granted.

§ 235. Rückwirkung einer gleichzeitigen Kapitalerhöhung

§ 235. Retroactive Effect of a Simultaneous Capital Increase

(1) Wird im Fall des § 234 zugleich mit der Kapitalherabsetzung eine Erhöhung des Grundkapitals beschlossen, so kann auch die Kapitalerhöhung in dem Jahresabschluß als vollzogen berücksichtigt werden. Die Beschlußfassung ist nur zulässig, wenn die neuen Aktien gezeichnet, keine Sacheinlagen festgesetzt sind und wenn auf jede Aktie die Einzahlung geleistet ist, die nach § 188 Abs. 2 zur Zeit der Anmeldung der Durchführung der Kapitalerhöhung bewirkt sein muß. Die Zeichnung und die Einzahlung sind dem Notar nachzuweisen, der den Beschluß über die Erhöhung des Grundkapitals beurkundet.

(1) If in the case of § 234 a capital reduction and a share capital increase have been resolved upon at the same time, the capital increase may also be treated in the annual financial statements as having been completed. Such a resolution may only be adopted if the new shares have been subscribed, no contributions in kind have been stipulated and the payment which is required to be made pursuant to § 188 (2) at the time of the report for registration of the completion of the capital increase has been made with respect to each share. Proof of the subscription and such payment shall be submitted to the notary who records the resolution on the share capital increase.

(2) Sämtliche Beschlüsse sind nichtig, wenn die Beschlüsse über die Kapitalherabsetzung und die Kapitalerhöhung und die Durchführung der Erhöhung nicht binnen drei Monaten nach der Beschlußfassung in das Handelsregister eingetragen worden sind. Der Lauf der Frist ist gehemmt, solange eine Anfechtungs-

(2) All resolutions shall be null and void if the resolutions on the capital reduction and the capital increase and the completion of the increase have not been registered in the commercial register within three months of the adoption of such resolutions. The running of such period shall be tolled for as long as an

oder Nichtigkeitsklage rechtshängig ist oder eine zur Kapitalherabsetzung oder Kapitalerhöhung beantragte staatliche Genehmigung noch nicht erteilt ist. Die Beschlüsse und die Durchführung der Erhöhung des Grundkapitals sollen nur zusammen in das Handelsregister eingetragen werden.

action to set aside or annul the resolution shall be pending or a governmental approval which has been applied for in connection with the capital reduction or capital increase has not yet been granted. The resolutions and the completion of the share capital increase shall only be registered together in the commercial register.

§ 236. Offenlegung

Die Offenlegung des Jahresabschlusses nach § 325 des Handelsgesetzbuchs darf im Fall des § 234 erst nach Eintragung des Beschlusses über die Kapitalherabsetzung, im Fall des § 235 erst ergehen, nachdem die Beschlüsse über die Kapitalherabsetzung und Kapitalerhöhung und die Durchführung der Kapitalerhöhung eingetragen worden sind.

§ 236. Disclosure

Disclosure of the annual financial statements pursuant to § 325 of the Commercial Code may only be made in the case of § 234 after registration of the resolution on the capital reduction, in the case of § 235 after the resolutions on the capital reduction and capital increase and the completion of the capital increase have been registered.

DRITTER UNTERABSCHNITT. KAPITALHERABSETZUNG DURCH EINZIEHUNG VON AKTIEN

SUBDIVISION THREE. CAPITAL REDUCTION BY CANCELLATION OF SHARES

§ 237. Voraussetzungen

(1) Aktien können zwangsweise oder nach Erwerb durch die Gesellschaft eingezogen werden. Eine Zwangseinziehung ist nur zulässig, wenn sie in der ursprünglichen Satzung oder durch eine Satzungsänderung vor Übernahme oder Zeichnung der Aktien angeordnet oder gestattet war.

(2) Bei der Einziehung sind die Vorschriften über die ordentliche Kapitalherabsetzung zu befolgen. In der Satzung oder in dem Beschluß der Hauptversammlung sind die Voraussetzungen für eine Zwangseinziehung und die Einzelheiten ihrer Durchführung festzulegen. Für die Zahlung des Entgelts, das Aktionären bei einer Zwangseinziehung oder bei einem Erwerb von Aktien zum Zwek-

§ 237. General Provisions

(1) Shares may be cancelled by means of mandatory redemption or acquisition by the company. A mandatory redemption may only be made if prescribed or permitted in the original articles or an amendment of the articles prior to acquisition or subscription of the shares.

(2) The provisions regarding an ordinary capital reduction shall govern such cancellation. The conditions governing a mandatory redemption and the respective procedure shall be stipulated in the articles or the resolution of the shareholders' meeting. § 225 (2) shall apply analogously to the payment of the consideration which is to be granted to shareholders in the case of a mandatory

ke der Einziehung gewährt wird, und für die Befreiung dieser Aktionäre von der Verpflichtung zur Leistung von Einlagen gilt § 225 Abs. 2 sinngemäß.

redemption or an acquisition of shares for the purpose of cancellation and to the release of such shareholders from the obligation to make contributions.

(3) Die Vorschriften über die ordentliche Kapitalherabsetzung brauchen nicht befolgt zu werden, wenn Aktien, auf die der Nennbetrag oder der höhere Ausgabebetrag voll geleistet ist,
1. der Gesellschaft unentgeltlich zur Verfügung gestellt oder
2. zu Lasten des Bilanzgewinns oder einer anderen Gewinnrücklage, soweit sie zu diesem Zweck verwandt werden können, eingezogen werden.

(3) The provisions regarding an ordinary capital reduction need not be observed if shares with respect to which the par value or the higher issue price has been fully paid:
1. are surrendered to the company gratis; or
2. are cancelled by a charge to distributable profits or another profit reserve, to the extent a charge against such items may be made for such purpose.

(4) Auch in den Fällen des Absatzes 3 kann die Kapitalherabsetzung durch Einziehung nur von der Hauptversammlung beschlossen werden. Für den Beschluß genügt die einfache Stimmenmehrheit. Die Satzung kann eine größere Mehrheit und weitere Erfordernisse bestimmen. Im Beschluß ist der Zweck der Kapitalherabsetzung festzusetzen. Der Vorstand und der Vorsitzende des Aufsichtsrats haben den Beschluß zur Eintragung in das Handelsregister anzumelden.

(4) A capital reduction by means of cancellation of shares shall also in the case of subsection (3) require a resolution of the shareholders' meeting. A simple majority of votes shall suffice for such resolution. The articles may provide for a larger capital majority and additional requirements. The resolution shall stipulate the purpose of the capital reduction. The management board and the chairman of the supervisory board shall report the resolution for registration in the commercial register.

(5) In den Fällen des Absatzes 3 ist in die Kapitalrücklage ein Betrag einzustellen, der dem Gesamtnennbetrag der eingezogenen Aktien gleichkommt.

(5) In the case of subsection (3) an amount shall be transferred to the capital reserve which is equal to the aggregate par value of the shares cancelled.

(6) Soweit es sich um eine durch die Satzung angeordnete Zwangseinziehung handelt, bedarf es eines Beschlusses der Hauptversammlung nicht. In diesem Fall tritt für die Anwendung der Vorschriften über die ordentliche Kapitalherabsetzung an die Stelle des Hauptversammlungsbeschlusses die Entscheidung des Vorstands über die Einziehung.

(6) If a mandatory redemption is prescribed by the articles, a resolution of the shareholders' meeting shall not be required. In such case, with respect to applicability of the provisions regarding an ordinary capital reduction, the decision of the management board regarding cancellation shall be substituted for the resolution of the shareholders' meeting.

§ 238. Wirksamwerden der Kapitalherabsetzung

Mit der Eintragung des Beschlusses oder, wenn die Einziehung nachfolgt, mit der Einziehung ist das Grundkapital um den Gesamtnennbetrag der eingezogenen Aktien herabgesetzt. Handelt es sich um eine durch die Satzung angeordnete Zwangseinziehung, so ist, wenn die Hauptversammlung nicht über die Kapitalherabsetzung beschließt, das Grundkapital mit der Zwangseinziehung herabgesetzt. Zur Einziehung bedarf es einer Handlung der Gesellschaft, die auf Vernichtung der Rechte aus bestimmten Aktien gerichtet ist.

§ 238. Effectiveness of Capital Reduction

The reduction of the share capital by the aggregate par value of the shares cancelled shall become effective upon registration of the resolution or, in the case of subsequent cancellation, upon cancellation. In the case of a mandatory redemption prescribed by the articles, the reduction of the share capital shall become effective upon such mandatory redemption, unless the shareholders' meeting resolves on such capital reduction. The cancellation shall require an act of the company which has the purpose of nullifying the rights arising with respect to specific shares.

§ 239. Anmeldung der Durchführung

(1) Der Vorstand hat die Durchführung der Herabsetzung des Grundkapitals zur Eintragung in das Handelsregister anzumelden. Dies gilt auch dann, wenn es sich um eine durch die Satzung angeordnete Zwangseinziehung handelt.

(2) Anmeldung und Eintragung der Durchführung der Herabsetzung können mit Anmeldung und Eintragung des Beschlusses über die Herabsetzung verbunden werden.

§ 239. Report of Completion of the Capital Reduction

(1) The management board shall report the completion of the share capital reduction for registration in the commercial register. The foregoing shall also apply in the case of a mandatory redemption prescribed by the articles.

(2) The report and registration of the completion of the reduction may be combined with the report and registration of the resolution on the reduction.

VIERTER UNTERABSCHNITT. AUSWEIS DER KAPITALHERABSETZUNG

§ 240.

Der aus der Kapitalherabsetzung gewonnene Betrag ist in der Gewinn- und Verlustrechnung als 'Ertrag aus der Kapitalherabsetzung' gesondert, und zwar hinter dem Posten 'Entnahmen aus Gewinnrücklagen', auszuweisen. Eine Ein-

SUBDIVISION FOUR. THE CAPITAL REDUCTION IN THE FINANCIAL STATEMENTS

§ 240.

The amount obtained in connection with the capital reduction shall be shown separately in the profit and loss statement as 'Income from capital reduction' after the item 'Releases from profit reserves'. A transfer to the capital reserve pursuant

stellung in die Kapitalrücklage nach § 229 Abs. 1 und § 232 ist als 'Einstellung in die Kapitalrücklage nach den Vorschriften über die vereinfachte Kapitalherabsetzung' gesondert auszuweisen. Im Anhang ist zu erläutern, ob und in welcher Höhe die aus der Kapitalherabsetzung und aus der Auflösung von Gewinnrücklagen gewonnenen Beträge

1. zum Ausgleich von Wertminderungen,

2. zur Deckung von sonstigen Verlusten oder

3. zur Einstellung in die Kapitalrücklage

verwandt werden.

to § 229 (1) and § 232 shall be shown separately as 'Transfer to the capital reserve pursuant to the provisions governing simplified procedure for capital reduction'. The notes shall explain whether and to what extent the amounts received in connection with the capital reduction and the release of profit reserves have been utilized:

1. to offset a decline in the value of assets;

2. to offset other losses; or

3. for transfer to the capital reserve.

Siebenter Teil. Nichtigkeit von Hauptversammlungsbeschlüssen und des festgestellten Jahresabschlusses. Sonderprüfung wegen unzulässiger Unterbewertung

Part Seven. Nullity of Resolutions of the Shareholders' Meeting and of the Approved Annual Financial Statements. Special Audit due to Illegal Undervaluation

Erster Abschnitt. Nichtigkeit von Hauptversammlungsbeschlüssen

Division One. Nullity of Resolutions of the Shareholders' Meeting

ERSTER UNTERABSCHNITT. ALLGEMEINES

SUBDIVISION ONE. GENERAL

§ 241. Nichtigkeitsgründe

Ein Beschluß der Hauptversammlung ist außer in den Fällen des § 192 Abs. 4, §§ 212, 217 Abs. 2, § 228 Abs. 2, § 234 Abs. 3 und § 235 Abs. 2 nur dann nichtig, wenn er

1. in einer Hauptversammlung gefaßt worden ist, die unter Verstoß gegen § 121 abs. 2 und 3 oder 4 einberufen war,

2. nicht nach § 130 Abs. 1, 2 und 4 beurkundet ist,

3. mit dem Wesen der Aktiengesellschaft nicht zu vereinbaren ist oder durch seinen Inhalt Vorschriften verletzt, die ausschießlich oder überwiegend zum Schutze der Gläubiger der Gesellschaft

§ 241. Grounds for Nullity

Except in the case of § 192 (4), §§ 212, 217 (2), § 228 (2), § 234 (3) and § 235 (2) a resolution of the shareholders' meeting shall be null and void only if it:

1. has been adopted in a shareholders' meeting which was called in violation of § 121(2) and (3) or (4);

2. was not recorded pursuant to § 130 (1), (2) and (4);

3. is not compatible with the nature of the stock corporation or by its terms violates provisions which exist exclusively or primarily for the protection of the com-

oder sonst im öffentlichen Interesse gegeben sind,

4. durch seinen Inhalt gegen die guten Sitten verstößt,

5. auf Anfechtungsklage durch Urteil rechtskräftig für nichtig erklärt worden ist,

6. nach § 144 Abs. 2 des Gesetzes über die Angelegenheiten der freiwilligen Gerichtsbarkeit auf Grund rechtskräftiger Entscheidung als nichtig gelöscht worden ist.

pany's creditors or otherwise in the public interest;

4. by its terms is unethical;

5. has been declared null and void by a judgement upon an action to set aside which is final and not subject to appeal;

6. has been cancelled as null and void pursuant to § 144 (2) of the Act on Court Procedure in Non-litigious Matters by virtue of a decision which is final and not subject to appeal.

§ 242. Heilung der Nichtigkeit

(1) Die Nichtigkeit eines Hauptversammlungsbeschlusses, der entgegen § 130 Abs. 1, 2 und 4 nicht oder nicht gehörig beurkundet worden ist, kann nicht mehr geltend gemacht werden, wenn der Beschluß in das Handelsregister eingetragen worden ist.

(2) Ist ein Hauptversammlungsbeschluß nach § 241 Nr. 1, 3 oder 4 nichtig, so kann die Nichtigkeit nicht mehr geltend gemacht werden, wenn der Beschluß in das Handelsregister eingetragen worden ist und seitdem drei Jahre verstrichen sind. Ist bei Ablauf der Frist eine Klage auf Feststellung der Nichtigkeit des Hauptversammlungsbeschlusses rechtshängig, so verlängert sich die Frist, bis über die Klage rechtskräftig entschieden ist oder sie sich auf andere Weise endgültig erledigt hat. Eine Löschung des Beschlusses von Amts wegen nach § 144 Abs. 2 des Gesetzes über die Angelegenheiten der freiwilligen Gerichtsbarkeit wird durch den Zeitablauf nicht ausgeschlossen. Ist ein Hauptversammlungsbeschluß wegen Verstoßes gegen § 121 Abs. 4 nach § 241 Nr. 1 nichtig, so kann die Nichtigkeit auch dann nicht mehr geltend gemacht werden, wenn der nicht ge-

§ 242. Curing of Nullity

(1) The nullity of a resolution of the shareholders' meeting which contrary to § 130 (1), (2) and (4) has not been recorded or has not been properly recorded, may no longer be asserted if the resolution has been registered in the commercial register.

(2) If a resolution of the shareholders' meeting is null and void pursuant to § 241 (1), (3) or (4), such nullity may no longer be asserted if the resolution has been registered in the commercial register and three years have since lapsed. If upon expiration of such period an action to annul the resolution of the shareholders' meeting is pending, such period shall be extended until a decision on the action has been issued which is final and not subject to appeal or the action has been otherwise finally disposed of. A cancellation of the resolution as null and void without application pursuant to § 144 (2) of the Act on Court Procedure in Non-Litigious Matters shall not be precluded by the expiration of such period. If a resolution of a shareholders' meeting is null and void pursuant to § 241 No. 1 for reason of a violation of § 121 (4) such nullity may no longer be asserted if the shareholder

ladene Aktionär den Beschluß genehmigt.

(3) Absatz 2 gilt entsprechend, wenn in den Fällen des § 217 Abs. 2, § 228 Abs. 2, § 234 Abs. 3 und § 235 Abs. 2 die erforderlichen Eintragungen nicht fristgemäß vorgenommen worden sind.

who was not called approves of the resolution.

(3) Subsection (2) shall apply analogously if in the case of § 217 (2), § 228 (2), § 234 (3) and § 235 (2) the necessary registration entries have not been made within the periods prescribed.

§ 243. Anfechtungsgründe

(1) Ein Beschluß der Hauptversammlung kann wegen Verletzung des Gesetzes oder der Satzung durch Klage angefochten werden.

(2) Die Anfechtung kann auch darauf gestützt werden, daß ein Aktionär mit der Ausübung des Stimmrechts für sich oder einen Dritten Sondervorteile zum Schaden der Gesellschaft oder der anderen Aktionäre zu erlangen suchte und der Beschluß geeignet ist, diesem Zweck zu dienen. Dies gilt nicht, wenn der Beschluß den anderen Aktionären einen angemessenen Ausgleich für ihren Schaden gewährt.

(3) Auf eine Verletzung des § 128 kann die Anfechtung nicht gestützt werden.

(4) Für eine Anfechtung, die auf die Verweigerung einer Auskunft gestützt wird, ist es unerheblich, daß die Hauptversammlung oder Aktionäre erklärt haben oder erklären, die Verweigerung der Auskunft habe ihre Beschlußfassung nicht beeinflußt.

§ 243. Grounds for an Action to set Aside

(1) A resolution of the shareholders' meeting may be set aside upon an action based on violation of law or the articles.

(2) An action to set aside may also be based on the grounds that a shareholder has attempted by exercising voting rights to attain special benefits for himself or another person to the detriment of the company or other shareholders and that the resolution is apt to serve such purpose. The foregoing shall not apply if the resolution grants to other shareholders adequate compensation for their losses.

(3) An action to set aside may not be based on a violation of § 128.

(4) In the case of an action to set aside which is based on a refusal to provide information it shall be immaterial whether the shareholders' meeting or the shareholders have declared or declare that the refusal of the information did not influence their decision.

§ 244. Bestätigung anfechtbarer Hauptversammlungsbeschlüsse

Die Anfechtung kann nicht mehr geltend gemacht werden, wenn die Hauptversammlung den anfechtbaren Beschluß

§ 244. Ratification of Voidable Resolutions of the Shareholders' Meeting

An action to set aside may no longer be brought if the shareholders' meeting has ratified a voidable resolution by a new

durch einen neuen Beschluß bestätigt hat und dieser Beschluß innerhalb der Anfechtungsfrist nicht angefochten oder die Anfechtung rechtskräftig zurückgewiesen worden ist. Hat der Kläger ein rechtliches Interesse, daß der anfechtbare Beschluß für die Zeit bis zum Bestätigungsbeschluß für nichtig erklärt wird, so kann er die Anfechtung weiterhin mit dem Ziel geltend machen, den anfechtbaren Beschluß für diese Zeit für nichtig zu erklären.

resolution and an action to set aside such resolution has not been instituted within the period of limitation for such action or such action to set aside has been denied in a decision which is final and not subject to appeal. If the plaintiff has a legal interest in having the voidable resolution declared null and void for the period of the resolution on ratification, he may continue to pursue such action for the purpose of having such voidable resolution declared null and void for such period.

§ 245. Anfechtungsbefugnis

Zur Anfechtung ist befugt

1. jeder in der Hauptversammlung erschienene Aktionär, wenn er gegen den Beschluß Widerspruch zur Niederschrift erklärt hat;
2. jeder in der Hauptversammlung nicht erschienene Aktionär, wenn er zu der Hauptversammlung zu Unrecht nicht zugelassen worden ist oder die Versammlung nicht ordnungsgemäß einberufen oder der Gegenstand der Beschlußfassung nicht ordnungsgemäß bekanntgemacht worden ist;
3. im Fall des § 243 Abs. 2 jeder Aktionär;
4. der Vorstand;
5. jedes Mitglied des Vorstands und des Aufsichtsrats, wenn durch die Ausführung des Beschlusses Mitglieder des Vorstands oder des Aufsichtsrats eine strafbare Handlung oder eine Ordnungswidrigkeit begehen oder wenn sie ersatzpflichtig werden würden.

§ 245. Standing

The following persons shall have standing to institute an action to set aside:

1. each shareholder who was present at the shareholders' meeting if he has objected to the resolution in the minutes;
2. each shareholder who was not present at the shareholders' meeting if he was wrongfully refused admission to the shareholders' meeting or if the meeting was not properly called or the object of the resolution was not properly announced;
3. in the case of § 243 (2) each shareholder;
4. the management board;
5. each member of the management board and supervisory board if by executing the resolution members of the management board or supervisory board would commit a criminal act or administrative offense or would be liable for damages.

§ 246. Anfechtungsklage

(1) Die Klage muß innerhalb eines Monats nach der Beschlußfassung erhoben werden.

§ 246. Action to Set Aside

(1) Any action to set aside must be instituted within one month after adoption of the resolution.

(2) Die Klage ist gegen die Gesellschaft zu richten. Die Gesellschaft wird durch Vorstand und Aufsichtsrat vertreten. Klagt der Vorstand oder ein Vorstandsmitglied, wird die Gesellschaft durch den Aufsichtsrat, klagt ein Aufsichtsratsmitglied, wird sie durch den Vorstand vertreten.

(2) The action shall be brought against the company. The company shall be represented by the management board and the supervisory board. If the action is brought by the management board or a member of the management board, the company shall be represented by the supervisory board; if the action is brought by a member of the supervisory board the company shall be represented by the management board.

(3) Zuständig für die Klage ist ausschließlich das Landgericht, in dessen Bezirk die Gesellschaft ihren Sitz hat. Die mündliche Verhandlung findet nicht vor Ablauf der Monatsfrist des Absatzes 1 statt. Mehrere Anfechtungsprozesse sind zur gleichzeitigen Verhandlung und Entscheidung zu verbinden.

(3) The District Court for the district of the company's domicile shall have exclusive jurisdiction over such action. No hearing shall be held prior to expiration of the one-month period mentioned in subsection (1). If more than one such action is brought such actions shall be consolidated in order to be heard and decided together.

(4) Der Vorstand hat die Erhebung der Klage und den Termin zur mündlichen Verhandlung unverzüglich in den Gesellschaftsblättern bekanntzumachen.

(4) The management board shall promptly announce the institution of any such action and the date for hearing in the company's journals.

§ 247. Streitwert

§ 247. Value of the Subject Matter of the Litigation

(1) Den Streitwert bestimmt das Prozeßgericht unter Berücksichtigung aller Umstände des einzelnen Falles, insbesondere der Bedeutung der Sache für die Parteien, nach billigem Ermessen. Er darf jedoch ein Zehntel des Grundkapitals oder, wenn dieses Zehntel mehr als eine Million Deutsche Mark beträgt, eine Million Deutsche Mark nur insoweit übersteigen, als die Bedeutung der Sache für den Kläger höher zu bewerten ist.

(1) The court shall in its discretion determine the value of the subject matter of the litigation by taking into consideration all circumstances of the respective case, in particular the importance of the matter for the parties. Such value shall, however, only exceed one tenth of the share capital or, if such one tenth exceeds DM 1 million, if the importance of the subject matter for the plaintiff requires a higher valuation.

(2) Macht eine Partei glaubhaft, daß die Belastung mit den Prozeßkosten nach dem gemäß Absatz 1 bestimmten Streitwert ihre wirtschaftliche Lage erheblich gefährden würde, so kann das Prozeßge-

(2) If a party presents evidence that the assessment of court costs on the basis of the value of the subject matter of the litigation pursuant to subsection (1) would materially impair its financial con-

richt auf ihren Antrag anordnen, daß ihre Verpflichtung zur Zahlung von Gerichtskosten sich nach einem ihrer Wirtschaftslage angepaßten Teil des Streitwerts bemißt. Die Anordnung hat zur Folge, daß die begünstigte Partei die Gebühren ihres Rechtsanwalts ebenfalls nur nach diesem Teil des Streitwerts zu entrichten hat. Soweit ihr Kosten des Rechtsstreits auferlegt werden oder soweit sie diese übernimmt, hat sie die von dem Gegner entrichteten Gerichtsgebühren und die Gebühren seines Rechtsanwalts nur nach dem Teil des Streitwerts zu erstatten. Soweit die außergerichtlichen Kosten dem Gegner auferlegt oder von ihm übernommen werden, kann der Rechtsanwalt der begünstigten Partei seine Gebühren von dem Gegner nach dem für diesen geltenden Streitwert beitreiben.

(3) Der Antrag nach Absatz 2 kann vor der Geschäftsstelle des Prozeßgerichts zur Niederschrift erklärt werden. Er ist vor der Verhandlung zur Hauptsache anzubringen. Später ist er nur zulässig, wenn der angenommene oder festgesetzte Streitwert durch das Prozeßgericht heraufgesetzt wird. Vor der Entscheidung über den Antrag ist der Gegner zu hören.

dition, the court may upon motion order the obligation to pay court costs to be computed on the basis of a value which has been adjusted to reflect such financial condition. As a consequence of such order, the benefitting party shall only be required to pay attorney fees which have been determined on the basis of such adjusted value. If costs of litigation are assessed against or assumed by such party, such party shall be required only to reimburse the court costs and attorney fees which have been paid by the other party on the basis of such adjusted value. If costs other than court fees are assessed against or assumed by the other party, the attorney of the benefitting party may collect his fees from the other party on the basis of the value applicable to such other party.

(3) The motion pursuant to subsection (2) may be made to the record of the court clerk. Such motion shall be made prior to the hearing of the subject matter. A subsequent motion may only be made if the value of the subject matter of the litigation which has been presumed or set shall be increased by the court. The other party shall be heard prior to any decision on such motion.

§ 248. Urteilswirkung

(1) Soweit der Beschluß durch rechtskräftiges Urteil für nichtig erklärt ist, wirkt das Urteil für und gegen alle Aktionäre sowie die Mitglieder des Vorstands und des Aufsichtsrats, auch wenn sie nicht Partei sind. Der Vorstand hat das Urteil unverzüglich zum Handelsregister einzureichen. War der Beschluß in das Handelsregister eingetragen, so ist auch das Urteil einzutragen. Die Eintragung des Urteils ist in gleicher Weise wie die des Beschlusses bekanntzumachen.

§ 248. Effect of Judgment

(1) If the resolution has been declared null and void by a judgment which is final and not subject to appeal, such judgment shall be binding on all shareholders and the members of the management board and the supervisory board, even if such persons were not parties to the action. The management board shall promptly submit the judgment to the commercial register. If the resolution has been registered in the commercial register, the judgment shall likewise be registered. The registration of the judgment

shall be announced in the same manner as the registration of the resolution.

(2) Hatte der Beschluß eine Satzungsänderung zum Inhalt, so ist mit dem Urteil der vollständige Wortlaut der Satzung, wie er sich unter Berücksichtigung des Urteils und aller bisherigen Satzungsänderungen ergibt, mit der Bescheinigung eines Notars über diese Tatsache zum Handelsregister einzureichen.

(2) In the case of a resolution on an amendment of the articles, the judgment shall be submitted to the commercial register together with the full text of the articles resulting from the judgment and all previous amendments to the articles and certification of a notary with respect to the completeness of such text.

§ 249. Nichtigkeitsklage

(1) Erhebt ein Aktionär, der Vorstand oder ein Mitglied des Vorstands oder des Aufsichtsrats Klage auf Feststellung der Nichtigkeit eines Hauptversammlungsbeschlusses gegen die Gesellschaft, so gelten § 246 Abs. 2, Abs. 3 Satz 1, Abs. 4, §§ 247 und 248 sinngemäß. Es ist nicht ausgeschlossen, die Nichtigkeit auf andere Weise als durch Erhebung der Klage geltend zu machen.

(2) Mehrere Nichtigkeitsprozesse sind zur gleichzeitigen Verhandlung und Entscheidung zu verbinden. Nichtigkeits- und Anfechtungsprozesse können verbunden werden.

§ 249. Action to Annul

(1) If a shareholder, the management board or a member of the management board or the supervisory board brings an action to declare a resolution of the shareholders' meeting to be null and void with respect to the company, § 246 (2), (3) sentence 1, (4), §§ 247 and 248 shall apply analogously. The nullity of such resolution may be asserted by means other than by bringing of an action.

(2) If more than one action to annul has been instituted, such actions shall be consolidated in order to be heard and decided together. Actions to set aside and to annul may be consolidated.

ZWEITER UNTERABSCHNITT. NICHTIGKEIT BESTIMMTER HAUPTVERSAMMLUNGSBESCHLÜSSE

§ 250. Nichtigkeit der Wahl von Aufsichtsratsmitgliedern

(1) Die Wahl eines Aufsichtsratsmitglieds durch die Hauptversammlung ist außer im Falle des § 241 Nr. 1, 2 und 5 nur dann nichtig, wenn

1. der Aufsichtsrat unter Verstoß gegen § 96 Abs. 2, § 97 Abs. 2 Satz 1 oder § 98 Abs. 4 zusammengesetzt wird;

SUBDIVISION TWO. NULLITY OF CERTAIN RESOLUTIONS OF THE SHAREHOLDERS' MEETING

§ 250. Nullity of the Election of Members of the Supervisory Board

(1) The election of a member of the supervisory board by the shareholders' meeting shall, besides the cases of § 241 numbers 1, 2 and 5, be null and void only if:

1. the supervisory board is composed in violation of § 96 (2), § 97 (2) sentence 1 or § 98 (4);

2. die Hauptversammlung, obwohl sie an Wahlvorschläge gebunden ist (§§ 6 und 8 des Montan-Mitbestimmungsgesetzes), eine nicht vorgeschlagene Person wählt;

3. durch die Wahl die gesetzliche Höchstzahl der Aufsichtsratsmitglieder überschritten wird (§ 95);

4. die gewählte Person nach § 100 Abs. 1 und 2 bei Beginn ihrer Amtszeit nicht Aufsichtsratsmitglied sein kann.

(2) Für die Klage auf Feststellung, daß die Wahl eines Aufsichtsratsmitglieds nichtig ist, sind parteifähig

1. der Gesamtbetriebsrat der Gesellschaft oder, wenn in der Gesellschaft nur ein Betriebsrat besteht, der Betriebsrat, sowie, wenn die Gesellschaft herrschendes Unternehmen eines Konzerns ist, der Konzernbetriebsrat,

2. der Gesamtbetriebsrat eines anderen Unternehmens, dessen Arbeitnehmer selbst oder durch Delegierte an der Wahl von Aufsichtsratsmitgliedern der Gesellschaft teilnehmen, oder, wenn in dem anderen Unternehmen nur ein Betriebsrat besteht, der Betriebsrat,

3. jede in der Gesellschaft oder in einem Unternehmen, dessen Arbeitnehmer selbst oder durch Delegierte an der Wahl von Aufsichtsratsmitgliedern der Gesellschaft teilnehmen, vertretene Gewerkschaft sowie deren Spitzenorganisation.

(3) Erhebt ein Aktionär, der Vorstand, ein Mitglied des Vorstands oder des Aufsichtsrats oder eine in Absatz 2 bezeichnete Organisation oder Vertretung der Arbeitnehmer gegen die Gesellschaft Klage auf Feststellung, daß die Wahl eines Aufsichtsratsmitglieds nichtig ist, so gelten § 246 Abs. 2, Abs. 3 Satz 1, Abs. 4, §§ 247, 248 Abs. 1 Satz 2 und

2. the shareholders' meeting, although bound by nominations (§ 6 and § 8 of the Coal and Steel Co-determination Act), has not elected a nominated person;

3. as a result of the election the maximum number of members of the supervisory board set by law has been exceeded (§ 95);

4. the person elected may not serve as a member of the supervisory board at the commencement of his term of office pursuant to § 100 (1) and (2).

(2) The following shall have standing to bring an action to declare the election of a member of the supervisory board to be null and void:

1. the company's central labour council or, if only one labour council exists in the company, such labour council, and, if the company is the controlling enterprise of a group, the group labour council,

2. the central labour council of another enterprise whose employees participate directly or through delegates in the election of members of the supervisory board of the company or, if only one labour council exists in the other enterprise, such labour council,

3. each labour union represented in the company or in an enterprise whose employees participate directly or through delegates in the election of members of the supervisory board of the company and the central organization of the labour union.

(3) If a shareholder, the management board, or a member of the management board or the supervisory board or an organization or the representatives of the employees designated in subsection (2) bring an action against the company to declare that the election of a member of the supervisory board is null and void, § 246 (2), (3) sentence 1, (4), §§ 247, 248

§ 249 Abs. 2 sinngemäß. Es ist nicht ausgeschlossen, die Nichtigkeit auf andere Weise als durch Erhebung der Klage geltend zu machen.

(1) sentence 2 and § 249 (2) shall apply analogously. The nullity of such election may be asserted by means other than bringing of an action.

§ 251. Anfechtung der Wahl von Aufsichtsratsmitgliedern

§ 251. Action to set aside the Election of Members of the Supervisory Board

(1) Die Wahl eines Aufsichtsratsmitglieds durch die Hauptversammlung kann wegen Verletzung des Gesetzes oder der Satzung durch Klage angefochten werden. Ist die Hauptversammlung an Wahlvorschläge gebunden, so kann die Anfechtung auch darauf gestützt werden, daß der Wahlvorschlag gesetzwidrig zustande gekommen ist. § 243 Abs. 4 und § 244 gelten.

(1) An action to set aside the election of a member of the supervisory board by the shareholders' meeting may be based on violation of law or the articles. If the shareholders' meeting is bound by nominations, such action may also be based on the fact that the nomination was made illegally. § 243 (4) and § 244 shall apply.

(2) Für die Anfechtungsbefugnis gilt § 245 Nr. 1, 2 und 4. Die Wahl eines Aufsichtsratsmitglieds, das nach dem Montan-Mitbestimmungsgesetz auf Vorschlag der Betriebsräte gewählt worden ist, kann auch von jedem Betriebsrat eines Betriebs der Gesellschaft, jeder in den Betrieben der Gesellschaft vertretenen Gewerkschaft oder deren Spitzenorganisation angefochten werden. Die Wahl eines weiteren Mitglieds, das nach dem Montan-Mitbestimmungsgesetz oder dem Mitbestimmungsergänzungsgesetz auf Vorschlag der übrigen Aufsichtratsmitglieder gewählt worden ist, kann auch von jedem Aufsichtsratsmitglied angefochten werden.

(2) § 245 nos. 1, 2 and 4 shall apply to the standing to bring an action. An action to set aside the election of a member of the supervisory board, who has been elected on the basis of a nomination by the labour councils pursuant to the Coal and Steel Co-determination Act, may also be brought by any labour council of an operation of the company, any labour union represented in the operations of the company or its central organization. An action to set aside the election of an additional member, who has been elected on the basis of a nomination by the other members of the supervisory board pursuant to the Coal and Steel Co-determination Act or the Supplemental Co-determination Act may also be brought by any member of the supervisory board.

(3) Für das Anfechtungsverfahren gelten §§ 246, 247 und 248 Abs. 1 Satz 2.

(3) §§ 246, 247 and 248 (1) sentence 2 shall govern the procedure in an action to set aside.

§ 252. Urteilswirkung

(1) Erhebt ein Aktionär, der Vorstand, ein Mitglied des Vorstands oder des Aufsichtsrats oder eine in § 250 Abs. 2 bezeichnete Organisation oder Vertretung der Arbeitnehmer gegen die Gesellschaft Klage auf Feststellung, daß die Wahl eines Aufsichtsratsmitglieds durch die Hauptversammlung nichtig ist, so wirkt ein Urteil, das die Nichtigkeit der Wahl rechtskräftig feststellt, für und gegen alle Aktionäre und Arbeitnehmer der Gesellschaft, alle Arbeitnehmer von anderen Unternehmen, deren Arbeitnehmer selbst oder durch Delegierte an der Wahl von Aufsichtsratsmitgliedern der Gesellschaft teilnehmen, die Mitglieder des Vorstands und des Aufsichtsrats sowie die in § 250 Abs. 2 bezeichneten Organisationen und Vertretungen der Arbeitnehmer, auch wenn sie nicht Partei sind.

(2) Wird die Wahl eines Aufsichtsratsmitglieds durch die Hauptversammlung durch rechtskräftiges Urteil für nichtig erklärt, so wirkt das Urteil für und gegen alle Aktionäre sowie die Mitglieder des Vorstands und Aufsichtsrats, auch wenn sie nicht Partei sind. Im Fall des § 251 Abs. 2 Satz 2 wirkt das Urteil auch für und gegen die nach dieser Vorschrift anfechtungsberechtigten Betriebsräte, Gewerkschaften und Spitzenorganisationen, auch wenn sie nicht Partei sind.

§ 252. Effect of Judgment

(1) If a shareholder, the supervisory board or an organization or the representatives of the employees designated in § 250 (2) bring an action against the company to declare the election of a member of the supervisory board by the shareholders' meeting to be null and void, a judgment which is final and not subject to appeal and which declares the election to be null and void shall be binding on all shareholders and employees of the company, all employees of other enterprises whose employees participate directly or by delegates in the election of members of the supervisory board of the company, the members of the management board and the supervisory board and the organizations and the representatives of the employees designated in subsection (2), even if they were not parties to the proceedings.

(2) If the election of a member of the supervisory board by the shareholders' meeting has been declared null and void by a judgment which is final and not subject to appeal, such judgment shall be binding on all shareholders and members of the management board and the supervisory board, even if they were not parties to the proceedings. In the case of § 251 (2) sentence 2 the judgment shall also be binding on the labor councils, labor unions and central organizations which pursuant to these provisions have standing to bring an action even if they were not parties to the proceedings.

§ 253. Nichtigkeit des Beschlusses über die Verwendung des Bilanzgewinns

(1) Der Beschluß über die Verwendung des Bilanzgewinns ist außer in den Fällen des § 173 Abs. 3, des § 217 Abs. 2 und des § 241 nur dann nichtig, wenn die

§ 253. Nullity of a Resolution on the Appropriation of Distributable Profits

(1) A resolution on the appropriation of distributable profits shall except in the case of § 173 (3), § 217 (2) and § 241 only be null and void if the approval of the an-

Feststellung des Jahresabschlusses, auf dem er beruht, nichtig ist. Die Nichtigkeit des Beschlusses aus diesem Grunde kann nicht mehr geltend gemacht werden, wenn die Nichtigkeit der Feststellung des Jahresabschlusses nicht mehr geltend gemacht werden kann.

(2) Für die Klage auf Feststellung der Nichtigkeit gegen die Gesellschaft gilt § 249.

nual financial statements on which such resolution is based is null and void. The nullity of such resolution may no longer be based on such ground if the nullity of the approval of the annual financial statements may no longer be asserted.

(2) § 249 shall apply to an action to declare such resolution to be null and void against the company.

§ 254. Anfechtung des Beschlusses über die Verwendung des Bilanzgewinns

(1) Der Beschluß über die Verwendung des Bilanzgewinns kann außer nach § 243 auch angefochten werden, wenn die Hauptversammlung aus dem Bilanzgewinn Beträge in Gewinnrücklagen einstellt oder als Gewinn vorträgt, die nicht nach Gesetz oder Satzung von der Verteilung unter die Aktionäre ausgeschlossen sind, obwohl die Einstellung oder der Gewinnvortrag bei vernünftiger kaufmännischer Beurteilung nicht notwendig ist, um die Lebens- und Widerstandsfähigkeit der Gesellschaft für einen hinsichtlich der wirtschaftlichen und finanziellen Notwendigkeiten übersehbaren Zeitraum zu sichern und dadurch unter die Aktionäre kein Gewinn in Höhe von mindestens vier vom Hundert des Grundkapitals abzüglich von noch nicht eingeforderten Einlagen verteilt werden kann.

(2) Für die Anfechtung gelten §§ 244 bis 248. Die Anfechtungsfrist beginnt auch dann mit der Beschlußfassung, wenn der Jahresabschluß nach § 316 Abs. 3 des Handelsgesetzbuchs erneut zu prüfen ist. Zu einer Anfechtung nach Absatz 1 sind Aktionäre nur befugt, wenn ihre Anteile zusammen den zwanzigsten Teil des Grundkapitals oder den Nennbetrag

§ 254. Action to Set Aside a Resolution on the Appropriation of Distributable Profits

(1) An action to set aside a resolution on the appropriation of distributable profits may, in addition to § 243, also be brought if the shareholders' meeting transfers amounts from distributable profits to profit reserves or carries such amounts forward as profit, and the payment of such amounts as dividends to the shareholders is not precluded by law or the articles, even though the transfer to reserves or carrying forward of profit is not necessary according to reasonable business judgment in order to secure the viability of the company for a period which is foreseeable with respect to economic and financial circumstances and therefore no dividend may be paid to shareholders in excess of four per cent of the share capital less any contributions not yet called.

(2) §§ 244 to 248 shall apply to the action to set aside. The period for bringing such action shall commence on the date of adoption of the resolution even if the annual financial statements are to be re-audited pursuant to § 316 (3) of the Commercial Code. Shareholders shall have standing to bring such action pursuant to subsection (1) only if their aggregate shareholdings amount to one twen-

von einer Million Deutsche Mark erreichen.

tieth of the share capital or the par value of one million Deutsche Mark.

§ 255. Anfechtung der Kapitalerhöhung gegen Einlagen

(1) Der Beschluß über eine Kapitalerhöhung gegen Einlagen kann nach § 243 angefochten werden.

(2) Die Anfechtung kann, wenn das Bezugsrecht der Aktionäre ganz oder zum Teil ausgeschlossen worden ist, auch darauf gestützt werden, daß der sich aus dem Erhöhungsbeschluß ergebende Ausgabebetrag oder der Mindestbetrag, unter dem die neuen Aktien nicht ausgegeben werden sollen, unangemessen niedrig ist. Dies gilt nicht, wenn die neuen Aktien von einem Dritten mit der Verpflichtung übernommen werden sollen, sie den Aktionären zum Bezug anzubieten.

(3) Für die Anfechtung gelten §§ 244 bis 248.

§ 255. Action to set aside a Capital Increase against Contributions

(1) An action to set aside a resolution on a capital increase against contributions may be brought pursuant to § 243.

(2) An action to set aside may, if the pre-emptive rights of the shareholders have been excluded in whole or in part, also be based on the ground that the issue price resulting from the resolution on the increase or the minimum price for the issuance of new shares are unreasonably low. The foregoing shall not apply if the new shares are to be acquired by a third person subject to the obligation to offer the shares to the shareholders for subscription.

(3) §§ 244 to 248 shall apply to the action to set aside.

Zweiter Abschnitt. Nichtigkeit des festgestellten Jahresabschlusses

§ 256. Nichtigkeit

(1) Ein festgestellter Jahresabschluß ist außer in den Fällen des § 173 Abs. 3, § 234 Abs. 3 und § 235 Abs. 2 nichtig, wenn

1. er durch seinen Inhalt Vorschriften verletzt, die ausschließlich oder überwiegend zum Schutze der Gläubiger der Gesellschaft gegeben sind,

2. er im Falle einer gesetzlichen Prüfungspflicht nicht nach § 316 Abs. 1 und 3 des Handelsgesetzbuchs geprüft worden ist,

3. er im Falle einer gesetzlichen Prüfungspflicht von Personen geprüft worden ist, die nicht zum Abschlußprüfer be-

Division Two. Nullity of the Approved Annual Financial Statements

§ 256. Nullity

(1) In addition to the cases specified in § 173 (3), § 234 (3) and § 235 (2), the approved annual financial statements shall be null and void if:

1. they by their terms violate provisions which exist exclusively or primarily for the protection of the company's creditors;

2. in case of a statutory audit requirement they have not been audited in accordance with § 316 (1) and (3) of the Commercial Code;

3. in case of a statutory audit requirement they have been audited by persons who were not appointed as external audi-

stellt sind oder nach § 319 Abs. 1 des Handelsgesetzbuchs oder nach Artikel 25 des Einführungsgesetzes zum Handelsgesetzbuche nicht Abschlußprüfer sind,

4. bei seiner Feststellung die Bestimmungen des Gesetzes oder der Satzung über die Einstellung von Beträgen in Kapital- oder Gewinnrücklagen oder über die Entnahme von Beträgen aus Kapital- oder Gewinnrücklagen verletzt worden sind.

(2) Ein von Vorstand und Aufsichtsrat festgestellter Jahresabschluß ist außer nach Absatz 1 nur nichtig, wenn der Vorstand oder der Aufsichtsrat bei seiner Feststellung nicht ordnungsgemäß mitgewirkt hat.

(3) Ein von der Hauptversammlung festgestellter Jahresabschluß ist außer nach Absatz 1 nur nichtig, wenn die Feststellung

1. in einer Hauptversammlung beschlossen worden ist, die unter Verstoß gegen § 121 Abs. 2 und 3 oder 4 einberufen war,

2. nicht nach § 130 Abs. 1, 2 und 4 beurkundet ist,

3. auf Anfechtungsklage durch Urteil rechtskräftig für nichtig erklärt worden ist.

(4) Wegen Verstoßes gegen die Vorschriften über die Gliederung des Jahresabschlusses sowie wegen der Nichtbeachtung von Formblättern, nach denen der Jahresabschluß zu gliedern ist, ist der Jahresabschluß nur nichtig, wenn seine Klarheit und Übersichtlichkeit dadurch wesentlich beeinträchtigt sind.

(5) Wegen Verstoßes gegen die Bewertungsvorschriften ist der Jahresabschluß nur nichtig, wenn

1. Posten überbewertet oder

tors or are not external auditors pursuant to § 319 (1) of the Commercial Code or Article 25 of the Introductory Act to the Commercial Code;

4. in connection with their approval the provisions of law or the articles regarding the transfer of amounts to the capital or profit reserves or regarding the release of amounts from the capital or profit reserves have been violated.

(2) In cases other than subsection (1), annual financial statements which have been approved by the management board and supervisory board shall only be null and void if the management board or the supervisory board has not properly taken part in the approval.

(3) In cases other than subsection (1), annual financial statements which have been approved by the shareholders' meeting shall only be null and void if the approval:

1. has been resolved by a shareholders' meeting which was called in violation of § 121 (2) and (3) or (4);

2. has not been recorded pursuant to § 130 (1), (2), and (4);

3. has been declared null and void by a judgment on an action to set aside which is final and not subject to appeal.

(4) The annual financial statements shall only be null and void on the ground of a violation of the provisions on the structure of the annual financial statements or failure to observe forms for the structure of the annual financial statements if the clearness of the presentation has been materially impaired thereby.

(5) The annual financial statements shall only be null and void for violation of the provisions on valuation if:

1. items have been overvalued; or

2. Posten unterbewertet sind und dadurch die Vermögens- und Ertragslage der Gesellschaft vorsätzlich unrichtig wiedergegeben oder verschleiert wird.

Überbewertet sind Aktivposten, wenn sie mit einem höheren Wert, Passivposten, wenn sie mit einem niedrigeren Betrag angesetzt sind, als nach §§ 253 bis 256 des Handelsgesetzbuchs in Verbindung mit §§ 279 bis 283 des Handelsgesetzbuchs zulässig ist. Unterbewertet sind Aktivposten, wenn sie mit einem niedrigeren Wert, Passivposten, wenn sie mit einem höheren Betrag angesetzt sind, als nach §§ 253 bis 256 des Handelsgesetzbuchs in Verbindung mit §§ 279 bis 283 des Handelsgesetzbuchs zulässig ist. Bei Kreditinstituten und Versicherungsunternehmen liegt ein Verstoß gegen die Bewertungsvorschriften nicht vor, soweit die Abweichung nach den für Kreditinstitute und Versicherungsunternehmen geltenden Vorschriften, insbesondere den §§ 340e bis 340g des Handelsgezetzbuchs für Kreditinstitute und den §§ 341b bis 341h des Handelsgesetzbuchs für Versicherungsunternehmen, zulässig ist.

(6) Die Nichtigkeit nach Absatz 1 Nr. 1, 3 und 4, Absatz 2, Absatz 3 Nr. 1 und 2, Absatz 4 und 5 kann nicht mehr geltend gemacht werden, wenn seit der Bekanntmachung nach § 325 Abs. 1 Satz 2 oder Abs. 2 Satz 1 des Handelsgesetzbuchs im Bundesanzeiger in den Fällen des Absatzes 1 Nr. 3 und 4, des Absatzes 2 und des Absatzes 3 Nr. 1 und 2 sechs Monate, in den anderen Fällen drei Jahre verstrichen sind. Ist bei Ablauf der Frist eine Klage auf Feststellung der Nichtigkeit des Jahresabschlusses rechtshängig, so verlängert sich die Frist, bis über die Klage rechtskräftig entschieden ist oder sie sich auf andere Weise endgültig erledigt hat.

2. items have been undervalued and the financial condition and profitability of the company has been intentionally mispresented or distorted thereby.

Asset items shall be deemed to be overvalued if they are shown at a higher value and liability items if they are shown at a lower value than permitted pursuant to §§ 253 to 256 of the Commercial Code in connection with §§ 279 to 283 of the Commercial Code. Asset items shall be deemed to be undervalued if they are shown at a lower value and liability items if they are shown at a higher value than permitted pursuant to §§ 253 to 256 of the Commercial Code in connection with §§ 279 to 283 of the Commercial Code. In case of credit institutions and insurance companies a violation of the provisions on valuation shall not exist if the deviation is permitted pursuant to the provisions applicable to credit institutions and insurance companies, in particular §§ 340e to 340g of the Commercial Code in the case of credit institutions, and §§ 341b to 341h of the Commercial Code in the cases of insurance enterprises.

(6) An action to annul pursuant to subsection (1) Nos. 1, 3 and 4, subsection (2), subsection (3) Nos. 1 and 2, subsections (4) and (5) may no longer be brought if, in the case of subsection (1) Nos. 3 and 4, subsection (2) and subsection (3) Nos. 1 and 2, six months have lapsed since publication in the Federal Gazette pursuant to § 325 (1) sentence 2 or (2) sentence 1 of the Commercial Code or, in other cases, three years have lapsed. If upon expiration of such period an action to declare the annual financial statements null and void is pending, such period shall be extended until a decision on the action has been issued which is final and not subject to appeal or the action has been otherwise finally disposed of.

(7) Für die Klage auf Feststellung der Nichtigkeit gegen die Gesellschaft gilt § 249 sinngemäß.

(7) § 249 shall apply analogously to an action against the company to declare the financial statements null and void.

§ 257. Anfechtung der Feststellung des Jahresabschlusses durch die Hauptversammlung

§ 257. Action to set aside Approval of the Annual Financial Statements by the Shareholders' Meeting

(1) Die Feststellung des Jahresabschlusses durch die Hauptversammlung kann nach § 243 angefochten werden. Die Anfechtung kann jedoch nicht darauf gestützt werden, daß der Inhalt des Jahresabschlusses gegen Gesetz oder Satzung verstößt.

(1) An action to set aside approval of the annual financial statements by the shareholders' meeting may be brought pursuant to § 243. Such action may, however, not be based on the ground that the contents of the annual financial statements violate law or the articles.

(2) Für die Anfechtung gelten die §§ 244 bis 248. Die Anfechtungsfrist beginnt auch dann mit der Beschlußfassung, wenn der Jahresabschluß nach § 316 Abs. 3 des Handelsgesetzbuchs erneut zu prüfen ist.

(2) §§ 244 to 248 apply to the action to set aside. The period for bringing such action shall commence on the date of adoption of the resolution, even if the annual financial statements are to be re-audited pursuant to § 316 (3) of the Commercial Code.

Dritter Abschnitt. Sonderprüfung wegen unzulässiger Unterbewertung

Division Seven. Special Audit due to Improper Undervaluation

§ 258. Bestellung der Sonderprüfer

§ 258. Appointment of Special Auditors

(1) Besteht Anlaß für die Annahme, daß

1. in einem festgestellten Jahresabschluß bestimmte Posten nicht unwesentlich unterbewertet sind (§ 256 Abs. 5 Satz 3) oder
2. der Anhang die vorgeschriebenen Angaben nicht oder nicht vollständig enthält und der Vorstand in der Hauptversammlung die fehlenden Angaben, obwohl nach ihnen gefragt worden ist, nicht gemacht hat und die Aufnahme der Frage in die Niederschrift verlangt worden ist,

so hat das Gericht auf Antrag Sonderprüfer zu bestellen. Die Sonderprüfer ha-

(1) The court shall upon motion appoint special auditors if there is reason to assume that:

1. certain items in the approved financial statements have been materially undervalued (§ 256 (5) sentence 3); or

2. the notes do not or do not fully contain the required information and the management board has not furnished such missing information at the shareholders' meeting even though such information has been requested and the inclusion of the respective question in the minutes has been demanded.

The special auditors shall examine the contested items as to whether they have

ben die bemängelten Posten darauf zu prüfen, ob sie nicht unwesentlich unterbewertet sind. Sie haben den Anhang darauf zu prüfen, ob die vorgeschriebenen Angaben nicht oder nicht vollständig gemacht worden sind und der Vorstand in der Hauptversammlung die fehlenden Angaben, obwohl nach ihnen gefragt worden ist, nicht gemacht hat und die Aufnahme der Frage in die Niederschrift verlangt worden ist.

been materially undervalued. Such auditors shall examine the notes as to whether the required information has not been or has not been fully furnished and whether the management board has not furnished the missing information at the shareholders' meeting even though such information has been requested and the inclusion of the respective question in the minutes has been demanded.

(1a) Bei Kreditinstituten kann ein Sonderprüfer nach Absatz 1 nicht bestellt werden, soweit die Unterbewertung oder die fehlenden Angaben im Anhang auf der Anwendung des § 340f des Handelsgesetzbuchs beruhen.

(1a) With respect to credit institutions a special auditor may not be appointed if the undervaluation or the missing information results from the application of § 340 of the Commercial Code.

(2) Der Antrag muß innerhalb eines Monats nach der Hauptversammlung über den Jahresabschluß gestellt werden. Dies gilt auch, wenn der Jahresabschluß nach § 316 Abs. 3 des Handelsgesetzbuchs erneut zu prüfen ist. Er kann nur von Aktionären gestellt werden, deren Anteile zusammen den zwanzigsten Teil des Grundkapitals oder den Nennbetrag von einer Million Deutsche Mark erreichen. Die Antragsteller haben die Aktien bis zur Entscheidung über den Antrag zu hinterlegen und glaubhaft zu machen, daß sie seit mindestens drei Monaten vor dem Tage der Hauptversammlung Inhaber der Aktien sind. Zur Glaubhaftmachung genügt eine eidesstattliche Versicherung vor einem Notar.

(2) Such motion must be made within one month after the shareholders' meeting regarding the annual financial statements. The foregoing shall also apply if the annual financial statements are to be re-audited pursuant to § 316 (3) of the Commercial Code. Such motion may only be made by shareholders whose shares in the aggregate amount to one twentieth of the share capital or a par value of DM 1 million. The persons making such motion shall deposit their shares until the motion has been decided and provide evidence that they have been holders of the shares for not less than three months prior to the date of the shareholders' meeting. An affidavit made before a notary shall suffice as evidence.

(3) Vor der Bestellung hat das Gericht den Vorstand, den Aufsichtsrat und den Abschlußprüfer zu hören. Gegen die Entscheidung ist die sofortige Beschwerde zulässig.

(3) Prior to such appointment the court shall hear the management board, the supervisory board and the external auditors. An immediate appeal against the decision of the court may be made.

(4) Sonderprüfer nach Absatz 1 können nur Wirtschaftsprüfer und Wirtschaftsprüfungsgesellschaften sein. Für die Auswahl gilt § 319 Abs. 2 und 3 des

(4) Special auditors pursuant to subsection (1) may only be certified public accountants and certified public accounting firms. § 319 (2) and (3) of the Com-

Handelsgesetzbuchs sinngemäß. Der Abschlußprüfer der Gesellschaft und Personen, die in den letzten drei Jahren vor der Bestellung Abschlußprüfer der Gesellschaft waren, können nicht Sonderprüfer nach Absatz 1 sein.

mercial Code shall apply analogously to their qualifications. The company's external auditors and persons who have served as external auditors of the company during the last three years prior to such appointment may not serve as special auditors pursuant to subsection (1).

(5) § 142 Abs. 6 über den Ersatz angemessener barer Auslagen und die Vergütung gerichtlich bestellter Sonderprüfer, § 145 Abs. 1 bis 3 über die Rechte der Sonderprüfer, § 146 über die Kosten der Sonderprüfung und § 323 des Handelsgesetzbuchs über die Verantwortlichkeit des Abschlußprüfers gelten sinngemäß. Die Sonderprüfer nach Absatz 1 haben die Rechte nach § 145 Abs. 2 auch gegenüber dem Abschlußprüfer der Gesellschaft.

(5) § 142 (6) regarding the reimbursement of reasonable cash expenses and remuneration of court-appointed special auditors, § 145 (1) to (3) regarding the rights of special auditors, § 146 regarding the expenses of the special audit and § 323 of the Commercial Code regarding the responsibility of the external auditor shall apply analogously. The special auditors pursuant to subsection (1) shall have the rights pursuant to § 145 (2) as against the company's external auditor.

§ 259. Prüfungsbericht. Abschließende Feststellungen

(1) Die Sonderprüfer haben über das Ergebnis der Prüfung schriftlich zu berichten. Stellen die Sonderprüfer bei Wahrnehmung ihrer Aufgaben fest, daß Posten überbewertet sind (§ 256 Abs. 5 Satz 2), oder daß gegen die Vorschriften über die Gliederung des Jahresabschlusses verstoßen ist oder Formblätter nicht beachtet sind, so haben sie auch darüber zu berichten. Für den Bericht gilt § 145 Abs. 4 sinngemäß.

(2) Sind nach dem Ergebnis der Prüfung die bemängelten Posten nicht unwesentlich unterbewertet (§ 256 Abs. 5 Satz 3), so haben die Sonderprüfer am Schluß ihres Berichts in einer abschließenden Feststellung zu erklären,

1. zu welchem Wert die einzelnen Aktivposten mindestens und mit welchem Betrag die einzelnen Passivposten höchstens anzusetzen waren;

§ 259. Audit Report; Findings

(1) The special auditors shall render a written report on the result of the audit. If the special auditors in carrying out their duties determine that items have been overvalued (§ 256 (5) sentence 2) or that the provisions governing the structure of the annual financial statements have been violated or the required forms have not been observed, they shall also include such findings in their report. § 145 (4) shall apply analogously to the report.

(2) If the special auditors determine that the contested items have been materially undervalued (§ 256 (5) sentence 3) they shall declare in the findings set out at the end of their report:

1. the minimum amount at which the individual asset items should be shown and the maximum amount at which the individual liability items should be shown;

2. um welchen Betrag der Jahresüberschuß sich beim Ansatz dieser Werte oder Beträge erhöht oder der Jahresfehlbetrag sich ermäßigt hätte.

2. the amount by which the annual net profit would have increased or the annual net loss would have decreased if such amounts had been applied.

Die Sonderprüfer haben ihrer Beurteilung die Verhältnisse am Stichtag des Jahresabschlusses zugrunde zu legen. Sie haben für den Ansatz der Werte und Beträge nach Nummer 1 diejenige Bewertungs- und Abschreibungsmethode zugrunde zu legen, nach der die Gesellschaft die zu bewertenden Gegenstände oder vergleichbare Gegenstände zuletzt in zulässiger Weise bewertet hat.

The special auditors shall base their opinion on the circumstances prevailing at the closing date of the annual financial statements. In determining the amounts in No. 1, they shall apply the same valuation and depreciation methods which the company used in its last proper valuation of the items to be valued or similar items.

(3) Sind nach dem Ergebnis der Prüfung die bemängelten Posten nicht oder nur unwesentlich unterbewertet (§ 256 Abs. 5 Satz 3), so haben die Sonderprüfer am Schluß ihres Berichts in einer abschließenden Feststellung zu erklären, daß nach ihrer pflichtmäßigen Prüfung und Beurteilung die bemängelten Posten nicht unzulässig unterbewertet sind.

(3) If the special auditors determine that the contested items have not been or have only been immaterially undervalued (§ 256 (5) sentence 3), the special auditors shall declare in the findings set out at the end of their report that in their opinion and in accordance with the audit carried out with due professional diligence the contested items have not been improperly undervalued.

(4) Hat nach dem Ergebnis der Prüfung der Anhang die vorgeschriebenen Angaben nicht oder nicht vollständig enthalten und der Vorstand in der Hauptversammlung die fehlenden Angaben, obwohl nach ihnen gefragt worden ist, nicht gemacht und ist die Aufnahme der Frage in die Niederschrift verlangt worden, so haben die Sonderprüfer am Schluß ihres Berichts in einer abschließenden Feststellung die fehlenden Angaben zu machen. Ist die Angabe von Abweichungen von Bewertungs- oder Abschreibungsmethoden unterlassen worden, so ist in der abschließenden Feststellung auch der Betrag anzugeben, um den der Jahresüberschuß oder Jahresfehlbetrag ohne die Abweichung, deren Angabe unterlassen wurde, höher oder niedriger gewesen wäre. Sind nach dem Ergebnis der Prüfung keine Angaben nach Satz 1 unterlas-

(4) If the special auditors determine that the notes do not or do not fully contain the required information and the management board has not furnished the missing information at the shareholders' meeting, even though such information has been requested and the inclusion of the respective question in the minutes has been demanded, the special auditors shall furnish the missing information in their findings set out at the end of their report. If information regarding inconsistencies in valuation or depreciation methods has been omitted, the findings shall state the amount by which the annual net profit or annual net loss would have been higher or lower without the inconsistencies which were omitted to be mentioned. If the special auditors determine that no information pursuant to subsection (1) has been omitted, the special auditors shall declare

sen worden, so haben die Sonderprüfer in einer abschließenden Feststellung zu erklären, daß nach ihrer pflichtmäßigen Prüfung und Beurteilung im Anhang keine der vorgeschriebenen Angaben unterlassen worden ist.

in their findings that in their opinion and in accordance with the audit carried out with due professional diligence no informations required to be given has been omitted in the notes.

(**5**) Der Vorstand hat die abschließenden Feststellungen der Sonderprüfer nach den Absätzen 2 bis 4 unverzüglich in den Gesellschaftsblättern bekanntzumachen.

(**5**) The management board shall promptly publish the findings of the special auditors pursuant to subsections (2) to (4) in the company's journals.

§ 260. Gerichtliche Entscheidung über die abschließenden Feststellungen der Sonderprüfer

§ 260. Judicial Decision on the Findings of the Special Auditors

(**1**) Gegen abschließende Feststellungen der Sonderprüfer nach § 259 Abs. 2 und 3 können die Gesellschaft oder Aktionäre, deren Anteile zusammen den zwanzigsten Teil des Grundkapitals oder den Nennbetrag von einer Million Deutsche Mark erreichen, innerhalb eines Monats nach der Veröffentlichung im Bundesanzeiger den Antrag auf Entscheidung durch das nach § 132 Abs. 1 zuständige Gericht stellen. § 258 Abs. 2 Satz 4 und 5 gilt sinngemäß. Der Antrag muß auf Feststellung des Betrags gerichtet sein, mit dem die im Antrag zu bezeichnenden Aktivposten mindestens oder die im Antrag zu bezeichnenden Passivposten höchstens anzusetzen waren. Der Antrag der Gesellschaft kann auch auf Feststellung gerichtet sein, daß der Jahresabschluß die in der abschließenden Feststellung der Sonderprüfer festgestellten Unterbewertungen nicht enthielt.

(**1**) The company or shareholders whose shares in the aggregate amount to one twentieth of the share capital or a par value of one million Deutsche Mark may make motion to the court with jurisdiction pursuant to § 132 (1) for a decision against the findings of the special auditors pursuant to § 259 (2) and (3) within one month after publication in the Federal Gazette. § 258 (2) sentences 4 and 5 shall apply analogously. The motion shall seek determination of the minimum amount at which the asset items specified in the motion should be shown or the maximum amount at which liability items specified in the motion should be shown. A motion by the company may also seek determination that the annual financial statements did not contain the undervaluations stated in the findings of the special auditors.

(**2**) Über den Antrag entscheidet das Gericht unter Würdigung aller Umstände nach freier Überzeugung. § 259 Abs. 2 Satz 2 und 3 ist anzuwenden. Soweit die volle Aufklärung aller maßgebenden Umstände mit erheblichen Schwierigkeiten verbunden ist, hat das Gericht die anzu-

(**2**) The court shall in its discretion decide on the motion with due regard to all circumstances. § 259 (2) sentences 2 and 3 shall apply. To the extent that a full investigation of all relevant circumstances would entail considerable difficulties, the court shall estimate the amounts to be shown.

setzenden Werte oder Beträge zu schätzen.

(3) § 99 Abs. 1, Abs. 2 Satz 1, Abs. 3 und 5 gilt sinngemäß. Das Gericht hat seine Entscheidung der Gesellschaft und, wenn Aktionäre den Antrag nach Absatz 1 gestellt haben, auch diesen zuzustellen. Es hat sie ferner ohne Gründe in den Gesellschaftsblättern bekanntzumachen. Die Beschwerde steht der Gesellschaft und Aktionären zu, deren Anteile zusammen den zwanzigsten Teil des Grundkapitals oder den Nennbetrag von einer Million Deutsche Mark erreichen. § 258 Abs. 2 Satz 4 und 5 gilt sinngemäß. Die Beschwerdefrist beginnt mit der Bekanntmachung der Entscheidung im Bundesanzeiger, jedoch für die Gesellschaft und, wenn Aktionäre den Antrag nach Absatz 1 gestellt haben, auch für diese nicht vor der Zustellung der Entscheidung.

(3) § 99 (1), (2) sentences 1, (3) and (5) shall apply analogously. The court shall serve its decision on the company and, if shareholders have made motion pursuant to subsection (1), also on such shareholders. The court shall in addition publish such decision, omitting the grounds therefor, in the company's journals. An appeal may be made by the company and shareholders whose shares in aggregate amount to one twentieth of the share capital or a par value of one million Deutsche Mark. § 258 (2) sentences 4 and 5 shall apply analogously. The period for appeal shall commence on the date of publication of the decision in the Federal Gazette but, in the case of the company and shareholders who have made motion pursuant to subsection (1), not prior to service of the decision.

(4) Für die Kosten des Verfahrens gilt die Kostenordnung. Für das Verfahren des ersten Rechtszugs wird das Doppelte der vollen Gebühr erhoben. Für den zweiten Rechtszug wird die gleiche Gebühr erhoben; dies gilt auch dann, wenn die Beschwerde Erfolg hat. Wird der Antrag oder die Beschwerde zurückgenommen, bevor es zu einer Entscheidung kommt, so ermäßigt sich die Gebühr auf die Hälfte. Der Geschäftswert ist von Amts wegen festzusetzen. Die Kosten sind, wenn dem Antrag stattgegeben wird, der Gesellschaft, sonst dem Antragsteller aufzuerlegen. § 247 gilt sinngemäß.

(4) The costs of the proceedings shall be governed by the Act on Court Costs. In proceedings before the court of first instance twice the full fee shall be assessed. For the second instance the same fee shall be assessed, the foregoing shall also apply if the appeal is successful. If the motion or appeal are withdrawn prior to a decision, the fee shall be reduced by one half. The court shall determine the value of the subject matter of the proceedings. The company shall be liable for the costs if the motion is granted, otherwise the party making motion shall be liable. § 247 shall apply analogously.

§ 261. Entscheidung über den Ertrag auf Grund höherer Bewertung

§ 261. Decision on Income based on Higher Valuation

(1) Haben die Sonderprüfer in ihrer abschließenden Feststellung erklärt, daß Posten unterbewertet sind, und ist gegen

(1) If the special auditors have determined in their findings that items have been undervalued, and no motion for

diese Feststellung nicht innerhalb der in § 260 Abs. 1 bestimmten Frist der Antrag auf gerichtliche Entscheidung gestellt worden, so sind die Posten in dem ersten Jahresabschluß, der nach Ablauf dieser Frist aufgestellt wird, mit den von den Sonderprüfern festgestellten Werten oder Beträgen anzusetzen. Dies gilt nicht, soweit auf Grund veränderter Verhältnisse, namentlich bei Gegenständen, die der Abnutzung unterliegen, auf Grund der Abnutzung, nach §§ 253 bis 256 des Handelsgesetzbuchs in Verbindung mit §§ 279 bis 283 des Handelsgesetzbuchs oder nach den Grundsätzen ordnungsmäßiger Buchführung für Aktivposten ein niedrigerer Wert oder für Passivposten ein höherer Betrag anzusetzen ist. In diesem Fall sind im Anhang die Gründe anzugeben und in einer Sonderrechnung die Entwicklung des von den Sonderprüfern festgestellten Wertes oder Betrags auf den nach Satz 2 angesetzten Wert oder Betrag darzustellen. Sind die Gegenstände nicht mehr vorhanden, so ist darüber und über die Verwendung des Ertrags aus dem Abgang der Gegenstände im Anhang zu berichten. Bei den einzelnen Posten der Jahresbilanz sind die Unterschiedsbeträge zu vermerken, um die auf Grund von Satz 1 und 2 Aktivposten zu einem höheren Wert oder Passivposten mit einem niedrigeren Betrag angesetzt worden sind. Die Summe der Unterschiedsbeträge ist auf der Passivseite der Bilanz und in der Gewinn- und Verlustrechnung als 'Ertrag auf Grund höherer Bewertung gemäß dem Ergebnis der Sonderprüfung' gesondert auszuweisen.

(2) Hat das gemäß § 260 angerufene Gericht festgestellt, daß Posten unterbewertet sind, so gilt für den Ansatz der Posten in dem ersten Jahresabschluß, der nach Rechtskraft der gerichtlichen Entscheidung aufgestellt wird, Absatz 1 sinngemäß. Die Summe der Unterschiedsbeträge ist als 'Ertrag auf Grund höherer Be-

judicial decision against such determination has been made within the period provided by § 260 (1), such items shall, in the first annual financial statements which are prepared after such period has lapsed, be shown at the amounts determined by the special auditors. The foregoing shall not apply to the extent that, by reason of changed circumstances, in particular, in the case of assets which are subject to wear and tear, by reason of such wear and tear in accordance with §§ 253 to 256 of the Commercial Code in conjunction with §§ 279 to 283 of the Commercial Code or generally accepted accounting principles, a lower amount should be shown for an asset item or a higher amount should be shown for a liability item. In such case the grounds therefor shall be specified in the notes and the means by which the amount pursuant to sentence 2 was computed from the amount determined by the special auditors shall be shown separately. If such assets no longer exist, the notes shall report such fact and the appropriation of the income from the disposal of such assets. Reference shall be made under the respective items in the annual balance sheet to the amounts by which asset items shown have been increased or liability items shown have been decreased pursuant to sentences 1 and 2. The sum of such increases and decreases shall be shown separately on the liability side of the balance sheet and in the profit and loss statement as 'Income Based on Higher Valuation in accordance with the Results of the Special Audit'.

(2) If the court to which motion has been made pursuant to § 260 shall determine that items have been undervalued, subsection (1) shall apply analogously to the valuation of items shown in the first annual financial statements prepared after the judicial decision has become final and not subject to appeal. The sum

wertung gemäß gerichtlicher Entscheidung' gesondert auszuweisen.

of such increases and decreases shall be shown separately as 'Income Based on Higher Valuation in accordance with Judicial Decision'.

(3) Der Ertrag aus höherer Bewertung nach Absätzen 1 und 2 rechnet für die Anwendung der §§ 58 und 86 Abs. 2 nicht zum Jahresüberschuß. Über die Verwendung des Ertrags abzüglich der auf ihn zu entrichtenden Steuern entscheidet die Hauptversammlung, soweit nicht in dem Jahresabschluß ein Bilanzverlust ausgewiesen wird, der nicht durch Kapital- oder Gewinnrücklagen gedeckt ist.

(3) The income based on higher valuation pursuant to subsections (1) and (2) shall not be considered part of the annual net profit for purposes of §§ 58 and 86 (2). The shareholders' meeting shall decide on appropriation of such income less the taxes payable thereon, to the extent that the annual financial statements do not show a balance sheet loss which is not offset by the capital or profit reserves.

Achter Teil. Auflösung und Nichtigerklärung der Gesellschaft

Part Eight. Dissolution and Declaration of Annulment of the Company

Erster Abschnitt. Auflösung

Division One. Dissolution

ERSTER UNTERABSCHNITT. AUFLÖSUNGSGRÜNDE UND ANMELDUNG

SUBDIVISION ONE. GROUNDS FOR DISSOLUTION AND REPORT FOR REGISTRATION

§ 262. Auflösungsgründe

(1) Die Aktiengesellschaft wird aufgelöst

1. durch Ablauf der in der Satzung bestimmten Zeit;
2. durch Beschluß der Hauptversammlung; dieser bedarf einer Mehrheit, die mindestens drei Viertel des bei der Beschlußfassung vertretenen Grundkapitals umfaßt; die Satzung kann eine größere Kapitalmehrheit und weitere Erfordernisse bestimmen;
3. durch die Eröffnung des Konkursverfahrens[1] über das Vermögen der Gesellschaft;

§ 262. Grounds for Dissolution

(1) The stock corporation is dissolved:

1. upon expiration of the period set in the articles;
2. upon resolution of the shareholders' meeting; such resolution shall require a majority of not less than three fourths of the share capital represented at the passing of the resolution; the articles may provide for a larger capital majority and additional requirements;
3. upon institution of bankruptcy proceedings[1] over the company's assets;

1. Mit Wirkung vom 1. Januar 1999 sind die Worte 'des Konkursverfahrens' durch die Worte 'des Insolvenzverfahrens' ersetzt.

1. Effective as of 1 January 1999 the words 'bankruptcy proceedings' will be substituted by the words 'insolvency proceedings'.

4. mit der Rechtskraft des Beschlusses, durch den die Eröffnung des Konkursverfahrens mangels einer den Kosten des Verfahrens entsprechenden Konkursmasse abgelehnt wird;[1]

5. mit der Rechtskraft einer Verfügung des Registergerichts, durch welche nach § 144a des Gesetzes über die Angelegenheiten der freiwilligen Gerichtsbarkeit ein Mangel der Satzung festgestellt worden ist.[2]

(2) Dieser Abschnitt gilt auch, wenn die Aktiengesellschaft aus anderen Gründen aufgelöst wird.

4. upon a decision which is final and not subject to appeal denying the institution of bankruptcy proceedings for lack of assets sufficient to cover the costs of the proceedings;[1]

5. upon an order of the court for registration, which is final and not subject to appeal, by which a deficiency in the articles pursuant to § 144a of the Act on Court Procedure in Non-Litigious Matters is determined.[2]

(2) The provisions of this subdivision shall also apply if the stock corporation is dissolved for other grounds.

§ 263. Anmeldung und Eintragung der Auflösung

Der Vorstand hat die Auflösung der Gesellschaft zur Eintragung in das Handelsregister anzumelden. Dies gilt nicht in den Fällen der Eröffnung und der Ablehnung der Eröffnung des Konkursverfahrens[3] (§ 262 Abs. 1 Nr. 3 und 4) sowie im Falle der gerichtlichen Feststellung eines Mangels der Satzung (§ 262 Abs. 1 Nr. 5). In diesen Fällen hat das Gericht die

§ 263. Report of the Dissolution for Registration

The management board shall report the dissolution of the company for registration in the commercial register. The foregoing shall not apply in the case of institution or denial of institution of bankruptcy proceedings[3] (§ 262 (1) sentences 3 and 4) or in the case of judicial determination of a deficiency in the articles (§ 262 (1) sentence 5). In such cases the court shall

1. Mit Wirkung vom 1. Januar 1999 ist § 262 Abs. 1 Nr. 4 wie folgt gefaßt:
   '4. mit der Rechtskraft des Beschlusses, durch den die Eröffnung des Insolvenzverfahrens mangels Masse abgelehnt wird;'
2. Mit Wirkung vom 1. Januar 1999 ist der Punkt am Ende von § 262 Abs. 1 Nr. 5 durch einen Strichpunkt ersetzt und die folgende neue Nummer 6 angefügt:
   '6. durch Löschung der Gesellschaft wegen Vermögenslosigkeit nach § 141a des Gesetzes über die Angelegenheiten der freiwilligen Gerichtsbarkeit.'
3. Mit Wirkung vom 1. Januar 1999 sind die Worte 'des Konkursverfahrens' durch die Worte 'des Insolvenzverfahrens' ersetzt.

1. Effective as of 1 January 1999 § 262 (1) No. 4 will read as follows:
   '4. upon a decision which is final and not subject to appeal denying the institution of insolvency proceedings for lack of assets;'
2. Effective as of 1 January 1999 the full stop at the end of § 262 (1) No. 5 will be substituted by a semicolon and the following No. 6 will be added:
   '6. by cancellation of the registration of the company for lack of any assets pursuant to § 141a of the Act on Court Procedure in Non-Litigious Matters.'
3. Effective as of 1 January 1999 the words 'bankruptcy proceedings' will be substituted by the words 'insolvency proceedings'.

Auflösung und ihren Grund von Amts wegen einzutragen.[1]

register the dissolution and the grounds therefor.[1]

ZWEITER UNTERABSCHNITT. ABWICKLUNG

SUBDIVISION TWO. LIQUIDATION

§ 264. Notwendigkeit der Abwicklung

(1) Nach der Auflösung der Gesellschaft findet die Abwicklung statt, wenn nicht über das Vermögen der Gesellschaft das Konkursverfahren[2] eröffnet worden ist.

(2)[3] Soweit sich aus diesem Unterabschnitt oder aus dem Zweck der Abwicklung nichts anderes ergibt, sind auf die Gesellschaft bis zum Schluß der Abwicklung die Vorschriften weiterhin anzuwenden, die für nicht aufgelöste Gesellschaften gelten.

§ 264. Requirement of Liquidation

(1) Upon dissolution of the company liquidation shall take place unless bankruptcy proceedings[2] have been instituted over the company's assets.

(2)[3] Unless this subdivision or the purpose of the liquidation require otherwise, the provisions governing companies which have not been dissolved shall continue to apply to the company up to the date of completion of liquidation.

§ 265. Abwickler

(1) Die Abwicklung besorgen die Vorstandsmitglieder als Abwickler.

(2) Die Satzung oder ein Beschluß der Hauptversammlung kann andere Per-

§ 265. Liquidators

(1) The members of the management board shall carry out the liquidation as liquidators.

(2) The articles or a resolution of the shareholders' meeting may designate

1. Mit Wirkung vom 1. Januar 1999 ist dem § 263 folgender neuer Satz 4 angefügt:
   'Im Falle der Löschung der Gesellschaft (§ 262 Abs. 1 Nr. 6) entfällt die Eintragung der Auflösung.'
2. Mit Wirkung vom 1. Januar 1999 ist das Wort 'Konkursverfahren' durch das Wort 'Insolvenzverfahren' ersetzt.
3. Mit Wirkung vom 1. Januar 1999 ist der Absatz 2 der neue Absatz 3, und der folgende neue § 264 Absatz 2 ist eingefügt:
   '(2) Ist die Gesellschaft durch Löschung wegen Vermögenslosigkeit aufgelöst, so findet eine Abwicklung nur statt, wenn sich nach der Löschung herausstelt, daß Vermögen vorhanden ist, das der Verteilung unterliegt. Die Abwickler sind auf Antrag eines Beteiligten durch das Gericht zu ernennen.'

1. Effective as of 1 January 1999 the following sentence 4 will be added to § 263:
   'The dissolution need not be registered in the event of a cancellation of the registration of the company (§ 262(1) No. 6).'
2. Effective as of 1 January 1999 the words 'bankruptcy proceedings' will be substituted by the words 'insolvency proceedings'.
3. Effective as of 1 January 1999 subsection (2) will become subsection (3) and the following § 264 (2) will be inserted:
   '(2) If the company is dissolved by cancellation of its registration for lack of any assets, a liquidation will only take place if it is found upon such cancellation that assets exist which qualify for distribution. The liquidators shall be appointed by the court upon motion by a party concerned.'

sonen als Abwickler bestellen. Für die Auswahl der Abwickler gilt § 76 Abs. 3 Satz 3 und 4 sinngemäß. Auch eine juristische Person kann Abwickler sein.

other persons as liquidators. § 76 (3) sentences 3 and 4 shall apply analogously to the qualifications of the liquidators. A legal entity may also act as liquidator.

(3) Auf Antrag des Aufsichtsrats oder einer Minderheit von Aktionären, deren Anteile zusammen den zwanzigsten Teil des Grundkapitals oder den Nennbetrag von einer Million Deutsche Mark erreichen, hat das Gericht bei Vorliegen eines wichtigen Grundes die Abwickler zu bestellen und abzuberufen. Die Aktionäre haben glaubhaft zu machen, daß sie seit mindestens drei Monaten Inhaber der Aktien sind. Zur Glaubhaftmachung genügt eine eidesstattliche Versicherung vor einem Gericht oder Notar. Gegen die Entscheidung ist die sofortige Beschwerde zulässig.

(3) The court shall appoint or remove liquidators for cause upon motion by the supervisory board or a minority of shareholders whose shares in the aggregate amount to one twentieth of the share capital or a par value of one million Deutsche Mark. The shareholders shall provide evidence that they have been holders of the shares for not less than three months. An affidavit made before a court or a notary shall suffice as evidence. An immediate appeal against the decision may be made.

(4) Die gerichtlich bestellten Abwickler haben Anspruch auf Ersatz angemessener barer Auslagen und auf Vergütung für ihre Tätigkeit. Einigen sich der gerichtlich bestellte Abwickler und die Gesellschaft nicht, so setzt das Gericht die Auslagen und die Vergütung fest. Gegen die Entscheidung ist die sofortige Beschwerde zulässig. Die weitere Beschwerde ist ausgeschlossen. Aus der rechtskräftigen Entscheidung findet die Zwangsvollstreckung nach der Zivilprozeßordnung statt.

(4) The liquidators appointed by the court shall be entitled to reimbursement of reasonable cash expenses and remuneration for their services. If the liquidator appointed by the court and the company shall not agree, the court shall stipulate the expenses and the remuneration. An immediate appeal against the decision may be made. Further appeal shall be precluded. A decision which is final and not subject to appeal shall be enforced in accordance with the Code of Civil Procedure.

(5) Abwickler, die nicht vom Gericht bestellt sind, kann die Hauptversammlung jederzeit abberufen. Für die Ansprüche aus dem Anstellungsvertrag gelten die allgemeinen Vorschriften.

(5) Liquidators who have not been appointed by the court may be removed by the shareholders' meeting at any time. General provisions of law shall apply to claims under a contract of employment.

(6) Die Absätze 2 bis 5 gelten nicht für den Arbeitsdirektor, soweit sich seine Bestellung und Abberufung nach den Vorschriften des Montan-Mitbestimmungsgesetzes bestimmen.

(6) Subsections (2) to (5) shall not apply to the labor director to the extent that his appointment and removal are governed by the provisions of the Coal and Steel Co-determination Act.

§ 266. Anmeldung der Abwickler

(1) Die ersten Abwickler sowie ihre Vertretungsbefugnis hat der Vorstand, jeden Wechsel der Abwickler und jede Änderung ihrer Vertretungsbefugnis haben die Abwickler zur Eintragung in das Handelsregister anzumelden.

(2) Der Anmeldung sind die Urkunden über die Bestellung oder Abberufung sowie über die Vertretungsbefugnis in Urschrift oder öffentlich beglaubigter Abschrift für das Gericht des Sitzes der Gesellschaft beizufügen.

(3) In der Anmeldung haben die Abwickler zu versichern, daß keine Umstände vorliegen, die ihrer Bestellung nach § 265 Abs. 2 Satz 2 entgegenstehen, und daß sie über ihre unbeschränkte Auskunftspflicht gegenüber dem Gericht belehrt worden sind. § 37 Abs. 2 Satz 2 ist anzuwenden.

(4) Die Bestellung oder Abberufung von Abwicklern durch das Gericht wird von Amts wegen eingetragen.

(5) Die Abwickler haben ihre Namensunterschrift zur Aufbewahrung beim Gericht zu zeichnen, wenn sie dies nicht schon als Vorstandsmitglieder getan haben.

§ 266. Report of the Liquidators for Registration

(1) The management board shall report the first liquidators and their authority to represent the company, and the liquidators shall report every change in the liquidators and in their authority to represent the company, for registration in the commercial register.

(2) The records regarding the appointment or removal or authority to represent the company shall be appended to the report in original or officially certified copy for the court of the company's domicile.

(3) In such report the liquidators shall state that no circumstances exist which preclude their appointment pursuant to § 265 (2) sentence 2 and that they have been informed of their obligation to make full disclosure to the court. § 37 (2) sentence 2 shall apply.

(4) The appointment or removal of liquidators by the court shall be registered by the court.

(5) The liquidators shall file their signatures with the court if they have not already done so in their capacity as members of the management board.

§ 267. Aufruf der Gläubiger

Die Abwickler haben unter Hinweis auf die Auflösung der Gesellschaft die Gläubiger der Gesellschaft aufzufordern, ihre Ansprüche anzumelden. Die Aufforderung ist dreimal in den Gesellschaftsblättern bekanntzumachen.

§ 267. Notice to Creditors

The liquidators shall give notice to the company's creditors to file their claims, referring in such notice to the dissolution of the company. Such notice shall be published three times in the company's journals.

§ 268. Pflichten der Abwickler

(1) Die Abwickler haben die laufenden Geschäfte zu beenden, die Forderungen einzuziehen, das übrige Vermögen in Geld umzusetzen und die Gläubiger zu befriedigen. Soweit es die Abwicklung erfordert, dürfen sie auch neue Geschäfte eingehen.

(2) Im übrigen haben die Abwickler innerhalb ihres Geschäftskreises die Rechte und Pflichten des Vorstands. Sie unterliegen wie dieser der Überwachung durch den Aufsichtsrat.

(3) Das Wettbewerbsverbot des § 88 gilt für sie nicht.

(4) Auf allen Geschäftsbriefen, die an einen bestimmten Empfänger gerichtet werden, müssen die Rechtsform und der Sitz der Gesellschaft, die Tatsache, daß die Gesellschaft sich in Abwicklung befindet, das Registergericht des Sitzes der Gesellschaft und die Nummer, unter der die Gesellschaft in das Handelsregister eingetragen ist, sowie alle Abwickler und der Vorsitzende des Aufsichtsrats mit dem Familiennamen und mindestens einem ausgeschriebenen Vornamen angegeben werden. Werden Angaben über das Kapital der Gesellschaft gemacht, so müssen in jedem Falle das Grundkapital sowie, wenn auf die Aktien der Nennbetrag oder der höhere Ausgabebetrag nicht vollständig eingezahlt ist, der Gesamtbetrag der ausstehenden Einlagen angegeben werden. Der Angaben nach Satz 1 bedarf es nicht bei Mitteilungen oder Berichten, die im Rahmen einer bestehenden Geschäftsverbindung ergehen und für die üblicherweise Vordrucke verwendet werden, in denen lediglich die im Einzelfall erforderlichen besonderen Angaben eingefügt zu werden brauchen. Bestellschei-

§ 268. Duties of the Liquidators

(1) The liquidators shall wind up all current transactions, collect claims, convert the remaining assets to cash and provide satisfaction to the creditors. To the extent required to carry out the liquidation, the liquidators may also enter into new transactions.

(2) The liquidators shall otherwise have the same rights and duties as the management board within the scope of their assigned functions. The liquidators shall in the same manner as the management board be subject to the supervision of the supervisory board.

(3) The prohibition on competition in § 88 shall not apply to the liquidators.

(4) All business letters which are addressed to a specific recipient shall state the company's legal form and domicile, the fact that the company is in liquidation, the court of registration of the company's domicile, the number under which the company has been registered in the commercial register, and the surname and at least one forename of all liquidators and the chairman of the supervisory board. If information with respect to the company's capital is provided, the share capital shall in any event be stated and the aggregate amount of outstanding contributions if the par value or the higher issue price of the shares has not been fully paid. The information pursuant to sentence 1 needs not be given in communications or reports which are made in the course of an existing business relationship and for which forms are customarily used in which only the details of the specific transaction need be added. Order forms shall be deemed to be business letters in the meaning of sentence 1; sentence 3 shall not apply thereto.

ne gelten als Geschäftsbriefe im Sinne des Satzes 1; Satz 3 ist auf sie nicht anzuwenden.

§ 269. Vertretung durch die Abwickler

(1) Die Abwickler vertreten die Gesellschaft gerichtlich und außergerichtlich.

(2) Sind mehrere Abwickler bestellt, so sind, wenn die Satzung oder die sonst zuständige Stelle nichts anderes bestimmt, sämtliche Abwickler nur gemeinschaftlich zur Vertretung der Gesellschaft befugt. Ist eine Willenserklärung gegenüber der Gesellschaft abzugeben, so genügt die Abgabe gegenüber einem Abwickler.

(3) Die Satzung oder die sonst zuständige Stelle kann auch bestimmen, daß einzelne Abwickler allein oder in Gemeinschaft mit einem Prokuristen zur Vertretung der Gesellschaft befugt sind. Dasselbe kann der Aufsichtsrat bestimmen, wenn die Satzung oder ein Beschluß der Hauptversammlung ihn hierzu ermächtigt hat. Absatz 2 Satz 2 gilt in diesen Fällen sinngemäß.

(4) Zur Gesamtvertretung befugte Abwickler können einzelne von ihnen zur Vornahme bestimmter Geschäfte oder bestimmter Arten von Geschäften ermächtigen. Dies gilt sinngemäß, wenn ein einzelner Abwickler in Gemeinschaft mit einem Prokuristen zur Vertretung der Gesellschaft befugt ist.

(5) Die Vertretungsbefugnis der Abwickler kann nicht beschränkt werden.

§ 269. Representation by the Liquidators

(1) The liquidators shall represent the company in and out of court.

(2) If more than one liquidator has been appointed, all liquidators shall only be authorized to represent the company jointly, unless the articles or the body with authority to make such appointment provide otherwise. If a statement with legally binding effect is to be made to the company, it shall suffice if such statement is made to one liquidator.

(3) The articles or the body with authority to make such appointment may also provide that individual liquidators are authorized to represent the company by acting solely or jointly with a registered authorized officer. The supervisory board may so provide if authorized to do so by the articles or resolution of the shareholders' meeting. Subsection (2) sentence 2 shall apply analogously in such cases.

(4) Liquidators authorized to represent the company by acting jointly may authorize individual liquidators to engage in certain transactions or kinds of transactions. The foregoing shall apply analogously if an individual liquidator is authorized to represent the company by acting jointly with a registered authorized officer.

(5) The authority of the liquidators to represent the company may not be restricted.

(6) Abwickler zeichnen für die Gesellschaft, indem sie der Firma einen die Abwicklung andeutenden Zusatz und ihre Namensunterschrift hinzufügen.

(6) Liquidators shall sign on behalf of the company by adding to the company name a reference to the liquidation and their signature.

§ 270. Eröffnungsbilanz. Jahresabschluß und Lagebericht

§ 270. Opening Balance Sheet; Annual Financial Statements and Annual Report

(1) Die Abwickler haben für den Beginn der Abwicklung eine Bilanz (Eröffnungsbilanz) und einen die Eröffnungsbilanz erläuternden Bericht sowie für den Schluß eines jeden Jahres einen Jahresabschluß und einen Lagebericht aufzustellen.

(1) The liquidators shall prepare a balance sheet as at the commencement of liquidation ('opening balance sheet') and an explanatory report regarding the opening balance sheet, and, as at the end of each year, annual financial statements and an annual report.

(2) Die Hauptversammlung beschließt über die Feststellung der Eröffnungsbilanz und des Jahresabschlusses sowie über die Entlastung der Abwickler und der Mitglieder des Aufsichtsrats. Auf die Eröffnungsbilanz und den erläuternden Bericht sind die Vorschriften über den Jahresabschluß entsprechend anzuwenden. Vermögensgegenstände des Anlagevermögens sind jedoch wie Umlaufvermögen zu bewerten, soweit ihre Veräußerung innerhalb eines übersehbaren Zeitraums beabsichtigt ist oder diese Vermögensgegenstände nicht mehr dem Geschäftsbetrieb dienen; dies gilt auch für den Jahresabschluß.

(2) The shareholders' meeting shall resolve an approval of the opening balance sheet and the annual financial statements and on the ratification of the acts of the liquidators and the members of the supervisory board. The provisions governing the annual financial statements shall apply analogously to the opening balance sheet and the explanatory report. Fixed assets shall, however, be shown in accordance with the valuation methods applicable to current assets to the extent that their sale is intended within a foreseeable period of time or such assets no longer serve the operation of the business; the foregoing shall also apply to the annual financial statements.

(3) Das Gericht kann von der Prüfung des Jahresabschlusses und des Lageberichts durch einen Abschlußprüfer befreien, wenn die Verhältnisse der Gesellschaft so überschaubar sind, daß eine Prüfung im Interesse der Gläubiger und Aktionäre nicht geboten erscheint. Gegen die Entscheidung ist die sofortige Beschwerde zulässig.

(3) The court may exempt the company from the requirement of an audit of the annual financial statements and the annual report by external auditors if the condition of the company is so readily apparent that an audit does not appear to be necessary in the interest of the creditors and the shareholders. An immediate appeal against the decision may be made.

§ 271. Verteilung des Vermögens

(1) Das nach der Berichtigung der Verbindlichkeiten verbleibende Vermögen der Gesellschaft wird unter die Aktionäre verteilt.

(2) Das Vermögen ist nach dem Verhältnis der Aktiennennbeträge zu verteilen, wenn nicht Aktien mit verschiedenen Rechten bei der Verteilung des Gesellschaftsvermögens vorhanden sind.

(3) Sind die Einlagen auf das Grundkapital nicht auf alle Aktien in demselben Verhältnis geleistet, so werden die geleisteten Einlagen erstattet und ein Überschuß nach dem Verhältnis der Aktiennennbeträge verteilt. Reicht das Vermögen zur Erstattung der Einlagen nicht aus, so haben die Aktionäre den Verlust nach dem Verhältnis der Aktiennennbeträge zu tragen; die noch ausstehenden Einlagen sind, soweit nötig, einzuziehen.

§ 271. Distribution of the Assets

(1) The assets of the company remaining after fulfillment of all liabilities shall be distributed among the shareholders.

(2) The assets shall be distributed in proportion to the par value of shares unless shares exist which grant different rights with respect to the distribution of the company's assets.

(3) If the contributions to share capital have not been made in the same proportion with respect to all shares, the contributions made shall be refunded and any surplus remaining distributed in proportion to the par values of shares. If the assets do not suffice to refund the contributions, the shareholders shall bear the loss in proportion to the par values of shares; the contributions still outstanding shall, to the extent necessary, be collected.

§ 272. Gläubigerschutz

(1) Das Vermögen darf nur verteilt werden, wenn ein Jahr seit dem Tage verstrichen ist, an dem der Aufruf der Gläubiger zum drittenmal bekanntgemacht worden ist.

(2) Meldet sich ein bekannter Gläubiger nicht, so ist der geschuldete Betrag für ihn zu hinterlegen, wenn ein Recht zur Hinterlegung besteht.

(3) Kann eine Verbindlichkeit zur Zeit nicht berichtigt werden oder ist sie streitig, so darf das Vermögen nur verteilt werden, wenn dem Gläubiger Sicherheit geleistet ist.

§ 272. Protection of Creditors

(1) The assets may only be distributed after one year has lapsed from the date on which the third publication of the notice to creditors has been made.

(2) If a creditor who is known shall not file his claim, the amount owed shall be placed on deposit for him, if a right to make such deposit exists.

(3) If a liability can not yet be fulfilled or is disputed, the assets may only be distributed if security has been provided to the creditor.

§ 273. Schluß der Abwicklung

(1) Ist die Abwicklung beendet und die Schlußrechnung gelegt, so haben die Abwickler den Schluß der Abwicklung zur Eintragung in das Handelsregister anzumelden. Die Gesellschaft ist zu löschen.

(2) Die Bücher und Schriften der Gesellschaft sind an einen vom Gericht bestimmten sicheren Ort zur Aufbewahrung auf zehn Jahre zu hinterlegen.

(3) Das Gericht kann den Aktionären und den Gläubigern die Einsicht der Bücher und Schriften gestatten.

(4) Stellt sich nachträglich heraus, daß weitere Abwicklungsmaßnahmen nötig sind, so hat auf Antrag eines Beteiligten das Gericht die bisherigen Abwickler neu zu bestellen oder andere Abwickler zu berufen. § 265 Abs. 4 gilt.

(5) Gegen die Entscheidungen nach den Absätzen 2, 3 und 4 Satz 1 ist die sofortige Beschwerde zulässig.

§ 273. Completion of Liquidation

(1) If the liquidation has been completed and the final statement of accounts rendered, the liquidators shall report the completion of the liquidation for registration in the commercial register. The registration of the company shall be cancelled.

(2) The company's books and records shall be deposited for safekeeping for ten years at a safe place to be designated by the court.

(3) The court may permit shareholders and creditors to inspect the books and records.

(4) If it subsequently becomes apparent that further liquidation measures are necessary, the court may upon motion by a party concerned reappoint the previous liquidators or appoint other liquidators. § 265 (4) shall apply.

(5) An immediate appeal against the decisions pursuant to subsections (2), (3) and (4) sentence 1 may be made.

§ 274. Fortsetzung einer aufgelösten Gesellschaft

(1) Ist eine Aktiengesellschaft durch Zeitablauf oder durch Beschluß der Hauptversammlung aufgelöst worden, so kann die Hauptversammlung, solange noch nicht mit der Verteilung des Vermögens unter die Aktionäre begonnen ist, die Fortsetzung der Gesellschaft beschließen. Der Beschluß bedarf einer Mehrheit, die mindestens drei Viertel des bei der Beschlußfassung vertretenen Grundkapitals umfaßt. Die Satzung kann eine größere Kapitalmehrheit und weitere Erfordernisse bestimmen.

§ 274. Continuation of a Dissolved Company

(1) If a stock corporation has been dissolved by expiration of a period of time or a resolution of the shareholders' meeting, the shareholders' meeting may resolve the continuation of the company if the distribution of assets among shareholders has not commenced. Such resolution shall require a majority of not less than three fourths of the share capital represented at the passing of the resolution. The articles may provide for a larger capital majority and additional requirements.

(2) Gleiches gilt, wenn die Gesellschaft

1. durch die Eröffnung des Konkursverfahrens aufgelöst, das Konkursverfahren aber auf Antrag der Gesellschaft eingestellt oder nach rechtskräftiger Bestätigung eines Zwangsvergleichs aufgehoben worden ist;[1]

2. durch die gerichtliche Feststellung eines Mangels der Satzung nach § 262 Abs. 1 Nr. 5 aufgelöst worden ist, eine den Mangel behebende Satzungsänderung aber spätestens zugleich mit der Fortsetzung der Gesellschaft beschlossen wird.

(3) Die Abwickler haben die Fortsetzung der Gesellschaft zur Eintragung in das Handelsregister anzumelden. Sie haben bei der Anmeldung nachzuweisen, daß noch nicht mit der Verteilung des Vermögens der Gesellschaft unter die Aktionäre begonnen worden ist.

(4) Der Fortsetzungsbeschluß wird erst wirksam, wenn er in das Handelsregister des Sitzes der Gesellschaft eingetragen worden ist. Im Falle des Absatzes 2 Nr. 2 hat der Fortsetzungsbeschluß keine Wirkung, solange er und der Beschluß über die Satzungsänderung nicht in das Handelsregister des Sitzes der Gesellschaft eingetragen worden sind; die beiden Beschlüsse sollen nur zusammen in das Handelsregister eingetragen werden.

(2) The foregoing shall apply if the company:

1. has been dissolved by the institution of bankruptcy proceedings, provided that such bankruptcy proceedings have been terminated upon motion by the company or cancelled following a confirmation, which is final and not subject to appeal, of a compulsory composition;[1]

2. has been dissolved by a judicial finding of a deficiency in the articles pursuant to § 262 (1) sentence 5, provided that an amendment to the articles which cures such deficiency has been resolved not later than the resolution for continuation of the company.

(3) The liquidators shall report the continuation of the company for registration in the commercial register. They shall furnish proof in connection with such report that the distribution of the assets of the company among the shareholders has not yet commenced.

(4) The resolution on continuation shall only become effective after it has been registered in the commercial register of the company's domicile. In the case of subsection (2) sentence 2 the resolution on continuation shall not be effective until it and the resolution on amendment of the articles have been registered in the commercial register of the company's domicile; both resolutions shall only be registered together in the commercial register.

1. Mit Wirkung vom 1. Januar 1999 ist § 274 Abs. 2 Nr. 1 wie folgt gefaßt:
'1. durch die Eröffnung des Insolvenzverfahrens aufgelöst, das Verfahren aber auf Antrag des Schuldners eingestellt oder nach der Bestätigung eines Insolvenzplans, der den Fortbestand der Gesellschaft vorsieht, aufgehoben worden ist;'

1. Effective as of 1 January 1999 § 274 (2) No. 1 will read as follows:
'1. has been dissolved by the institution of insolvency proceedings, provided that such proceedings have been terminated upon motion by the debtor or have been rescinded following the approval of an insolvency plan which provides for the continuation of the company;'

Zweiter Abschnitt. Nichtigerklärung der Gesellschaft

§ 275. Klage auf Nichtigerklärung

(1) Enthält die Satzung keine Bestimmungen über die Höhe des Grundkapitals oder über den Gegenstand des Unternehmens oder sind die Bestimmungen der Satzung über den Gegenstand des Unternehmens nichtig, so kann jeder Aktionär und jedes Mitglied des Vorstands und des Aufsichtsrats darauf klagen, daß die Gesellschaft für nichtig erklärt werde. Auf andere Gründe kann die Klage nicht gestützt werden.

(2) Kann der Mangel nach § 276 geheilt werden, so kann die Klage erst erhoben werden, nachdem ein Klageberechtigter die Gesellschaft aufgefordert hat, den Mangel zu beseitigen, und sie binnen drei Monaten dieser Aufforderung nicht nachgekommen ist.

(3) Die Klage muß binnen drei Jahren nach Eintragung der Gesellschaft erhoben werden. Eine Löschung der Gesellschaft von Amts wegen nach § 144 Abs. 1 des Gesetzes über die Angelegenheiten der freiwilligen Gerichtsbarkeit wird durch den Zeitablauf nicht ausgeschlossen.

(4) Für die Klage gelten § 246 Abs. 2 bis 4, §§ 247, 248 Abs. 1 Satz 1, § 249 Abs. 2 sinngemäß. Der Vorstand hat eine beglaubigte Abschrift der Klage und das rechtskräftige Urteil zum Handelsregister einzureichen. Die Nichtigkeit der Gesellschaft auf Grund rechtskräftigen Urteils ist einzutragen.

Division Two. Declaration of Annulment of the Company

§ 275. Action for Declaration of Annulment

(1) If the articles do not contain provisions regarding the amount of the share capital or the company's purpose or the provisions of the articles regarding the company's purpose are null and void, each shareholder and each member of the management board and the supervisory board may bring an action for declaration of annulment of the company. Such action may not be based on any other grounds.

(2) If the deficiency shall be capable of being cured pursuant to § 276, the action may only be instituted after a party with standing to bring such action has demanded that the company cure such deficiency and the company has failed to comply with such demand within three months.

(3) Such action must be brought within three years after registration of the company. A cancellation of the registration of the company by the court pursuant to § 144 (1) of the Act on Court Procedure in Non-Litigious Matters shall not be precluded by the expiration of such period.

(4) § 246 (2) to (4), §§ 247, 248 (1) sentence 1, § 249 (2) shall apply analogously to such action. The management board shall submit to the commercial register a certified copy of the complaint and a decision which is final and not subject to appeal. The annulment of the company by virtue of such judgment shall be registered.

§ 276. Heilung von Mängeln

Ein Mangel, der die Bestimmungen über den Gegenstand des Unternehmens betrifft, kann unter Beachtung der Bestimmungen des Gesetzes und der Satzung über Satzungsänderungen geheilt werden.

§ 276. Curing of Deficiencies

Any deficiency which relates to the provisions governing the company's purpose may be cured in accordance with the provisions of law and the articles regarding amendments of the articles.

§ 277. Wirkung der Eintragung der Nichtigkeit

(1) Ist die Nichtigkeit einer Gesellschaft auf Grund rechtskräftigen Urteils oder einer Entscheidung des Registergerichts in das Handelsregister eingetragen, so findet die Abwicklung nach den Vorschriften über die Abwicklung bei Auflösung statt.

(2) Die Wirksamkeit der im Namen der Gesellschaft vorgenommenen Rechtsgeschäfte wird durch die Nichtigkeit nicht berührt.

(3) Die Gesellschafter haben die Einlagen zu leisten, soweit es zur Erfüllung der eingegangenen Verbindlichkeiten nötig ist.

§ 277. Effectiveness of Registration of Annulment

(1) If the annulment of the company by virtue of a judgment which is final and not subject to appeal or a decision by the court of registration has been registered in the commercial register, liquidation shall be carried out in accordance with the provisions regarding liquidation in the case of dissolution.

(2) The validity of transactions entered into in the name of the company shall not be affected by the annulment.

(3) The shareholders shall make contributions to the extent necessary to fulfill the liabilities incurred.

Zweites Buch. Kommanditgesellschaft auf Aktien

Book Two. Partnership Limited by Shares

§ 278. Wesen der Kommanditgesellschaft auf Aktien

§ 278. Nature of the Partnership Limited by Shares

(1) Die Kommanditgesellschaft auf Aktien ist eine Gesellschaft mit eigener Rechtspersönlichkeit, bei der mindestens ein Gesellschafter den Gesellschaftsgläubigern unbeschränkt haftet (persönlich haftender Gesellschafter) und die übrigen an dem in Aktien zerlegten Grundkapital beteiligt sind, ohne persönlich für die Verbindlichkeiten der Gesellschaft zu haften (Kommanditaktionäre).

(1) The partnership limited by shares is a company which constitutes a separate legal entity and in which not less than one partner who has unlimited liability with regard to the creditors of the company ('general partner') and the other shareholders who are not personally liable for the obligations of the company ('limited shareholders') participate in the share capital.

(2) Das Rechtsverhältnis der persönlich haftenden Gesellschafter untereinander und gegenüber der Gesamtheit der Kommanditaktionäre sowie gegenüber Dritten, namentlich die Befugnis der persönlich haftenden Gesellschafter zur Geschäftsführung und zur Vertretung der Gesellschaft, bestimmt sich nach den Vorschriften des Handelsgesetzbuchs über die Kommanditgesellschaft.

(2) The legal relations of the general partners among themselves and with respect to the body of limited shareholders and to third parties, in particular the authority of the general partners to manage the business and represent the company, shall be governed by the provisions of the Commercial Code regarding limited partnerships.

(3) Im übrigen gelten für die Kommanditgesellschaft auf Aktien, soweit sich aus den folgenden Vorschriften oder aus dem Fehlen eines Vorstands nichts anderes ergibt, die Vorschriften des Ersten Buchs über die Aktiengesellschaft sinngemäß.

(3) The provisions of Book One regarding the stock corporation shall apply analogously to the partnership limited by shares unless the following provisions or the absence of a management board necessitate otherwise.

§ 279. Firma

(1) Die Firma der Kommanditgesellschaft auf Aktien ist in der Regel dem Gegenstand des Unternehmens zu entnehmen. Sie muß die Bezeichnung 'Kommanditgesellschaft auf Aktien' enthalten.

(2) Führt die Kommanditgesellschaft auf Aktien die Firma eines auf sie übergegangenen Handelsgeschäfts fort (§ 22 des Handelsgesetzbuchs), so muß sie die Bezeichnung 'Kommanditgesellschaft auf Aktien' in die Firma aufnehmen.

§ 279. Name

(1) The name of the partnership limited by shares shall as a rule be derived from the company's purpose. The name shall contain the designation 'Kommanditgesellschaft auf Aktien'.

(2) If the partnership limited by shares retains the name of a business which it has acquired (§ 22 of the Commercial Code), it shall add to the name the designation 'Kommanditgesellschaft auf Aktien'.

§ 280. Feststellung der Satzung. Gründer

(1) Die Satzung muß von mindestens fünf Personen durch notarielle Beurkundung festgestellt werden. In der Urkunde sind der Nennbetrag, der Ausgabebetrag und, wenn mehrere Gattungen bestehen, die Gattung der Aktien anzugeben, die jeder Beteiligte übernimmt. Bevollmächtigte bedürfen einer notariell beglaubigten Vollmacht.

(2) Alle persönlich haftenden Gesellschafter müssen sich bei der Feststellung der Satzung beteiligen. Außer ihnen müssen die Personen mitwirken, die als Kommanditaktionäre Aktien gegen Einlagen übernehmen.

(3) Die Gesellschafter, die die Satzung festgestellt haben, sind die Gründer der Gesellschaft.

§ 280. Establishment of the Articles; Incorporators

(1) The articles shall be established by not less than five persons in the form of a notarial deed. The deed shall specify the par value, the issue price and, if there is more than one class of shares, the class of shares acquired by each partner. Attorneys-in-fact shall require a power of attorney certified by a notary.

(2) All general partners shall participate in the establishment of the articles. In addition to the general partners the persons who as limited shareholders subscribe to shares against contributions shall participate in the establishment of the articles.

(3) The general partners and limited shareholders, who have established the articles are the incorporators of the company.

§ 281. Inhalt der Satzung

(1) Die Satzung muß außer den Festsetzungen nach § 23 Abs. 3 und 4 den Na-

§ 281. Contents of the Articles

(1) The articles shall contain, in addition to the stipulations pursuant to § 23

men, Vornamen, Beruf und Wohnort jedes persönlich haftenden Gesellschafters enthalten.

(2) Vermögenseinlagen der persönlich haftenden Gesellschafter müssen, wenn sie nicht auf das Grundkapital geleistet werden, nach Höhe und Art in der Satzung festgesetzt werden.

(3) (*aufgehoben*)

§ 282. Eintragung der persönlich haftenden Gesellschafter

Bei der Eintragung der Gesellschaft in das Handelsregister sind statt der Vorstandsmitglieder die persönlich haftenden Gesellschafter anzugeben. Ferner ist einzutragen, welche Vertretungsbefugnis die persönlich haftenden Gesellschafter haben.

§ 283. Persönlich haftende Gesellschafter

Für die persönlich haftenden Gesellschafter gelten sinngemäß die für den Vorstand der Aktiengesellschaft geltenden Vorschriften über

1. die Anmeldungen, Einreichungen, Erklärungen und Nachweise zum Handelsregister sowie über Bekanntmachungen;
2. die Gründungsprüfung;
3. die Sorgfaltspflicht und Verantwortlichkeit;
4. die Pflichten gegenüber dem Aufsichtsrat;
5. die Zulässigkeit einer Kreditgewährung;
6. die Einberufung der Hauptversammlung;
7. die Sonderprüfung;
8. die Geltendmachung von Ersatzansprüchen wegen der Geschäftsführung;

(3) and (4) the surname, forename, profession and place of residence of each general partner.

(2) The articles shall stipulate the amount and kind of any contributions of assets by general partners which are not made against the issuance of share capital.

(3) (*repealed*)

§ 282. Registration of the General Partners

The registration of the company in the commercial register shall, in lieu of the members of the management board, designate the general partners. In addition the authority of the general partners to represent the company shall be registered.

§ 283. General Partners

The provisions governing the management board of the stock corporation with regard to the following subjects shall apply analogously to the general partners:

1. reports, submissions, declarations, and proof to be furnished to the commercial register and announcements;
2. the formation audit;
3. duty of diligence and responsibility;
4. duties in relation to the supervisory board;
5. permission to extend credit;
6. notice of a shareholders' meeting;
7. special audits;
8. assertion of claims for damages in connection with the management of the business;

9. die Aufstellung und Vorlegung des Jahresabschlusses, des Lageberichts und des Vorschlags für die Verwendung des Bilanzgewinns;

10. die Prüfung des Jahresabschlusses;

11. die Rechnungslegung im Konzern;

12. die Ausgabe von Aktien bei bedingter Kapitalerhöhung, bei genehmigtem Kapital und bei Kapitalerhöhung aus Gesellschaftsmitteln;

13. die Nichtigkeit und Anfechtung von Hauptversammlungsbeschlüssen;

14. den Antrag auf Eröffnung des Konkursverfahrens oder des gerichtlichen Vergleichsverfahrens.[1]

9. preparation and submission of the annual financial statements, the annual report and the proposal for the appropriation of distributable profits;

10. audit of the annual financial statements;

11. group statement of accounts;

12. issuance of shares in the case of a contingent capital increase, authorized capital or a capital increase from the company's reserves;

13. annulment and setting aside of resolutions of the shareholders' meeting;

14. petition for institution of bankruptcy proceedings or judicial composition proceedings.[1]

§ 284. Wettbewerbsverbot

(1) Ein persönlich haftender der Gesellschafter darf ohne ausdrückliche Einwilligung der übrigen persönlich haftenden Gesellschafter und des Aufsichtsrats weder im Geschäftszweig der Gesellschaft für eigene oder fremde Rechnung Geschäfte machen noch Mitglied des Vorstands oder Geschäftsführer oder persönlich haftender Gesellschafter einer anderen gleichartigen Handelsgesellschaft sein. Die Einwilligung kann nur für bestimmte Arten von Geschäften oder für bestimmte Handelsgesellschaften erteilt werden.

(2) Verstößt ein persönlich haftender Gesellschafter gegen dieses Verbot, so kann die Gesellschaft Schadenersatz fordern. Sie kann statt dessen von dem Gesellschafter verlangen, daß er die für eigene Rechnung gemachten Geschäfte als für Rechnung der Gesellschaft eingegangen gelten läßt und die aus Geschäften für

§ 284. Prohibition of Competition

(1) A general partner may not without the express consent of the other general partners and of the supervisory board enter into transactions on his own behalf or on behalf of another person in the company's field of business or become member of the management board, manager or general partner of a similar commercial enterprise. The consent may only be granted for specific kinds of business or specific commercial enterprises.

(2) If a general partner violates such prohibition, the company may claim damages. In lieu thereof the company may require that the partner treat the transactions made for his own account as having been made on behalf of the company and remit any remuneration obtained for transactions made on behalf of

1. Mit Wirkung vom 1. Januar 1999 ist § 283 Nr. 14 wie folgt gefaßt:
'14. den Antrag auf Eröffnung des Insolvenzverfahrens.'

1. Effective as of 1 January 1999 § 283 No. 14 will read as follows:
'14. petition for institution of insolvency proceedings.'

fremde Rechnung bezogene Vergütung herausgibt oder seinen Anspruch auf die Vergütung abtritt.

(**3**) Die Ansprüche der Gesellschaft verjähren in drei Monaten seit dem Zeitpunkt, in dem die übrigen persönlich haftenden Gesellschafter und die Aufsichtsratsmitglieder von der zum Schadenersatz verpflichtenden Handlung Kenntnis erlangen. Sie verjähren ohne Rücksicht auf diese Kenntnis in fünf Jahren seit ihrer Entstehung.

another person or assign his claim to such remuneration.

(**3**) Such claims of the company shall be barred after three months from the date on which the other general partners and the members of the supervisory board obtain knowledge of the act giving rise to the claim for damages. Such claims shall be barred five years after they have arisen irrespective of such knowledge.

§ 285. Hauptversammlung

(**1**) In der Hauptversammlung haben die persönlich haftenden Gesellschafter nur ein Stimmrecht für ihre Aktien. Sie können das Stimmrecht weder für sich noch für einen anderen ausüben bei Beschlußfassungen über
1. die Wahl und Abberufung des Aufsichtsrats;
2. die Entlastung der persönlich haftenden Gesellschafter und der Mitglieder des Aufsichtsrats;
3. die Bestellung von Sonderprüfern;
4. die Geltendmachung von Ersatzansprüchen;
5. den Verzicht auf Ersatzansprüche;
6. die Wahl von Abschlußprüfern.

Bei diesen Beschlußfassungen kann ihr Stimmrecht auch nicht durch einen anderen ausgeübt werden.

(**2**) Die Beschlüsse der Hauptversammlung bedürfen der Zustimmung der persönlich haftenden Gesellschafter, soweit sie Angelegenheiten betreffen, für die bei einer Kommanditgesellschaft das Einverständnis der persönlich haftenden Gesellschafter und der Kommanditisten erforderlich ist. Die Ausübung der Befugnisse, die der Hauptversammlung oder einer Minderheit von Kommanditaktionä-

§ 285. Shareholders' Meeting

(**1**) In the shareholders' meeting the general partners shall have only voting rights in respect of the shares held by them. They may not exercise voting rights on behalf of themselves or other persons in the case of resolutions regarding:
1. election or removal of the supervisory board;
2. ratification of the acts of the general partners and members of the supervisory board;
3. appointment of special auditors;
4. assertion of claims for damages;
5. waiver of claims for damages;
6. appointment of external auditors.

In the case of resolutions regarding such matters their voting rights may also not be exercised by any other person.

(**2**) The resolutions of the shareholders' meeting shall require the consent of the general partners to the extent that they relate to matters which in the case of a limited partnership require the agreement of the general partners and the limited partners. Consent of the general partners shall not be required for the exercise of the authority of the shareholders' meeting or of a minority of limited shareholders to

ren bei der Bestellung von Prüfern und der Geltendmachung von Ansprüchen der Gesellschaft aus der Gründung oder der Geschäftsführung zustehen, bedarf nicht der Zustimmung der persönlich haftenden Gesellschafter.

appoint auditors or assert claims of the company arising from the formation or management of the company.

(3) Beschlüsse der Hauptversammlung, die der Zustimmung der persönlich haftenden Gesellschafter bedürfen, sind zum Handelsregister erst einzureichen, wenn die Zustimmung vorliegt. Bei Beschlüssen, die in das Handelsregister einzutragen sind, ist die Zustimmung in der Verhandlungsniederschrift oder in einem Anhang zur Niederschrift zu beurkunden.

(3) Resolutions of the shareholders' meeting which require the consent of the general partners may be submitted to the commercial register only after such consent has been granted. Such consent shall, in the case of resolutions which are required to be registered in the commercial register, be recorded in the minutes of the meeting or in an appendix to the minutes.

§ 286. Jahresabschluß. Lagebericht

§ 286. Annual Financial Statements; Annual Report

(1) Die Hauptversammlung beschließt über die Feststellung des Jahresabschlusses. Der Beschluß bedarf der Zustimmung der persönlich haftenden Gesellschafter.

(1) The shareholders' meeting shall resolve upon approval of the annual financial statements. Such resolution shall require the consent of the general partners.

(2) In der Jahresbilanz sind die Kapitalanteile der persönlich haftenden Gesellschafter nach dem Posten 'Gezeichnetes Kapital' gesondert auszuweisen. Der auf den Kapitalanteil eines persönlich haftenden Gesellschafters für das Geschäftsjahr entfallende Verlust ist von dem Kapitalanteil abzuschreiben. Soweit der Verlust den Kapitalanteil übersteigt, ist er auf der Aktivseite unter der Bezeichnung 'Einzahlungsverpflichtungen persönlich haftender Gesellschafter' unter den Forderungen gesondert auszuweisen, soweit eine Zahlungsverpflichtung besteht; besteht keine Zahlungsverpflichtung, so ist der Betrag als 'Nicht durch Vermögenseinlagen gedeckter Verlustanteil persönlich haftender Gesellschafter' zu bezeichnen und gemäß § 268 Abs. 3 des Handelsgesetzbuchs auszuweisen. Unter § 89 fallende Kredite, die die Ge-

(2) The capital participations of the general partners shall be shown separately in the annual balance sheet following the item 'Subscribed Capital'. The share of a general partner in any loss for the fiscal year shall be deducted from such capital participation. If the amount of the loss exceeds such capital participation, such excess shall be shown separately on the asset side as account receivable designated 'Payment Obligation of General Partner', to the extent that a payment obligation exists; if no payment obligation exists, such excess shall be designated as 'Share of General Partners in Losses which are not Offset by Contributions of Assets' and shown in accordance with § 268 (3) of the Commercial Code. Credits falling under § 89 which the company has extended to general partners, to their spouses or minor children or to third

sellschaft persönlich haftenden Gesellschaftern, deren Ehegatten oder minderjährigen Kindern oder Dritten, die für Rechnung dieser Personen handeln, gewährt hat, sind auf der Aktivseite bei den entsprechenden Posten unter der Bezeichnung 'davon an persönlich haftende Gesellschafter und deren Angehörige' zu vermerken.

persons which are acting on behalf of such persons, shall be shown on the asset side under the appropriate items with the designation 'thereof credits extended to general partners and their relatives'.

(**3**) In der Gewinn- und Verlustrechnung braucht der auf die Kapitalanteile der persönlich haftenden Gesellschafter entfallende Gewinn oder Verlust nicht gesondert ausgewiesen zu werden.

(**3**) The profit or loss attributable to the capital participations of the general partners need not be shown separately in the profit and loss statement.

(**4**) § 285 Nr. 9 Buchstaben a und b des Handelsgesetzbuchs gilt für die persönlich haftenden Gesellschafter mit der Maßgabe, daß der auf den Kapitalanteil eines persönlich haftenden Gesellschafters entfallende Gewinn nicht angegeben zu werden braucht.

(**4**) § 285 No. 9 a and b of the Commercial Code shall apply to general partners, provided, however, that the profit attributable to the capital participation of a general partner shall not be required to be shown separately.

§ 287. Aufsichtsrat

(**1**) Die Beschlüsse der Kommanditaktionäre führt der Aufsichtsrat aus, wenn die Satzung nichts anderes bestimmt.

(**2**) In Rechtsstreitigkeiten, die die Gesamtheit der Kommanditaktionäre gegen die persönlich haftenden Gesellschafter oder diese gegen die Gesamtheit der Kommanditaktionäre führen, vertritt der Aufsichtsrat die Kommanditaktionäre, wenn die Hauptversammlung keine besonderen Vertreter gewählt hat. Für die Kosten des Rechtsstreits, die den Kommanditaktionären zur Last fallen, haftet die Gesellschaft unbeschadet ihres Rückgriffs gegen die Kommanditaktionäre.

(**3**) Persönlich haftende Gesellschafter können nicht Aufsichtsratsmitglieder sein.

§ 287. Supervisory Board

(**1**) The supervisory board shall carry out the resolutions of the limited shareholders unless the articles provide otherwise.

(**2**) The supervisory board shall represent the limited shareholders, unless the shareholders' meeting has elected special representatives, in the case of litigation by the limited shareholders as a body against the general partners or in the case of litigation by the general partners against the limited shareholders as a body. The company shall be liable for the costs of the litigation which are incurred by the limited shareholders irrespective of the company's right to recourse against the limited shareholders.

(**3**) General partners may not also be members of the supervisory board.

§ 288. Entnahmen der persönlich haftenden Gesellschafter. Kreditgewährung

(1) Entfällt auf einen persönlich haftenden Gesellschafter ein Verlust, der seinen Kapitalanteil übersteigt, so darf er keinen Gewinn auf seinen Kapitalanteil entnehmen. Er darf ferner keinen solchen Gewinnanteil und kein Geld auf seinen Kapitalanteil entnehmen, solange die Summe aus Bilanzverlust, Einzahlungsverpflichtungen, Verlustanteilen persönlich haftender Gesellschafter und Forderungen aus Krediten an persönlich haftende Gesellschafter und deren Angehörige die Summe aus Gewinnvortrag, Kapital- und Gewinnrücklagen sowie Kapitalanteilen der persönlich haftenden Gesellschafter übersteigt.

(2) Solange die Voraussetzung von Absatz 1 Satz 2 vorliegt, darf die Gesellschaft keinen unter § 286 Abs. 2 Satz 4 fallenden Kredit gewähren. Ein trotzdem gewährter Kredit ist ohne Rücksicht auf entgegenstehende Vereinbarungen sofort zurückzugewähren.

(3) Ansprüche persönlich haftender Gesellschafter auf nicht vom Gewinn abhängige Tätigkeitsvergütungen werden durch diese Vorschriften nicht berührt. Für eine Herabsetzung solcher Vergütungen gilt § 87 Abs. 2 Satz 1 sinngemäß.

§ 288. Withdrawals by General Partners; Extension of Credits

(1) A general partner may not withdraw any profit with respect to his capital participation if his share of a loss exceeds his capital participation. He also may not withdraw any share of profits or cash for his capital participation as long as the sum of any balance sheet loss, any payment obligations, the share of general partners in any losses of the partnership and any amounts owed under credits extended to general partners and their relatives exceeds the sum of any profit carried forward, the capital and profit reserves and the capital participations of the general partners.

(2) The company may not extend any credit falling under § 286 (2) sentence 4 as long as the conditions set forth in subsection (1) sentence 2 apply. Any such credit which has been extended in violation of the foregoing shall be required to be repaid immediately irrespective of any agreements to the contrary.

(3) The foregoing provisions shall not affect the claims of general partners for remuneration for services which are not related to profits. § 87 (2) sentence 1 shall apply analogously to any reduction of such remuneration.

§ 289. Auflösung

(1) Die Gründe für die Auflösung der Kommanditgesellschaft auf Aktien und das Ausscheiden eines von mehreren persönlich haftenden Gesellschaftern aus der Gesellschaft richten sich, soweit in den Absätzen 2 bis 6 nichts anderes bestimmt ist, nach den Vorschriften des Handelsgesetzbuchs über die Kommanditgesellschaft.

§ 289. Dissolution

(1) The grounds for dissolution of a partnership limited by shares and for the resignation of one of the general partners from the company shall be governed by the provisions of the Commercial Code regarding limited partnerships, unless subsections (2) to (6) provide otherwise.

(2) Die Kommanditgesellschaft auf Aktien wird auch aufgelöst

1. mit der Rechtskraft des Beschlusses, durch den die Eröffnung des Konkursverfahrens mangels einer den Kosten des Verfahrens entsprechenden Konkursmasse abgelehnt wird;[1]

2. mit der Rechtskraft einer Verfügung des Registergerichts, durch welche nach § 144a des Gesetzes über die Angelegenheiten der freiwilligen Gerichtsbarkeit ein Mangel der Satzung festgestellt worden ist.[2]

(2) The partnership limited by shares shall be dissolved:

1. upon a decision which is final and which may not be appealed denying the institution of bankruptcy proceedings for lack of assets sufficient to cover the costs of the proceedings;[1]

2. upon an order of the court of registration, which is final and which may not be appealed, which finds a deficiency in the articles pursuant to § 144a of the Act on Court Procedure in Non-Litigious Matters.[2]

(3) Durch die Eröffnung des Konkursverfahrens[3] über das Vermögen eines Kommanditaktionärs wird die Gesellschaft nicht aufgelöst. Die Gläubiger eines Kommanditaktionärs sind nicht berechtigt, die Gesellschaft zu kündigen.

(3) The company shall not be dissolved by reason of the institution of bankruptcy proceedings[3] over the assets of a limited shareholder. The creditors of a limited shareholder shall not be entitled to terminate the company.

(4) Für die Kündigung der Gesellschaft durch die Kommanditaktionäre und für ihre Zustimmung zur Auflösung der Gesellschaft ist ein Beschluß der Hauptversammlung nötig. Gleiches gilt für den Antrag auf Auflösung der Gesellschaft durch gerichtliche Entscheidung. Der Beschluß bedarf einer Mehrheit, die mindestens drei Viertel des bei der Beschlußfassung vertretenen Grundkapitals umfaßt. Die Satzung kann eine größere Kapitalmehrheit und weitere Erfordernisse bestimmen.

(4) Termination of the company by the limited shareholders or their consent to the dissolution of the company shall require a resolution of the shareholders' meeting. The foregoing shall apply to a motion for dissolution of the company by judicial decision. Such resolution shall require a majority of not less than three fourths of the share capital represented at the passing of the resolution. The articles may provide for a larger capital majority and additional requirements.

1. Mit Wirkung vom 1. Januar 1999 ist § 289 Abs. 2 Nr. 1 wie folgt gefaßt:
'1. mit der Rechtskraft des Beschlusses, durch den die Eröffnung des Insolvenzverfahrens mangels Masse abgelehnt wird;'.
2. Mit wirkung vom 1. Januar 1999 ist der Punkt durch einen Strichpunkt ersetzt und die folgende neue Nummer 3 angefügt:
'3. durch die Löschung der Gesellschaft wegen Vermögenslosigkeit nach § 141a des Gesetzes über die Angelegenheiten der freiwilligen Gerichtsbarkeit.'
3. Mit Wirkung vom 1. Januar 1999 sind die Worte 'des Konkursverfahrens' durch die Worte 'des Insolvenzverfahrens' ersetzt.

1. Effective as of 1 January 1999 § 289 (2) No. 1 will read as follows:
'1. Upon a decision which is final and which may not be appealed denying the institution of insolvency proceedings for lack of assets;'
2. Effective as of 1 January 1999 the full stop will be substituted by a semicolon and the following new No. 3 will be inserted:
'3. upon cancellation of the registration of the company for lack of any assets pursuant to § 141a of the Act on Court Procedure in Non-Litigious Matters.'
3. Effective as of 1 January 1999 the words 'bankruptcy proceedings' will be substituted by the words 'insolvency proceedings'.

(5) Persönlich haftende Gesellschafter können außer durch Ausschließung nur ausscheiden, wenn es die Satzung für zulässig erklärt.

(5) General partners may, except in the case of expulsion, resign only when the articles so permit.

(6) Die Auflösung der Gesellschaft und das Ausscheiden eines persönlich haftenden Gesellschafters ist von allen persönlich haftenden Gesellschaftern zur Eintragung in das Handelsregister anzumelden. § 143 Abs. 3 des Handelsgesetzbuchs gilt sinngemäß.[1]

(6) All general partners shall report the dissolution of the company or the resignation of the general partner for registration in the commercial register. § 143 (3) of the Commercial Code shall apply analogously.[1]

§ 290. Abwicklung

§ 290. Liquidation

(1) Die Abwicklung besorgen alle persönlich haftenden Gesellschafter und eine oder mehrere von der Hauptversammlung gewählte Personen als Abwickler, wenn die Satzung nichts anderes bestimmt.

(1) All general partners and one or more persons elected by the shareholders' meeting shall carry out the liquidation of the company as liquidators, unless the articles provide otherwise.

(2) Die Bestellung oder Abberufung von Abwicklern durch das Gericht kann auch jeder persönlich haftende Gesellschafter beantragen.[2]

(2) Each general partner may also make motion for the appointment or removal of liquidators by the court.[2]

1. Dem § 289 Abs. 6 sind mit Wirkung vom 1. Januar 1999 folgende neue Sätze angefügt:
'In den Fällen des Absatzes 2 hat das Gericht die Auflösung und ihren Grund von Amts wegen einzutragen. Im Falle des Absatzes 2 Nr. 3 entfällt die Eintragung der Auflösung.'
2. Mit Wirkung vom 1. Januar 1999 ist an § 290 folgender neuer Absatz 3 angefügt:
'(3) Ist die Gesellschaft durch Löschung wegen Vermögenslosigkeit aufgelöst, so findet eine Abwicklung nur statt, wenn sich nach der Löschung herausstellt, daß Vermögen vorhanden ist, das der Verteilung unterliegt. Die Abwickler sind auf Antrag eines Beteiligten durch das Gericht zu ernennen.'

1. Effective as of 1 January 1999 the following will be added to § 289 (6):
'In the cases of subsection (2) the court shall register on its own initiative the dissolution and the reasons therefor. In case of subsection (2) No. 3 the dissolution shall not be registered.'
2. Effective as of 1 January 1999 the following subsection (3) will be added to § 290:
'(3) If the company is dissolved by cancellation of its registration for lack of any assets, a liquidation will only take place if it is found upon such cancellation that assets exist which qualify for distribution. The liquidators shall be appointed by the court upon motion by a party concerned.'

Drittes Buch. Verbundene Unternehmen

Book Three. Affiliated Enterprises

Erster Teil. Unternehmensverträge

Part One. Enterprise Agreements

Erster Abschnitt. Arten von Unternehmensverträgen

Division One. Forms of Enterprise Agreements

§ 291. Beherrschungsvertrag. Gewinnabführungsvertrag

§ 291. Control Agreement; Profit Transfer Agreement

(**1**) Unternehmensverträge sind Verträge, durch die eine Aktiengesellschaft oder Kommanditgesellschaft auf Aktien die Leitung ihrer Gesellschaft einem anderen Unternehmen unterstellt (Beherrschungsvertrag) oder sich verpflichtet, ihren ganzen Gewinn an ein anderes Unternehmen abzuführen (Gewinnabführungsvertrag). Als Vertrag über die Abführung des ganzen Gewinns gilt auch ein Vertrag, durch den eine Aktiengesellschaft oder Kommanditgesellschaft auf Aktien es übernimmt, ihr Unternehmen für Rechnung eines anderen Unternehmens zu führen.

(**1**) An agreement in which a stock corporation or partnership limited by shares submits the direction of the company to another enterprise ('control agreement') or undertakes to transfer its entire profits to another enterprise ('profit transfer agreements') shall constitute enterprise agreements. An agreement in which a stock corporation or partnership limited by shares agrees to conduct its business on behalf of another enterprise shall also constitute a profit transfer agreement.

(**2**) Stellen sich Unternehmen, die voneinander nicht abhängig sind, durch Vertrag unter einheitliche Leitung, ohne daß dadurch eines von ihnen von einem anderen vertragschließenden Unternehmen abhängig wird, so ist dieser Vertrag kein Beherrschungsvertrag.

(**2**) If enterprises which are not controlled by one another submit by agreement to common direction, without one of such enterprises becoming controlled by another contracting enterprise, such agreement shall not constitute a control agreement.

(**3**) Leistungen der Gesellschaft auf Grund eines Beherrschungs- oder eines Gewinnabführungsvertrags gelten nicht als Verstoß gegen die §§ 57, 58 und 60.

(**3**) Payments made by a company pursuant to a control agreement or profit transfer agreement shall not constitute a violation of §§ 57, 58 and 60.

§ 292. Andere Unternehmensverträge

(1) Unternehmensverträge sind ferner Verträge, durch die eine Aktiengesellschaft oder Kommanditgesellschaft auf Aktien

1. sich verpflichtet, ihren Gewinn oder den Gewinn einzelner ihrer Betriebe ganz oder zum Teil mit dem Gewinn anderer Unternehmen oder einzelner Betriebe anderer Unternehmen zur Aufteilung eines gemeinschaftlichen Gewinns zusammenzulegen (Gewinngemeinschaft),

2. sich verpflichtet, einen Teil ihres Gewinns oder den Gewinn einzelner ihrer Betriebe ganz oder zum Teil an einen anderen abzuführen (Teilgewinnabführungsvertrag),

3. den Betrieb ihres Unternehmens einem anderen verpachtet oder sonst überläßt (Betriebspachtvertrag, Betriebsüberlassungsvertrag).

(2) Ein Vertrag über eine Gewinnbeteiligung mit Mitgliedern von Vorstand und Aufsichtsrat oder mit einzelnen Arbeitnehmern der Gesellschaft sowie eine Abrede über eine Gewinnbeteiligung im Rahmen von Verträgen des laufenden Geschäftsverkehrs oder Lizenzverträgen ist kein Teilgewinnabführungsvertrag.

(3) Ein Betriebspacht- oder Betriebsüberlassungsvertrag und der Beschluß, durch den die Hauptversammlung dem Vertrag zugestimmt hat, sind nicht deshalb nichtig, weil der Vertrag gegen die §§ 57, 58 und 60 verstößt. Satz 1 schließt die Anfechtung des Beschlusses wegen dieses Verstoßes nicht aus.

§ 292. Other Enterprise Agreements

(1) Agreements in which a stock corporation or partnership limited by shares:

1. undertakes to pool its profits or the profits of certain operations in whole or in part with the profits of other enterprises or certain operations of other enterprises for the purpose of dividing the pool's profits ('profit pool');

2. undertakes to transfer a share of its profit or the profit of certain operations in whole or in part to another person ('agreement to transfer a share of profits');

3. leases or otherwise surrenders the operation of its business to another person ('agreement to lease operations', 'agreement to surrender operations')

shall also constitute enterprise agreements.

(2) An agreement on profit sharing with members of the management board and the supervisory board or with individual employees of the company or an arrangement as to profit sharing under agreements entered into in the ordinary course of business or under licensing agreements shall not constitute an agreement to transfer a share of profits.

(3) The fact that an agreement violates §§ 57, 58 and 60 shall not render any agreement to lease or surrender operations, or the resolution by which the shareholders' meeting has consented to such agreement, null and void. Sentence 1 shall not preclude an action to set aside such resolution on the grounds that such agreement violates such provisions.

Zweiter Abschnitt. Abschluß, Änderung und Beendigung von Unternehmensverträgen

Division Two. Execution, Amendment and Termination of Enterprise Agreements

§ 293. Zustimmung der Hauptversammlung

§ 293. Consent of the Shareholders' Meeting

(1) Ein Unternehmensvertrag wird nur mit Zustimmung der Hauptversammlung wirksam. Der Beschluß bedarf einer Mehrheit, die mindestens drei Viertel des bei der Beschlußfassung vertretenen Grundkapitals umfaßt. Die Satzung kann eine größere Kapitalmehrheit und weitere Erfordernisse bestimmen. Auf den Beschluß sind die Bestimmungen des Gesetzes und der Satzung über Satzungsänderungen nicht anzuwenden.

(1) An enterprise agreement shall only become effective upon the consent of the shareholders' meeting. The relevant resolution shall require a majority of not less than three fourths of the share capital represented at the passing of the resolution. The articles may provide for a larger capital majority and additional requirements. The provisions of law and of the articles governing amendments of the articles shall not apply to such resolution.

(2) Ein Beherrschungs- oder ein Gewinnabführungsvertrag wird, wenn der andere Vertragsteil eine Aktiengesellschaft oder Kommanditgesellschaft auf Aktien ist, nur wirksam, wenn auch die Hauptversammlung dieser Gesellschaft zustimmt. Für den Beschluß gilt Absatz 1 Satz 2 bis 4 sinngemäß.

(2) A control agreement or profit transfer agreement shall, if the other party to the agreement is a stock corporation or partnership limited by shares, become effective only if also the shareholders' meeting of such other company consents thereto. Subsection (1) sentences 2 to 4 shall apply analogously to any such resolution by such other company.

(3) Der Vertrag bedarf der schriftlichen Form.

(3) Any such agreement shall be in writing.

(4) (*aufgehoben*)

(4) (*repealed*)

§ 293a. Bericht über den Unternehmensvertrag

§ 293a. Report on the Enterprise Agreement

(1) Der Vorstand jeder an einem Unternehmensvertrag beteiligten Aktiengesellschaft oder Kommanditgesellschaft auf Aktien hat, soweit die Zustimmung der Hauptversammlung nach § 293 erforderlich ist, einen ausführlichen schriftlichen Bericht zu erstatten, in dem der Abschluß des Unternehmensvertrags, der Vertrag im einzelnen und insbesondere

(1) If pursuant to § 293 the consent of the shareholders' meeting is required, the management board of each of the stock corporations or partnerships limited by shares party to the enterprise agreement shall give a comprehensive written report in which the entry into the enterprise agreement, the individual terms of such agreement and especially the form and

Art und Höhe des Ausgleichs nach § 304 und der Abfindung nach § 305 rechtlich und wirtschaftlich erläutert und begründet werden; der Bericht kann von den Vorständen auch gemeinsam erstattet werden. Auf besondere Schwierigkeiten bei der Bewertung der vertragschließenden Unternehmen sowie auf die Folgen für die Beteiligungen der Aktionäre ist hinzuweisen.

(2) In den Bericht brauchen Tatsachen nicht aufgenommen zu werden, deren Bekanntwerden geeignet ist, einem der vertragschließenden Unternehmen oder einem verbundenen Unternehmen einen nicht unerheblichen Nachteil zuzufügen. In diesem Falle sind in dem Bericht die Gründe, aus denen die Tatsachen nicht aufgenommen worden sind, darzulegen.

(3) Der Bericht ist nicht erforderlich, wenn alle Anteilsinhaber aller beteiligten Unternehmen auf seine Erstattung durch öffentlich beglaubigte Erklärung verzichten.

§ 293b. Prüfung des Unternehmensvertrags

(1) Der Unternehmensvertrag ist für jede vertragschließende Aktiengesellschaft oder Kommanditgesellschaft auf Aktien durch sachverständige Prüfer (Vertragsprüfer) zu prüfen, es sei denn, daß sich alle Aktien der abhängigen Gesellschaft in der Hand des herrschenden Unternehmens befinden.

(2) § 293a Abs. 3 ist entsprechend anzuwenden.

amount of the compensation pursuant to § 304 and the consideration pursuant to § 305 shall be explained and substantiated from the legal and financial perspective; the report may be given jointly by the management boards. Such report shall refer to any specific difficulties regarding the valuation of the contracting enterprises and the consequences for the interests of the shareholders.

(2) Such report need not include facts whose disclosure is likely to cause material damage to a contracting enterprise or an affiliated enterprise. In such event the report shall set forth the reasons for not including such facts.

(3) The report need not be given if all shareholders of all participating enterprises waive the giving of the report by officially certified declaration.

§ 293b. Audit of the Enterprise Agreement

(1) The enterprise agreement shall be audited by qualified auditors ('agreement auditors') for each contracting stock corporation or partnership limited by shares unless all shares of the controlled company are held by the controlling company.

(2) § 293a (3) shall apply analogously.

§ 293c. Bestellung der Vertragsprüfer

(1) Die Vertragsprüfer werden von dem Vorstand der abhängigen Gesellschaft oder auf dessen Antrag vom Gericht bestellt. Zuständig ist das Landgericht, in dessen Bezirk die abhängige Gesellschaft ihren Sitz hat. Ist bei dem Landgericht eine Kammer für Handelssachen gebildet, so entscheidet diese an Stelle der Zivilkammer. Für den Ersatz von Auslagen und für die Vergütung der vom Gericht bestellten Prüfer gilt § 318 Abs. 5 des Handelsgesetzbuchs.

(2) Die Landesregierung kann die Entscheidung durch Rechtsverordnung für die Bezirke mehrerer Landgerichte einem der Landgerichte übertragen, wenn dies der Sicherung einer einheitlichen Rechtsprechung dient. Die Landesregierung kann die Ermächtigung auf die Landesjustizverwaltung übertragen.

§ 293c. Appointment of the Agreement Auditors

(1) The agreement auditors shall be appointed by the management board of the controlled company or upon its motion by the court. Jurisdiction shall lie with the district court of the domicile of the controlled company. If the district court maintains a chamber for commercial matters such chamber shall have jurisdiction in lieu of the chamber for civil matters. § 318 (5) of the Commercial Code shall apply to reimbursement of the expenses and fees of the auditors appointed by the court.

(2) The appropriate state government may by regulation transfer jurisdiction for several district courts to one district court if such transfer is required to ensure uniformity of decisions. Such state government may transfer such authority to the ministry of justice of such state.

§ 293d. Auswahl, Stellung und Verantwortlichkeit der Vertragsprüfer

(1) Für die Auswahl und das Auskunftsrecht der Vertragsprüfer gelten § 319 Abs. 1 bis 3, § 320 Abs. 1 Satz 2 und Abs. 2 Satz 1 und 2 des Handelsgesetzbuchs entsprechend. Das Auskunftsrecht besteht gegenüber den vertragschließenden Unternehmen und gegenüber einem Konzernunternehmen sowie einem abhängigen und einem herrschenden Unternehmen.

(2) Für die Verantwortlichkeit der Vertragsprüfer, ihrer Gehilfen und der bei der Prüfung mitwirkenden gesetzlichen Vertreter einer Prüfungsgesellschaft gilt § 323 des Handelsgesetzbuchs entsprechend. Die Verantwortlichkeit besteht ge-

§ 293d. Selection, Position and Responsibility of the Agreement Auditors

(1) § 319 (1) to (3), § 320 (1) sentence 2 and (2) sentences 1 and 2 of the Commercial Code shall apply analogously to the selection and the right to information of the agreement auditors. The right to information exists towards the contracting enterprises, any member of a group and the controlled and controlling enterprises.

(2) § 323 of the Commercial Code shall apply analogously to the responsibility of the agreement auditors, their assistants and the legal representatives of an auditing firm which participates in the audit. The responsibility exists towards the

genüber den vertragschließenden Unternehmen und deren Anteilsinhabern.

contracting enterprises and their shareholders.

§ 293e. Prüfungsbericht

(1) Die Vertragsprüfer haben über das Ergebnis der Prüfung schriftlich zu berichten. Der Prüfungsbericht ist mit einer Erklärung darüber abzuschließen, ob der vorgeschlagene Ausgleich oder die vorgeschlagene Abfindung angemessen ist. Dabei ist anzugeben,

1. nach welchen Methoden Ausgleich und Abfindung ermittelt worden sind;

2. aus welchen Gründen die Anwendung dieser Methoden angemessen ist;

3. welcher Ausgleich oder welche Abfindung sich bei der Anwendung verschiedener Methoden, sofern mehrere angewandt worden sind, jeweils ergeben würde; zugleich ist darzulegen, welches Gewicht den verschiedenen Methoden bei der Bestimmung des vorgeschlagenen Ausgleichs oder der vorgeschlagenen Abfindung und der ihnen zugrunde liegenden Werte beigemessen worden ist und welche besonderen Schwierigkeiten bei der Bewertung der vertragschließenden Unternehmen aufgetreten sind.

(2) § 293a Abs. 2 und 3 ist entsprechend anzuwenden.

§ 293e. Audit Report

(1) The agreement auditors shall report in writing on the findings of the audit. The audit report shall end with a statement whether or not the proposed compensation pursuant to § 304 or the proposed consideration pursuant to § 305 is appropriate. In such context it shall be stated:

1. according to which methods the compensation and consideration have been determined;

2. for which reasons the application of these methods is appropriate;

3. if several methods have been applied, which compensation or which consideration would have resulted from the application of the different methods; at the same time it shall be set forth which weight has been attached to the different methods in determining the proposed compensation or the proposed consideration and to the values taken as basis and which specific difficulties appeared in valuating the contracting enterprises.

(2) § 293a (2) and (3) shall apply analogously.

§ 293f. Vorbereitung der Hauptversammlung

(1) Von der Einberufung der Hauptversammlung an, die über die Zustimmung zu dem Unternehmensvertrag beschließen soll, sind in dem Geschäftsraum jeder der beteiligten Aktiengesellschaften oder Kommanditgesellschaften auf Aktien zur Einsicht der Aktionäre auszulegen

§ 293f. Preparation of the Shareholders' Meeting

(1) As from the date of calling that shareholders' meeting which is to resolve on the consent to the enterprise agreement, the following documents shall be made available for inspection by the shareholders in the offices of each of the participating stock corporations or partnerships limited by shares:

1. der Unternehmensvertrag;
2. die Jahresabschlüsse und die Lageberichte der vertragschließenden Unternehmen für die letzten drei Geschäftsjahre;
3. die nach § 293a erstatteten Berichte der Vorstände und die nach § 293e erstatteten Berichte der Vertragsprüfer.

1. the enterprise agreement;
2. the annual financial statements and annual reports of the contracting enterprises for the last three fiscal years;
3. the reports given by the management boards pursuant to § 293a and the reports given by the agreement auditors pursuant to § 293e.

(**2**) Auf Verlangen ist jedem Aktionär unverzüglich und kostenlos eine Abschrift der in Absatz 1 bezeichneten Unterlagen zu erteilen.

(**2**) Upon request each shareholder shall promptly and free of charge be provided with a copy of the documents mentioned in subsection (1).

§ 293g. Durchführung der Hauptversammlung

§ 293g. The Shareholders' Meeting

(**1**) In der Hauptversammlung sind die in § 293f Abs. 1 bezeichneten Unterlagen auszulegen.

(**1**) The documents named in § 293f (1) shall be displayed at the shareholders' meeting.

(**2**) Der Vorstand hat den Unternehmensvertrag zu Beginn der Verhandlung mündlich zu erläutern. Er ist der Niederschrift als Anlage beizufügen.

(**2**) The management board shall comment on the enterprise agreement at the commencement of deliberations. The agreement shall be appended to the minutes.

(**3**) Jedem Aktionär ist auf Verlangen in der Hauptversammlung Auskunft auch über alle für den Vertragschluß wesentlichen Angelegenheiten des anderen Vertragsteils zu geben.

(**3**) Upon request each shareholder shall be provided at the shareholders' meeting also with information regarding all matters relating to the other enterprise which is a party to the agreement which are material in the context of such agreement.

§ 294. Eintragung. Wirksamwerden

§ 294. Registration; Date of Effectiveness

(**1**) Der Vorstand der Gesellschaft hat das Bestehen und die Art des Unternehmensvertrags sowie den Namen des anderen Vertragsteils, bei Teilgewinnabführungsverträgen außerdem die Vereinbarung über die Höhe des abzuführenden Gewinns, zur Eintragung in das Handels-

(**1**) The management board of the company shall report for registration in the commercial register the existence and kind of the enterprise agreement and the name of the other contracting party, and further, in the case of agreements to transfer a share of profit, the arrangement as to

register anzumelden. Der Anmeldung sind der Vertrag sowie, wenn er nur mit Zustimmung der Hauptversammlung des anderen Vertragsteils wirksam wird, die Niederschrift dieses Beschlusses und ihre Anlagen in Urschrift, Ausfertigung oder öffentlich beglaubigter Abschrift beizufügen.

the share of profit to be transferred. The agreement and, if such agreement shall become effective only upon the consent of the shareholders' meeting of the other contracting party, the minutes of the resolution of the other contracting party and documents pertaining thereto shall be appended to the report in original, duplicate or officially certified copy.

(2) Der Vertrag wird erst wirksam, wenn sein Bestehen in das Handelsregister des Sitzes der Gesellschaft eingetragen worden ist.

(2) The agreement shall only become effective upon registration thereof in the commercial register of the company's domicile.

§ 295. Änderung

§ 295. Amendment

(1) Ein Unternehmensvertrag kann nur mit Zustimmung der Hauptversammlung geändert werden. §§ 293 bis 294 gelten sinngemäß.

(1) An enterprise agreement may be amended only with the consent of the shareholders' meeting. §§ 293 to 294 shall apply analogously.

(2) Die Zustimmung der Hauptversammlung der Gesellschaft zu einer Änderung der Bestimmungen des Vertrags, die zur Leistung eines Ausgleichs an die außenstehenden Aktionäre der Gesellschaft oder zum Erwerb ihrer Aktien verpflichten, bedarf, um wirksam zu werden, eines Sonderbeschlusses der außenstehenden Aktionäre. Für den Sonderbeschluß gilt § 293 Abs. 1 Satz 2 und 3. Jedem außenstehenden Aktionär ist auf Verlangen in der Versammlung, die über die Zustimmung beschließt, Auskunft auch über alle für die Änderung wesentlichen Angelegenheiten des anderen Vertragsteils zu geben.

(2) The consent of the shareholders' meeting of the company to any amendment of the terms of the agreement which would obligate the company to pay compensation to its outside shareholders or to acquire their shares shall require a separate resolution of the outside shareholders in order to become effective. § 293 (1) sentences 2 and 3 shall apply to such separate resolution. At the shareholders' meeting resolving upon such consent, each outside shareholder shall upon request be provided with information regarding all matters relating to the other contracting party which are material in the context of such amendment.

§ 296. Aufhebung

§ 296. Cancellation

(1) Ein Unternehmensvertrag kann nur zum Ende des Geschäftsjahrs oder des sonst vertraglich bestimmten Abrechnungszeitraums aufgehoben werden. Eine rückwirkende Aufhebung ist unzu-

(1) An enterprise agreement may be cancelled only by mutual agreement at the end of the fiscal year or the accounting period otherwise agreed upon. A retroactive cancellation may not be made. Any

lässig. Die Aufhebung bedarf der schriftlichen Form.

such cancellation shall be made in writing.

(2) Ein Vertrag, der zur Leistung eines Ausgleichs an die außenstehenden Aktionäre oder zum Erwerb ihrer Aktien verpflichtet, kann nur aufgehoben werden, wenn die außenstehenden Aktionäre durch Sonderbeschluß zustimmen. Für den Sonderbeschluß gilt § 293 Abs. 1 Satz 2 und 3, § 295 Abs. 2 Satz 3 sinngemäß.

(2) An agreement which obligates the company to pay compensation to outside shareholders or to acquire their shares may be cancelled by mutual agreement if the outside shareholders consent thereto by separate resolution. § 293 (1) sentences 2 and 3, § 295 (2) sentence 3 shall apply analogously to such separate resolution.

§ 297. Kündigung

§ 297. Termination

(1) Ein Unternehmensvertrag kann aus wichtigem Grunde ohne Einhaltung einer Kündigungsfrist gekündigt werden. Ein wichtiger Grund liegt namentlich vor, wenn der andere Vertragsteil voraussichtlich nicht in der Lage sein wird, seine auf Grund des Vertrags bestehenden Verpflichtungen zu erfüllen.

(1) An enterprise agreement may be terminated for cause without observing any period of notice. Cause shall in particular exist if it is likely that the other contracting party will not be able to fulfill its obligations arising under the agreement.

(2) Der Vorstand der Gesellschaft kann einen Vertrag, der zur Leistung eines Ausgleichs an die außenstehenden Aktionäre der Gesellschaft oder zum Erwerb ihrer Aktien verpflichtet, ohne wichtigen Grund nur kündigen, wenn die außenstehenden Aktionäre durch Sonderbeschluß zustimmen. Für den Sonderbeschluß gilt § 293 Abs. 1 Satz 2 und 3, § 295 Abs. 2 Satz 3 sinngemäß.

(2) The management board of the company may only terminate without cause an agreement which obligates the company to pay compensation to the outside shareholders or to acquire their shares if the outside shareholders consent thereto by separate resolution. § 293 (1) sentences 2 and 3, § 295 (2) sentence 3 shall apply analogously to such separate resolution.

(3) Die Kündigung bedarf der schriftlichen Form.

(3) The notice of termination shall be made in writing.

§ 298. Anmeldung und Eintragung

§ 298. Report and Registration

Der Vorstand der Gesellschaft hat die Beendigung eines Unternehmensvertrags, den Grund und den Zeitpunkt der Beendigung unverzüglich zur Eintragung in das Handelsregister anzumelden.

The management board of the company shall promptly report the cancellation or termination of an enterprise agreement, the grounds and the date of cancellation or termination for registration in the commercial register.

§ 299. Ausschluß von Weisungen

Auf Grund eines Unternehmensvertrags kann der Gesellschaft nicht die Weisung erteilt werden, den Vertrag zu ändern, aufrechtzuerhalten oder zu beendigen.

§ 299. Prohibition of Instructions

An enterprise agreement may not serve as the basis for an instruction to the company to amend, continue or cancel or terminate the agreement.

Dritter Abschnitt. Sicherung der Gesellschaft und der Gläubiger

§ 300. Gesetzliche Rücklage

In die gesetzliche Rücklage sind an Stelle des in § 150 Abs. 2 bestimmten Betrags einzustellen,

1. wenn ein Gewinnabführungsvertrag besteht, aus dem ohne die Gewinnabführung entstehenden, um einen Verlustvortrag aus dem Vorjahr geminderten Jahresüberschuß der Betrag, der erforderlich ist, um die gesetzliche Rücklage unter Hinzurechnung einer Kapitalrücklage innerhalb der ersten fünf Geschäftsjahre, die während des Bestehens des Vertrags oder nach Durchführung einer Kapitalerhöhung beginnen, gleichmäßig auf den zehnten oder den in der Satzung bestimmten höheren Teil des Grundkapitals aufzufüllen, mindestens aber der in Nummer 2 bestimmte Betrag;
2. wenn ein Teilgewinnabführungsvertrag besteht, der Betrag, der nach § 150 Abs. 2 aus dem ohne die Gewinnabführung entstehenden, um einen Verlustvortrag aus dem Vorjahr geminderten Jahresüberschuß in die gesetzliche Rücklage einzustellen wäre;
3. wenn ein Beherrschungsvertrag besteht, ohne daß die Gesellschaft auch zur Abführung ihres ganzen Gewinns verpflichtet ist, der zur Auffüllung der gesetzlichen Rücklage nach Nummer 1 erforderliche Betrag, mindestens aber der in § 150 Abs. 2 oder, wenn die Gesellschaft verpflichtet ist, ihren Gewinn zum

Division Three. Protection of the Company and Creditors

§ 300. Legal Reserve

The following amounts are to be transferred to the legal reserve in lieu of the amount specified in § 150 (2):

1. in the case of a profit transfer agreement, that share of the annual net profit accruing prior such profit transfer, after deducting any loss carried forward from the previous year, which is required in order to increase, during the first five fiscal years commencing during the term of such agreement or upon completion of a capital increase, the legal reserve, plus the amount of any capital reserve, in equal instalments to one-tenth of the share capital or a higher proportion specified by the articles, but in any event not less than the amount specified in No. 2;
2. in the case of an agreement to transfer a share of profits, that share of the annual net profit accruing prior to such profit transfer, after deducting any loss carried forward from the previous year, which would be transferred pursuant to § 150 (2);
3. in the case of a control agreement which does not obligate the company to transfer its entire profit, that amount which is required to increase the legal reserve in accordance with No. 1, but in any event not less than the amount specified in § 150 (2) or, if the company is obligated to transfer a share of its profit, the amount specified in No. 2.

Teil abzuführen, der in Nummer 2 bestimmte Betrag.

§ 301. Höchstbetrag der Gewinnabführung

Eine Gesellschaft kann, gleichgültig welche Vereinbarungen über die Berechnung des abzuführenden Gewinns getroffen worden sind, als ihren Gewinn höchstens den ohne die Gewinnabführung entstehenden Jahresüberschuß, vermindert um einen Verlustvortrag aus dem Vorjahr und um den Betrag, der nach § 300 in die gesetzliche Rücklage einzustellen ist, abführen. Sind während der Dauer des Vertrags Beträge in andere Gewinnrücklagen eingestellt worden, so können diese Beträge den anderen Gewinnrücklagen entnommen und als Gewinn abgeführt werden.

§ 301. Maximum Amount of Profit Transfer

Irrespective of any agreements made regarding the computation of the amount of profit to be transferred, a company may in no event transfer as profit an amount exceeding the annual net profit accruing prior to such profit transfer, after deducting any loss carried forward from the previous year, plus the amount to be transferred to the legal reserve pursuant to § 300. If during the term of the agreement amounts have been transferred to other profit reserves, such amounts may be withdrawn from such other profit reserves and transferred as profit.

§ 302. Verlustübernahme

(1) Besteht ein Beherrschungs- oder ein Gewinnabführungsvertrag, so hat der andere Vertragsteil jeden während der Vertragsdauer sonst entstehenden Jahresfehlbetrag auszugleichen, soweit dieser nicht dadurch ausgeglichen wird, daß den anderen Gewinnrücklagen Beträge entnommen werden, die während der Vertragsdauer in sie eingestellt worden sind.

(2) Hat eine abhängige Gesellschaft den Betrieb ihres Unternehmens dem herrschenden Unternehmen verpachtet oder sonst überlassen, so hat das herrschende Unternehmen jeden während der Vertragsdauer sonst entstehenden Jahresfehlbetrag auszugleichen, soweit die vereinbarte Gegenleistung das angemessene Entgelt nicht erreicht.

(3) Die Gesellschaft kann auf den Anspruch auf Ausgleich erst drei Jahre

§ 302. Assumption of Losses

(1) In the case of a control agreement or profit transfer agreement, the other contracting party shall compensate any annual net loss occurring during the term of the agreement to the extent that such loss is not compensated by withdrawing amounts from the profit reserves which were transferred to such reserves during the term of the agreement.

(2) If a controlled company has leased or otherwise surrendered the operation of its business to its controlling enterprise, such controlling enterprise shall compensate any annual net loss occurring during the term of the agreement to the extent that the consideration agreed upon for such lease or surrender of operation does not constitute adequate compensation.

(3) The company may only waive or compromise any claim for compensation

nach dem Tage, an dem die Eintragung der Beendigung des Vertrags in das Handelsregister nach § 10 des Handelsgesetzbuchs als bekanntgemacht gilt, verzichten oder sich über ihn vergleichen. Dies gilt nicht, wenn der Ausgleichspflichtige zahlungsunfähig ist und sich zur Abwendung oder Beseitigung des Konkursverfahrens mit seinen Gläubigern vergleicht.[1] Der Verzicht oder Vergleich wird nur wirksam, wenn die außenstehenden Aktionäre durch Sonderbeschluß zustimmen und nicht eine Minderheit, deren Anteile zusammen den zehnten Teil des bei der Beschlußfassung vertretenen Grundkapitals erreichen, zur Niederschrift Widerspruch erhebt.

after the expiration of three years from the date on which the registration of the cancellation or termination of the agreement in the commercial register shall be deemed to have been announced pursuant to § 10 of the Commercial Code. The foregoing shall not apply if the party obligated to compensate is insolvent and enters into composition with its creditors to avoid or terminate bankruptcy proceedings.[1] Such waiver or composition shall only become effective if the outside shareholders consent thereto by separate resolution and no minority whose holding in the aggregate equals or exceeds one tenth of the share capital represented at the passing of the resolution has recorded an objection in the minutes.

§ 303. Gläubigerschutz

(1) Endet ein Beherrschungs- oder ein Gewinnabführungsvertrag, so hat der andere Vertragsteil den Gläubigern der Gesellschaft, deren Forderungen begründet worden sind, bevor die Eintragung der Beendigung des Vertrags in das Handelsregister nach § 10 des Handelsgesetzbuchs als bekanntgemacht gilt, Sicherheit zu leisten, wenn sie sich binnen sechs Monaten nach der Bekanntmachung der Eintragung zu diesem Zweck bei ihm melden. Die Gläubiger sind in der Bekanntmachung der Eintragung auf dieses Recht hinzuweisen.

§ 303. Protection of Creditors

(1) If a control agreement or profit transfer agreement is cancelled or terminated, the other contracting part shall provide security to the creditors of the company whose claims arose prior to the date on which the registration of the cancellation or termination of the agreement in the commercial register shall be deemed to have been announced pursuant to § 10 of the Commercial Code, provided that such creditors have applied to such contracting party for such purpose within six months from the date of the announcement of the registration. The announcement of the registration shall advise the creditors of such right.

1. Mit Wirkung vom 1. Januar 1999 ist § 302 Abs. 3 Satz 2 wie folgt gefaßt:
'Dies gilt nicht, wenn der Ausgleichspflichtige zahlungsunfähig ist und sich zur Abwendung des Insolvenzverfahrens mit seinen Gläubigern vergleicht oder wenn die Ersatzpflicht in einem Insolvenzplan geregelt wird.'

1. Effective as of 1 January 1999 § 302 (3) sentence 2 will read as follows:
'The foregoing shall not apply if the party obliged to compensate is insolvent and enters into composition with its creditors to avoid insolvency proceedings or if the obligation to compensation is subject to an insolvency plan.'

(2) Das Recht, Sicherheitsleistung zu verlangen, steht Gläubigern nicht zu, die im Fall des Konkurses[1] ein Recht auf vorzugsweise Befriedigung aus einer Dekkungsmasse haben, die nach gesetzlicher Vorschrift zu ihrem Schutz errichtet und staatlich überwacht ist.

(2) Creditors who in the case of bankruptcy[1] have a right to preferential satisfaction from a fund which has been established pursuant to statutory provisions for their protection and is subject to governmental supervision shall not have the right to demand security.

(3) Statt Sicherheit zu leisten, kann der andere Vertragsteil sich für die Forderung verbürgen. § 349 des Handelsgesetzbuchs über den Ausschluß der Einrede der Vorausklage ist nicht anzuwenden.

(3) The other contracting party may in lieu of security guarantee the claim. The provisions of § 349 of the Commercial Code which exclude the defense of failure to pursue remedy against the principal debtor, shall not apply.

Vierter Abschnitt. Sicherung der außenstehenden Aktionäre bei Beherrschungs- und Gewinnabführungsverträgen

Division Four. Protection of Outside Shareholders in the Case of Control Agreements and Profit Transfer Agreements

§ 304. Angemessener Ausgleich

(1) Ein Gewinnabführungsvertrag muß einen angemessenen Ausgleich für die außenstehenden Aktionäre durch eine auf die Aktiennennbeträge bezogene wiederkehrende Geldleistung (Ausgleichszahlung) vorsehen. Ein Beherrschungsvertrag muß, wenn die Gesellschaft nicht auch zur Abführung ihres ganzen Gewinns verpflichtet ist, den außenstehenden Aktionären als angemessenen Ausgleich einen bestimmten jährlichen Gewinnanteil nach der für die Ausgleichszahlung bestimmten Höhe garantieren. Von der Bestimmung eines angemessenen Ausgleichs kann nur abgesehen werden, wenn die Gesellschaft im Zeitpunkt der Beschlußfassung ihrer Hauptversammlung über den Vertrag keinen außenstehenden Aktionär hat.

§ 304. Adequate Compensation

(1) A profit transfer agreement shall provide for adequate compensation for outside shareholders by recurring payments in proportion to the par value of shares ('compensation payment'). A control agreement shall, if the company is not obligated to transfer its entire profit, guarantee to the outside shareholders as adequate compensation a certain annual share of profit in the same amount as in the case of a compensation payment. Provision for adequate compensation may be omitted only if the company does not have any outside shareholders at the time of the adoption of the resolution of the shareholders' meeting on the agreement.

1. Mit Wirkung vom 1. Januar 1999 sind die Worte 'des Konkurses' durch die Worte 'des Insolvenzverfahrens' ersetzt.

1. Effective as of 1 January 1999 the word 'bankruptcy' will be substituted by the words 'insolvency proceedings'.

(2) Als Ausgleichszahlung ist mindestens die jährliche Zahlung des Betrags zuzusichern, der nach der bisherigen Ertragslage der Gesellschaft und ihren künftigen Ertragsaussichten unter Berücksichtigung angemessener Abschreibungen und Wertberichtigungen, jedoch ohne Bildung anderer Gewinnrücklagen, voraussichtlich als durchschnittlicher Gewinnanteil auf die einzelne Aktie verteilt werden könnte. Ist der andere Vertragsteil eine Aktiengesellschaft oder Kommanditgesellschaft auf Aktien, so kann als Ausgleichszahlung auch die Zahlung des Betrags zugesichert werden, der auf Aktien der anderen Gesellschaft mit mindestens dem entsprechenden Nennbetrag jeweils als Gewinnanteil entfällt. Der entsprechende Nennbetrag bestimmt sich nach dem Verhältnis, in dem bei einer Verschmelzung auf eine Aktie der Gesellschaft Aktien der anderen Gesellschaft zu gewähren wären.

(2) The annual amount to be provided as compensation payment shall be not less than the amount which could be expected to be distributed as the average dividend for each share in view of the past profitability of the company and its prospective profits, taking into account adequate depreciation and reserves for declines in value but exclusive of other profit reserves. If the other contracting party is a stock corporation or a partnership limited by shares, the amount to be provided as compensation payment may be the amount which is paid as dividend on shares of the other company which have at least an equivalent par value. Such equivalent par value shall be determined by the proportion in which shares of the company, in the case of a merger, would be entitled to shares of the other company.

(3) Ein Vertrag, der entgegen Absatz 1 überhaupt keinen Ausgleich vorsieht, ist nichtig. Die Anfechtung des Beschlusses, durch den die Hauptversammlung der Gesellschaft dem Vertrag oder einer unter § 295 Abs. 2 fallenden Änderung des Vertrags zugestimmt hat, kann nicht auf § 243 Abs. 2 oder darauf gestützt werden, daß der im Vertrag bestimmte Ausgleich nicht angemessen ist. Ist der im Vertrag bestimmte Ausgleich nicht angemessen, so hat das in § 306 bestimmte Gericht auf Antrag den vertraglich geschuldeten Ausgleich zu bestimmen, wobei es, wenn der Vertrag einen nach Absatz 2 Satz 2 berechneten Ausgleich vorsieht, den Ausgleich nach dieser Vorschrift zu bestimmen hat.

(3) An agreement which contrary to subsection (1) does not provide for any compensation payment shall be null and void. An action to set aside the resolution by which the shareholders' meeting of the company has consented to the agreement or to an amendment of the agreement falling under § 295 (2), may not be based on § 243 (2) or on the grounds that the compensation provided for in the agreement is inadequate. If the compensation provided for in the agreement shall be inadequate, the court with jurisdiction pursuant to § 306 shall upon motion determine the compensation due under the agreement, provided that, if the agreement provides for a compensation payment computed pursuant to subsection (2) sentence 2, the court shall determine the compensation pursuant to such provision.

(4) Antragsberechtigt ist jeder außenstehende Aktionär. Der Antrag kann

(4) Each outside shareholder shall have standing to make such motion. Such

nur binnen zwei Monaten seit dem Tage gestellt werden, an dem die Eintragung des Bestehens oder einer unter § 295 Abs. 2 fallenden Änderung des Vertrags im Handelsregister nach § 10 des Handelsgesetzbuchs als bekanntgemacht gilt.

motion may be made not less than two months after the date on which the registration in the commercial register of the agreement, or an amendment thereto falling under § 295 (2), shall be deemed to have been announced pursuant to § 10 of the Commercial Code.

(5) Bestimmt das Gericht den Ausgleich, so kann der andere Vertragsteil den Vertrag binnen zwei Monaten nach Rechtskraft der Entscheidung ohne Einhaltung einer Kündigungsfrist kündigen.

(5) If the court determines the amount of the compensation payment, the other contracting party may terminate the agreement without complying with any notice period within two months of the date on which the decision has become final and may not be appealed.

§ 305. Abfindung

§ 305. Consideration

(1) Außer der Verpflichtung zum Ausgleich nach § 304 muß ein Beherrschungs- oder ein Gewinnabführungsvertrag die Verpflichtung des anderen Vertragsteils enthalten, auf Verlangen eines außenstehenden Aktionärs dessen Aktien gegen eine im Vertrag bestimmte angemessene Abfindung zu erwerben.

(1) A control agreement or profit transfer agreement shall, in addition to the obligation to provide compensation pursuant to § 304, include the obligation of the other contracting party to acquire the shares of any outside shareholder upon demand by such shareholder against an adequate consideration specified in the agreement.

(2) Als Abfindung muß der Vertrag,

1. wenn der andere Vertragsteil eine nicht abhängige und nicht in Mehrheitsbesitz stehende Aktiengesellschaft oder Kommanditgesellschaft auf Aktien mit Sitz im Inland ist, die Gewährung eigener Aktien dieser Gesellschaft,

2. wenn der andere Vertragsteil eine abhängige oder in Mehrheitsbesitz stehende Aktiengesellschaft oder Kommanditgesellschaft auf Aktien und das herrschende Unternehmen eine Aktiengesellschaft oder Kommanditgesellschaft auf Aktien mit Sitz im Inland ist, entweder die Gewährung von Aktien der herrschenden oder mit Mehrheit beteiligten Gesellschaft oder eine Barabfindung,

(2) The agreement shall provide for the following consideration:

1. if the other contracting party is a stock corporation or partnership limited by shares with domestic domicile which is not a controlled enterprise or subsidiary, shares of such other company;

2. if the other contracting party is a stock corporation or partnership limited by shares which is a controlled enterprise or subsidiary and the controlling enterprise is a stock corporation or partnership limited by shares with domestic domicile, either shares of the controlling enterprise or of the parent or a cash payment;

3. in allen anderen Fällen eine Barabfindung
vorsehen.

3. in all other cases a cash payment.

(3) Werden als Abfindung Aktien einer anderen Gesellschaft gewährt, so ist die Abfindung als angemessen anzusehen, wenn die Aktien in dem Verhältnis gewährt werden, in dem bei einer Verschmelzung auf eine Aktie der Gesellschaft Aktien der anderen Gesellschaft zu gewähren wären, wobei Spitzenbeträge durch bare Zuzahlungen ausgeglichen werden können. Die angemessene Barabfindung muß die Verhältnisse der Gesellschaft im Zeitpunkt der Beschlußfassung ihrer Hauptversammlung über den Vertrag berücksichtigen. Sie ist nach Ablauf des Tages, an dem der Beherrschungs- oder Gewinnabführungsvertrag wirksam geworden ist, mit jährlich zwei vom Hundert über dem jeweiligen Diskontsatz der Deutschen Bundesbank zu verzinsen; die Geltendmachung eines weiteren Schadens ist nicht ausgeschlossen.

(3) If shares of another company are provided as consideration, such consideration shall be considered to be adequate if the shares are provided in the same proportion in which shares of the company would, in the case of a merger, be entitled to shares of the other company, provided that fractional amounts may be compensated by additional cash payments. The determination of the adequate cash payment shall take into account the conditions of the company at the time of adoption by its shareholders' meeting of the resolution on the agreement. The adequate cash payment shall bear interest at the rate of two percent per annum above the from time to time prevailing discount rate of the German Federal Bank as from the end of the day on which the control agreement or the profit transfer agreement has become effective; claims for further damages shall not be precluded.

(4) Die Verpflichtung zum Erwerb der Aktien kann befristet werden. Die Frist endet frühestens zwei Monate nach dem Tage, an dem die Eintragung des Bestehens des Vertrags im Handelsregister nach § 10 des Handelsgesetzbuchs als bekanntgemacht gilt. Ist ein Antrag auf Bestimmung des Ausgleichs oder der Abfindung durch das in § 306 bestimmte Gericht gestellt worden, so endet die Frist frühestens zwei Monate nach dem Tage, an dem die Entscheidung über den zuletzt beschiedenen Antrag im Bundesanzeiger bekanntgemacht worden ist.

(4) The obligation to acquire shares may be limited to a specified period of time. Such period of time shall expire not earlier than two months after the date on which the registration of the agreement in the commercial register shall be deemed to have been announced pursuant to § 10 of the Commercial Code. If motion has been made for determination of the amount of the compensation or consideration by the court with jurisdiction pursuant to § 306, such period of time shall expire not earlier than two months after the date on which the decision on the last motion disposed of has been announced in the Federal Gazette.

(5) Die Anfechtung des Beschlusses, durch den die Hauptversammlung der Gesellschaft dem Vertrag oder einer unter § 295 Abs. 2 fallenden Änderung des Ver-

(5) An action to set aside the resolution by which the shareholders' meeting of the company has consented to the agreement, or to an amendment thereto

trags zugestimmt hat, kann nicht darauf gestützt werden, daß der Vertrag keine angemessene Abfindung vorsieht. Sieht der Vertrag überhaupt keine oder eine den Absätzen 1 bis 3 nicht entsprechende Abfindung vor, so hat das in § 306 bestimmte Gericht auf Antrag die vertraglich zu gewährende Abfindung zu bestimmen. Dabei hat es in den Fällen des Absatzes 2 Nr. 2, wenn der Vertrag die Gewährung von Aktien der herrschenden oder mit Mehrheit beteiligten Gesellschaft vorsieht, das Verhältnis, in dem diese Aktien zu gewähren sind, wenn der Vertrag nicht die Gewährung von Aktien der herrschenden oder mit Mehrheit beteiligten Gesellschaft vorsieht, die angemessene Barabfindung zu bestimmen. § 304 Abs. 4 und 5 gilt sinngemäß.

falling under § 295 (2), may not be based on the ground that the agreement does not provide for an adequate consideration. If the agreement does not provide for any consideration or for consideration which does not comply with subsections (1) to (3), the court with jurisdiction pursuant to § 306 shall upon motion determine the amount of the consideration due under the agreement. In the case of subsection (2) No. 2, if the agreement provides for the granting of shares of the controlling enterprise or parent company, the court shall determine the ratio in which such shares are to be granted, and if the agreement does not provide for the granting of shares of the controlling enterprise or parent company, the court shall determine the appropriate cash consideration. § 304 (4) and (5) shall apply analogously.

§ 306. Verfahren

(1) Zuständig ist das Landgericht, in dessen Bezirk die Gesellschaft, deren außenstehende Aktionäre antragsberechtigt sind, ihren Sitz hat. § 132 Abs. 1 Satz 2 bis 4 sowie § 306 Abs. 2 Satz 2 und 3 des Umwandlungsgesetzes sind anzuwenden.

(2) § 99 Abs. 1, Abs. 3 Satz 1, 2, 4 bis 9, Abs. 5 gilt sinngemäß.

(3) Das Landgericht hat den Antrag in den Gesellschaftsblättern der Gesellschaft, deren außenstehende Aktionäre antragsberechtigt sind, bekanntzumachen. Außenstehende Aktionäre können noch binnen einer Frist von zwei Monaten nach dieser Bekanntmachung eigene Anträge stellen. Auf dieses Recht ist in der Bekanntmachung hinzuweisen.

(4) Das Landgericht hat die Vertragsteile des Unternehmensvertrags zu hören. Es hat den außenstehenden Aktionären,

§ 306. Procedure

(1) Jurisdiction shall lie with the District Court for the domicile of the company whose outside shareholders have standing to make motion. § 132 (1) sentences 2 to 4 and § 306 (2) sentences 2 and 3 of the Act on Transformation shall apply.

(2) § 99 (1), (3) sentences 1, 2, 4 to 9, (5) shall apply analogously.

(3) The District Court shall announce the motion in the designated journals of the company whose outside shareholders have standing to make motion. Other outside shareholders may file motions within a period of two months after the date of such announcement. Such announcement shall advise the outside shareholders of such right.

(4) The District Court shall hear the parties to the enterprise agreement. The court shall appoint a common repre-

die nicht Antragsteller nach § 304 Abs. 4 oder § 305 Abs. 5 sind oder eigene Anträge nach Absatz 3 Satz 2 gestellt haben, zur Wahrung ihrer Rechte einen gemeinsamen Vertreter zu bestellen, der die Stellung eines gesetzlichen Vertreters hat. Werden die Festsetzung des angemessenen Ausgleichs und die Festsetzung der angemessenen Abfindung beantragt, so hat es für jeden Antrag einen gemeinsamen Vertreter zu bestellen. Die Bestellung kann unterbleiben, wenn die Wahrung der Rechte dieser außenstehenden Aktionäre auf andere Weise sichergestellt ist. Die Bestellung des gemeinsamen Vertreters hat das Landgericht in den Gesellschaftsblättern bekanntzumachen. Der Vertreter kann von der Gesellschaft den Ersatz angemessener barer Auslagen und eine Vergütung für seine Tätigkeit verlangen. Die Auslagen und die Vergütung setzt das Landgericht fest. Es kann der Gesellschaft auf Verlangen des Vertreters die Zahlung von Vorschüssen aufgeben. Aus der Festsetzung findet die Zwangsvollstreckung nach der Zivilprozeßordnung statt. § 308 Abs. 3 des Umwandlungsgesetzes ist anzuwenden.

(5) Das Landgericht hat seine Entscheidung den Vertragsteilen des Unternehmensvertrags sowie den Antragstellern nach § 304 Abs. 4, § 305 Abs. 5, den außenstehenden Aktionären, die eigene Anträge nach Absatz 3 Satz 2 gestellt haben, und, wenn ein gemeinsamer Vertreter bestellt ist, diesem zuzustellen.

(6) Der Vorstand der Gesellschaft hat die rechtskräftige Entscheidung ohne Gründe in den Gesellschaftsblättern bekanntzumachen.

(7) Für die Kosten des Verfahrens gilt die Kostenordnung. Für das Verfahren des ersten Rechtszugs wird das Doppelte der vollen Gebühr erhoben. Für den

sentative, with the status of a legal representative, for the outside shareholders who have not made motion pursuant to § 304 (4) or § 305 (5) or have made motions pursuant to subsection (3) sentence 2 to protect their rights. If motion has been made to determine the amount of the compensation and the consideration, the court shall appoint a common representative for each motion. The court may refrain from such appointment if the protection of the rights of such outside shareholders is otherwise ensured. The District Court shall announce the appointment of the common representative in the company's designated journals. Such representative shall be entitled to receive from the company reimbursement of reasonable cash expenses and remuneration for services. The District Court shall determine the amount of reasonable expenses and remuneration. The court may instruct the company to make advance payments upon request by such representative. Such determination may be enforced in accordance with the provisions of the Code of Civil Procedure. § 308 (3) of the Act on Transformation shall apply.

(5) The District Court shall serve its decision on the parties to the enterprise agreement, the parties making motion pursuant to § 304 (4) and § 305 (5), the outside shareholders who have made motions pursuant to subsection (3) sentence 2, and the common representative, if any such representative has been appointed.

(6) The management board shall publish any decision, omitting the grounds, which has become final and which may not be appealed, in the company's designated journals.

(7) The costs of the proceedings shall be determined by the Act on Court Costs. In proceedings before the court of first instance twice the full fee shall be as-

zweiten Rechtszug wird die gleiche Gebühr erhoben; dies gilt auch dann, wenn die Beschwerde Erfolg hat. Wird der Antrag oder die Beschwerde zurückgenommen, bevor es zu einer Entscheidung kommt, so ermäßigt sich die Gebühr auf die Hälfte. Der Geschäftswert ist von Amts wegen festzusetzen. Er bestimmt sich nach § 30 Abs. 1 der Kostenordnung. Schuldner der Kosten sind die Vertragsteile des Unternehmensvertrags. Die Kosten können jedoch ganz oder zum Teil einem anderen Beteiligten auferlegt werden, wenn dies der Billigkeit entspricht.

sessed. In proceedings before the court of the second instance the same fee shall be assessed; the foregoing shall also apply if the appeal is successful. If the motion or the appeal are withdrawn before a decision is rendered, the fees shall be reduced by one half. The court shall determine the value of the subject matter of the proceedings. Such value shall be determined in accordance with § 30 (1) of the Act on Court Costs. The costs shall be borne by the parties to the enterprise agreement. The costs may, however, be imposed in whole or in part on another party concerned if equity so requires.

§ 307. Vertragsbeendigung zur Sicherung außenstehender Aktionäre

Hat die Gesellschaft im Zeitpunkt der Beschlußfassung ihrer Hauptversammlung über einen Beherrschungs- oder Gewinnabführungsvertrag keinen außenstehenden Aktionär, so endet der Vertrag spätestens zum Ende des Geschäftsjahrs, in dem ein außenstehender Aktionär beteiligt ist.

§ 307. Termination of Agreement in the Interests of Outside Shareholders

If the company does not have any outside shareholder at the date of the resolution by its shareholders' meeting on a control agreement or profit transfer agreement, such agreement shall terminate no later than at the end of the fiscal year in which an outside shareholder acquires a shareholding in the company.

Zweiter Teil. Leitungsmacht und Verantwortlichkeit bei Abhängigkeit von Unternehmen

Part Two. Power to direct and Liability in the Case of Controlled Enterprises

Erster Abschnitt. Leitungsmacht und Verantwortlichkeit bei Bestehen eines Beherrschungsvertrags

Division One. Power to direct and Liability in the Case of a Control Agreement

§ 308. Leitungsmacht

(1) Besteht ein Beherrschungsvertrag, so ist das herrschende Unternehmen berechtigt, dem Vorstand der Gesellschaft hinsichtlich der Leitung der Gesellschaft Weisungen zu erteilen. Bestimmt der Vertrag nichts anderes, so können auch Weisungen erteilt werden, die

§ 308. Power to Direct

(1) In the case of a control agreement, the controlling enterprise shall be entitled to issue instructions to the management board of the controlled company with respect to the management of the controlled company. Unless otherwise provided in such agreement, instructions

für die Gesellschaft nachteilig sind, wenn sie den Belangen des herrschenden Unternehmens oder der mit ihm und der Gesellschaft konzernverbundenen Unternehmen dienen.

may be issued which are disadvantageous to the controlled company, provided that such instructions serve the interests of the controlling enterprise or of affiliated enterprises which are members of the same group as such controlling enterprise and such controlled company.

(2) Der Vorstand ist verpflichtet, die Weisungen des herrschenden Unternehmens zu befolgen. Er ist nicht berechtigt, die Befolgung einer Weisung zu verweigern, weil sie nach seiner Ansicht nicht den Belangen des herrschenden Unternehmens oder der mit ihm und der Gesellschaft konzernverbundenen Unternehmen dient, es sei denn, daß sie offensichtlich nicht diesen Belangen dient.

(2) The management board of the controlled company shall be obligated to comply with the instructions of the controlling enterprise. The management board may not refuse compliance with an instruction on the grounds that such instruction does not in its opinion serve the interests of the controlling enterprise or of affiliated enterprises which are members of the same group as such controlling enterprise and such controlled company unless such instruction manifestly does not serve such interests.

(3) Wird der Vorstand angewiesen, ein Geschäft vorzunehmen, das nur mit Zustimmung des Aufsichtsrats der Gesellschaft vorgenommen werden darf, und wird diese Zustimmung nicht innerhalb einer angemessenen Frist erteilt, so hat der Vorstand dies dem herrschenden Unternehmen mitzuteilen. Wiederholt das herrschende Unternehmen nach dieser Mitteilung die Weisung, so ist die Zustimmung des Aufsichtsrats nicht mehr erforderlich; die Weisung darf, wenn das herrschende Unternehmen einen Aufsichtsrat hat, nur mit dessen Zustimmung wiederholt werden.

(3) If the management board of the controlled company has been instructed to undertake a transaction which requires the consent of the controlled company's supervisory board, and such consent has not been granted within a reasonable period of time, the management board of the controlled company shall inform the controlling enterprise thereof. If after such notification the controlling enterprise renews its instruction, the consent of the supervisory board of the controlled company shall no longer be required; if the controlling enterprise has a supervisory board, such instruction may only be renewed with the consent of such supervisory board.

§ 309. Verantwortlichkeit der gesetzlichen Vertreter des herrschenden Unternehmens

§ 309. Liability of the Legal Representatives of the Controlling Enterprise

(1) Besteht ein Beherrschungsvertrag, so haben die gesetzlichen Vertreter (beim Einzelkaufmann der Inhaber) des

(1) In the case of a control agreement, the legal representatives (in the case of a sole proprietor the owner) of the

herrschenden Unternehmens gegenüber der Gesellschaft bei der Erteilung von Weisungen an diese die Sorgfalt eines ordentlichen und gewissenhaften Geschäftsleiters anzuwenden.

controlling enterprise shall, in issuing instructions to the controlled company, employ the care of a diligent and conscientious manager.

(2) Verletzen sie ihre Pflichten, so sind sie der Gesellschaft zum Ersatz des daraus entstehenden Schadens als Gesamtschuldner verpflichtet. Ist streitig, ob sie die Sorgfalt eines ordentlichen und gewissenhaften Geschäftsleiters angewandt haben, so trifft sie die Beweislast.

(2) If such legal representatives violate their duties they shall be jointly and severally liable to the company for any resulting damage. In the event of a dispute as to whether such legal representatives have employed the care of a diligent and conscientious manager, they shall bear the burden of proof.

(3) Die Gesellschaft kann erst drei Jahre nach der Entstehung des Anspruchs und nur dann auf Ersatzansprüche verzichten oder sich über sie vergleichen, wenn die außenstehenden Aktionäre durch Sonderbeschluß zustimmen und nicht eine Minderheit, deren Anteile zusammen den zehnten Teil des bei der Beschlußfassung vertretenen Grundkapitals erreichen, zur Niederschrift Widerspruch erhebt. Die zeitliche Beschränkung gilt nicht, wenn der Ersatzpflichtige zahlungsunfähig ist und sich zur Abwendung oder Beseitigung des Konkursverfahrens mit seinen Gläubigern vergleicht.[1]

(3) The company may waive or compromise any claim for damages not made prior to the expiration of three years from the date on which such claim has arisen and only if the outside shareholders consent thereto by separate resolution and no minority whose holding in the aggregate equals or exceeds one tenth of the share capital represented at the passing of the resolution records an objection in the minutes. Such period shall not apply if the person liable for damages is insolvent and enters into composition with its creditors to avoid or terminate bankruptcy proceedings.[1]

(4) Der Ersatzanspruch der Gesellschaft kann auch von jedem Aktionär geltend gemacht werden. Der Aktionär kann jedoch nur Leistung an die Gesellschaft fordern. Der Ersatzanspruch kann ferner von den Gläubigern der Gesellschaft geltend gemacht werden, soweit sie von dieser keine Befriedigung erlangen können. Den Gläubigern gegenüber wird die Ersatzpflicht durch einen Verzicht oder Ver-

(4) Any claim of the company for damages may also be asserted by any shareholder. The shareholders may, however, only demand that compensation be paid directly to the company. Such claim for damages may also be asserted by the creditors of the company, provided that such creditors are unable to obtain satisfaction from the company. Liability for damages with respect to the creditors

1. Mit Wirkung vom 1. Januar 1999 ist § 309 Abs. 3 Satz 2 wie folgt gefaßt:
'Die zeitliche Beschränkung gilt nicht, wenn der Ersatzpflichtige zahlungsunfähig ist und sich zur Abwendung des Insolvenzverfahrens mit seinen Gläubigern vergleicht oder wenn die Ersatzpflicht in einem Insolvenzplan geregelt wird.'

1. Effective as of 1 January 1999 § 309 (3) sentence 2 will read as follows:
'Such period shall not apply if the party liable for damages is insolvent and enters into composition with its creditors to avoid insolvency proceedings or if the liability for damages is subject to an insolvency plan.'

gleich der Gesellschaft nicht ausgeschlossen. Ist über das Vermögen der Gesellschaft das Konkursverfahren eröffnet, so übt während dessen Dauer der Konkursverwalter das Recht der Aktionäre und Gläubiger, den Ersatzanspruch der Gesellschaft geltend zu machen, aus.[1]

shall be extinguished neither by a waiver nor by a composition of the company. If bankruptcy proceedings have been instituted over the assets of the company, the receiver in bankruptcy shall exercise the rights of the shareholders and creditors to assert any claim of the company for damages during the course of such proceedings.[1]

(5) Die Ansprüche aus diesen Vorschriften verjähren in fünf Jahren.

(5) Claims under the foregoing provisions shall be barred after expiration of a period of five years.

§ 310. Verantwortlichkeit der Verwaltungsmitglieder der Gesellschaft

§ 310. Liability of the Board Members

(1) Die Mitglieder des Vorstands und des Aufsichtsrats der Gesellschaft haften neben dem Ersatzpflichtigen nach § 309 als Gesamtschuldner, wenn sie unter Verletzung ihrer Pflichten gehandelt haben. Ist streitig, ob sie die Sorgfalt eines ordentlichen und gewissenhaften Geschäftsleiters angewandt haben, so trifft sie die Beweislast.

(1) The members of the management board and the supervisory board of the company shall, in addition to any person liable pursuant to § 309, be jointly and severally liable if they have acted in violation of their duties. In the event of a dispute as to whether they have employed the care of diligent and conscientious manager, they shall bear the burden of proof.

(2) Dadurch, daß der Aufsichtsrat die Handlung gebilligt hat, wird die Ersatzpflicht nicht ausgeschlossen.

(2) The consent of the supervisory board to such act shall not preclude liability for damages.

(3) Eine Ersatzpflicht der Verwaltungsmitglieder der Gesellschaft besteht nicht, wenn die schädigende Handlung auf einer Weisung beruht, die nach § 308 Abs. 2 zu befolgen war.

(3) The board members of the company shall not be liable for damages if the act causing damages was based on an instruction which is binding pursuant to § 308 (2).

(4) § 309 Abs. 3 bis 5 ist anzuwenden.

(4) § 309 (3) to (5) shall apply.

1. Mit Wirkung vom 1. Januar 1999 ist § 309 Abs. 4 Satz 5 wie folgt gefaßt:
'Ist über das Vermögen der Gesellschaft das Insolvenzverfahren eröffnet, so übt während dessen Dauer der Insolvenzverwalter oder der Sachwalter das Recht der Aktionäre und Gläubiger, den Ersatzanspruch der Gesellschaft geltend zu machen, aus.'

1. Effective as of 1 January 1999 § 309 (4) sentence 5 will read as follows:
'If insolvency proceedings have been instituted over the assets of the company, the receiver or the trustee, as the case may be, shall exercise the rights of the shareholders and creditors to assert any claim of the company for damages during the course of such proceedings.'

Zweiter Abschnitt. Vcrantwortlichkeit bei Fehlen eines Beherrschungsvertrags

§ 311. Schranken des Einflusses

(1) Besteht kein Beherrschungsvertrag, so darf ein herrschendes Unternehmen seinen Einfluß nicht dazu benutzen, eine abhängige Aktiengesellschaft oder Kommanditgesellschaft auf Aktien zu veranlassen, ein für sie nachteiliges Rechtsgeschäft vorzunehmen oder Maßnahmen zu ihrem Nachteil zu treffen oder zu unterlassen, es sei denn, daß die Nachteile ausgeglichen werden.

(2) Ist der Ausgleich nicht während des Geschäftsjahrs tatsächlich erfolgt, so muß spätestens am Ende des Geschäftsjahrs, in dem der abhängigen Gesellschaft der Nachteil zugefügt worden ist, bestimmt werden, wann und durch welche Vorteile der Nachteil ausgeglichen werden soll. Auf die zum Ausgleich bestimmten Vorteile ist der abhängigen Gesellschaft ein Rechtsanspruch zu gewähren.

§ 312. Bericht des Vorstands über Beziehungen zu verbundenen Unternehmen

(1) Besteht kein Beherrschungsvertrag, so hat der Vorstand einer abhängigen Gesellschaft in den ersten drei Monaten des Geschäftsjahrs einen Bericht über die Beziehungen der Gesellschaft zu verbundenen Unternehmen aufzustellen. In dem Bericht sind alle Rechtsgeschäfte, welche die Gesellschaft im vergangenen Geschäftsjahr mit dem herrschenden Unternehmen oder einem mit ihm verbundenen Unternehmen oder auf Veranlassung oder im Interesse dieser Unternehmen vorgenommen hat, und alle anderen Maßnahmen, die sie auf Veranlassung oder im Interesse dieser Unternehmen im vergangenen Geschäftsjahr getroffen oder unter-

Division Two. Liability in the Absence of a Control Agreement

§ 311. Limitation on the Excercise of Influence

(1) In the absence of a control agreement, a controlling enterprise may not exercise its influence to cause a controlled stock corporation or partnership limited by shares to undertake a disadvantageous transaction or to undertake, or refrain from undertaking, to the detriment of the company, any action, unless any disadvantage is compensated.

(2) If such compensation is not actually made during the fiscal year, the time and means by which such disadvantage shall be compensated, shall be determined no later than the end of the fiscal year in which the controlled company has suffered such disadvantage. The controlled company shall be granted an entitlement to the measures designated to serve as compensation.

§ 312. Report of the Management Board on Relations with Affiliated Enterprises

(1) In the absence of a control agreement, the management board of a controlled company shall, within the first three months of each fiscal year, render a report on the company's relations with affiliated enterprises. Such report shall specify all transactions entered into by the company during the previous fiscal year with the controlling enterprise or any enterprise affiliated with such controlling enterprise or at the instruction or in the interest of any such enterprise and all other acts which the controlled company has undertaken or refrained from undertaking at the instruction or in the interest of any such enterprise. Such report shall,

lassen hat, aufzuführen. Bei den Rechtsgeschäften sind Leistung und Gegenleistung, bei den Maßnahmen die Gründe der Maßnahme und deren Vorteile und Nachteile für die Gesellschaft anzugeben. Bei einem Ausgleich von Nachteilen ist im einzelnen anzugeben, wie der Ausgleich während des Geschäftsjahrs tatsächlich erfolgt ist, oder auf welche Vorteile der Gesellschaft ein Rechtsanspruch gewährt worden ist.

(2) Der Bericht hat den Grundsätzen einer gewissenhaften und getreuen Rechenschaft zu entsprechen.

(3) Am Schluß des Berichts hat der Vorstand zu erklären, ob die Gesellschaft nach den Umständen, die ihm in dem Zeitpunkt bekannt waren, in dem das Rechtsgeschäft vorgenommen oder die Maßnahme getroffen oder unterlassen wurde, bei jedem Rechtsgeschäft eine angemessene Gegenleistung erhielt und dadurch, daß die Maßnahme getroffen oder unterlassen wurde, nicht benachteiligt wurde. Wurde die Gesellschaft benachteiligt, so hat er außerdem zu erklären, ob die Nachteile ausgeglichen worden sind. Die Erklärung ist auch in den Lagebericht aufzunehmen.

in the case of transactions, specify any consideration given or received and, in the case of acts undertaken, shall state the reasons for such acts and the advantages and disadvantages for the controlled company. Such report shall, in the case of compensation for disadvantages, specify the manner in which such compensation was made during the fiscal year and to which advantages the company has been granted an entitlement.

(2) Such report shall comply with the principles of conscientious and accurate accounting.

(3) The management board shall, at the end of such report, comment on whether the company, under the circumstances known to the board at the date on which the company entered into such transaction or undertook or refrained from undertaking such act, received adequate consideration for each such transaction and did not suffer any disadvantage by reason of undertaking or refraining from undertaking such act. If the company suffered any disadvantage, the management board shall further comment on whether such disadvantage has been compensated. Such comments shall be included in the annual report.

§ 313. Prüfung durch den Abschlußprüfer

(1) Ist der Jahresabschluß durch einen Abschlußprüfer zu prüfen, so ist gleichzeitig mit dem Jahresabschluß und dem Lagebericht auch der Bericht über die Beziehungen zu verbundenen Unternehmen dem Abschlußprüfer vorzulegen. Er hat zu prüfen, ob

1. die tatsächlichen Angaben des Berichts richtig sind,

2. bei den im Bericht aufgeführten Rechtsgeschäften nach den Umständen, die im Zeitpunkt ihrer Vornahme bekannt

§ 313. Audit by External Auditors

(1) If the annual financial statements are to be audited by an external auditor, the report on relations with affiliated enterprises shall be submitted to the external auditor together with the annual financial statements and the annual report. The auditor shall examine whether:

1. the factual statements in such report are accurate;

2. the consideration given by the company for the transaction specified in such report was unreasonably high in view of

waren, die Leistung der Gesellschaft nicht unangemessen hoch war; soweit sie dies war, ob die Nachteile ausgeglichen worden sind,

3. bei den im Bericht aufgeführten Maßnahmen keine Umstände für eine wesentlich andere Beurteilung als die durch den Vorstand sprechen.

§ 320 Abs. 1 Satz 2 und Abs. 2 Satz 1 und 2 des Handelsgesetzbuchs gilt sinngemäß. Die Rechte nach dieser Vorschrift hat der Abschlußprüfer auch gegenüber einem Konzernunternehmen sowie gegenüber einem abhängigen oder herrschenden Unternehmen.

(2) Der Abschlußprüfer hat über das Ergebnis der Prüfung schriftlich zu berichten. Stellt er bei der Prüfung des Jahresabschlusses, des Lageberichts und des Berichts über die Beziehungen zu verbundenen Unternehmen fest, daß dieser Bericht unvollständig ist, so hat er auch hierüber zu berichten. Der Abschlußprüfer hat seinen Bericht zu unterzeichnen und dem Vorstand vorzulegen.

(3) Sind nach dem abschließenden Ergebnis der Prüfung keine Einwendungen zu erheben, so hat der Abschlußprüfer dies durch folgenden Vermerk zum Bericht über die Beziehungen zu verbundenen Unternehmen zu bestätigen:

Nach meiner/unserer pflichtmäßigen Prüfung und Beurteilung bestätige ich/ bestätigen wir, daß

1. die tatsächlichen Angaben des Berichts richtig sind,
2. bei den im Bericht aufgeführten Rechtsgeschäften die Leistung der Gesellschaft nicht unangemessen hoch war oder Nachteile ausgeglichen worden sind,
3. bei den im Bericht aufgeführten Maßnahmen keine Umstände für

the circumstances known at the time such transactions were entered into; and, if this was the case, whether the disadvantages have been compensated;

3. circumstances would justify a materially different opinion in respect of the acts specified in the report than the opinion of the management board.

§ 320 (1) sentence 2 and (2) sentences 1 and 2 of the Commercial Code shall apply analogously. The external auditor shall have the rights pursuant to the foregoing provisions also with respect to a member of an affiliated group or a controlled or controlling enterprise.

(2) The external auditor shall report in writing on the findings of the audit. If the auditor shall determine in the course of the audit of the annual financial statements, the annual report and the report on the relations with affiliated enterprises that such report on relations with affiliated enterprises is incomplete, he shall also report thereon. The external auditor shall sign and submit the audit report to the management board.

(3) The external auditor shall confirm the absence of any objections based on the findings of the audit by the following note to the report on relations with affiliated enterprises:

On the basis of my/our diligent examination and judgment I/we hereby confirm that:

1. the factual statements in the report are accurate;
2. the consideration given by the company for the transactions specified in the report was not unreasonably high and any disadvantages incurred have been compensated;
3. no circumstances would justify, in respect of the acts specified in the re-

eine wesentlich andere Beurteilung als die durch den Vorstand sprechen.

Führt der Bericht kein Rechtsgeschäft auf, so ist Nummer 2, führt er keine Maßnahme auf, so ist Nummer 3 des Vermerks fortzulassen. Hat der Abschlußprüfer bei keinem im Bericht aufgeführten Rechtsgeschäft festgestellt, daß die Leistung der Gesellschaft unangemessen hoch war, so ist Nummer 2 des Vermerks auf diese Bestätigung zu beschränken.

(4) Sind Einwendungen zu erheben oder hat der Abschlußprüfer festgestellt, daß der Bericht über die Beziehungen zu verbundenen Unternehmen unvollständig ist, so hat er die Bestätigung einzuschränken oder zu versagen. Hat der Vorstand selbst erklärt, daß die Gesellschaft durch bestimmte Rechtsgeschäfte oder Maßnahmen benachteiligt worden ist, ohne daß die Nachteile ausgeglichen worden sind, so ist dies in dem Vermerk anzugeben und der Vermerk auf die übrigen Rechtsgeschäfte oder Maßnahmen zu beschränken.

(5) Der Abschlußprüfer hat den Bestätigungsvermerk mit Angabe von Ort und Tag zu unterzeichnen. Der Bestätigungsvermerk ist auch in den Prüfungsbericht aufzunehmen.

§ 314. Prüfung durch den Aufsichtsrat

(1) Der Vorstand hat den Bericht über die Beziehungen zu verbundenen Unternehmen und, wenn der Jahresabschluß durch einen Abschlußprüfer zu prüfen ist, den Prüfungsbericht des Abschlußprüfers zusammen mit den in § 170 angegebenen Vorlagen dem Aufsichtsrat vorzulegen. Jedes Aufsichtsratsmitglied hat das

ports, a materially different opinion than the opinion of the management board.

No. 2 shall be omitted from such note if the report does not specify any transactions and No. 3 shall be omitted from such note if the report does not specify any acts. If the external auditor has not determined that the consideration given by the company for any transaction specified in the report was unreasonably high, no. 2 of such note shall be limited to confirmation of such fact.

(4) If objections are to be made or the external auditor has determined that the report on relations with affiliated enterprises is incomplete the auditors shall either restrict the wording of the confirmation note or refuse to provide any confirmation. If the management board has stated that the company has suffered a disadvantage as a result of certain transactions or acts, and that such disadvantages have not been compensated, such fact shall be stated in the note and the note shall be restricted to any other transactions or acts.

(5) The external auditor shall sign the confirmation note stating the place and date of signature. Such note shall also be included in the audit report.

§ 314. Examination by the Supervisory Board

(1) The management board shall submit to the supervisory board the report on relations with affiliated enterprises and, if the annual financial statements are to be audited by an external auditor, the audit report of the external auditor together with the documents specified in § 170. Each member of the supervisory board

Recht, von den Berichten Kenntnis zu nehmen. Die Berichte sind auch jedem Aufsichtsratsmitglied auf Verlangen auszuhändigen, soweit der Aufsichtsrat nichts anderes beschlossen hat.

shall be entitled to take cognizance of such reports. Such reports shall also be delivered to each member of the supervisory board upon request, unless the supervisory board has decided otherwise.

(2) Der Aufsichtsrat hat den Bericht über die Beziehungen zu verbundenen Unternehmen zu prüfen und in seinem Bericht an die Hauptversammlung (§ 171 Abs. 2) über das Ergebnis der Prüfung zu berichten. Ist der Jahresabschluß durch einen Abschlußprüfer zu prüfen, so hat der Aufsichtsrat in diesem Bericht ferner zu dem Ergebnis der Prüfung des Berichts über die Beziehungen zu verbundenen Unternehmen durch den Abschlußprüfer Stellung zu nehmen. Ein von dem Abschlußprüfer erteilter Bestätigungsvermerk ist in den Bericht aufzunehmen, eine Versagung des Bestätigungsvermerks ausdrücklich mitzuteilen.

(2) The supervisory board shall examine the report on relations with affiliated enterprises and comment on the findings of such examination in its report to the shareholders' meeting (§ 171 (2)). If the annual financial statements are to be audited by an external auditor, the supervisory board shall in its report further comment on the findings of the audit of the report on relations with affiliated enterprises by the external auditor. The confirmation note of the external auditor shall be included in such report and the refusal to provide such note shall be explicitly stated.

(3) Am Schluß des Berichts hat der Aufsichtsrat zu erklären, ob nach dem abschließenden Ergebnis seiner Prüfung Einwendungen gegen die Erklärung des Vorstands am Schluß des Berichts über die Beziehungen zu verbundenen Unternehmen zu erheben sind.

(3) The supervisory board shall, at the end of the report, state whether or not based on the findings of its examination, objections are to be made to the comments of the management board at the end of the report on relations with affiliated enterprises.

(4) Ist der Jahresabschluß durch einen Abschlußprüfer zu prüfen, so hat der Abschlußprüfer auf Verlangen des Aufsichtsrats an dessen Verhandlung über den Bericht über die Beziehungen zu verbundenen Unternehmen teilzunehmen.

(4) If the annual financial statements are to be audited by an external auditor, the external auditor shall, at the request of the supervisory board, attend the deliberations of the supervisory board regarding the report on relations with affiliated enterprises.

§ 315. Sonderprüfung

Auf Antrag eines Aktionärs hat das Gericht Sonderprüfer zur Prüfung der geschäftlichen Beziehungen der Gesellschaft zu dem herrschenden Unternehmen oder einem mit ihm verbundenen Unternehmen zu bestellen, wenn

§ 315. Special Audit

The court shall upon motion by a shareholder appoint special auditors to audit the business relations of the company with its controlling enterprise or an enterprise affiliated with such controlling enterprise if:

1. der Abschlußprüfer den Bestätigungsvermerk zum Bericht über die Beziehungen zu verbundenen Unternehmen eingeschränkt oder versagt hat,

2. der Aufsichtsrat erklärt hat, daß Einwendungen gegen die Erklärung des Vorstands am Schluß des Berichts über die Beziehungen zu verbundenen Unternehmen zu erheben sind,

3. der Vorstand selbst erklärt hat, daß die Gesellschaft durch bestimmte Rechtsgeschäfte oder Maßnahmen benachteiligt worden ist, ohne daß die Nachteile ausgeglichen worden sind.

Gegen die Entscheidung ist die sofortige Beschwerde zulässig. Hat die Hauptversammlung zur Prüfung derselben Vorgänge Sonderprüfer bestellt, so kann jeder Aktionär den Antrag nach § 142 Abs. 4 stellen.

1. the external auditor has restricted the wording of or refused to provide a confirmation note on the report on relations with affiliated enterprises;

2. the supervisory board has stated that objections are to be made to the comments of the management board at the end of the report on relations with affiliated enterprises;

3. the management board has stated that the company has suffered a disadvantage as a result of certain transactions or acts, and such disadvantages have not been compensated.

An immediate appeal may be made against the decision. If the shareholders' meeting has appointed special auditors to audit the same matters, each shareholder may make motion pursuant to § 142 (4).

§ 316. Kein Bericht über Beziehungen zu verbundenen Unternehmen bei Gewinnabführungsvertrag

§§ 312 bis 315 gelten nicht, wenn zwischen der abhängigen Gesellschaft und dem herrschenden Unternehmen ein Gewinnabführungsvertrag besteht.

§ 316. No Report on Relations with Affiliated Enterprises in the Case of a Profit Transfer Agreement

§§ 312 to 315 shall not apply in the case of a profit transfer agreement between the controlled company and the controlling enterprise.

§ 317. Verantwortlichkeit des herrschenden Unternehmens und seiner gesetzlichen Vertreter

(1) Veranlaßt ein herrschendes Unternehmen eine abhängige Gesellschaft, mit der kein Beherrschungsvertrag besteht, ein für sie nachteiliges Rechtsgeschäft vorzunehmen oder zu ihrem Nachteil eine Maßnahme zu treffen oder zu unterlassen, ohne daß es den Nachteil bis zum Ende des Geschäftsjahrs tatsächlich ausgleicht oder der abhängigen Gesellschaft einen Rechtsanspruch auf einen zum Ausgleich bestimmten Vorteil ge-

§ 317. Liability of the Controlling Enterprise and its Legal Representatives

(1) If a controlling enterprise causes a controlled company with which a control agreement does not exist to enter into a transaction which is disadvantageous to such controlled company or to undertake or refrain from undertaking any act which is disadvantageous to such controlled company, without compensating such disadvantage by the end of the fiscal year or granting to the controlled company an entitlement to any measures serving as

währt, so ist es der Gesellschaft zum Ersatz des ihr daraus entstehenden Schadens verpflichtet. Es ist auch den Aktionären zum Ersatz des ihnen daraus entstehenden Schadens verpflichtet, soweit sie, abgesehen von einem Schaden, der ihnen durch Schädigung der Gesellschaft zugefügt worden ist, geschädigt worden sind.

compensation therefor, such controlling enterprise shall be liable for any resulting damage to such controlled company. Such controlling enterprise shall also be liable to the shareholders of the controlled company for any resulting damage to the shareholders insofar as they have suffered damage in addition to any loss incurred as a result of the damage to the company.

(2) Die Ersatzpflicht tritt nicht ein, wenn auch ein ordentlicher und gewissenhafter Geschäftsleiter einer unabhängigen Gesellschaft das Rechtsgeschäft vorgenommen oder die Maßnahme getroffen oder unterlassen hätte.

(2) The controlled enterprise shall not be liable if a prudent and conscientious manager of an independant company would have entered into such transaction or undertaken or refrained from undertaking such act.

(3) Neben dem herrschenden Unternehmen haften als Gesamtschuldner die gesetzlichen Vertreter des Unternehmens, die die Gesellschaft zu dem Rechtsgeschäft oder der Maßnahme veranlaßt haben.

(3) The legal representatives of the controlling enterprise who have caused the controlled company to enter into such transaction or undertake or refrain from undertaking such act shall, in addition to the controlling enterprise, be jointly and severally liable.

(4) § 309 Abs. 3 bis 5 gilt sinngemäß.

(4) § 309 (3) to (5) shall apply analogously.

§ 318. Verantwortlichkeit der Verwaltungsmitglieder der Gesellschaft

§ 318. Liability of Board Members of the Company

(1) Die Mitglieder des Vorstands der Gesellschaft haften neben den nach § 317 Ersatzpflichtigen als Gesamtschuldner, wenn sie es unter Verletzung ihrer Pflichten unterlassen haben, das nachteilige Rechtsgeschäft oder die nachteilige Maßnahme in dem Bericht über die Beziehungen der Gesellschaft zu verbundenen Unternehmen aufzuführen oder anzugeben, daß die Gesellschaft durch das Rechtsgeschäft oder die Maßnahme benachteiligt wurde und der Nachteil nicht ausgeglichen worden war. Ist streitig, ob sie die Sorgfalt eines ordentlichen und gewis-

(1) The members of the management board of the company shall be jointly and severally liable together with the persons liable pursuant to § 317 if, in violation of their duties, they have failed to include any disadvantageous transaction or act in their report on relations of the company with affiliated enterprises or to state that the company has suffered a disadvantage as a result of such transaction or act and that such disadvantage has not been compensated. In the event of a dispute as to whether such board members have employed the care of a diligent and conscien-

senhaften Geschäftsleiters angewandt haben, so trifft sie die Beweislast.

tious manager, they shall bear the burden of proof.

(2) Die Mitglieder des Aufsichtsrats der Gesellschaft haften neben den nach § 317 Ersatzpflichtigen als Gesamtschuldner, wenn sie hinsichtlich des nachteiligen Rechtsgeschäfts oder der nachteiligen Maßnahme ihre Pflicht, den Bericht über die Beziehungen zu verbundenen Unternehmen zu prüfen und über das Ergebnis der Prüfung an die Hauptversammlung zu berichten (§ 314), verletzt haben; Absatz 1 Satz 2 gilt sinngemäß.

(2) The members of the supervisory board of the company shall be jointly and severally liable together with persons liable pursuant to § 317, with respect to any disadavantageous transaction or act, if they have violated their duty to examine the report on relations with affiliated enterprises and to report to the shareholders' meeting on the findings of such examination (§ 314); subsection (1) sentence 2 shall apply analogously.

(3) Der Gesellschaft und auch den Aktionären gegenüber tritt die Ersatzpflicht nicht ein, wenn die Handlung auf einem gesetzmäßigen Beschluß der Hauptversammlung beruht.

(3) The board members shall not be liable to the company and the shareholders if any such act was based on a lawful resolution of the shareholders' meeting.

(4) § 309 Abs. 3 bis 5 gilt sinngemäß.

(4) § 309 (3) to (5) shall apply analogously.

Dritter Teil. Eingegliederte Gesellschaften

Part Three. Integrated Companies

§ 319. Eingliederung

§ 319. Integration

(1) Die Hauptversammlung einer Aktiengesellschaft kann die Eingliederung der Gesellschaft in eine andere Aktiengesellschaft mit Sitz im Inland (Hauptgesellschaft) beschließen, wenn sich alle Aktien der Gesellschaft in der Hand der zukünftigen Hauptgesellschaft befinden. Auf den Beschluß sind die Bestimmungen des Gesetzes und der Satzung über Satzungsänderungen nicht anzuwenden.

(1) The shareholders' meeting of a stock corporation may resolve to integrate the company into another stock corporation with domestic domicile ('principal company'), if all shares of such company are held by the prospective principal company. The statutory provisions and the provisions of the articles governing amendments shall not apply to such resolution.

(2) Der Beschluß über die Eingliederung wird nur wirksam, wenn die Hauptversammlung der zukünftigen Hauptgesellschaft zustimmt. Der Beschluß über

(2) The resolution on integration shall become effective only upon consent by the shareholders' meeting of the prospective principal company. The resolu-

die Zustimmung bedarf einer Mehrheit, die mindestens drei Viertel des bei der Beschlußfassung vertretenen Grundkapitals umfaßt. Die Satzung kann eine größere Kapitalmehrheit und weitere Erfordernisse bestimmen. Absatz 1 Satz 2 ist anzuwenden.

tion on such consent shall require a majority of not less than three fourths of the share capital represented at the passing of the resolution. The articles may provide for a larger capital majority and for additional requirements. Subsection (1) sentence 2 shall apply.

(**3**) Von der Einberufung der Hauptversammlung der zukünftigen Hauptgesellschaft an, die über die Zustimmung zur Eingliederung beschließen soll, sind in dem Geschäftsraum dieser Gesellschaft zur Einsicht der Aktionäre auszulegen

1. der Entwurf des Eingliederungsbeschlusses;
2. die Jahresabschlüsse und die Lageberichte der beteiligten Gesellschaften für die letzten drei Geschäftsjahre;
3. ein ausführlicher schriftlicher Bericht des Vorstands der zukünftigen Hauptgesellschaft, in dem die Eingliederung rechtlich und wirtschaftlich erläutert und begründet wird (Eingliederungsbericht).

(**3**) As from the date of calling that shareholders' meeting of the prospective principal company which is to resolve on the consent to the integration, the following documents shall be made available for inspection by the shareholders in the offices of such company:

1. the draft of the resolution on the integration;
2. the annual financial statements and annual reports of the participating companies for the last three fiscal years;
3. a comprehensive written report of the management board of the prospective principal company in which the integration shall be explained and substantiated from the legal and financial perspective ('integration report').

Auf Verlangen ist jedem Aktionär der zukünftigen Hauptgesellschaft unverzüglich und kostenlos eine Abschrift der in Satz 1 bezeichneten Unterlagen zu erteilen. In der Hauptversammlung sind diese Unterlagen auszulegen. Jedem Aktionär ist in der Hauptversammlung auf Verlangen Auskunft auch über alle im Zusammenhang mit der Eingliederung wesentlichen Angelegenheiten der einzugliedernden Gesellschaft zu geben.

Upon request each shareholder of the prospective principal company shall promptly and free of charge be provided with a copy of the documents mentioned in sentence 1. The documents shall be displayed at the shareholders' meeting. Upon request each shareholder shall be provided at the shareholders' meeting also with information regarding all matters of the company to be integrated which are material in the context of such integration.

(**4**) Der Vorstand der einzugliedernden Gesellschaft hat die Eingliederung und die Firma der Hauptgesellschaft zur Eintragung in das Handelsregister anzumelden. Der Anmeldung sind die Niederschriften der Hauptversammlungsbeschlüsse und ihre Anlagen in Ausferti-

(**4**) The management board of the company to be integrated shall report the integration and the name of the principal company for registration in the commercial register. The minutes of the resolutions of the shareholders' meetings and the appendices thereto shall be appended

gung oder öffentlich beglaubigter Abschrift beizufügen.

(5) Bei der Anmeldung nach Absatz 4 hat der Vorstand zu erklären, daß eine Klage gegen die Wirksamkeit eines Hauptversammlungsbeschlusses nicht oder nicht fristgemäß erhoben oder eine solche Klage rechtskräftig abgewiesen oder zurückgenommen worden ist; hierüber hat der Vorstand dem Registergericht auch nach der Anmeldung Mitteilung zu machen. Liegt die Erklärung nicht vor, so darf die Eingliederung nicht eingetragen werden, es sei denn, daß die klageberechtigten Aktionäre durch notariell beurkundete Verzichtserklärung auf die Klage gegen die Wirksamkeit des Hauptversammlungsbeschlusses verzichten.

(6) Der Erklärung nach Absatz 5 Satz 1 steht es gleich, wenn nach Erhebung einer Klage gegen die Wirksamkeit eines Hauptversammlungsbeschlusses das für diese Klage zuständige Landgericht auf Antrag der Gesellschaft, gegen deren Hauptversammlungsbeschluß sich die Klage richtet, durch rechtskräftigen Beschluß festgestellt hat, daß die Erhebung der Klage der Eintragung nicht entgegensteht. Der Beschluß nach Satz 1 darf nur ergehen, wenn die Klage gegen die Wirksamkeit des Hauptversammlungsbeschlusses unzulässig oder offensichtlich unbegründet ist oder wenn das alsbaldige Wirksamwerden der Eingliederung nach freier Überzeugung des Gerichts unter Berücksichtigung der Schwere der mit der Klage geltend gemachten Rechtsverletzungen zur Abwendung der vom Antragsteller dargelegten wesentlichen Nachteile für die Gesellschaft und ihre Aktionäre vorrangig erscheint. Der Beschluß kann in dringenden Fällen ohne

to such report in duplicate of officially certified copy.

(5) In connection with the report pursuant to subsection (4), the management board shall state that an action against the validity of a resolution of a shareholders' meeting has not been brought or not been brought within the period of time for bringing such action or that any such action has been dismissed in a decision which is final and no longer subject to appeal or that any such action has been withdrawn; the management board shall inform the commercial registry on such facts also subsequent to the making of such report. If such statement has not been made, the integration may not be registered, unless the shareholders entitled to bring action waive their right for bringing action against the validity of the resolution of the shareholders' meeting in a declaration certified by a notary.

(6) It shall be equal to the statement pursuant to subsection (5) sentence 1 if upon the bringing of an action against the validity of a resolution of a shareholders' meeting, the district court with jurisdiction for such action, upon motion by the company against which the action is directed, determines by a decree which is final and no longer subject to appeal that the bringing of the action does not hinder the registration. The decree pursuant to sentence 1 may only be rendered if the action against the validity of the resolution of the shareholders' meeting is inadmissibile or manifestly unfounded or if the early effectiveness of the integration in the judgment of the court should take priority in order to prevent material disadvantages to the company and its shareholders as contended in the motion giving regard to the weight of the violations of law claimed by the action. In urgent cases the decree may be rendered without oral hearing. For the facts submitted, on the

mündliche Verhandlung ergehen. Die vorgebrachten Tatsachen, aufgrund derer der Beschluß nach Satz 2 ergehen kann, sind glaubhaft zu machen. Gegen den Beschluß findet die sofortige Beschwerde statt. Erweist sich die Klage als begründet, so ist die Gesellschaft, die den Beschluß erwirkt hat, verpflichtet, dem Antragsgegner den Schaden zu ersetzen, der ihm aus einer auf dem Beschluß beruhenden Eintragung der Eingliederung entstanden ist.

basis of which the decree pursuant to sentence 2 may be rendered, *prima facie* evidence shall be presented. Immediate appeal against such decree is admitted. If the action proves to be founded, the company which has obtained the decree shall compensate those damages of the motion's opponent which were caused by the registration of the integration based on the decree.

(7) Mit der Eintragung der Eingliederung in das Handelsregister des Sitzes der Gesellschaft wird die Gesellschaft in die Hauptgesellschaft eingegliedert.

(7) The integration of the company into the principal company shall become effective upon registration of the integration in the commercial register of the integrated company's domicile.

§ 320. Eingliederung durch Mehrheitsbeschluß

§ 320. Integration by Majority Resolution

(1) Die Hauptversammlung einer Aktiengesellschaft kann die Eingliederung der Gesellschaft in eine andere Aktiengesellschaft mit Sitz im Inland auch dann beschließen, wenn sich Aktien der Gesellschaft im Gesamtnennbetrag von fünfundneunzig vom Hundert des Grundkapitals in der Hand der zukünftigen Hauptgesellschaft befinden. Eigene Aktien und Aktien, die einem anderen für Rechnung der Gesellschaft gehören, sind vom Grundkapital abzusetzen. Für die Eingliederung gelten außer § 319 Abs. 1 Satz 2, Abs. 2 bis 7 die Absätze 2 bis 4.

(1) The shareholders's meeting of a stock corporation may also resolve to integrate the company into another stock corporation with domestic domicile if the prospective principal company holds shares of the company with an aggregate par value of not less than ninety-five per cent of the share capital. Company shares held by the company to be integrated and shares held by another person on behalf of such company shall be deducted from the share capital. Subsections (2) to (4) shall, in addition to § 319 (1) sentence 2, (2) to (7), apply to the integration.

(2) Die Bekanntmachung der Eingliederung als Gegenstand der Tagesordnung ist nur ordnungsgemäß, wenn

1. sie die Firma und den Sitz der zukünftigen Hauptgesellschaft enthält,

2. ihr eine Erklärung der zukünftigen Hauptgesellschaft beigefügt ist, in der diese den ausscheidenden Aktionären als Abfindung für ihre Aktien eigene Aktien,

(2) The announcement of the integration as an item on the agenda shall be considered to have been duly made only if:

1. such announcement includes the name and domicile of the prospective principal company;

2. a statement of the prospective principal company has been appended to such announcement in which such prospective principal company offers its own shares

im Falle des § 320b Abs.1 Satz 3 außerdem eine Barabfindung anbietet.

to shareholders of the company to be integrated as compensation for their shares, and, in the case of § 320b (1) sentence 3, a cash payment.

Satz 1 Nr. 2 gilt auch für die Bekanntmachung der zukünftigen Hauptgesellschaft.

Sentence 1 No. 2 shall also apply to the announcement of the prospective principal company.

(3) Die Eingliederung ist durch sachverständige Prüfer (Eingliederungsprüfer) zu prüfen. Diese werden von dem Vorstand der zukünftigen Hauptgesellschaft bestellt. § 293a Abs. 3, §§ 293c bis 293e sind sinngemäß anzuwenden.

(3) The integration shall be audited by qualified auditors ('integration auditors'). Such auditors shall be appointed by the management board of the prospective principal company. § 293a (3), §§ 293c to 293e shall apply analogously.

(4) Die in § 319 Abs. 3 Satz 1 bezeichneten Unterlagen sowie der Prüfungsbericht nach Absatz 3 sind jeweils von der Einberufung der Hauptversammlung an, die über die Zustimmung zur Eingliederung beschließen soll, in dem Geschäftsraum der einzugliedernden Gesellschaft und der Hauptgesellschaft zur Einsicht der Aktionäre auszulegen. In dem Eingliederungsbericht sind auch Art und Höhe der Abfindung nach § 320b rechtlich und wirtschaftlich zu erläutern und zu begründen; auf besondere Schwierigkeiten bei der Bewertung der beteiligten Gesellschaften sowie auf die Folgen für die Beteiligungen der Aktionäre ist hinzuweisen. § 319 Abs. 3 Satz 2 bis 4 gilt sinngemäß für die Aktionäre beider Gesellschaften.

(4) As the relevant date of calling of that shareholders' meeting which is to resolve on the consent to the integration the documents mentioned in § 319 (3) sentence 1 and the audit report pursuant to subsection 3 shall be made available for inspection by the shareholders in the offices of the company to be integrated and the principal company. The integration report shall explain and substantiate form and amount of the compensation pursuant to § 320b from the legal and financial perspective; specific difficulties in the valuation of the participating companies and the consequences for the interests of the shareholders shall be indicated. § 319 (3) sentences 2 to 4 shall apply analogously to the shareholders of both companies.

§ 320a. Wirkungen der Eingliederung

Mit der Eintragung der Eingliederung in has Handelsregister gehen alle Aktien, die sich nicht in der Hand der Hauptgesellschaft befinden, auf diese über. Sind über diese Aktien Aktienurkunden ausgegeben, so verbriefen sie bis zu ihrer Aushändigung an die Hauptgesellschaft nur den Anspruch auf Abfindung.

§ 320a. Effects of the Integration

Upon the registration of the integration in the commercial register title to all shares which were not held by the principal company shall be transferred to the principal company. If share certificates have been issued for such shares, such share certificates shall, prior to delivery to the principal company, constitute only the right to compensation.

§ 320b. Abfindung der ausgeschiedenen Aktionäre

(1) Die ausgeschiedenen Aktionäre der eingegliederten Gesellschaft haben Anspruch auf angemessene Abfindung. Als Abfindung sind ihnen eigene Aktien der Hauptgesellschaft zu gewähren. Ist die Hauptgesellschaft eine abhängige Gesellschaft, so sind den ausgeschiedenen Aktionären nach deren Wahl eigene Aktien der Hauptgesellschaft oder eine angemessene Barabfindung zu gewähren. Werden als Abfindung Aktien der Hauptgesellschaft gewährt, so ist die Abfindung als angemessen anzusehen, wenn die Aktien in dem Verhältnis gewährt werden, in dem bei einer Verschmelzung auf eine Aktie der Gesellschaft Aktien der Hauptgesellschaft zu gewähren wären, wobei Spitzenbeträge durch bare Zuzahlungen ausgeglichen werden können. Die Barabfindung muß die Verhältnisse der Gesellschaft im Zeitpunkt der Beschlußfassung ihrer Hauptversammlung über die Eingliederung berücksichtigen. Die Barabfindung sowie bare Zuzahlungen sind von der Bekanntmachung der Eintragung der Eingliederung an mit jährlich zwei vom Hundert über dem jeweiligen Diskontsatz der Deutschen Bundesbank zu verzinsen; die Geltendmachung eines weiteren Schadens ist nich ausgeschlossen.

(2) Die Anfechtung des Beschlusses, durch den die Hauptversammlung der eingegliederten Gesellschaft die Eingliederung der Gesellschaft beschlossen hat, kann nicht auf § 243 Abs. 2 oder darauf gestützt werden, daß die von der Hauptgesellschaft nach § 320 Abs. 2 Nr. 2 angebotene Abfindung nicht angemessen ist. Ist die angebotene Abfindung nicht angemessen, so hat das in § 306 bestimmte Gericht auf Antrag die angemessene Abfindung zu bestimmen. Das gleiche gilt, wenn die Hauptgesellschaft eine Abfindung nicht oder nicht ordnungsgemäß an-

§ 320b. Compensation for Former Shareholders

(1) The former shareholders of the integrated company shall be entitled to adequate compensation. As compensation they shall be granted own shares of the principal company. If the principal company is a controlled company, the former shareholders may elect to receive shares of the principal company or an adequate cash compensation. If shares of the principal company are granted as compensation, such compensation shall be deemed to be adequate if such shares are to be granted in the same proportion in which, in case of a merger, a share of the integrated company would be entitled to shares of the principal company, provided that fractional shares may be compensated by additional cash payments. The cash compensation shall take into account the conditions of the company at the time of the adoption of the resolution of its shareholders' meeting on the integration. The cash compensation and any additional cash payments shall bear interest at the rate of two percent per annum above the from time to time prevailing discount rate of the German Federal Bank as from the date of the announcement of the registration of the integration; claims for further damages shall not be precluded.

(2) An action to set aside the resolution of the shareholders' meeting of the integrated company on the integration of the company may not be based on § 243 (2) or on the ground that the compensation offered by the principal company pursuant to § 320 (2) No. 2 is not adequate. If the compensation offered is not adequate, the court with jurisdiction pursuant to § 306 shall upon motion determine the amount of adequate compensation. The foregoing shall also apply if the principal company has not or has not properly offered compensation and an ac-

geboten hat und eine hierauf gestützte Abfechtungsklage innerhalb der Anfechtungsfrist nicht erhoben oder zurückgenommen oder rechtskräftig abgewiesen worden ist.

tion to set aside which is based on such fact has not been brought within the period of time for bringing such action or has been withdrawn or has been dismissed in a decision which is final and which may not be appealed.

(3) Antragsberechtigt ist jeder ausgeschiedene Aktionär. Der Antrag kann nur binnen zwei Monaten nach dem Tage gestellt werden, an dem die Eintragung der Eingliederung in das Handelsregister nach § 10 des Handelsgesetzbuchs als bekanntgemacht gilt. Für das Verfahren gilt § 306 sinngemäß.

(3) Each former shareholder shall have standing to make such motion. Such motion may be made only within a period of two months from the date on which the registration of the integration in the commercial register shall be deemed to have been announced pursuant to § 10 of the Commercial Code. § 306 shall apply analogously to the procedure.

§ 321. Gläubigerschutz

§ 321. Protection of Creditors

(1) Den Gläubigern der eingegliederten Gesellschaft, deren Forderungen begründet worden sind, bevor die Eintragung der Eingliederung in das Handelsregister bekanntgemacht worden ist, ist, wenn sie sich binnen sechs Monaten nach der Bekanntmachung zu diesem Zweck melden, Sicherheit zu leisten, soweit sie nicht Befriedigung verlangen können. Die Gläubiger sind in der Bekanntmachung der Eintragung auf dieses Recht hinzuweisen.

(1) Creditors of the integrated company whose claims arose prior to the registration of the integration in the commercial register shall be provided with security insofar as they are not able to demand satisfaction, provided that they have made application for this purpose within six months after the date of such announcement. The announcement of the registration shall advise the creditors of such right.

(2) Das Recht, Sicherheitsleistung zu verlangen, steht Gläubigern nicht zu, die im Falle des Konkurses[1] ein Recht auf vorzugsweise Befriedigung aus einer Deckungsmasse haben, die nach gesetzlicher Vorschrift zu ihrem Schutz errichtet und staatlich überwacht ist.

(2) Creditors shall not be entitled to demand provision of security if they have a right to preferential satisfaction in the case of bankruptcy[1] from a fund which has been created for their protection pursuant to statutory provisions and which is subject to governmental supervision.

1. Mit Wirkung vom 1. Januar 1999 sind die Worte 'des Konkurses' durch die Worte 'des Insolvenzverfahrens' ersetzt.

1. Effective as of 1 January 1999 the word 'bankruptcy' will be substituted by the words 'insolvency proceedings'.

§ 322. Haftung der Hauptgesellschaft

(1) Von der Eingliederung an haftet die Hauptgesellschaft für die vor diesem Zeitpunkt begründeten Verbindlichkeiten der eingegliederten Gesellschaft den Gläubigern dieser Gesellschaft als Gesamtschuldner. Die gleiche Haftung trifft sie für alle Verbindlichkeiten der eingegliederten Gesellschaft, die nach der Eingliederung begründet werden. Eine entgegenstehende Vereinbarung ist Dritten gegenüber unwirksam.

(2) Wird die Hauptgesellschaft wegen einer Verbindlichkeit der eingegliederten Gesellschaft in Anspruch genommen, so kann sie Einwendungen, die nicht in ihrer Person begründet sind, nur insoweit geltend machen, als sie von der eingegliederten Gesellschaft erhoben werden können.

(3) Die Hauptgesellschaft kann die Befriedigung des Gläubigers verweigern, solange der eingegliederten Gesellschaft das Recht zusteht, das ihrer Verbindlichkeit zugrunde liegende Rechtsgeschäft anzufechten. Die gleiche Befugnis hat die Hauptgesellschaft, solange sich der Gläubiger durch Aufrechnung gegen eine fällige Forderung der eingegliederten Gesellschaft befriedigen kann.

(4) Aus einem gegen die eingegliederte Gesellschaft gerichteten vollstreckbaren Schuldtitel findet die Zwangsvollstreckung gegen die Hauptgesellschaft nicht statt.

§ 322. Liability of the Principal Company

(1) The principal company shall be liable to the creditors of the integrated company as joint and several debtor for the obligations of such company incurred prior to such date. The principal company shall also be liable for all obligations of the integrated company incurred after the integration. Such liability shall not be extinguished by any agreement to the contrary between the integrated company and the principal company.

(2) If a claim is made against the principal company regarding an obligation of the integrated company, such principal company may raise defenses other than those it has in its own right only if such defenses may be raised by the integrated company.

(3) The principal company may refuse to satisfy a creditor for as long as the integrated company has the right to rescind the transaction giving rise to such obligation. The principal company shall have to the same right for as long as the creditor may obtain satisfaction by setting off against a claim of the integrated company which is due.

(4) A judgment or other judicial decision which is enforceable against the integrated company may not be enforced against the principal company.

§ 323. Leitungsmacht der Hauptgesellschaft und Verantwortlichkeit der Vorstandsmitglieder

(1) Die Hauptgesellschaft ist berechtigt, dem Vorstand der eingegliederten Gesellschaft hinsichtlich der Leitung der

§ 323. Power of the Principal Company to direct and Liability of Members of the Management Board

(1) The principal company shall be entitled to issue instructions to the management board of the integrated company

Gesellschaft Weisungen zu erteilen. § 308 Abs. 2 Satz 1, Abs. 3, §§ 309, 310 gelten sinngemäß. §§ 311 bis 318 sind nicht anzuwenden.

regarding the management of the company. § 308 (2) sentence 1, (3), §§ 309, 310 shall apply analogously. §§ 311 to 318 shall not apply.

(2) Leistungen der eingegliederten Gesellschaft an die Hauptgesellschaft gelten nicht als Verstoß gegen die §§ 57, 58 und 60.

(2) Payments and other forms of consideration given by the integrated company to the principal company shall not be deemed to constitute a violation of §§ 57, 58 and 60.

§ 324. Gesetzliche Rücklage. Gewinnabführung. Verlustübernahme

§ 324. Legal Reserve; Profit Transfer; Assumption of Losses

(1) Die gesetzlichen Vorschriften über die Bildung einer gesetzlichen Rücklage, über ihre Verwendung und über die Einstellung von Beträgen in die gesetzliche Rücklage sind auf eingegliederte Gesellschaften nicht anzuwenden.

(1) The statutory provisions governing the creation of a legal reserve, the use thereof and the transfer of amounts to the legal reserve shall not apply to integrated companies.

(2) Auf einen Gewinnabführungsvertrag, eine Gewinngemeinschaft oder einen Teilgewinnabführungsvertrag zwischen der eingegliederten Gesellschaft und der Hauptgesellschaft sind die §§ 293 bis 296, 298 bis 303 nicht anzuwenden. Der Vertrag, seine Änderung und seine Aufhebung bedürfen der schriftlichen Form. Als Gewinn kann höchstens der ohne die Gewinnabführung entstehende Bilanzgewinn abgeführt werden. Der Vertrag endet spätestens zum Ende des Geschäftsjahrs, in dem die Eingliederung endet.

(2) §§ 293 to 296, 298 to 303 shall not apply to a profit transfer agreement, a profit sharing arrangement or an agreement to transfer a share of profits between an integrated company and the principal company. The agreement, any amendments thereto and the cancellation thereof shall be in writing. The amount to be transferred as profit may not exceed the distributable profit accruing prior to the profit transfer. The agreement shall expire not later than at the end of the fiscal year in which the integration terminates.

(3) Die Hauptgesellschaft ist verpflichtet, jeden bei der eingegliederten Gesellschaft sonst entstehenden Bilanzverlust auszugleichen, soweit dieser den Betrag der Kapitalrücklagen und der Gewinnrücklagen übersteigt.

(3) The principal company shall be obligated to compensate any accumulated loss of the integrated company which may otherwise arise insofar as such loss exceeds the amount of the capital reserves and profit reserves.

§ 325. (aufgehoben)

§ 325. (repealed)

§ 326. Auskunftsrecht der Aktionäre der Hauptgesellschaft

Jedem Aktionär der Hauptgesellschaft ist über Angelegenheiten der eingegliederten Gesellschaft ebenso Auskunft zu erteilen wie über Angelegenheiten der Hauptgesellschaft.

§ 326. Right of the Principal Company's Shareholders to Information

Each shareholder of the principal company shall be entitled to be provided with information regarding matters relating to the integrated company to the same extent he is entitled to be provided with information regarding matters relating to the principal company.

§ 327. Ende der Eingliederung

(1) Die Eingliederung endet

1. durch Beschluß der Hauptversammlung der eingegliederten Gesellschaft,
2. wenn die Hauptgesellschaft nicht mehr eine Aktiengesellschaft mit Sitz im Inland ist,
3. wenn sich nicht mehr alle Aktien der eingegliederten Gesellschaft in der Hand der Hauptgesellschaft befinden,
4. durch Auflösung der Hauptgesellschaft.

(2) Befinden sich nicht mehr alle Aktien der eingegliederten Gesellschaft in der Hand der Hauptgesellschaft, so hat die Hauptgesellschaft dies der eingegliederten Gesellschaft unverzüglich schriftlich mitzuteilen.

(3) Der Vorstand der bisher eingegliederten Gesellschaft hat das Ende der Eingliederung, seinen Grund und seinen Zeitpunkt unverzüglich zur Eintragung in das Handelsregister des Sitzes der Gesellschaft anzumelden.

(4) Die Ansprüche gegen die frühere Hauptgesellschaft aus Verbindlichkeiten der bisher eingegliederten Gesellschaft verjähren in fünf Jahren seit dem Tage, an dem die Eintragung des Endes der Eingliederung in das Handelsregister nach § 10 des Handelsgesetzbuchs als bekanntgemacht gilt, sofern nicht der An-

§ 327. Termination of Integration

(1) Integration shall terminate:

1. upon resolution of the shareholders' meeting of the integrated company;
2. if the principal company is no longer a stock corporation with domestic domicile;
3. if the principal company no longer holds all shares of the integrated company;
4. upon dissolution of the principal company.

(2) If the principal company no longer holds all shares of the integrated company, the principal company shall promptly advise the integrated company thereof in writing.

(3) The management board of the previously integrated company shall promptly report the termination of integration, the reason therefor and the date thereof for registration in the commercial register of such company's domicile.

(4) Any claim against the previous principal company arising from obligations of the previously integrated company shall be barred after the expiration of five years from the date on which the registration of the termination of integration in the commercial register shall be deemed to have been announced pursuant

spruch gegen die bisher eingegliederte Gesellschaft einer kürzeren Verjährung unterliegt. Wird der Anspruch des Gläubigers erst nach dem Tage, an dem die Eintragung des Endes der Eingliederung in das Handelsregister als bekanntgemacht gilt, fällig, so beginnt die Verjährung mit dem Zeitpunkt der Fälligkeit.

to § 10 of the Commercial Code, unless the claim against the previously integrated company is barred within a shorter period of time. If the claim of the creditor shall become due only after the date on which the registration of the termination of integration in the commercial register shall be deemed to have been announced, such period of time shall commence on the date on which such claim becomes due.

Vierter Teil. Wechselseitig beteiligte Unternehmen

§ 328. Beschränkung der Rechte

(1) Sind eine Aktiengesellschaft oder Kommanditgesellschaft auf Aktien und ein anderes Unternehmen wechselseitig beteiligte Unternehmen, so können, sobald dem einen Unternehmen das Bestehen der wechselseitigen Beteiligung bekannt geworden ist oder ihm das andere Unternehmen eine Mitteilung nach § 20 Abs. 3 oder § 21 Abs. 1 gemacht hat, Rechte aus den Anteilen, die ihm an dem anderen Unternehmen gehören, nur für höchstens den vierten Teil aller Anteile des anderen Unternehmens ausgeübt werden. Dies gilt nicht für das Recht auf neue Aktien bei einer Kapitalerhöhung aus Gesellschaftsmitteln. § 16 Abs. 4 ist anzuwenden.

(2) Die Beschränkung des Absatzes 1 gilt nicht, wenn das Unternehmen seinerseits dem anderen Unternehmen eine Mitteilung nach § 20 Abs. 3 oder § 21 Abs. 1 gemacht hatte, bevor es von dem anderen Unternehmen eine solche Mitteilung erhalten hat und bevor ihm das Bestehen der wechselseitigen Beteiligung bekannt geworden ist.

Part Four. Enterprises with Cross-Shareholdings

§ 328. Limitation of Rights

(1) If a stock corporation or partnership limited by shares and another enterprise constitute enterprises with cross-shareholdings, rights arising from shares which are held by any such enterprise in the other enterprise may not be exercised with respect to more than one fourth of all shares of such other enterprise as from the date on which such other enterprise has received knowledge of the existence of such cross-shareholding or the enterprise has given notice to such enterprise pursuant to § 20 (3) or § 21 (1). The foregoing shall not apply to the right to new shares in the case of a capital increase from the company's reserves. § 16 (4) shall apply.

(2) The restriction on exercise of rights pursuant to subsection (1) shall not apply if such enterprise has given notice to the other enterprise pursuant to § 20 (3) or § 21 (1) prior to receiving such notice from the other enterprise and prior to having received knowledge of the cross-shareholding.

(3) Sind eine Aktiengesellschaft oder Kommanditgesellschaft auf Aktien und ein anderes Unternehmen wechselseitig beteiligte Unternehmen, so haben die Unternehmen einander unverzüglich die Höhe ihrer Beteiligung und jede Änderung schriftlich mitzuteilen.

(3) If a stock corporation or partnership limited by shares and another enterprise constitute enterprises with cross-shareholdings, such enterprises shall promptly give notice in writing to one another of the amount of such holding and any change therein.

Fünfter Teil. Rechnungslegung im Konzern

Part Five. Group Financial Statements

§§ 329–336. (aufgehoben)

§§ 329–336. (repealed)

§ 337. Vorlage des Konzernabschlusses und des Konzernlageberichts

§ 337. Submission of the Group Financial Statements and Group Annual Report

(1) Unverzüglich nach Eingang des Prüfungsberichts des Abschlußprüfers hat der Vorstand des Mutterunternehmens den Konzernabschluß, den Konzernlagebericht und den Prüfungsbericht dem Aufsichtsrat des Mutterunternehmens zur Kenntnisnahme vorzulegen. Jedes Aufsichtsratsmitglied hat das Recht, von den Vorlagen Kenntnis zu nehmen. Die Vorlagen sind auch jedem Aufsichtsratsmitglied auf Verlangen auszuhändigen, soweit der Aufsichtsrat nichts anderes beschlossen hat.

(1) The management board of the parent enterprise shall, upon receipt of the audit report of the external auditor, promptly submit to the supervisory board of the parent enterprise for its information the group financial statements, the group annual report and the audit report. Each member of the supervisory board shall be entitled to take cognizance of such documents. Such documents shall upon request be delivered to each member of the supervisory board unless the supervisory board has decided otherwise.

(2) Ist der Konzernabschluß auf den Stichtag des Jahresabschlusses des Mutterunternehmens aufgestellt worden, so sind der Konzernabschluß und der Konzernlagebericht der Hauptversammlung vorzulegen, die diesen Jahresabschluß entgegennimmt oder festzustellen hat. Weicht der Stichtag des Konzernabschlusses vom Stichtag des Jahresabschlusses des Mutterunternehmens ab, so sind der Konzernabschluß und der Konzernlagebericht der Hauptversammlung vorzulegen, die den nächsten auf den Stichtag des Konzernabschlusses folgenden Jahresabschluß entgegennimmt oder festzustellen hat.

(2) If the group financial statements have the same record date as the annual financial statements of the parent enterprise, the group financial statements and the group annual report shall be submitted to the shareholders' meeting which is to consider or approve such annual financial statements. If the record date of the group financial statements differs from the record date of the annual financial statements of the parent enterprise, the group financial statements and the group annual report shall be submitted to the shareholders' meeting which is to consider or approve the annual financial

statements next following the record date of the group financial statements.

(**3**) Auf die Auslegung des Konzernabschlusses und des Konzernlageberichts und die Erteilung von Abschriften ist § 175 Abs. 2, auf die Vorlage an die Hauptversammlung und die Berichterstattung des Vorstandes ist § 176 Abs. 1 entsprechend anzuwenden.

(**3**) § 175 (2) shall apply analogously to the display for inspection of the group financial statements and the group annual report and to the distribution of copies; § 176 (1) shall apply analogously to the submission to the shareholders' meeting and the report of the management board.

(**4**) Die Auskunftspflicht des Vorstands des Mutterunternehmens in der Hauptversammlung, der der Konzernabschluß und der Konzernlagebericht vorgelegt werden, erstreckt sich auch auf die Lage des Konzerns und der in den Konzernabschluß einbezogenen Unternehmen.

(**4**) The duty of the management board of the parent enterprise to provide information at the shareholders' meeting to which the group financial statements and group annual report are submitted shall include information on the condition of the group and the enterprises included in the group financial statements.

§§ 338–393. (aufgehoben)

§§ 338–393. (repealed)

Viertes Buch. Sonder-, Straf- und Schlußvorschriften

Book Four. Special, Criminal and Final Provisions

Erster Teil. Sondervorschriften bei Beteiligung von Gebietskörperschaften

Part One. Special Provisions concerning the Participation of Municipalities

§ 394. Berichte der Aufsichtsratsmitglieder

Aufsichtsratsmitglieder, die auf Veranlassung einer Gebietskörperschaft in den Aufsichtsrat gewählt oder entsandt worden sind, unterliegen hinsichtlich der Berichte, die sie der Gebietskörperschaft zu erstatten haben, keiner Verschwiegenheitspflicht. Für vertrauliche Angaben und Geheimnisse der Gesellschaft, namentlich Betriebs- oder Geschäftsgeheimnisse, gilt dies nicht, wenn ihre Kenntnis für die Zwecke der Berichte nicht von Bedeutung ist.

§ 394. Reports of the Members of the Supervisory Board

Persons who have been elected or delegated to the supervisory board by a municipality shall not be bound by a duty of secrecy with respect to reports which they are required to make to the municipality. The foregoing shall not apply to confidential information and secrets of the company, in particular trade and business secrets, if knowledge thereof is not material in the context of such reports.

§ 395. Verschwiegenheitspflicht

(1) Personen, die damit betraut sind, die Beteiligungen einer Gebietskörperschaft zu verwalten oder für eine Gebietskörperschaft die Gesellschaft, die Betätigung der Gebietskörperschaft als Aktionär oder die Tätigkeit der auf Veranlassung der Gebietskörperschaft gewählten oder entsandten Aufsichtsratsmitglieder zu prüfen, haben über vertrauliche Angaben und Geheimnisse der Gesellschaft, namentlich Betriebs- oder Geschäftsgeheimnisse, die ihnen aus Berichten nach

§ 395. Duty of Secrecy

(1) Persons who are charged with administering the participations of a municipality or auditing on behalf of a municipality the company, the activities of the municipality in its capacity as shareholder or the activities of members in the supervisory board who have been elected or delegated by the municipality, shall not disclose any confidential information or secrets of the company, in particular trade or business secrets which have become known to them in connection with reports

§ 394 bekanntgeworden sind, Stillschweigen zu bewahren; dies gilt nicht für Mitteilungen im dienstlichen Verkehr.

(2) Bei der Veröffentlichung von Prüfungsergebnissen dürfen vertrauliche Angaben und Geheimnisse der Gesellschaft, namentlich Betriebs- oder Geschäftsgeheimnisse, nicht veröffentlicht werden.

pursuant to § 394; the foregoing shall not apply to internal governmental communications.

(2) Confidential information and secrets of the company, in particular trade and business secrets, may not be disclosed when the findings of audits are published.

Zweiter Teil. Gerichtliche Auflösung

Part Two. Judicial Dissolution

§ 396. Voraussetzungen

(1) Gefährdet eine Aktiengesellschaft oder Kommanditgesellschaft auf Aktien durch gesetzwidriges Verhalten ihrer Verwaltungsträger das Gemeinwohl und sorgen der Aufsichtsrat und die Hauptversammlung nicht für eine Abberufung der Verwaltungsträger, so kann die Gesellschaft auf Antrag der zuständigen obersten Landesbehörde des Landes, in dem die Gesellschaft ihren Sitz hat, durch Urteil aufgelöst werden. Ausschließlich zuständig für die Klage ist das Landgericht, in dessen Bezirk die Gesellschaft ihren Sitz hat.

(2) Nach der Auflösung findet die Abwicklung nach den §§ 264 bis 273 statt. Den Antrag auf Abberufung oder Bestellung der Abwickler aus einem wichtigen Grund kann auch die in Absatz 1 Satz 1 bestimmte Behörde stellen.

§ 396. General Provisions

(1) If a stock corporation or a partnership limited by shares endangers the public welfare as a result of unlawful conduct of its board members and the supervisory board or the shareholders' meeting, as the case may be, do not procure the dismissal of such board members, the company may be dissolved by judicial decree upon motion by the appropriate highest authority of the state in which the company is domiciled. The district court of the district in which the company is domiciled shall have exclusive jurisdiction with respect to any such action.

(2) After dissolution the company shall be liquidated pursuant to §§ 264 to 273. A motion to dismiss or appoint liquidators for cause may also be made by the authority designated in subsection (1) sentence 1.

§ 397. Anordnungen bei der Auflösung

Ist die Auflösungsklage erhoben, so kann das Gericht auf Antrag der in § 396 Abs. 1 Satz 1 bestimmten Behörde durch

§ 397. Preliminary Injunctions in Connection with Dissolution

If an action for dissolution has been brought, the court may upon motion by the authority designated in § 396 (1) sen-

einstweilige Verfügung die nötigen Anordnungen treffen.

tence 1 undertake any necessary measures by preliminary injunction.

§ 398. Eintragung

Die Entscheidungen des Gerichts sind dem Registergericht mitzuteilen. Dieses trägt sie, soweit sie eintragungspflichtige Rechtsverhältnisse betreffen, in das Handelsregister ein.

§ 398. Registration

The decisions of the court shall be communicated to the court maintaining the commercial register. Such court shall enter such decisions in the commercial register to the extent that they concern legal relations requiring registration.

Dritter Teil. Straf- und Bußgeldvorschriften. Schlußvorschriften

Part Three. Criminal Provisions and Fines; Final Provisions

§ 399. Falsche Angaben

(1) Mit Freiheitsstrafe bis zu drei Jahren oder mit Geldstrafe wird bestraft, wer

1. als Gründer oder als Mitglied des Vorstands oder des Aufsichtsrats zum Zweck der Eintragung der Gesellschaft über die Übernahme der Aktien, die Einzahlung auf Aktien, die Verwendung eingezahlter Beträge, den Ausgabebetrag der Aktien, über Sondervorteile, Gründungsaufwand, Sacheinlagen, Sachübernahmen und Sicherungen für nicht voll einbezahlte Geldeinlagen,

2. als Gründer oder als Mitglied des Vorstands oder des Aufsichtsrats im Gründungsbericht, im Nachgründungsbericht oder im Prüfungsbericht,

3. in der öffentlichen Ankündigung nach § 47 Nr. 3,

4. als Mitglied des Vorstands oder des Aufsichtsrats zum Zweck der Eintragung einer Erhöhung des Grundkapitals (§§ 182 bis 206) über die Einbringung des bisherigen, die Zeichnung oder Einbringung des neuen Kapitals, den Ausgabebetrag der Aktien, die Ausgabe der Bezugsaktien oder über Sacheinlagen,

5. als Abwickler zum Zweck der Ein-

§ 399. False Statements

(1) Whoever makes false statements or fails to disclose material facts:

1. as incorporator or member of the management board or supervisory board, for purpose of registration of the company, with respect to the acquisition of shares, payment of contributions, appropriation of contributions, the share issue price, special benefits, formation expenses, contributions in kind, acquisitions of assets and security for contributions in cash which have not been paid in full;

2. as incorporator or member of the management board or supervisory board in the formation report, the report on post-formation acquisition or the audit report;

3. in the official announcement pursuant to § 47 No. 3;

4. as member of the management board or supervisory board, for purposes of registration of a share capital increase (§§ 182 to 206), with respect to contributions to the previously existing capital, subscription or contribution of the new capital, the share issue price, the issuance of new shares, or contributions in kind;

5. as liquidator, for purposes of reg-

tragung der Fortsetzung der Gesellschaft in dem nach § 274 Abs. 3 zu führenden Nachweis oder

6. als Mitglied des Vorstands in der nach § 37 Abs. 2 Satz 1 oder § 81 Abs. 3 Satz 1 abzugebenden Versicherung oder als Abwickler in der nach § 266 Abs. 3 Satz 1 abzugebenden Versicherung

falsche Angaben macht oder erhebliche Umstände verschweigt.

(2) Ebenso wird bestraft, wer als Mitglied des Vorstands oder des Aufsichtsrats zum Zweck der Eintragung einer Erhöhung des Grundkapitals die in § 210 Abs. 1 Satz 2 vorgeschriebene Erklärung der Wahrheit zuwider abgibt.

istration of the continuation of the company, in connection with the proof to be furnished pursuant to § 274 (3); or

6. as a member of the management board, in the statement to be made pursuant to § 37 (2) sentence 1 or § 81 (3) sentence 1 or as liquidator in the statement to be made pursuant to § 266 (3) sentence 1

shall be punished by imprisonment of up to three years or by fine.

(2) Whoever as member of the management board or the supervisory board, for purposes of registration of a share capital increase, with respect to the statement required pursuant to § 210 (1) sentence 2 makes a false statement, shall be punished in the same manner.

§ 400. Unrichtige Darstellung

(1) Mit Freiheitsstrafe bis zu drei Jahren oder mit Geldstrafe wird bestraft, wer als Mitglied des Vorstands oder des Aufsichtsrats oder als Abwickler

1. die Verhältnisse der Gesellschaft einschließlich ihrer Beziehungen zu verbundenen Unternehmen in Darstellungen oder Übersichten über den Vermögensstand, in Vorträgen oder Auskünften in der Hauptversammlung unrichtig wiedergibt oder verschleiert, wenn die Tat nicht in § 331 Nr. 1 des Handelsgesetzbuchs mit Strafe bedroht ist, oder

2. in Aufklärungen oder Nachweisen, die nach den Vorschriften dieses Gesetzes einem Prüfer der Gesellschaft oder eines verbundenen Unternehmens zu geben sind, falsche Angaben macht oder die Verhältnisse der Gesellschaft unrichtig wiedergibt oder verschleiert, wenn die Tat nicht in § 331 Nr. 4 des Handelsgesetzbuchs mit Strafe bedroht ist.

§ 400. Misrepresentation

(1) Whoever as a member of the management board or the supervisory board:

1. misrepresents or conceals the condition of the company, including its relations with affiliated enterprises, in presentations on the financial condition of the company, statements or information provided at the shareholders' meeting, unless such act constitutes a criminal offense pursuant to § 331 No. 1 of the Commercial Code, or

2. makes false statements or misrepresents or conceals the condition of the company in disclosures or statements which are required to be made to an auditor of the company or an affiliated enterprise pursuant to the provisions of this Act, unless such act constitutes a criminal offense pursuant to § 331 No. 4 of the Commercial Code

shall be punished by imprisonment of up to three years or by fine.

(2) Ebenso wird bestraft, wer als Gründer oder Aktionär in Aufklärungen oder Nachweisen, die nach den Vorschriften dieses Gesetzes einem Gründungsprüfer oder sonstigen Prüfer zu geben sind, falsche Angaben macht oder erhebliche Umstände verschweigt.

(2) Whoever, as incorporator or shareholder, makes false statements or conceals material facts in disclosures or evidence which are required to be made to a formation auditor or other auditor pursuant to the provisions of this Act, shall be punished in the same manner.

§ 401. Pflichtverletzung bei Verlust, Überschuldung oder Zahlungsunfähigkeit

§ 401. Violation of Duty in the Event of Loss of Capital, Overindebtedness or Insolvency

(1) Mit Freiheitsstrafe bis zu drei Jahren oder mit Geldstrafe wird bestraft, wer es

1. als Mitglied des Vorstands entgegen § 92 Abs. 1 unterläßt, bei einem Verlust in Höhe der Hälfte des Grundkapitals die Hauptversammlung einzuberufen und ihr dies anzuzeigen, oder

2. als Mitglied des Vorstands entgegen § 92 Abs. 2 oder als Abwickler entgegen § 268 Abs. 2 Satz 1 unterläßt, bei Zahlungsunfähigkeit oder Überschuldung die Eröffnung des Konkursverfahrens oder des gerichtlichen Vergleichsverfahrens[1] zu beantragen.

(1) Whoever:

1. as member of the management board in violation of § 92 (1) fails to call a shareholders' meeting and to disclose at such meeting a loss equal or exceeding one half of the share capital; or

2. as member of the management board, in violation of § 92 (2) or as liquidator in violation of § 268 (2) sentence 1, fails to apply for the institution of bankruptcy proceedings or judicial composition proceedings[1] in the event of insolvency or overindebtedness

shall be punished by imprisonment of up to three years or by fine.

(2) Handelt der Täter fahrlässig, so ist die Strafe Freiheitsstrafe bis zu einem Jahr oder Geldstrafe.

(2) If the offender acts negligently, the punishment shall be imprisonment up to one year or a fine.

1. Mit Wirkung vom 1. Januar 1999 sind die Worte 'des Konkursverfahrens oder des gerichtlichen Vergleichsverfahrens' durch die Worte 'des Insolvenzverfahrens' ersetzt.

1. Effective as of 1 January 1999 the words 'bankruptcy proceedings or judicial composition proceedings' will be substituted by the words 'insolvency proceedings'.

§ 402. Falsche Ausstellung oder Verfälschung von Hinterlegungsbescheinigungen

(1) Wer über die Hinterlegung von Aktien oder Zwischenscheinen Bescheinigungen, die zum Nachweis des Stimmrechts in einer Hauptversammlung oder in einer gesonderten Versammlung dienen sollen, falsch ausstellt oder verfälscht, wird mit Freiheitsstrafe bis zu drei Jahren oder mit Geldstrafe bestraft, wenn die Tat nicht in anderen Vorschriften über Urkundenstraftaten mit schwererer Strafe bedroht ist.

(2) Ebenso wird bestraft, wer von einer falschen oder verfälschten Bescheinigung der in Absatz 1 bezeichneten Art zur Ausübung des Stimmrechts Gebrauch macht.

(3) Der Versuch ist strafbar.

§ 402. False Issuance or Falsification of Deposit Certificates

(1) Whoever issues falsely or falsifies certificates concerning the deposit of share certificates or interim certificates which are to serve as proof at a shareholders' meeting or separate meeting, shall be punished by imprisonment of up to three years or by fine, unless such act is subject to a more severe punishment in other criminal provisions concerning documents.

(2) Whoever makes use of a false or falsified certificate of the kind specified in subsection (1) for the purpose of exercising voting rights shall be punished in the same manner.

(3) The attempt shall also be punishable.

§ 403. Verletzung der Berichtspflicht

(1) Mit Freiheitsstrafe bis zu drei Jahren oder mit Geldstrafe wird bestraft, wer als Prüfer oder als Gehilfe eines Prüfers über das Ergebnis der Prüfung falsch berichtet oder erhebliche Umstände im Bericht verschweigt.

(2) Handelt der Täter gegen Entgelt oder in der Absicht, sich oder einen anderen zu bereichern oder einen anderen zu schädigen, so ist die Strafe Freiheitsstrafe bis zu fünf Jahren oder Geldstrafe.

§ 403. Violation of Duty to Report

(1) Whoever as auditor or assistant to an auditor renders a false report on findings of an audit or fails to disclose material facts in such report shall be punished by imprisonment up to three years or by fine.

(2) If the offender acted for remuneration or with the intent to enrich himself or another person or causing damage to another person, the punishment shall be imprisonment up to five years or payment of a fine.

§ 404. Verletzung der Geheimhaltungspflicht

(1) Mit Freiheitsstrafe bis zu einem Jahr oder mit Geldstrafe wird bestraft,

§ 404. Violation of the Duty of Confidentiality

(1) Whoever without authorization discloses a secret of the company, in par-

wer ein Geheimnis der Gesellschaft, namentlich ein Betriebs- oder Geschäftsgeheimnis, das ihm in seiner Eigenschaft als

1. Mitglied des Vorstands oder des Aufsichtsrats oder Abwickler,
2. Prüfer oder Gehilfe eines Prüfers

bekanntgeworden ist, unbefugt offenbart; im Falle der Nummer 2 jedoch nur, wenn die Tat nicht in § 333 des Handelsgesetzbuchs mit Strafe bedroht ist.

ticular a trade or business secret, shall be punished by imprisonment of up to one year or by fine if such secret became known to him in his capacity as:

1. a member of the management board or supervisory board or liquidator;
2. auditor or assistant to an auditor;

in the case of no. 2, however, only if such act does not constitute a criminal offense pursuant to § 333 of the Commercial Code.

(2) Handelt der Täter gegen Entgelt oder in der Absicht, sich oder einen anderen zu bereichern oder einen anderen zu schädigen, so ist die Strafe Freiheitsstrafe bis zu zwei Jahren oder Geldstrafe. Ebenso wird bestraft, wer ein Geheimnis der in Absatz 1 bezeichneten Art, namentlich ein Betriebs- oder Geschäftsgeheimnis, das ihm unter den Voraussetzungen des Absatzes 1 bekanntgeworden ist, unbefugt verwertet.

(2) If such offender acted for remuneration or with the intent to enrich himself or another person or causing damage to another person, the punishment shall be imprisonment of up to two years or a fine. Whoever unlawfully uses a secret of the kind specified in subsection (1), in particular a trade or business secret, which has become known to him under the circumstances of subsection (1) shall be punished in the same manner.

(3) Die Tat wird nur auf Antrag der Gesellschaft verfolgt. Hat ein Mitglied des Vorstands oder ein Abwickler die Tat begangen, so ist der Aufsichtsrat, hat ein Mitglied des Aufsichtsrats die Tat begangen, so sind der Vorstand oder die Abwickler antragsberechtigt.

(3) Such act shall be prosecuted only upon complaint by the company. Such complaint may be made by the supervisory board if a member of the management board or liquidator committed such act; such complaint may be made by the management board or the liquidators if a member of the supervisory board committed such act.

§ 405. Ordnungswidrigkeiten

(1) Ordnungswidrig handelt, wer als Mitglied des Vorstands oder des Aufsichtsrats oder als Abwickler

1. Namensaktien ausgibt, in denen der Betrag der Teilleistung nicht angegeben ist, oder Inhaberaktien ausgibt, bevor auf sie der Nennbetrag oder der höhere Ausgabebetrag voll geleistet ist,
2. Aktien oder Zwischenscheine aus-

§ 405. Administrative Offenses

(1) Any member of the management board or supervisory board or liquidator shall be guilty of an administrative offence who:

1. issues registered share certificates in which the amount of partial contributions is not stated or issues bearer shares prior to contribution in full of the par value or higher issue price;
2. issues share certificates or interim

gibt, bevor die Gesellschaft oder im Fall einer Kapitalerhöhung die Durchführung der Erhöhung des Grundkapitals oder im Fall einer bedingten Kapitalerhöhung oder einer Kapitalerhöhung aus Gesellschaftsmitteln der Beschluß über die bedingte Kapitalerhöhung oder die Kapitalerhöhung aus Gesellschaftsmitteln eingetragen ist,

3. Aktien oder Zwischenscheine ausgibt, die auf einen geringeren als den nach § 8 zulässigen Mindestnennbetrag lauten, oder

4. (a) entgegen § 71 Abs. 1 Nr. 1 bis 4 oder Abs. 2 eigene Aktien der Gesellschaft erwirbt oder, in Verbindung mit § 71e Abs. 1, als Pfand nimmt,

(b) zu veräußernde eigene Aktien (§ 71c Abs. 1 und 2) nicht anbietet oder

(c) die zur Vorbereitung der Beschlußfassung über die Einziehung eigener Aktien (§ 71c Abs. 3) erforderlichen Maßnahmen nicht trifft.

(2) Ordnungswidrig handelt auch, wer als Aktionär oder als Vertreter eines Aktionärs die nach § 129 in das Verzeichnis aufzunehmenden Angaben nicht oder nicht richtig macht.

(3) Ordnungswidrig handelt ferner, wer

1. Aktien eines anderen, zu dessen Vertretung er nicht befugt ist, ohne dessen Einwilligung zur Ausübung von Rechten in der Hauptversammlung oder in einer gesonderten Versammlung benutzt,

2. zur Ausübung von Rechten in der Hauptversammlung oder in einer gesonderten Versammlung Aktien eines anderen benutzt, die er sich zu diesem Zweck durch Gewähren oder Versprechen besonderer Vorteile verschafft hat,

3. Aktien zu dem in Nummer 2 bezeichneten Zweck gegen Gewähren oder Versprechen besonderer Vorteile einem anderen überläßt,

4. Aktien eines anderen, für die er oder

certificates prior to registration of the company or, in the case of a capital increase, the completion of the share capital increase, or, in the case of a contingent capital increase or a capital increase from the company's reserves, the resolution on the contingent capital increase or the capital increase from the company's reserves;

3. issues share certificates or interim certificates which have a par value less than the minimum par value pursuant to § 8;

4.(a) acquires shares held by the company in violation of § 71 (1) No. 1 to 4 or (2) or, in connection with § 71e (1), takes a pledge on such shares;

(b) fails to offer company shares held by the company which are to be disposed of (§ 71c (1) and (2));

(c) fails to take measures necessary for preparation of a resolution on the cancellation of company shares (§ 71c (3)).

(2) Whoever as shareholder or proxy fails to provide or provides incorrectly the information to be included in the list pursuant to § 129 shall be guilty of an administrative offense.

(3) Whoever:

1. uses shares of another person, without authorization to act as proxy and without the approval of such other person, to exercise rights at a shareholders' meeting or a separate meeting;

2. uses shares of another person which he has acquired by granting or promising special benefits, to exercise rights at a shareholders' meeting or a separate meeting;

3. permits the use of shares for the purpose specified in No. 2 against the grant or promise of special benefits;

4. uses shares of another person to

der von ihm Vertretene das Stimmrecht nach § 135 nicht ausüben darf, zur Ausübung des Stimmrechts benutzt,

5. Aktien, für die er oder der von ihm Vertretene das Stimmrecht nach § 20 Abs. 7, § 21 Abs. 4, §§ 71b, 71d Satz 4, § 134 Abs. 1, §§ 135, 136, 142 Abs. 1 Satz 2, § 285 Abs. 1 nicht ausüben darf, einem anderen zum Zweck der Ausübung des Stimmrechts überläßt oder solche ihm überlassene Aktien zur Ausübung des Stimmrechts benutzt,

6. besondere Vorteile als Gegenleistung dafür fordert, sich versprechen läßt oder annimmt, daß er bei einer Abstimmung in der Hauptversammlung oder in einer gesonderten Versammlung nicht oder in einem bestimmten Sinne stimme oder

7. besondere Vorteile als Gegenleistung dafür anbietet, verspricht oder gewährt, daß jemand bei einer Abstimmung in der Hauptversammlung oder in einer gesonderten Versammlung nicht oder in einem bestimmten Sinne stimme.

(**4**) Die Ordnungswidrigkeit kann mit einer Geldbuße bis zu fünfzigtausend Deutsche Mark geahndet werden.

§ 406. (aufgehoben)

§ 407. Zwangsgelder

(**1**) Vorstandsmitglieder oder Abwickler, die § 52 Abs. 2 Satz 2 und 3, § 71c, § 73 Abs. 3 Satz 2, §§ 80, 90, 104 Abs. 1, § 111 Abs. 2, § 145, §§ 170, 171 Abs. 3, §§ 175, 179a Abs. 2 Satz 1 und 2, § 214 Abs. 1, § 246 Abs. 4, § 259 Abs. 5, § 268 Abs. 4, § 270 Abs. 1, § 273 Abs. 2, §§ 293f, 293g Abs 1, § 306 Abs. 6, § 312 Abs. 1, § 313 Abs. 1, § 314 Abs. 1 nicht befolgen, sind hierzu vom Registerge-

exercise voting rights, for which neither he nor any person represented by him may exercise voting rights pursuant to § 135;

5. permits the use of shares or uses such shares to exercise voting rights which neither he nor any person represented by him may exercise pursuant to § 20 (7), § 21 (4), §§ 71b, 71d sentence 4, § 134 (1), §§ 135, 136, 142 (1) sentence 2 and § 285 (1);

6. demands, obtains a promise of or accepts special benefits as consideration for refraining from voting or voting in a prescribed manner at a shareholders' meeting or a separate meeting;

7. offers, promises or grants special benefits as consideration to another person for refraining from voting or voting in a prescribed manner at a shareholders' meeting or a separate meeting;

shall be guilty of an administrative offence.

(**4**) An administrative offence shall be punished by a fine up to fifty thousand Deutsche Mark.

§ 406. (repealed)

§ 407. Compliance Fines

(**1**) The court maintaining the commercial register shall threaten to impose fines in order to insure compliance by members of the management board and liquidators who fail to comply with § 52 (2) sentences 2 and 3, § 71c, § 73 (3) sentence 2, §§ 80, 90, 104 (1), § 111 (2), § 145, §§ 170, 171 (3), §§ 175, 179a (2) sentences 1 and 2, § 214 (1), § 246 (4), § 259 (5), § 268 (4), § 270 (1), § 273 (2),

richt durch Festsetzung von Zwangsgeld anzuhalten; § 14 des Handelsgesetzbuchs bleibt unberührt. Das einzelne Zwangsgeld darf den Betrag von zehntausend Deutsche Mark nicht übersteigen.

(2) Die Anmeldungen zum Handelsregister nach den §§ 36, 45, 52, 181 Abs. 1, §§ 184, 188, 195, 210, 223, 237 Abs. 4, §§ 274, 294 Abs. 1, § 319 Abs. 3 werden durch Festsetzung von Zwangsgeld nicht erzwungen. Für die Einreichung der der Zahl der Zweigniederlassungen entsprechenden Stückzahl der Anmeldungen verbleibt es bei § 14 des Handelsgesetzbuchs.

§§ 293f, 293g (1), § 306 (6), § 312 (1), § 313 (1), § 314 (1); § 14 of the Commercial Code shall remain unaffected. Each such fine may not exceed ten thousand Deutsche Mark.

(2) The court maintaining the commercial register may not threaten to impose fines in order to ensure that reports to the commercial register for registration pursuant to §§ 36, 45, 52, 181 (1), §§ 184, 188, 195, 210, 223, 237 (4), §§ 274, 294 (1), § 319 (3) are made. § 14 of the Commercial Code shall apply with respect to the submission of reports in a number corresponding to the number of branches.

§ 408. Strafbarkeit persönlich haftender Gesellschafter einer Kommanditgesellschaft auf Aktien

Die §§ 399 bis 407 gelten sinngemäß für die Kommanditgesellschaft auf Aktien. Soweit sie Vorstandsmitglieder betreffen, gelten sie bei der Kommanditgesellschaft auf Aktien für die persönlich haftenden Gesellschafter.

§ 408. Criminal Liability of General Partners of a Partnership Limited by Shares

§§ 399 to 407 shall apply analogously to partnerships limited by shares. Insofar as such provisions refer to members of the management board, such provisions shall in the case of a partnership limited by shares apply to the general partners.

§ 409. Geltung in Berlin

(*überholt*)

§ 409. Berlin Clause

(*obsolete*)

§ 410. Inkrafttreten

Dieses Gesetz tritt am 1. Januar 1966 in Kraft.

§ 410. Effective Date

This Act shall come into effect on 1 January 1966.

3 Index

Index

(Numbers refer to Sections of Stock Corporation Law)

A

F

G

N

O

P

R

S

W

Z